5th Edition

SUPERVISION

CONCEPTS AND PRACTICES OF MANAGEMENT

RAYMOND L. HILGERT

Professor of Management and Industrial Relations
John M. Olin School of Business
Washington University

THEO HAIMANN

The Mary Louise Murray
Professor of Management
School of Business and Administration
Saint Louis University

COLLEGE DIVISION South-Western Publishing Co.

CINCINNATI   DALLAS   LIVERMORE

Publisher: Roger Ross
Developmental Editor: Edward A. Parker
Production Editor: Sue Ellen Brown
Production House: York Production Services
Cover and Interior Designer: Joseph M. Devine
Photo Researcher: Diana Fears
Marketing Manager: David L. Shaut
Cover Photo: COMSTOCK

GZ94EA

Copyright © 1991
by South-Western Publishing Co.
Cincinnati, Ohio

1 2 3 4 5 6 7 AG 6 5 4 3 2 1 0

Printed in the United States of America

Hilgert, Raymond L.
   Supervision: concepts and practices of management / Raymond L.
Hilgert, Theo Haimann. — 5th ed.
     p.   cm.
   Fourth ed. written by Theo Haimann and Raymond L. Hilgert.
   Includes bibliographical references.
   "GZ94EA."
   ISBN 0-538-81082-3
   1. Supervision of employees. 2. Personnel management.
I. Haimann, Theo. II. Title.
HF5549.H265   1991
658.3'02—dc20

                         90-39499
                           CIP

Preface

In writing this fifth edition of *Supervision: Concepts and Practices of Management,* the authors have retained the general format and major concepts contained in the previous editions. At the same time, we have updated all of the text and integrated new developments and considerations that are vital to the performance of today's supervisors.

This text is written primarily for practicing, newly appointed, or potential supervisors and managers who hold or will hold from first-line up to middle-level management positions. However, most of the contents probably will be of interest to top management executives as well as staff personnel, nonmanagerial employees, and students who desire to understand the supervisory position. The common denominator of all supervisors is the part they play as managers within the structure of any organization. Most supervisors are acutely aware of their need for developing broader perspectives, for gaining new insights into organizational behavior and human relations, and for staying on top of their jobs—in brief, the need to improve their managerial skills. This text is intended as an aid in that direction. Our purpose is to demonstrate to the supervisor or the student of supervision that proficiency in management will enable him or her to make the supervisor a more valuable part of the management team.

Increasingly, it is recognized that regardless of the technical specialties or particular organizational conditions that may exist, there are managerial aspects that are common to every supervisory position. In many organizations, however, supervisory training and development in management have not kept pace with technical and scientific progress and change. The future holds an ever-increasing challenge for supervisors who are capable of managing in more complex situations, whether they are in business, professional, health-care, government, scientific, educational, or other types of organizations. More than ever before, higher management is aware of the need for capable, knowledgeable, and broadly trained supervisors who are able to manage their departments competently and efficiently.

Since it is the supervisor's job to get things done with and through the help of people, we have emphasized human, behavioral aspects as being the most pervasive component of a supervisor's position. The text is not an all-inclusive text on management and human factors in supervision. It would be presumptuous to assume that one short volume possibly could cover all supervisory problems. We have tried to emphasize balance in this text. Employee relations are kept in perspective with many other aspects of the demanding responsibilities of the supervisor.

This book is introductory in the sense that it assumes no previous management knowledge on the part of the reader. However, it does include some material of a relatively sophisticated nature that can be understood without undue difficulties. The language of the book is direct and understandable. It is not intended as a book for academic theoreticians.

An objective of the book is to assist the student, the potential supervisor, or the newly appointed supervisor to analyze the many issues and problems that confront supervisors, and the book offers practical advice for their solutions. For experienced supervisors, the text is intended to refresh thinking, to widen horizons, and to challenge them to look at their positions and examine how they are managing and relating with employees, other supervisors, and higher management.

Materials for this text have been drawn from writings and research of scholars in management and the behavioral sciences and from reported experiences of many supervisors, managers, and administrators. In addition to the authors' own experience in management practice, the text reflects our backgrounds in teaching management courses, in participating in many stimulating discussions in supervisory management development programs, and in consulting activities for numerous companies and organizations.

We have retained a text structure that focuses upon the *managerial process,* examining the managerial functions of *planning, organizing, staffing, directing,* and *controlling* and their relations to the daily job of the supervisor. In reality, these functions are closely interrelated and a distinct classification is scarcely discernible. However, such a presentation makes possible a more methodical, clear, and comprehensive analysis of the managerial functions of a supervisor.

All of the 22 chapters have been edited, updated, and rewritten. New illustrations of concepts and issues are part of the text presentation. Among the areas involving significant changes or updating are the chapters on managing in a non-discriminatory way, building positive discipline, the human resources department, labor relations, group dynamics, and motivation. New and updated topics reflect recent laws, rulings, and trends. We have added sections on ethical decision making in supervisory management, family care issues in supervision, and "pay for performance" compensation programs.

For each part of the text we have included a number of short case problems (a total of 44 cases throughout the text). These cases provide users of the book with an opportunity to apply concepts and principles presented in the text to realistic problem situations involving supervisors. The cases, six of which are new to this edition, are actual situations that have come to the attention of the authors through various sources. Students of supervisory management, whether in class or seminar sessions, usually find it interesting and challenging to discuss these cases in order to apply their knowledge to realistic problems that have faced other supervisors.

Again available for use in conjunction with the text is a *Student Supple-*

ment and Study Guide, which has been developed by Dr. Taggart Smith of the Department of Supervision of the School of Technology at Purdue University. This supplement/study guide includes a chapter review of text materials, key terms and concepts, review questions, and application projects that the instructor can assign or that students can study independently to enrich their comprehension of supervision.

In order to assist the instructor, the authors have prepared an *Instructor's Manual* that contains general comments and suggestions for use of the text; comments on the end-of-chapter questions; discussion of the case problems; commentary on the application projects in the *Student Supplement and Study Guide;* a test bank of objective questions that can be used for examination purposes; and an extensive set of transparency masters.

In writing this book, the authors are indebted to so many persons that it is impossible to give all of them credit. However, special thanks go to those organizations and individuals who provided the materials for the cases. The authors are particularly grateful to the following professors who reviewed the text and who offered numerous suggestions and comments:

Tommy Gilbreath of the University of Texas at Tyler;
Dewey Johnson of the California State University at Fresno;
John Kohl of the University of Nevada at Las Vegas;
Fred Sutton of Cuyahoga Community College in Cleveland, Ohio;
Ed White of Danville Community College in Danville, Virginia.

The authors also express their appreciation to Professors Arthur Carlson and Sterling Schoen of Washington University for case study contributions; to Kelley Crowder and Sandra Jost, graduate assistants at Washington University, who developed new objective test questions and case discussion notes for the *Instructor's Manual;* and to the Washington University School of Business secretarial staff who typed and processed the manuscripts.

Raymond L. Hilgert and **Theo Haimann**

About the Authors

Dr. Raymond Hilgert graduated from Westminster College, Fulton, Missouri, with a Bachelor of Arts Degree. He received his Master's and Doctor's degrees from Washington University. His business experience includes management positions at Southwestern Bell Telephone Company and a market research position with an advertising company. Dr. Hilgert has taught at Washington University since 1961. He has published over seventy articles in management, business, and educational journals and has co-authored six books on personnel/human resources management, supervision, and industrial relations, two of which are in their fifth and sixth editions.

Dr. Hilgert is a member of the Academy of Management, the Industrial Relations Research Association, the Society for Human Resource Management, and the American Management Association. He has participated in or directed numerous management, supervisory, and economics programs and seminars. Dr. Hilgert is an arbitrator certified by the Federal Mediation and Conciliation Service and the American Arbitration Association, and he holds the Senior Professional in Human Resources (SPHR) accreditation from the Personnel Accreditation Institute.

Dr. Theo Haimann received his MBA from Washington University, St. Louis, and his Ph.D. from the University of Bonn, Germany. His business experience includes over 20 years as President and General Manager for a midwestern manufacturing concern. Dr. Haimann has been teaching at St. Louis University since 1958 and is currently The Mary Louise Murray Professor of Management Sciences. In addition to this text, Dr. Haimann has written a number of other scholarly works and textbooks.

Dr. Haimann is a member of the Academy of Management and the American Economics Association. He has lectured widely on supervision and management topics for the past 25 years.

Both Dr. Hilgert and Dr. Haimann are included in the current edition of *Who's Who in America*.

Contents

PART 4   STAFFING   241

PART 5   DIRECTING   313

PART 6   CONTROLLING   399

PART 1

MANAGEMENT OVERVIEW

CHAPTER 1

Supervisory Management in the 1990s: The Challenge of Leadership

CHAPTER OBJECTIVES

1. To discuss a number of the major demographic and societal trends that will impact on contemporary supervisory management during the 1990s.
2. To identify the principal trends associated with shifting employee values and expectations, motivation, and behavior patterns that affect the supervisory position.
3. To discuss the leadership component of supervision, with emphasis upon supervisory leadership as residing in a supervisor's ability to blend organizational needs and objectives with the employees' needs and objectives.
4. To emphasize that supervisors must continually grow and develop as professionals.

Virtually every aspect of contemporary life has experienced major changes during the past several decades. There is little doubt that major changes will continue to take place in most parts of our society during coming years, and continuing change will be a regular part of every organization's problems as well as challenges. Managers at all levels will be at the forefront of planning and coping with trends, factors, and problems requiring attention and sound management if they and their organizations are to survive, grow, and prosper.

Our concerns in this book will focus primarily on the first tier of management, which generally is referred to as the supervisory level, or **supervisory management**. Like all aspects of modern life, concepts and practices of supervisory management are undergoing major changes.

Joe D. Batten, a leading management authority and consultant, has written that:

> The decade of the 1980s has witnessed a volatile series of changes in the way leadership is viewed in America.
>
> Increasingly, it is moving beyond the level of craft to the level of profession.
>
> ★　★　★
>
> The very nature of management must be perceived in a new way. In practical reality, management is an ever-changing, ever-dynamic system of interacting minds. In the future—and the future is almost here—managing minds and spirits will be the name of the game.[1]

Batten comments further to the effect that the old idea of getting a job done through power and formal weight of authority is no longer recognized as effective. Today's managers and supervisors, whether they are in a machine shop, a factory, a nursing care unit, a business office, a retail store, a bank, or a government agency, realize that reliance on authoritarian direction and close control usually will not bring about the desired results. The supervisory job has become more complex, sophisticated, and demanding, and requires the knowledge and development of professional and personal skills.

Although every supervisor is responsible for the management of numerous resources, unquestionably the most important, overriding aspect of supervision is the management of people. A fundamental question which all supervisors ask is, "What can I do to be a more effective manager of people?" This question always has been the major challenge of supervisory management, and it will continue to be the major concern of supervisors in the future.

---

[1] Joe D. Batten, *Tough Minded Leadership* (New York: AMACOM Division of the American Management Association, 1989), pp. 1–2.

FACTORS AND TRENDS IN THE 1990s

Throughout the foreseeable future, supervisors will necessarily have to understand and deal with many complex factors and trends. It is therefore appropriate at the outset of this text to examine some of the major demographic and societal factors and trends that are likely to affect the supervisory management position. The supervisor who is sensitive to these factors and trends should be better prepared to deal with them in a positive fashion, if and when they become a reality.

Population and Labor Force Growth[2]

Since supervisory management focuses primarily on the management of people, the nature of the labor force should be of vital concern to the supervisor who plans for the future. Finding and developing qualified people have always been among the most important of supervisory responsibilities and tasks.

Despite the rather low birth rates of recent decades, the population and labor force are growing. It is estimated that the U.S. population will grow at a modest rate from a 1990 level of about 250 million people to nearly 270 million people by the year 2000.

Growing at a faster rate than the population is the labor force. From a 1990 level of about 120 million workers, the U.S. labor force is projected to increase to nearly 140 million by the year 2000, a growth of over 15 percent for the decade. It can be seen from these estimates that a somewhat higher percentage of the total population will be employed in the labor force—a continuation of a trend that has existed over the previous two decades. This, in turn, will increase the need for more and better supervisors.

Changes in Age Categories

Both the overall population and the labor force of the United States will reflect changes by age categories. The most obvious trend is that our nation is becoming older, both statistically and in reality. For example, in 1990 about 40% of the labor force was between 35 and 54 years of age; this age group will comprise about 50% of the labor force by the year 2000. Since this "mature" or

---

[2]Most of the demographic statistics and projections included in this and other sections to follow are drawn from various U.S. governmental publications. These projections assume that there will not be a major war or severe economic depression, and that the aggregate economy will grow about 2 to 3% annually.

For extensive discussion and analysis of future trends as introduced in this chapter, see *Workforce 2000*, a report published by the Hudson Institute, Indianapolis, Indiana (June, 1987); or, "Special Report—Needed; Human Capital," *Business Week* (Sept. 19, 1988, pp. 100–141.

"middle-aged" group normally provides the highest percentage of people who are promotable to supervisory and other management positions, during the 1990s more people will be available from this age group. At the same time, there will also be a corresponding increase in the need for those who possess management skills. Some authorities estimate that about 30 percent more supervisors and managers will be needed in the labor force during the decade. In order to find and develop supervisors, organizations will have an ample pool of so-called middle-aged workers, but other age categories, both younger and older employees, also will be available.

A federal law prohibits discrimination on the basis of age in the employment status of most individuals beyond 40 years of age. This law requires that hiring, promotion, and retirement decisions cannot be based on age considerations for employees who are over forty. Thus, many employees will choose to continue working as long as they are capable, which means that there will be higher numbers of people in the older age categories in the labor force. This factor will bring additional pressures on management to devote considerable attention to employee health, retirement, and pension plans which reflect these realities.

At the opposite end of the age spectrum, there will be relatively fewer young people entering the labor force. As of 1990, about 30% of the labor force was between 25 and 34 years of age; this is expected to drop to about 23% by the year 2000. Similarly, the 16-24 year age group will constitute only 16% of the labor force in the year 2000, down from 20% ten years earlier. Analysts attribute this to a so-called "baby-bust" of recent decades; some believe that the 1990s will be troubled by labor shortages because of a shortage of new entrants to the labor force. Unlikely to change, however, is the fact that many younger employees tend to possess attitudes, values, and behavior styles which are quite different from those possessed by more mature supervisors. Supervisors may well be confronted with the so-called generation gap for the foreseeable future, even if younger people are becoming more "conservative" in their political views as suggested by recent trends.

Women in the Labor Force

Probably the most dramatic change in the labor force has been the fact that both the number and percentage of women in the U.S. labor force have increased rapidly. In 1990, about 45 percent of the labor force was female. By 2000, it is estimated that this percentage will increase to nearly 50 percent of the labor force, as roughly three out of every five new entrants into the labor force during the 1990s will be women.

The Civil Rights Act of 1964 and other laws and governmental regulations prohibit employers from discriminating against women in hiring and job practices. Some of these laws and regulations require or imply special efforts or programs to upgrade and develop female employees' job opportunities. As a result women have assumed many jobs formerly dominated by men; women now hold over one-third of the nation's administrative, supervisory, and other managerial positions. Nevertheless, some companies still seem to relegate women to secondary or clerical-type positions and have not fully utilized the potential contributions that many women have to offer. As more women move into supervision and management and other upgraded positions, many will continue to need an effective combination of educational and job-related experiences to provide them with opportunities to further develop their talents and abilities.

The movement of women into the labor force, however, has brought with it a number of problems for employers that are likely to continue. For example, more than half of all mothers are employed, and more demands are being made for child-care facilities, parental leave, and other arrangements that will assist women in balancing both career and family responsibilities. Supervisors, both male and female, will be affected in many areas by the continuing "conflict" between job and family obligations faced by many women, and it is likely that many companies will find more flexible ways of accommodating women's particular needs in order to continue utilizing their services and contributions.

Growth of Racial Minorities in the Labor Force

The Civil Rights Act of 1964 and other laws and regulations prohibit employers from discrimination in employment practices on the basis of race, creed, color, religion, sex, or national origin. Other legislation has extended certain protection to individuals who are physically or otherwise handicapped. These laws and regulations have had and will continue to have a major impact on most organizations.

During the 1990s, racial minorities will enter the labor force in much greater numbers than ever before. By the year 2000, it is projected that about one out of every four workers will be nonwhite, compared to one out of every five workers at the end of the 1980s. The principal minority groups—blacks, Hispanics, and Asians—will comprise 12%, 10%, and 4%, respectively, of the labor force by the year 2000.

Not only will companies and organizations be expected to practice nondiscrimination in all employment policies, but continuing attention will be given to programs designed to give preferential access to employment and development of minority employees for positions at all levels and skills. Legally, ethically, and economically it is vital that minority persons be provided the full range of opportunities open to everyone else.

Although progress has been made in bringing minorities into and upgrading them in many organizations, progress in certain areas has been slow. Minority persons, especially blacks and Hispanics, still occupy many of the lower paying and lower skill level jobs in the work force. Further, as preferential employment policies for minorities are implemented, charges of "reverse discrimination" have been raised by certain employees, particularly white males. Supervisors in the 1990s, perhaps more than ever before, will have to cope with these types of tensions by striving to be scrupulously fair in supervising diverse groups of employees through nondiscriminatory and progressive policies and actions.

Educational Preparation

Accompanying the social changes in the racial and ethnic composition of the work force are educational preparation factors that also will challenge supervisors in the 1990s. Much of the labor force is better educated today than at any other time in history. About 85% of new entrants to the labor force have or will complete at least a high school education. More people than ever before have some college education. College graduates in 1990 made up almost a quarter of the civilian work force, compared to about 20% just ten years previously. It is estimated that about 12 million students will be enrolled in colleges and universities annually; of these, about 15% will be pursuing graduate degrees. Part-time academic and continuing-education programs for adults already employed will be a major and growing component of many institutions of higher education. Some 45% of the students pursuing academic degrees will be doing so on a part-time basis. Some forecasters believe that we may soon encounter problems with an "over-educated" labor force. That is to say, more and more college-trained employees will compete for jobs that do not necessarily require a college education to perform.

Yet we must keep in mind the other side of the picture; namely, that millions of young workers entering the labor force will not have completed a secondary education. Of those who complete high school, many will receive an inferior education because their schools do not offer the variety or quality of classes that other schools offer. Thousands more will not have completed grade school. Thus on the one hand, there will be a continual increase in better educated employees; on the other hand literally millions of people—particularly among certain minorities—will not be educationally prepared to compete for better jobs. In addition, there are many individuals entering the labor force who have had considerable formal education, but this education has not prepared them with a specific skill or talent that is directly applicable to the job market. All of these factors will put pressures on companies to provide employment and training opportunities for the unprepared and unskilled and then to train and develop those who have limited specific skills—despite their level of formal education—but who are motivated to work.[3]

---

[3]See Amanda Bennett, "Firms Become a Crucial Agent of Social Change," *The Wall Street Journal Centennial Edition* (June 23, 1989), p.A22.

Occupational and Industry Trends

Recent occupational and industry trends should continue well through the 1990s. Relatively high demands for professional, managerial, technical, clerical, sales, and skilled workers will probably continue. In total, the U.S. Department of Labor expects that some 20 million new jobs will be added to the economy during the 1990s, although growth in various job categories will be uneven.

Occupational and industry forecasts expect that there will be a steady need for more people in white-collar occupational categories and in the service industries. Among the industries expected to show the greatest job growth during coming years are: business services (e.g., computers), retail trade, health-care services, transportation, and banking and financial services. Although government services will not grow substantially, combined federal, state, and local government employment will continue to constitute some 15% of total employment in the United States. All levels of government will compete with private industry for competent and qualified workers, particularly those who have the requisite education and skills.

On the negative side, many manufacturing industries are expected to show little change or slow growth in overall employment during the 1990s. There actually may be fewer positions available in blue-collar unskilled and semi-skilled jobs in some manufacturing companies. Part of this will be the result of changing technology, which increasingly aims at substituting mechanization for labor, as well as the loss of many manufacturing jobs due to international competition, relocation of facilities outside of the United States, and foreign imports.

Changing Technology and Business Conditions

Many business organizations have been completely revamped because of technological advances, computers, robotics, automation, changing markets, and other competitive influences, which cause both internal and external adaptations. Although the pace of corporate buyouts, mergers, and acquisitions probably will be slower in the 1990s compared to the 1980s, they nevertheless will continue to occur as many companies attempt to cope with intensive pressures of domestic and foreign competition. Movement of plants, offices, and personnel will be constant and commonplace, influencing job positions, management policies, and supervisory practices.

For the foreseeable future, the "computer revolution" will continue to be apparent throughout most businesses and other organizations. Adaptations and uses for personal and desktop computers will grow as more specialized software is developed for specific purposes. It is likely that a majority of supervisors will become familiar with and/or learn how to operate computers as part of their day-to-day responsibilities.

Fig 1-1.
The "computer revolution" will continue to be apparent throughout most businesses.

Since it is difficult to forecast specifically when and how technological change may directly impact upon a supervisor's position, every supervisor will have to continue to be better educated in the broadest sense of the word. Supervisors will have to prepare themselves and their employees, both technologically and psychologically, for anticipated changes. Supervisors who keep up to date and progress with all of the changes taking place unquestionably will be more valuable to their organizations.

The story is told of a supervisor who suggested to her boss a procedure by which her own job as supervisor could be eliminated as a result of certain technological and computer changes in the company's information system. Although the supervisor's job was eliminated as a result of this suggestion, she stayed with the company; in fact, she received an increase in salary and a promotion to a higher position!

Work Scheduling and Employment Conditions

Other general conditions of work are not likely to change as rapidly as some of the other factors discussed to this point. Somewhat longer vacations, additional holidays, shorter working days, and more flexible workweeks may be granted to some workers. However, most forecasters believe that additional benefits in these areas will not expand in the 1990s, primarily because of competitive pressures in the marketplace for businesses to contain costs and maintain productivity. The average workweek will remain in the 35–40 hours a week range, and there will be a growing use of part-time employees by many companies. Part timers, also called "contingent workers," constituted some 25%

of the labor force in 1989; many employers will expand the use of such workers in the 1990s in their efforts to reduce wage and benefit costs associated with full-time employees.[4]

Many employers in the 1990s will experiment with different types of work-days and workweeks, such as flextime (where employees choose their work schedules within certain limits), job sharing (where two or more employees share a job position), and the four-day, ten-hour-a-day workweek. For those in supervisory and managerial positions, however, forecasts of shorter or flexible working hours are probably meaningless. Supervisors will be expected to work many long hours each week in order to stay on top of their broad and complex responsibilities.

Personal security is a job factor that workers are going to continue to seek in the future, particularly those who are not well equipped to cope with rapid changes in technology. Unions and minority groups in particular will continue to place pressure on companies for protection against technological change, ups and downs in the business cycle, and business disruptions. Similarly, government officials and leaders from all segments of society will become concerned about problems of job creation, job displacement, and job security. It is likely that supervisors and managers, of necessity, will devote more attention to these areas in their personnel and organizational planning.

Other Governmental and Societal Issues

Other governmental and societal issues have emerged and will continue to emerge, which will complicate the supervisory management position during the 1990s. For example, numerous environmental concerns remain as serious long-term problems for business, government, and the general public. Energy availability and costs may be determined by international and domestic political and economic changes. These types of issues and societal pressures often become part of business planning and operations.

There are already in place extensive laws and regulations that may be expanded in relation to supervisory responsibilities. For example, the Federal Occupational Safety and Health Act enables the federal government to both set and enforce safety standards in most work organizations. Numerous states have adopted their own safety laws, which require compliance by management to provide safer and healthier work environments. In addition, federal, state, and local governments have laws and regulations regarding environmental pollution and waste disposal by businesses. The effect of such legislation can be

---

[4]See Gene Koretz, ''Taking Stock of the Flexible Work Force,'' *Business Week* (July 24, 1989), p. 12. In Chapter 16, we discuss the impact on employee morale and productivity that is often associated with the expanding numbers of ''contingent workers.''

quite costly, and supervisors may be required to change their departmental operations in order to comply with environmental regulations.

Additionally, other governmental legislation regarding pension benefits, age discrimination, minimum wage and maximum hour requirements, and workers' compensation for accidental injuries on the job must be complied with by most companies and organizations. Supervisors are both directly and indirectly influenced by such governmental requirements and they must continue to stay abreast of any legislation that may influence their operations.

Further, supervisors must be sensitive to pressures that have been exerted by various special-interest groups. Consumer groups, in particular, have demanded better products and services from business, labor, and government. Environmentalists seek to influence company decisions that may have an adverse environmental impact. Some employees (especially parents of young children) will demand that their employers provide day-care facilities so that they may better combine their parental and job responsibilities. It would seem likely that numerous other permanent and temporary special-interest groups will continue to place community and political demands on ways that managers and supervisors will operate during the 1990s.

All indications are that these pressures on supervisors and managers will remain intense. A utility company supervisor said recently, ''I have to be more of a lawyer and political scientist these days than a manager!'' Although a bit overstated, this supervisor's comment reflects a realistic aspect of every supervisor's contemporary role.

SUPERVISION IN THE 1990s: PREDICTIONS AND CHALLENGES

Although it is always precarious to make forecasts, several predictions can be suggested that are likely to be part of supervisory management in future years. Experienced supervisors will recognize that most of these items already exist to a certain degree. It is vital that all supervisors are sensitive to them and plan for their continued presence.

Shifting Employee Values and Expectations

Employee values and expectations will continue to vex supervisors and managers in the 1990s. During periods of economic recession, employees typically are content to have and hold their jobs in order to survive economically. But over the long run, particularly when economic conditions are favorable, most individuals have higher expectations and aspirations about their employment situations. Work has become more than just a way of preserving life and limb. As educational levels are increased and the types of job positions that people want and hold are upgraded, work tends to become an integral part of making life more meaningful to vast numbers of people. Most professional, technical, and managerial positions offer considerable personal satisfaction as well as financial rewards. People holding these types of positions—including supervisors—usually find personal involvement, a sense of achievement, and satisfaction in the work they perform.

Many employees, however, do not find these types of personal satisfactions present in their jobs. For example, assembly-line workers and employees who perform other types of unskilled, routine, or repetitive jobs tend to find their daily work boring and unrewarding, even though they may be highly paid. When better educated people are placed in routine, monotonous jobs—whether in the factory or in the office—stresses develop, which can become more serious over time. Younger employees, in particular, tend to expect that their employment should contribute to their development as individuals, and they expect personal involvement in their jobs.

Supervisors in the 1990s will have to give greater attention to planning of jobs and the organizational structures they design. Managers at all levels will be asked to consider ways by which jobs can be upgraded and made more meaningful to employees, while at the same time being productive and efficient in contributing to organizational objectives.

Attitudes About Behavior and Authority

Shifting values and expectations concerning work have been accompanied by widespread changes in traditional attitudes and behavior patterns regarding other aspects of modern life. The decades of the 1960s and 1970s saw sweeping and even radical changes in the values that many people held concerning morality, customs, and attitudes toward established authority. However, in the 1980s, there appeared to be a swing back to more conservative social and political values, even among many young people. It is speculative whether or not this will be a temporary or permanent change in attitudes and behavior patterns during the 1990s.

However, it does appear likely that a large segment of the work force, particularly younger people, will continue to question and challenge the role of higher authority both in their personal and work lives. The traditional supremacy of management's authority in the workplace will often be criticized and challenged. Supervisors will have to be flexible—within reasonable limits—in their attitudes and responses toward employee behavior, dress, and other facets of work life. At the same time, supervisors will have to be firm in dealing with those types of unacceptable employee behavior that cannot be tolerated in any workplace situation.

Throughout the 1990s, it seems apparent that higher management everywhere will make constant, on-going demands on supervisors to obtain better productivity from all of their human resources. This pressure will foster serious strains in many organizations given the nature of the work force as it exists.

Employee Participation in Decision Making

Related to these considerations is an already established trend: employees will continue to expect a greater voice in workplace decision making. Whether or not a labor union or employee association represents employees in an organization, supervisors will come to recognize that large numbers of employees want more from their jobs and will demand a voice or influence in the kinds of decisions that are made concerning their employment. This does not have to be objectionable to a supervisor. In fact, when supervisors are willing to acknowledge that their employees have something to contribute, they will welcome employee participation in decisions rather than fear it.

Many companies and organizations already have accepted the premise that employee involvement in making suggestions and participating in decisions affecting their jobs can and should be supported. Various approaches described as "Quality Circles," "Quality of Work Life," "Japanese Style Management," and the like have been implemented in both unionized and non-unionized firms. It is likely that these types of approaches will continue to be utilized by companies during the 1990s.[5]

Some supervisors become worried when workers challenge what are referred to as management prerogatives and rights, and they prefer to think that certain areas should be beyond employee challenge. But there will continue to be pressures from employees, labor unions, minorities, and other groups for more influence in decisions surrounding the workplace. Supervisors will become accustomed to the practice of **participative management,** which essentially means a willingness to permit employees to influence or share in managerial decisions. If supervisors learn to react to this in a positive rather than a negative way, it actually should be helpful and improve their own and their company's performance.

Acquiring and Developing Human Resources

Several implications concerning the upgrading of skill levels through training and development already have been suggested. Additionally, supervisors will be required to do a better job in the selection, upgrading, and development of employees. Information and technological changes will make imperative heavy outlays of time, talent, and funds to acquire and develop human resources to their full potential. Supervisors will be asked to provide more opportunities for employee training and development in order to upgrade people from rank-and-file positions to more demanding responsibilities.

---

[5]These concepts and approaches will be discussed in more detail in Chapters 4 and 15.

Selecting Personnel.   Any human resources development program depends upon the initial selection of employees. Employers will have to become more thorough and accurate in recruitment and selection. In the past, some supervisors have approached the selection task in terms of filling a quota or finding enough people to fill available jobs. That kind of hiring pattern often backfires in turnover, employee dissatisfaction, and, most seriously, what the employee actually contributes. Better selection procedures will be a necessity in suitably matching job applicants to the kinds of positions available. At the same time, of course, all such procedures must be scrupulously fair and meet legal standards for nondiscrimination.

Matching Jobs to People.   Supervisors also will need to devote more attention to the problem of matching jobs to people, rather than simply trying to fit people to jobs. Many firms will be pressured by minorities, women, handicapped, and other groups to develop jobs to fit people who have something to contribute and who are motivated to work, even if someone does not fit the exact job specifications set by supervisors. Although this approach contradicts what appears to be the customary policy of matching people to jobs available, it can be a significant contribution toward meeting a firm's employment needs as well as its social responsibilities. This approach may be somewhat impracticable in many work situations, but too often supervisors overlook promising talents because they refuse to pursue enough creative thinking about the problem of matching jobs to people.

Fig 1–2.
Supervisors
should be
concerned with
matching jobs
to people.

Identifying and Developing Supervisors. A continuing major problem facing organizations everywhere is that some capable people shun or resist promotion to supervisory positions. They do not want the longer hours, the lessened security, and the greater pressures of supervisory management. Throughout the 1990s, supervisors must play a major role in identifying and developing those individuals who are capable of and willing to assume supervisory management and other advanced responsibilities. In fact, many supervisors will find that their own performance to some extent will be judged by higher management on the basis of whether or not they have been able to find and develop future supervisors.

Employee Motivation and Supervisory Management

All of the foregoing factors are part of the fundamental problem area of employee motivation. In order to be successful, a supervisor must effectively guide, direct, and lead employees so that they become more positively motivated and contribute fully to the objectives of the department and the total organization. Throughout the 1990s, this will remain as the primary concern and challenge facing most supervisors.

Understanding Motivation. Some supervisors believe that if their companies paid higher wages and offered better benefits, they would receive superior employee work performance in return. These supervisors should recognize, however, that wages and benefits may be determined by forces or situations over which they as supervisors have little direct control. For example, union contracts, legal requirements, the competitive ability of a firm, and other economic pressures typically are outside a supervisor's sphere of influence. Further, once salaries or wages reach a relatively high or at least a satisfactory level, monetary income may play a secondary role in the employees' attitudes and behavior.

Wages, benefits, and good working conditions are not the only influences on an employee's motivation and work performance. Of course, if these items are not satisfactory to employees, their morale will tend to be low and their work performance probably will suffer. But even where wages and benefits are good or excellent, there is no guarantee that employees will be motivated to perform beyond an average performance level. The never-ending task before a supervisor is to supervise employees in a manner that is conducive to positive employee motivation and superior work performance. Behavioral research studies have suggested that approaches which provide employees with a sense of greater responsibility, a chance to achieve, recognition, and opportunities to advance are factors that generally will have a more lasting influence on employee motivation and performance.

Better Performance Standards. Good performance standards are another important aspect of employee motivation. This problem is one which many supervisors in the past have rationalized by saying, "It can't be done because the job can't be measured." For example, many companies have few or no performance standards for most aspects of their clerical operations. Yet, many offices typically are inefficient and wasteful because supervisors have not taken the time and interest to develop adequate standards of performance.

How many companies have performance standards for technical and professional positions? This is an even greater problem. Too often supervisors of these positions have claimed, "Well, for these people, it's just not possible to develop good performance standards." Here, too, supervisors of the 1990s will be expected to formulate better, more realistic standards of performance, both quantitative and qualitative, enabling them to have adequate measures of employee performance, abilities, and contributions.

One approach that has become widely used by supervisors as a motivational device is called "management by objectives" (MBO) or "results-oriented management." This approach is based on the idea of having certain employees set their own target standards of performance (within agreed-upon limits) and later appraise themselves within the parameters of these objectives. This approach is consistent with behavioral research findings concerning employee motivation, but it requires careful and patient supervision to implement and maintain.[6]

LEADERSHIP: THE CORE OF SUPERVISORY MANAGEMENT

Although many supervisors are aware of the importance of individual and group motivation, there still is considerable misunderstanding concerning the supervisor's leadership role in influencing employee motivation and work performance. This misunderstanding often stems from a misconception regarding the meaning of leadership itself. Some supervisors believe that, because they occupy a position of responsibility and authority, this identifies them as leaders who should be followed by their subordinates. This, of course, is an oversimplified and dubious assumption.

The Test of Supervisory Leadership

Actually, it is not the supervisor's position alone that defines the supervisor as a leader. Properly understood, **leadership** is the ability to guide and influence

---

[6]The "management by objectives" approach and other aspects of employee motivation and supervisory management are discussed extensively in Chapter 4 and Chapter 7.

Fig 1–3.
Being in a
position of
authority does
not necessarily
make a leader.

the opinions, attitudes, and behavior of others. This means that anyone who is able to direct or influence others toward objectives can function as a leader.

In a workplace situation, leadership roles often are assumed by members of the work group; the direction of informal employee leadership can be supportive of or contrary to the direction the supervisor desires. For example, employee resistance to changes in work arrangements, work rules, or procedures is a common phenomenon. Such resistance usually is the result of some informal group leadership within the work group itself.

Thus leadership in the general sense should be understood as a process rather than just a positional relationship. Leadership includes what the followers or group members think and do; it does not just consist of what the supervisor does or has done. Nor does leadership necessarily occur as a result of a supervisor's authority and position, since employees obviously will have to obey certain supervisory directives as a condition of retaining their employment. *The real test of supervisory leadership occurs in the process of following on the part of the work group. It resides in a supervisor's ability to obtain the work group's willingness and enthusiasm to follow, a willingness based on commonly shared goals and objectives and a mutual effort to achieve them in a superior fashion.*

Leadership Can Be Developed

Supervisors often believe that any definition of leadership should include considerable recognition of "basic traits" possessed by a leader. That is, they

Fig 1–4.
Supervisory
leadership
results in a
work group's
willingness to
follow.

consider effective leadership as some special quality or qualities possessed by
the leader, and they point to certain successful supervisors and managers as
being representative of outstanding leadership.

Are there natural qualities or traits necessary in order to become an effective leader? Generally, the ability to lead is something that can be learned;
leaders are made, not born. Many studies have shown that there is no significant relationship between one's ability to lead and characteristics such as age,
height, weight, sex, race, and other physical attributes. Although there are
indications that successful supervisors tend to be somewhat more intelligent
than the average of their subordinates, they are not so superior in intelligence
that they cannot be understood. Intelligence is partially hereditary, but for the
most part it depends on environmental factors, such as the amount of a person's formal education and diversity of experiences. Successful supervisors
do tend to be well-rounded individuals from the standpoint of interests and
aptitudes; they are good communicators; they are mentally and emotionally
mature; and they possess a strong inner drive and personal motivation. Most
important, they tend to rely on their supervisory and managerial skills to a
greater extent than on their technical skills. These are essentially learned characteristics, rather than innate qualities or traits with which individuals are
born.

Putting this in perspective, supervisory leadership is something that an
individual supervisor can develop if the supervisor has a real desire to be a
leader and not just be someone in charge of a group of people. Most supervi-

sors can become more effective leaders if they earnestly strive to develop their managerial and human relations capacities and skills.

Effective Supervisory Leadership as a Dynamic Process

It long has been recognized that effective supervisory leadership is a dynamic process that takes place between the supervisor, the work group, and various situations confronting the supervisor.

Good communication is a central part of effective supervisory leadership. The ability to communicate well, to keep the lines of communication open at all times, and to be able to communicate in such a way that the expectations and needs of workers are met are essential requisites for any supervisor to be a leader.

The nature of the work environment, the size of the work group, and the type of people involved also are important. Generally, the larger the work group, the more important it is for the supervisor to be an effective planner, organizer, and coordinator of activities. The larger the work group, the more the supervisor will have to delegate authority. The smaller the work group and the closer the supervisor physically is located to the employees, the more he or she must consider and deal with the individual expectations and needs of those in the group.

Understanding the expectations of employees is vital in effective supervision. As discussed previously, today's employees desire some degree of participation in decisions that are made concerning their jobs. However, there are times when a supervisor must exercise authority and make decisions that may not be popular with the work group. The ability of the supervisor to assess the expectations of employees and the demands of the job situation and then to act appropriately are skills that can be developed with experience and practice.

Although many such studies have been made, one of the most famous series of studies focusing upon employees' needs and expectations, supervisory leadership, and productivity was conducted by behavioral science researchers from the University of Michigan a number of years ago.[7] In studies made of office employees, railroad workers, and factory employees, it was established that a similar type of supervisory leadership pattern consistently was associated with high productivity and a high degree of job satisfaction experienced

---

[7] For a review of these studies, as well as a review of other research findings concerning supervisory style, productivity, and employee job satisfaction, see: Rensis Likert, *New Patterns of Management* (New York: McGraw-Hill Book Company, Inc., 1967), pp. 13–46. See also Leslie Rue and Lloyd Byars, *Management: Theory and Application* (4th ed.; Homewood, Illinois; Richard D. Irwin, Inc., 1986), pp. 389–390.

by work-group members. This effective supervisory leadership pattern included the following significant characteristics:

1. General supervision rather than close, detailed supervision of employees.
2. More time devoted to supervisory activities than in doing work normally assigned to employees.
3. Much attention to planning of work and special tasks.
4. A willingness to permit employees to participate in the decision making process.
5. An approach to the job situation described as being employee centered (that is, showing a sincere interest in the needs and problems of employees as individuals), as well as being interested in high production.

HUMAN ASPECTS OF SUPERVISORY MANAGEMENT ARE CONSTANT

The above model still appears to be a useful approach for supervisors to utilize in the 1990s, because the fundamental human aspects of the supervisory management position have not changed significantly over the years, nor are they likely to change in the future. As an illustration, consider the results of a major survey involving respondents from a dozen business organizations and two major governmental agencies. In this survey, supervisors, managers, and employees identified what they considered to be the ten most important qualities and practices of an effective supervisor/manager. These were as follows:[8]

1. Providing direction by establishing clear goals, communicating those goals, involving others in setting goals, and delegating effectively.
2. Encouraging open, two-way communication by being candid and honest in dealings with others.
3. Coaching and supporting people.
4. Providing "objective recognition." This was defined as recognizing individuals for good performance, rather than just criticizing them for performance problems; and relating rewards to the excellence of job performance.
5. Establishing reasonable controls by following up and giving subordinates feedback on how they are doing.
6. Selecting the right people to staff the organization.
7. Understanding the financial implications of decisions.
8. Encouraging innovation and new ideas.
9. Giving subordinates clear-cut decisions when they are needed.
10. Consistently demonstrating high levels of integrity.

---

[8]The survey was conducted by Harbridge House, Inc., a Boston-based management consulting firm, and it was summarized in *The Right Report*, (Volume 2, Number 4, Fall, 1984, issue), a publication of Right Associates Management Consultants.

It would appear from these and other studies that "the more things change, the more they stay the same" in identifying effective leadership in supervision. As in the past, the success of a supervisor in the 1990s will usually reside in a supervisor's ability to blend the requirements for high work performance with a personal approach to employees that recognizes and respects them as human beings. For example, a number of studies have shown that employees in high-producing work groups tend to describe their supervisors as taking a personal interest in them, as being less authoritarian and punitive than other supervisors, and as being helpful in training them for higher positions. At the same time, however, these same high-producing work groups recognize their supervisors as leaders who expect and accept nothing less than high productivity and good performance.

Looking at this another way, most successful supervisors are those who can reach a degree of mutual harmony between company and departmental objectives and the needs, objectives, and activities of the people they supervise. Although this relationship is often difficult to implement and to achieve, it is essential to successful supervisory management. Of course, the nature of the organization, top management policies, the technology and types of work involved, and many other factors will influence how to apply this type of supervisory leadership approach within an organization.[9] But supervisors should continually strive to develop a sound leadership pattern, one which offers the greatest possibilities for achieving objectives and excellent performance within their departments.

SUPERVISION: A PROFESSIONAL PERSPECTIVE

Supervisors have a primary managerial responsibility for the utilization of what we consider to be the most important resource that must be managed— the human resource. It is the human resource upon which any organization ultimately depends. This starts with the selection and training of people to fill job openings, and it continues with the ongoing development, motivation, and leadership of people and with helping prepare them for jobs in the future.

Thus supervisors throughout the 1990s will have to become true professionals with a growing professional perspective. Supervisors will have to develop as innovators and idea people. They must look to the future with a

---

[9]Two books that have received widespread publicity concerning management practices of successful major corporations are, Thomas J. Peters and Robert H. Waterman, Jr., *In Search of Excellence* (New York; Harper & Row Publishers, 1982); and Robert Levering and Michael Katz, *The 100 Best Companies to Work for in America* (Reading, Mass.: Addison-Wesley Publishing Co., 1984). Although these books involve various factors and considerations that are rather broad in dimension, the companies reported on consistently were shown to have a high concern for their human resources, both in terms of their well-being and to motivate individuals to strive for high levels of achievement and contributions to their organizations.

professional awareness of the trends influencing human behavior and observe how these trends have an impact on the management of people in a complex society.

In all of this, there is an imperative thread. This is the professional perspective, which recognizes the need for constant self-improvement and self-renewal. No amount of formal or informal education can ever be considered enough for a supervisor's personal program of self-improvement. Supervisors must recognize that they, too, can become obsolete unless they constantly take measures to update their own fund of knowledge through a program of continuous self-development.

The supervisor who masters the managerial concepts and skills discussed in this text should make considerable progress in terms of personal development, but just knowing concepts and approaches is not enough. The supervisor must constantly seek new ways to apply this knowledge in the very challenging, complex, and dynamic situations that will be encountered.

SUMMARY

Supervisory management focuses primarily on the management of people. Consequently, supervisors must recognize and understand the many factors and trends surrounding the labor force that will have an impact on how most organizations will operate.

During the 1990s, the labor force will grow at a somewhat faster rate than the overall population, and the age composition of the labor force will be a changing one. Women will continue to enter the labor force in increasing numbers, and they will be utilized more fully than they have been in the past, including further advancement in supervisory and management positions. Similarly, minority persons and other categories of people who are protected by laws and regulations will continue to press for nondiscriminatory treatment and opportunities for upgrading in their employment. Educational levels of the work force generally will reflect an increase in better educated workers; but millions of people will not be prepared educationally to qualify for many of the employment opportunities available.

Occupational and industry trends, changing technology and business conditions, and governmental and societal pressures will be major influences on supervisory management. Governmental laws and regulations will continue to have a major impact upon the policies and activities of most organizations.

Supervisors in the 1990s will have to be sensitive to existing and expected employee trends. For example, more employees than ever before will expect their jobs to have greater personal meaning to them as individuals. Varying employee behavior patterns and attitudes toward authority, especially among younger workers, mean that supervisors will have to be somewhat flexible in their approaches to managing. Employees will continue to expect a greater voice in workplace decision making. There will be increasing demands on supervisors to select, train, and develop human resources to the fullest extent that is feasible under the circumstances.

Effective supervisory management means that supervisors must become leaders in the true sense of the word. Supervisory leadership primarily resides in the ability of a supervisor to influence the opinions, attitudes, and performance of employees. The test of supervisory leadership is found in the ability to obtain the willingess and enthusiasm of workers to follow the supervisor's lead in accomplishing goals and objectives. The supervisor who aspires to become a more effective leader needs to have a professional outlook and must recognize the necessity for a personal program of continuous self-development.

QUESTIONS FOR DISCUSSION

1. Discuss how each of the following factors or trends may influence supervisory management in the 1990s:
   a. Population and labor force growth.
   b. Age distributions of the labor force.
   c. Women in the labor force.
   d. Minorities and other legally protected groups in the labor force.
   e. Educational trends.
   f. Organizational and industry trends.
   g. Changing technology and business conditions.
   h. Work scheduling and employment conditions
   i. Other governmental and societal issues.
2. Analyze how each of the following may influence a supervisor's planning and functioning in the future:
   a. Shifting values and expectations of employees.
   b. Employee attitudes about behavior and authority.
   c. Employee desires to participate in workplace decision making.
   d. The ongoing need to acquire and develop human resources, including supervisors.
   e. Employee motivational factors as related to supervisory management.
3. Define supervisory leadership. What is ''the real test'' of supervisory leadership?
4. Why is it generally correct to say that ''Leaders are made, not born''?
5. Discuss the dynamic factors involved in effective supervisory leadership. Why is the concept of blending organizational (supervisory) objectives with the employees' needs and objectives at the heart of effective supervisory leadership?
6. Why will supervisors have to grow as professionals if they are to keep up with the demands of their positions? Why is continuous self-development vital to the supervisory role?

CHAPTER 2

The Managerial Functions

CHAPTER OBJECTIVES

1. To identify the managerial role of the supervisor, who serves as the link between employees and higher management.
2. To emphasize the importance and benefits of the managerial capabilities and skills, even more so than technical skills, in supervisory performance.
3. To define and discuss the primary management functions and how these are interrelated, with emphasis on their special meaning for the supervisor.
4. To introduce the concept of authority as a requirement of any managerial position.
5. To discuss the attainment of coordination and cooperation in supervision and how these depend on the proper performance of the managerial functions.

The supervisory position within the management structure of most organizations has long been acknowledged as a difficult and demanding role. Supervisors have been depicted as being ''people in the middle,'' since supervisors are the principal link between higher management and the employees (see Figure 2–1).

To employees, a supervisor may be viewed as being *the* management of the organization; their supervisor is the primary contact that employees have with management. Employees expect a supervisor to be technically competent and to be a good leader and boss who can show them how to get a job done. But the supervisor also must be a competent subordinate to higher management—for example, to the division head or plant superintendent. In this role the supervisor must be a good follower. Further, the supervisor is expected to maintain satisfactory relationships with management heads of other departments and units. Thus a supervisor's relationship to other supervisors is that of a colleague who must cooperate and coordinate the department's efforts with others in order to reach the overall objectives and goals of the organization.

In general, the job of any supervisor has two main requirements. First, the supervisor must have a sufficient knowledge of the jobs to be performed and should be technically competent to accomplish the tasks assigned. The second—and more significant—aspect of the supervisor's job is managing, that is, running the department. It is the managerial competence of a supervisor that usually determines the effectiveness of his or her performance. Further, supervisory management often is the first level in a career of managerial positions that will demand more and more managerial competence on the way up.

Fig 2–1.
A supervisor is the principal link between employees and higher management.

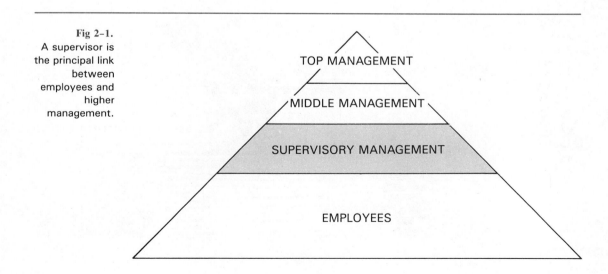

TOP MANAGEMENT

MIDDLE MANAGEMENT

SUPERVISORY MANAGEMENT

EMPLOYEES

THE SUPERVISOR'S MANAGERIAL ROLE

In most organizations there are supervisors who typically appear to be under constant pressure and who continuously are involved in doing the work at hand. They are "getting by," although they claim that they are overburdened with work. These supervisors endure hard and long hours, they may be very devoted to their jobs, and they are willing to do everything themselves. They are supervisors who want to be effective, although they admit that they seldom have enough time to actually supervise. In the same organizations there are other supervisors who usually appear to be on top of their jobs and whose departments function in a smooth and orderly manner. These supervisors find time to sit at their desks at least part of the day, and they are able to keep their desk work up to date. Why is there a difference?

Managerial Capabilities and Skills

Of course, there are some supervisors who essentially are more capable than others, just as there are poor and better mechanics. However, if we were to compare two maintenance supervisors who are equally good mechanics, who have similar equipment under their care, and who operate under about the same conditions, why might one be more effective than the other? The answer probably is that the one has learned to manage the departmental operations in a manner that gets the job done through and with the efforts of his or her people. The difference between a good supervisor and a poor supervisor,

Fig 2–2. The effective supervisor is on top of the job rather than "snowed under."

assuming that their technical skills are basically similar, is the difference in their managerial capabilities and skills.

The managerial aspects of the supervisor's position too often have been neglected in the selection and development of supervisors. Consider the background of many supervisors. Typically they were selected for their supervisory positions on the basis of their education or technical competence, their seniority or past performance, and their willingness to work hard. When appointed supervisors, they were expected to assume responsibilities of management, but little was done to train or develop them to carry out these management responsibilities. In other words, little was done to help these individuals cope with the managerial aspects of their new supervisory jobs. Thus, more or less overnight, the supervisors were made a part of management without having been prepared to be managers. So, they do the best they can by imitating and learning from their predecessors. Their departments may even function reasonably well. But over time, unless supervisors learn and understand the managerial aspects of their positions and apply them systematically, they find that the departments are running them instead of their running the departments.

Some writers have grouped managerial capabilities and skills needed by supervisors into four major classifications. These are: (1) **conceptual skills**—the ability to obtain, utilize, interpret, and apply the necessary information in order to make sound decisions; (2) **human relations skills**—the ability to deal with and work with and through people; (3) **administrative skills**—the ability to plan, to organize, to coordinate, and to handle the administrative and paper work components of the position; and (4) **technical skills**—the knowledge of and ability to perform the actual jobs within the area of responsibility of the supervisor. All of these capabilities and skills are important to a supervisor's performance, but increasingly it is recognized that the possession of technical skills alone will not be sufficient to identify and develop a good manager at the supervisory level.

The Need for Technical Competence in Supervision

Although a supervisor should strive to become a good manager, this does not mean that the supervisor's departmental responsibilities, which are job-oriented in nature, can be neglected. A competent supervisor of a department must thoroughly understand the specific, technical aspects of its operations. Perhaps the supervisor actually is the most skilled person within the department and is able to do a quicker, more efficient job than most of the subordinates. Yet, the supervisor must learn to avoid "stepping in" and personally doing the employees' jobs except for the purpose of instruction or in short-handed or emergency situations.[1] The responsibility of a supervisor as a man-

---

[1] In some companies a union contract may severely restrict supervisors from performing "bargaining unit" work.

ager is to see that the employees do their jobs and do them properly. As a manager, the supervisor must plan, guide, and supervise.

In this regard, however, we are not referring to those supervisors who are considered to be *working supervisors,* or *lead persons,* whose responsibilities include performing certain jobs within their departments. Supervisors of very small departments, for example, often are expected to perform a certain share of the workload assigned to their units. Similarly, supervisors in retail stores and supervisors in many service occupations and organizations typically work along with their employees in order to get the work accomplished. Nevertheless, it should be recognized that whenever a supervisor is occupied with a job that could be performed by an employee, the supervisor's managerial functions necessarily are neglected.

At the other extreme are those departments that are involved in varied and complex operations and where individual jobs may be quite diversified and even specialized. In these situations, it would be impossible for a supervisor to comprehend the exact details of each job. Here, too, it still remains important for the supervisor to at least understand the broad technical aspects of each job under his or her supervision—and to know where to get help and assistance when it is needed.

The Relationship Between Managerial and Technical Skills

As stated above, supervisors should possess or be acquainted with the technical knowledge and skills and specific know-how of the particular jobs and fields which they supervise. For example, a nursing supervisor must know the profession of nursing. A construction supervisor must know the skills of the construction trades, such as carpentry and bricklaying. A word-processing supervisor who is not knowledgeable in the computer field would be at a great disadvantage. This supervisor would first have to learn and understand the department's computer and word-processing system in order to become an effective manager of the department.

However, mere technical know-how or knowledge would not be sufficient. Besides being technically competent or knowledgeable, supervisors should also possess the skills of a manager. Further, as supervisors advance upward in the managerial ranks, they will rely less on their technical skills and will find it increasingly more important to apply their managerial capabilities and skills. Most top executives usually possess fewer specific technical skills than those who are employed in lower level managerial positions. In moving to the top, an executive probably has acquired numerous managerial capabilities and skills which are utilized in directing the entire organization. For example, the chief executive of a company is concerned primarily with the management of overall activities, and the executive's duties for the most part are conceptual, managerial, and administrative. Most of the top executive's time is spent applying broad managerial skills to guide and coordinate the efforts of all subordinate managers and supervisors towards common objectives.

Managerial Capabilities and Skills Can Be Learned and Developed

Many people believe that good managers, like good athletes, are born, not made. Much research has indicated that this belief is generally incorrect, even though it cannot be denied that people are born with different physiological potential and that, to some degree, heredity does play a role in some people's intelligence. An athlete who is not endowed with natural physical advantages is not likely to run a hundred yards in record time. On the other hand, many individuals who are "natural athletes" have not come close to that goal either.

Most superior athletes are individuals who have developed their natural endowments into mature skills by practice, learning, effort, sacrifice, and experience. The same holds true for a good manager. The skills involved in managing are as learnable as are the skills used in playing tennis. It does take time, effort, and determination for a supervisor to develop managerial capabilities and skills, as these are not acquired instantaneously. As the supervisor performs the job, some mistakes will be made; but learning comes from mistakes as well as successes. By applying the principles and guidelines discussed in this text, the supervisor will become more effective, and will be able to prevent many of the difficulties which can make the supervisory job a burden instead of a challenging and satisfying career.

Benefits from Better Supervisory Management

Many significant benefits will accrue to a supervisor who learns to be a better manager. A supervisor has daily opportunities to apply managerial principles and managerial knowledge in the present job. Proper application of the principles of management to supervisory work will contribute to a smoother functioning department where the work gets done on time and where the workers more willingly and enthusiastically contribute toward stated objectives. The application of management principles will put supervisors on top of the job, instead of being "swallowed up" by it. Supervisors who manage well are more likely to contribute with suggestions and advice to higher management and to other supervisors in areas where they were not consulted previously. Effective supervisors become aware of the needs and objectives of other departments as well as the interrelationships between those other departments and their own. They seek to work in closer harmony with colleagues who supervise other departments. Briefly, better supervisory management means doing a more effective job with much less effort.

In addition to direct benefits, there are indirect benefits. The supervisor who manages well will grow in stature and, as time goes on, will be capable of handling larger and more complicated assignments. The supervisor who develops as a manager will be ready for more responsible and higher paying positions within the managerial hierarchy. An additional satisfying thought is that the functions of management are applicable in any organization and at all managerial and supervisory levels, regardless of where a supervisor's future career may lead.

THE FUNCTIONS OF MANAGEMENT

In this text the terms ''supervisor'' and ''manager'' are used interchangeably. However, the term supervisor primarily is used to describe a person occupying the first-line level of management, that is, one who is in charge of a department of rank-and-file employees. We use the terms ''executive'' and ''administrator'' to identify an individual who is at a higher level in the organization than a ''supervisor.'' References will be made to supervisory, managerial, and administrative functions as being the same. There are some theoretical distinctions that could be considered, but for our purposes we consider the major functions of management to be the same throughout all levels of management.

Also, throughout the text we use the terms ''employee,'' ''worker,'' and ''subordinate'' interchangeably to refer generally to individuals who report to and carry out directives from their supervisors or managers.

Definition of Supervisory Management

The term management has been defined in many ways. One general definition of **management** is that it is a process involving the effective and efficient integration and coordination of all resources, both human and technical, to accomplish various desired objectives.[2]

At the supervisory level, a more focused definition would be that **supervisory management** is the process of getting things accomplished with and through people by guiding and motivating their efforts toward common objectives. In most endeavors one person can accomplish relatively little. Therefore, individuals join forces with others in order to attain the goals of any group or organization. In a business enterprise, top managers are responsible for achieving the goals of the organization, but this requires the efforts of all subordinate managers and employees. Those who hold supervisory positions significantly influence the effectiveness with which people work together and utilize the resources available in order to attain stated objectives and goals. The managerial role of a supervisor is to have assigned tasks accomplished

---

[2]Michael Hitt, R. Dennis Middlemist, and Robert Mathis, *Management: Concepts and Practice* (2d ed; Saint Paul: West Publishing Company, 1986), p. 11.

with and through the help of employees. Thus the better the supervisor manages, the better will be the departmental results.

Although we do not stress legal distinctions in this text, it is interesting to note that the National Labor Relations Act (as amended), which governs federal labor relations policy, only defines the term "supervisor" and does not use or define the term "manager." Section 2(11) of this Act defines a supervisor as follows:

> The term "supervisor" means any individual having authority, in the interest of the employer, to hire, transfer, suspend, lay off, recall, promote, discharge, assign, reward, or discipline other employees, or responsibility to direct them, or to adjust their grievances, or effectively to recommend such action, if in connection with the foregoing the exercise of such authority is not of a merely routine or clerical nature, but requires the use of independent judgment.

Managerial Functions Are the Same in All Managerial Positions

The managerial functions of all supervisors are the same, regardless of the technical functions in which they are engaged. The managerial functions of a supervisory position are similar whether it involves supervision of a production line, a housekeeping division, a laboratory, a maintenance department, or word-processing services. Further, the primary managerial functions are the same regardless of the level within the hierarchy of management. It does not matter whether one is a supervisor "on the firing line," whether one is in middle-level management, or whether one is part of the top-management (or executive) group. Nor does it matter in what kind of organization one is working. Managerial functions are the same whether the supervisor is working in an industrial enterprise, a commercial enterprise, a nonprofit organization, a fraternal organization, a government office, a school, or a hospital. Supervisors, as well as other managers in all organizations, perform the same basic managerial functions. The "labels" used to identify these functions may vary somewhat in management literature. For purposes of familiarity and convenience, in this text we classify these functions under the major categories of *planning, organizing, staffing, directing,* and *controlling.* The following description of these functions is general and brief, since most of this text is devoted to discussing and expanding upon the meaning and ramifications of these functions—particularly at the supervisory level.

Planning.   The initial managerial function, which consists of determining what should be done in the future, is called **planning.** It consists of setting goals, objectives, policies, procedures, and other plans needed to achieve the purposes of the organization. In planning, the manager contemplates and decides from various alternative courses that are available. Planning is primarily conceptual and intellectual in nature. It means thinking before acting, looking ahead and preparing for the future, laying out in advance the road to be followed, and thinking about what and how the job should be done. It includes collecting and sorting data and information from numerous sources in order to make decisions.

Many supervisors find that they are constantly confronted with one crisis after another. The probable reason for this is that they neglect to plan; they do not look much beyond the day's events. It is every supervisor's responsibility to plan, and this cannot be delegated to someone else. Certain specialists, such as a budget officer, a production scheduler, or an engineer, may provide the supervisor with assistance in planning. But it is up to each supervisor, as the manager of a department, to make specific departmental plans which must coincide with the general objectives established by higher management.

As the supervisor proceeds with other managerial functions, planning continues, previous plans are revised, and different alternatives are chosen as the need arises. This is particularly true as a supervisor evaluates the results of previous plans and adjusts future plans accordingly. Planning is the managerial function that comes first, and a supervisor will continue to plan while performing the other managerial functions.

Organizing.   Once plans have been made, the **organizing** function primarily answers the question, "How will the work be divided and accomplished?" This means that the supervisor defines the various activities and job duties, and groups these activities into distinct areas, subdepartments, sections, units, or teams. The supervisor must determine and enumerate the duties required, assign them, and, at the same time, provide subordinates with the authority needed to carry out their tasks. Organizing means designing the department's structural framework within which job duties are to be performed and deciding how such duties are related to one another.

The structural framework of a department must fit into the organization's overall framework. When designing the organization's overall structural framework, top management must make sure that authority relationships among departmental supervisors are appropriately established. This requires that top management delegate authority to middle managers and that there is further delegation to supervisors. It is essential for a supervisor to possess authority in order to manage effectively (as discussed in this and other chapters). In performing the departmental organizing function, the supervisor in turn clarifies boundaries of authority and responsibility within the department itself. By organizing, the supervisor creates an *activity–authority network* for the department in accordance with and within the overall organization structure.

Staffing.   The managerial tasks of recruiting, selecting, orienting, and training employees may be grouped within the function called **staffing.** This function includes appraising the performance of employees, promoting employees where appropriate, and providing them with further opportunities for development. In addition, staffing includes devising an equitable compensation system and rates of pay. Some of the specific technical activities involved in the staffing function are handled and facilitated by the human resources (or personnel) department in many companies. However, day-to-day responsibility for essential aspects of the staffing function remains with the supervisor.

Directing.   To direct means to issue orders and instructions so that jobs are done and objectives are accomplished. The **directing** function of management involves guiding, teaching, and supervising subordinates. This includes developing the abilities of employees to their maximum potential by directing, teaching, and coaching them effectively. It is not sufficient for a supervisor just to plan, organize, and have enough employees available. The supervisor must attempt to positively motivate them as they go about their work. Directing is the day-to-day process around which all supervisory performance revolves.

Directing is also known as **leading, motivating,** or **influencing,** since it plays a major role in employee morale, job satisfaction, productivity, and communication. It is through the directing function that the supervisor seeks to create a climate which is conducive to employee satisfaction and at the same time achieves the objectives of the department. A supervisor will spend a large part of each day directing subordinates. As a matter of fact, probably most of a supervisor's time is spent on the directing function, since it is the function around which departmental performance revolves.

Controlling.   The managerial function of **controlling** involves those activities that are necessary to make certain that objectives are achieved and plans are followed. Controlling means to determine whether plans are being met; to decide whether progress is being made toward objectives; and, if necessary, to correct deviations and shortcomings. Here, too, the importance of planning as the first function of management should be obvious. It would not be possible for a supervisor to determine whether work was proceeding properly if there were no plans against which to check. If plans or standards are superficial or poorly conceived, the controlling function is severely limited in scope. Thus controlling means not only to make sure that objectives are achieved, but also to take corrective action in case of failure to achieve planned objectives. It also means revising plans if circumstances require it.

The Continuous Flow of Managerial Functions

The five managerial functions can be viewed as a circular, continuous movement. (Yet in daily supervisory activities, the supervisor may feel that the job is a "vicious circle" with neither a beginning nor an end!) If we view the managerial process as a circular flow (Figure 2–3) consisting of the five functions, we can see that the functions flow into each other and that each affects the performance of the others. At times there is no clear line to mark where one function ends and the other begins. Also, it is not possible for a supervisor to set aside a certain amount of time for one or another function, since the effort spent in each function will vary as conditions and circumstances change. But there is no doubt that planning must come first. Without plans, the supervisor cannot organize, staff, direct, or control.

Managerial Functions Relative to Time and Position

Managerial functions essentially are the same for all managers, whether they are board chairpersons, top executives, middle managers, or supervisors on the "firing line." This concept has been referred to as the **principle of universality of managerial functions.**

However, the time and effort devoted to each of these functions will vary, depending on a person's level within the management hierarchy. It is likely that the top executive will spend most of the time carrying out the planning, organizing, and controlling functions and less time in staffing and directing. Typically, the first-line supervisor of a department will spend more time directing and controlling, and less time planning, organizing, and staffing. The chief executive will tend to plan for at least one year ahead, or for five or even ten or twenty years ahead. The supervisor normally will make plans for much shorter periods. There are times when the supervisor will plan for only the next few weeks, for the present week, for the present day, or even for the present shift. Thus both the span and the magnitude of the first-line supervisor's plans will be smaller. For example, an executive may plan for a capital investment program involving millions of dollars and the entire plant. By com-

Fig 2–3.
The circular concept illustrates the close and continuous relationship among the managerial functions.

parison, the first-line supervisor typically plans for the use of employees, equipment, and material for a rather short period of time and involving restricted amounts of money and resources.

The same is true for the directing function. The top executive, who delegates and depends on subordinate managers to carry out assignments, normally will spend a minimum of time directing and supervising. The first-line supervisor, however, will be concerned with getting the job done each day and will have to spend considerable time and effort directing.

Therefore, to review what has been emphasized: all managers perform the same managerial functions regardless of their level in the hierarchy. The time and effort involved in each of these functions will vary and depend on the rung of the management ladder the manager occupies. This is illustrated in Figure 2–4.

COMPONENTS OF A MANAGERIAL POSITION

Two essential components must be present to determine whether a member of an organization truly is a manager. These components (or characteristics) are defined by answers to the following two questions: (1) Does the person perform all the managerial functions? and (2) Does the person possess managerial authority? If both of these questions can be answered affirmatively, then the individual is acting as a manager in the accepted sense of the word. If either of these components is lacking, regardless of the best intentions or of outward

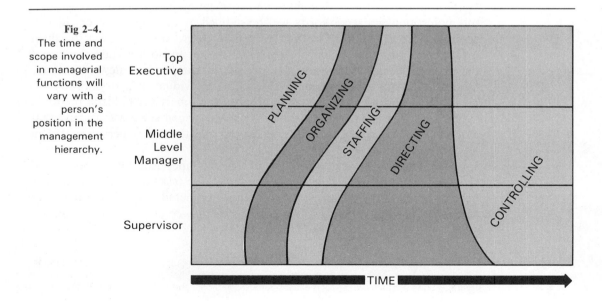

Fig 2–4. The time and scope involved in managerial functions will vary with a person's position in the management hierarchy.

Top Executive

Middle Level Manager

Supervisor

PLANNING ORGANIZING STAFFING DIRECTING CONTROLLING

TIME

Fig 2–5. Performance of managerial functions and possession of authority are essential components of a managerial position.

signs or titles, the individual is not really a manager in the true sense of the word.

MANAGERIAL AUTHORITY

Without authority, an individual in an organization cannot be a manager. At this point **managerial authority** will be defined as the legitimate or rightful power to direct others, the right to order and to act.[3] It is the power by which a manager can require subordinates to do or not to do a certain thing that the manager deems appropriate and necessary in order to achieve objectives. Managerial authority does not adhere to the individual; it is organizational, positional authority attached to the position the supervisor holds at the time. When the supervisor leaves the job or is replaced, he or she ceases to have that authority. When a successor takes over this position, that person will then have that authority.

Having managerial authority means that the supervisor has the power and right to issue directives in order to accomplish the tasks and duties that have been assigned to the department. This authority includes the right and power to impose sanctions, if necessary. Without such leverage to enforce an order,

---

[3]Technically, this is *line* or *scalar* authority. As the text progresses, other concepts of managerial authority are discussed from additional points of view that supervisors must consider in their positions. Further, we do not make any legal distinctions, such as are included in federal and state laws.

an enterprise would become disorganized and possibly even chaotic. In the case where a worker refuses to carry out a directive, a supervisor's authority includes the power and right to take disciplinary action, even to the extent of discharging the subordinate. Of course, this power, like all authority, has limitations in many respects. For example, a union contract and legal restrictions may require that certain steps or conditions be fulfilled before a worker can be discharged.

Avoiding Reliance on Managerial Authority

Most successful supervisors know that in order to persuade and motivate workers to perform their required duties, it usually is best not to rely on their formal managerial authority but to utilize other approaches. Generally, it is better for a supervisor not to ''show'' power and formal authority, and in practice it has come to the point where many supervisors prefer not even to speak about their authority. They prefer to speak of ''responsibility,'' ''tasks,'' or ''duties'' which they have, instead of stating that they possess authority. Some supervisors consider it better to say that they have responsibility for certain activities, instead of saying that they have authority within that area. Using the words responsibility, tasks, and duties in this sense—although these certainly are not the same as authority—helps the supervisor to avoid showing the ''club'' of authority.

Regardless of how a supervisor applies authority, the point to remember is that the supervisory position must have it. Without managerial authority, a supervisor cannot adequately perform as a manager. Without the right to give directives to workers, the supervisor-subordinate relationship is weakened and confusion or chaos inevitably will result.

Delegating Authority

Included within positional managerial authority is the right and duty to delegate authority. Delegation of authority is the process by which the supervisor receives authority from a higher level manager and, in turn, entrusts some of this authority to subordinates. Just as the possession of authority is a required component of any managerial position, the process of delegating authority to lower levels within the hierarchy is required for an organization to have effective managers, supervisors, and employees. In the next chapter, we discuss in considerable detail the concepts of authority, responsibility, and the delegation of authority.

COORDINATION

Supervisory management was generally defined as a process of getting things done through and with the help of people by directing their efforts toward common objectives. In a sense, all levels of management could be broadly visualized as involving the coordination of efforts of all the members and resources of an organization toward overall objectives. Some writers, therefore, have included the concept of coordination as a separate managerial function.

Coordination is the orderly synchronization (or putting together) of efforts of the members and resources of an organization to provide the proper amount, timing, and quality of execution that will bring about the accomplishment of the organization's objectives. We prefer to view coordination as being an implicit, interrelated aspect of the five major managerial functions previously cited. That is, coordination is fostered whenever a manager performs any and all of the managerial functions appropriately, and we believe that it should not be viewed as a separate function. A supervisor achieves coordination while properly performing the managerial functions of planning, organizing, staffing, directing, and controlling. In a sense, coordination can be best understood as being a direct result of good management, rather than being thought of as a managerial function in itself.

Achieving coordination typically is more difficult at the executive level than at the supervisory level. The chief executive officer has to achieve synchronization of use of resources and human efforts throughout the entire organization, that is, throughout numerous departments and levels. A supervisor of one department has the responsibility to achieve coordination primarily within the department. However, this, too, can be quite difficult to achieve, especially during periods of rapid change.

Cooperation As Related to Coordination

The concept of coordination should not be confused with cooperation, since there is considerable difference between them. **Cooperation** indicates the degree of willingness of individuals to work with and help each other. It primarily involves the attitudes of a group of people. Coordination is much more inclusive, requiring more than the mere desire and willingness of participants.

For example, consider a group of workers attempting to move a heavy object. They are sufficient in number, willing and eager to cooperate with each other, and trying their best to move the object. They are also fully aware of their common purpose. However, in all likelihood their efforts will be of little avail until one of them—the supervisor—gives the proper orders to apply the right amount of effort at the right place at the right time. Then they can move the object. It is possible that by sheer coincidence mere cooperation could have brought about the desired result in this instance; but no supervisor can afford to rely upon such a coincidental occurrence. Although cooperation is desirable and helpful, and the lack of it could prevent or impede coordination, its presence alone will not assure coordination. Coordination is ''superior'' in order of importance to cooperation.

Attaining Coordination

Coordination is not easily attained, and the task of achieving coordination is becoming more complex. As an organization grows, coordinating the many activities of various departments becomes an increasingly complicated problem for higher management. At the supervisory level, as the number and types of positions within a department increase, the need for coordination in order to obtain desired results similarly increases.

Complexities of human nature present additional problems of coordination. Many employees understandably are preoccupied with their own work because, in the final analysis, they primarily are evaluated on how they do their jobs. Therefore, they tend not to become involved in other areas, and often they are indifferent to the fact that their activities may have a significant bearing on other departments of the company.

Coordination As Part of the Managerial Functions.   While performing the managerial functions, the supervisor should recognize that coordination is a desired result of effective management. Proper attention to coordination within each of the five managerial functions contributes to overall coordination.

The planning stage is the critical and ideal time for fostering coordination, since a supervisor must see to it that the various plans within the department are properly interrelated. For example, a supervisor may wish to discuss departmental job assignments with the workers who are to carry them out. In this way they have the opportunity to express their opinions or objections, which need to be reconciled in advance. Further, employees may be encouraged to make suggestions and to participate in discussing the merits of proposed plans and alternatives. If employees are involved in departmental planning at the initial stages, the supervisor's chances for achieving coordination usually will be improved.

This same concern for coordination should be prevalent when a supervisor organizes. The purpose of setting up a structural framework concerning who is to do what, when, where, and how is to obtain coordination. For example, whenever a new and different job is to be done, a supervisor assigns it to the unit that has employees who are best suited or best able to be trained to accomplish the work. Thus whenever a supervisor groups activities and assigns subordinates to them, the thought of coordination should be uppermost. Achieving coordination also should be of concern as a supervisor establishes authority relationships within the department and among employees. Clear statements as to specific duties and reporting relationships in the department will foster coordination and prevent duplication of efforts and confusion.

Similarly, coordination should be a high priority when a supervisor performs the staffing function. There must be the right number of workers possessing the proper skills in all of the positions to assure the group's effective performance. The supervisor must see to it that employees have the abilities and job training that will contribute to the coordination of their efforts.

When directing, the supervisor is significantly involved in coordination. The essence of giving instructions is to coordinate the activities of employees in such a manner that the overall objectives will be reached in the most efficient way possible. In addition, a supervisor must assess and reward the performance of employees in order to maintain a reasonably harmonious work group.

Last, but certainly not least, the supervisor is concerned with coordination when performing the controlling function. By checking, monitoring, and observing, the supervisor makes certain that activities are being performed in conformance with established plans. If there are any discrepancies, the supervisor should take immediate remedial action and, in so doing, may achieve coordination at least from then on. The very nature of the controlling process contributes to coordination and keeps the organization moving toward its stated and desired objectives.

Coordination with Other Departments.   Not only must supervisors be concerned with coordination within their own departments, but they also must coordinate the efforts of their departments with those of other departments. For example, a production department supervisor will have to meet with supervisors of scheduling, quality control, maintenance, shipping, and the like, to coordinate various activities. Similarly, an accounting supervisor typically has to meet on numerous occasions with supervisors from production, sales, shipping, and the like to coordinate cost accounting, inventory records, billing, etc. It should be readily apparent in all of this that achieving coordination is an essential and major component of the supervisory management position.

SUMMARY

In most organizations supervisors have been rightly depicted as being ''people in the middle.'' Employees see their supervisors as being management, but supervisors are subordinates to their own bosses in higher management. Toward supervisors of other departments, they are colleagues.

Although it is vital that supervisors possess technical knowledge or competence in departmental tasks, increasingly it is recognized that they must perform as managers of their departments. Supervisory management primarily is the process of getting things done with and through people. The way supervisors handle the managerial aspects of their jobs will make the difference between running their departments effectively or being run by their departments. Management skills can be learned and developed. The supervisor who learns to manage the department effectively will be capable of handling more difficult assignments, including the opportunity for moving into higher management positions.

The five major managerial functions are: planning, organizing, staffing, directing, and controlling. Planning is recognized as being the first function of management, upon which the performance of all other managerial functions depends. The five managerial functions are universal regardless of the job environment, the activity involved, or a person's position in the management hierarchy. However, the scope and time a manager will devote to each of these functions will vary depending on the level of management. Typically, first-line supervisors spend most of their time directing and controlling. A supervisor's planning will cover a much shorter time and narrower focus than that of a top executive.

A supervisor must possess authority in order to really perform as a manager. Managerial authority is the legitimate or rightful power to direct others. Authority is delegated from top management through middle management to supervisors. All supervisors must be delegated appropriate authority to manage their departments. Most supervisors, rather than relying primarily on formal managerial authority, prefer to utilize other approaches for gaining good employee performance.

Coordination is the orderly synchronization of efforts of all members of an organization toward the attainment of stated objectives. Cooperation—as distinguished from coordination—indicates the degree of willingness of individuals to work with and help each other. From a management perspective, coordination is a more important consideration than cooperation. However, a supervisor who performs the managerial functions properly will recognize that both coordination and cooperation are attainable through good management practices.

QUESTIONS FOR DISCUSSION

1. Why are supervisors ''people in the middle''? Discuss the supervisory position as the principal ''link'' between employees, other supervisors, and other levels of management.
2. Identify four of the major managerial capabilities or skills needed by every supervisor.
3. Does managerial ability really make the major difference between a good supervisor and a poor supervisor? Could a supervisor adequately manage a department if he or she were totally unfamiliar with the technical aspects of the departmental operation? Discuss.
4. Evaluate the definitions of management and supervisory management. Develop improved definitions if you consider the text's definitions to be inadequate.
5. Are managerial functions identical in different industries and at different levels within an industry? Why or why not?
6. Define each of the five managerial functions. Evaluate the ''overlaps'' in these functions. Are these functions adequate to describe the complexities of a managerial position? Discuss.
7. Discuss the concept of management as a continuous, circular flow.
8. How will the time spent on and the scope of each of the managerial functions usually vary with a person's position within the management structure?
9. Define authority and discuss its part in identifying a management position.
10. What is coordination? Some writers prefer to consider coordination as a separate managerial function. Why do the authors of this text prefer to consider

coordination as an integral goal which a supervisor always has in mind as a manager?

11. Define the concept of cooperation. Why is coordination ''superior'' in order of importance to cooperation? How are coordination and cooperation usually interrelated?

12. Compare the problem of attaining coordination from the standpoint of a chief executive to that of a first-line supervisor.

CHAPTER 3

Delegation: The Supervisor's Leverage

CHAPTER OBJECTIVES

1. To discuss managerial authority from various points of view and the meaning of authority to supervisory management.
2. To define the three major components of the process of delegation and to show how they are interrelated.
3. To discuss delegation at the supervisory level.
4. To compare the authoritarian approach with the general approach to supervision.
5. To emphasize that proper delegation does not mean losing control and that supervisors must exercise their authority as the situation requires.

In the training of military personnel, there have been two major principles embodied in the following statements, which have been repeated countless times in one form or another:

> In order to learn how to give an order, you must first learn how to take an order.
>
> If you give a man a job to do, give him the authority he needs to carry out his job responsibilities.

These statements are as relevant to a civilian supervisor as they are to a military person, and they both primarily focus on the importance of delegating authority commensurate with responsibility as a major component of the managerial role.

As stated before, a supervisor must be a good subordinate and follower in relation to his or her own boss. Supervisors are delegated a certain amount of authority from their bosses in order to manage their departments. Supervisors, in turn, must learn to delegate authority to their employees if the work and objectives of the department are to be accomplished. Delegation, as the title of this chapter suggests, is typically the leverage by which most effective supervisors achieve desired results.

Since authority is an integral characteristic of being a manager, it is essential for supervisors to know what authority means and how to use it. The way a supervisor uses authority usually makes the difference between grudging compliance or willing acceptance of supervisory directives by subordinates. Although most competent supervisors find it unnecessary to "throw their weight around" when giving orders and instructions, firm leadership is sometimes needed. Before these aspects can be discussed further, it is necessary to understand the concept of managerial authority and its origin.

UNDERSTANDING MANAGERIAL AUTHORITY

In Chapter 2, we defined managerial authority as the legitimate right or power to direct or request subordinates to perform a task or to refrain from doing something. Ultimately it includes the right to take disciplinary action in the event that a subordinate should refuse to carry out an order or legitimate request. This latter aspect, of course, is something to be avoided if possible, and disciplinary action normally should not be relied on consistently in daily activities. In order for employees to be motivated to perform their required duties willingly and enthusiastically, it is preferable to use other approaches rather than to rely on formal authority. For supervisors to apply their managerial authority appropriately, they must first understand where their authority comes from.

Origin of Formal Authority

Every supervisor can trace formal authority that has been delegated directly by an immediate superior. The supervisor receives authority, for example, from a division superintendent who, in turn, receives authority from a plant manager, who, in turn, traces authority directly back to the chief executive. This is the traditional, or formal, way of looking at the origin of authority, which is the power arising from the recognition of private property rights.[1] Owners delegate this power to those whom they have placed in managerial positions to run the enterprise. From the chief executive position, authority flows down through the chain of command until it reaches the supervisor.

The Acceptance Theory of Authority

Although the foregoing is a realistic way for a supervisor to view the source of formal authority, a supervisor should not rely solely on formal authority in day-to-day relations with employees, as the following story illustrates. An argument occurred between a supervisor and a worker concerning an order which had been given. When the argument intensified, the supervisor finally shouted, "Jack, unless you do what I tell you, you're fired!" Jack, in the same heated manner, replied, "You can't fire me, I quit!" When Jack walked off the job, he was no longer with the company because he chose to lose his job rather than accept the supervisor's authority. His remark, "You can't fire me, I quit," illustrates why a supervisor should be concerned about other forms of leverage and not depend solely on the sheer weight of formal authority.

The **acceptance theory of authority** states that a manager does not possess any authority until and unless the subordinate employee accepts it. For example, a supervisor may instruct an employee to carry out a certain work assignment. The employee has several alternatives from which to choose. Although it is not likely, the employee can refuse to obey, thus rejecting the supervisor's authority and becoming exposed to possible disciplinary action. More likely, the employee may only grudgingly accept the supervisor's direction and carry out the assignment in a mediocre or minimal fashion. Or the employee may accept the order and carry it out with varying degrees of performance and enthusiasm. For example, the employee may go well beyond the requirements

---

[1]It has been said humorously that this is a modern version of the "Golden Rule," i.e., "Those who have the gold make the rules!" Although it is difficult to generalize for not-for-profit organizations—such as governmental entities, public educational institutions, hospitals, etc.— it can be said that formal authority mostly resides in those boards and executives who are appointed or elected to manage/control the assets and resources of the organization in order to achieve the desired objectives.

of the supervisor and do far more than was expected. Thus the degree to which the employee accepts the supervisor's authority—or the amount of "upward authority" granted the supervisor—is an important part of the employee's choice of alternatives. The acceptance theory states that unless employees accept managerial authority, the supervisor actually does not possess such authority. Of course, employees sometimes have little choice between accepting authority or not accepting it; the other alternative they obviously have is to leave the job. Since this is not a desirable choice, there is merit in considering authority as something that must be accepted by the employees if authority is to bring about the desired results.

Briefly stated, then, the origin of authority can be considered from two viewpoints: (a) the formal way of looking at authority as something that originates with ownership rights—formally handed from the top all the way down to the first-line supervisor; and (b) by contrast, the consideration of authority as something that subordinates confer on a supervisor, i.e., by the degree of willingness with which they accept or respond to the supervisor's direction.

There is some validity in each point of view. A supervisor would be well advised to consider both approaches to looking at authority, since, in reality, each weighs heavily in the practice of supervision. Few supervisors in this day and age rely solely on the weight of formal authority to motivate workers to perform their jobs, although there will be some occasions when supervisors have to resort to it. Even when a supervisor has to invoke and rely on formal authority, the manner in which it is applied will be critical in determining whether the authority will be resented or accepted. There will be supervisory decisions which the subordinate dislikes but which cannot be avoided at the time. The prudent manner in which the supervisor invokes authority can make the difference between being resented or being accepted as a fair supervisor.

Limitations to Authority

There are definite limitations to authority—both explicit and implicit, external and internal. Over a period of time many political, legal, ethical, moral, social, and economic considerations place limitations on the exercise of authority. For example, many companies have adopted various policies and practices of nondiscrimination in employment, in part because they recognize that these policies are socially and ethically desirable, but in part also because they are required to do so by law. A company's articles of incorporation may limit the authority of the chief executive, and the bylaws may present further restrictions. Many laws and contracts clearly limit the authority of management. For example, wage and hour laws require employers to pay certain minimum wages and overtime rates and restrict the use of child labor. Union contracts limit a manager's freedom to take various actions, such as in disciplining employees. In addition, every manager or supervisor in a particular position is subject to the specific limitations stemming from the assignment of duties and delegation of authority.

Generally speaking, there are more limitations on the scope of authority the further one descends in the managerial hierarchy (see Figure 3–1). Usually, the lower the level at which managers or supervisors are located in the management hierarchy, the more restrictions are placed on their authority. First-line supervisors, for example, usually find that there are rather definite limits placed on their authority to utilize resources and to make certain types of managerial decisions. This should not be resented by a supervisor since it is a natural part of the process of delegating authority in any organization.

DELEGATION: THE "ENERGY FLOW" OF SUPERVISION

Just as authority is a major component of the managerial job, so the delegation of authority is essential to the creation and operation of an organization. It is the process of delegating authority commensurate with responsibility that breathes life into the organization. In a very real sense, delegation is the "energy flow" of supervisory management.

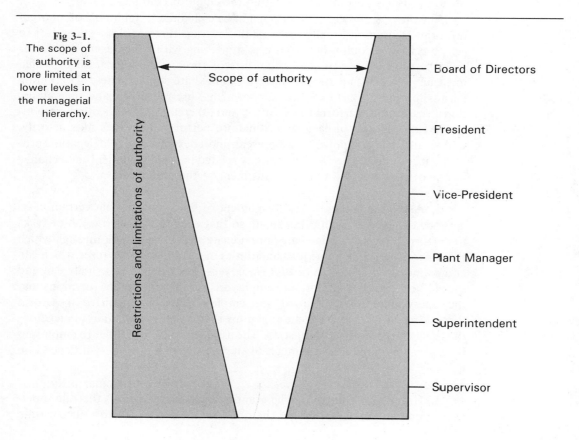

Fig 3–1. The scope of authority is more limited at lower levels in the managerial hierarchy.

Scope of authority

Restrictions and limitations of authority

— Board of Directors

— President

— Vice-President

— Plant Manager

— Superintendent

— Supervisor

Delegation of authority means the granting of enough power to subordinates so that they can perform within prescribed limits. The subordinate manager receives authority from a superior through the process of delegation, but this does not mean that the higher level manager surrenders all authority. Overall authority is still retained by the higher level manager to such a degree that he or she can, if need be, revoke all or part of whatever authority was granted to a subordinate. An analogy can be made between delegating authority and imparting knowledge in school. The teacher in school shares knowledge with the students, who then acquire that knowledge, but the teacher also personally retains the knowledge that has been imparted to the students.

The Process of Delegation

In the process of delegation, authority is distributed throughout the organization. It flows downward from the source of authority at the top through the various levels of management to the first-line supervisors. It is possible that by the time this flow of authority reaches the lower levels, the supervisor feels that it has been narrowed to barely a "trickle" instead of a broad flow. But the supervisor's position is still within the chain of command.

The process of delegation also might be called the "lifeblood" of an organization. Delegation usually provides the leverage that enables a supervisor to get objectives accomplished, and it is something with which every supervisor must be thoroughly familiar. It consists of three components, all of which must be present: (1) assigning duties to immediate subordinates; (2) granting permission (authority) to make commitments, use resources, and take all actions necessary to perform these duties; and (3) creating an obligation (responsibility) on the part of each subordinate to perform the duties satisfactorily. Unless all three components are present and coextensive, the delegation process is incomplete. They are inseparably related in such a manner that a change in one of the three will require adjustment of the other two.

1. Assigning Duties. The assignment of duties means that certain tasks must be assigned to each subordinate so that each has a specific job or tasks to perform. Job descriptions may provide a general framework through which the supervisor can examine jobs and duties in the department to see which can and cannot be assigned to certain employees. Routine duties usually can and should be assigned to almost any employee. But there are other functions that the supervisor can assign only to those employees who are qualified to perform them. And then there are some functions that a supervisor cannot delegate—those which the supervisor must do. The assignment of job duties to employees is of great significance, and much of the supervisor's success will depend on it.

2. Granting Authority. The granting of authority means that the supervisor confers upon subordinates the right and power to act, to utilize certain resources, and to make decisions within predetermined or prescribed limits. Of course, the supervisor must determine the scope of authority that is to be delegated. How much authority can be delegated will depend in part on the amount of authority the supervisor possesses. The degree of authority is also related to the employees and jobs to be done. In every instance enough authority must be granted to each employee to enable that person to adequately and successfully perform his or her assigned tasks. There is no need for the amount of authority to be larger than the tasks assigned, but the authority granted must be sufficient to meet the employee's obligations. However, just to delegate authority to someone who has no specific tasks to perform only leads to confusion and resentment.

Defining Limitations.   A supervisor must be specific in telling employees what authority they have and what they can or cannot do. It is very uncomfortable for employees to have to guess how far their authority extends. For example, one employee may be expected to order certain materials as a regular part of the job. This employee must know the limits within which materials can be ordered, perhaps in terms of time and costs, and when permission from the supervisor is needed before ordering additional materials. If the supervisor does not state this clearly, the employee probably will be forced to test the limits and to experiment by trial and error. Further, if it becomes necessary to change an employee's job assignment, the degree of authority should be checked to make certain that the authority delegated is still appropriate. If it is less (or more) than needed, it should be adjusted.

Many supervisors have found themselves in the deplorable position where their own boss was not explicit concerning how much authority they really had. This is a frustrating situation, which should be avoided. If a supervisor is unclear about the authority delegated, he or she should check with the boss to clear up any possible misunderstanding in this regard.

Unity-of-Command Principle.   Throughout the process of delegation, employees must be reassured that their orders and authority will come from their immediate supervisor. That delegation of authority normally should come only from a single supervisor to an employee, and that each employee should report directly to only one supervisor is known as the **unity-of-command principle.** It is one of the most widely recognized principles of organization within management.[2]

Situations often occur where two superiors give orders and try to delegate authority to the same subordinates. Since Biblical times, at least, it has been

---

[2]There are some situations and organizational structures where the unity-of-command principle will not always be observed. In Chapter 9, the matrix organizational structure and the use of functional staff authority, which are examples of this, are described. Similarly, the use of task forces, project groups, and committees to handle certain types of assignments may blur the unity-of-command concept. Committees and problem-solving groups are discussed in Chapter 11.

recognized that it is difficult, if not impossible, to serve two masters. Having more than one boss usually leads to unsatisfactory performance by the employee due to confusion of authority. Where this basic principle of unity of command—having one boss—is disregarded or violated in practice, conflicts and organizational difficulties usually result. Therefore, a supervisor should make certain that—unless there is a valid reason for it—there is only one boss who gives directives to an employee.

3. Creating Responsibility. The third component of the process of delegation is the creation of an obligation on the part of the subordinate toward a superior to perform satisfactorily the assigned duties. Acceptance of this obligation creates responsibility; without responsibility, delegation is not complete.

The terms responsibility and authority are closely related to each other. Like the concept of authority, the concept of responsibility has often been misunderstood and misused. It is common practice for supervisors to use expressions such as "keeping subordinates responsible," "delegating responsibilities," and "carrying out responsibilities." Simply stated, however, **responsibility** is the obligation of a subordinate to perform duties as required by a superior. By accepting a job position or by accepting an obligation to perform assigned duties, the employee implies acceptance of responsibility. Responsibility recognizes a contractual or implied agreement in which the employee agrees to perform duties in return for rewards, such as a paycheck. The most important facet is that responsibility is something that a subordinate must recognize and accept.

Supervisory Accountability Cannot be Delegated. Although a supervisor can and must delegate authority to subordinates to accomplish specific jobs, the supervisor's own personal accountability cannot be delegated. Assigning duties to employees does not relieve the supervisor of the responsibility for these duties. Thus, when delegating assignments to subordinates, the supervisor still remains accountable for the actions of the subordinates in carrying out these assignments. "The buck stops here" is an old but ever true concept in this regard.

To reiterate, responsibility includes: (1) the obligation of a subordinate to perform assigned tasks; and (2) an obligation that is owed to one's boss, or **accountability.** Thus, for example, when a supervisor is called on by a higher level manager to explain performance within the department, the supervisor cannot plead as a defense that the responsibility for performance has been delegated to employees in the group. The supervisor remains accountable and must answer to the boss. Regardless of the extent to which a supervisor creates an obligation on the part of employees to perform satisfactorily, the supervisor retains the ultimate responsibility along with the authority that are part of the supervisor's departmental position.

This may be a worrisome thought for some supervisors, but the fact remains that responsibility is something that goes with the supervisory position. Of course, reality must be taken into account; delegation and redelegation are necessary for jobs to be accomplished. Although a supervisor may use sound managerial practices, not every employee will always use the best judgment or perform in a superior fashion. Therefore, allowances must be made for errors. Although the responsibility remains with supervisors, it is understood that they must depend on their employees. If employees fail to carry out their assigned tasks, the employees are accountable to the supervisor who must then correct or discipline the employees as appropriate. When appraising a supervisor's performance, higher level managers usually will take into consideration how much care the supervisor has taken in selecting employees, training them, supervising them thoroughly, and controlling their activities.

The Parity Principle of Delegation

The three components of delegation must go together and generally be equal in scope in order to make the process of delegation successful. This is referred to as the **parity principle** of delegation. There must be enough authority granted to each subordinate to do the job. Tasks and duties assigned should not be beyond the scope of authority that has been granted. Nor should subordinates be expected to accept responsibility for activities for which they do not have proper authority. Inconsistencies among assigned tasks, delegated authority, and responsibility will produce undesirable results. In some organizations supervisors have a large amount of authority delegated to them but have only limited duties to perform. This creates frustrations and disturbances. In many companies the responsibilities of some supervisors are far in excess of their delegated authority. This is an even more frustrating situation. Thus the three components necessary to a successful process of delegation should be of equal magnitude; whenever one is changed, the other two must be changed accordingly.

Organizational Approaches to Delegation of Authority

We have clearly stated that an essential element in the energy flow of an organization is delegation of authority. If authority has not been delegated, we can hardly speak of an organization in the true sense of the word. The overall approach to delegation chosen by top management generally will determine much of the "character" of the enterprise and the constraints under which subordinate managers and supervisors will operate.

For example, there are many small companies described as "one-person organizations." There is little if any delegation of authority from the president or owner of the company to anyone else. The consequences are usually disastrous to this type of company when the "one person" becomes incapacitated,

Fig 3–2.
Effective
delegation
requires an
equal mix of the
assignment,
authority, and
responsibility.

dies, or for some other reason leaves the scene. Since there is no real organization, the company usually collapses or must be restructured under someone else.

However, in most organizations the problem of delegating authority is not a question of whether authority will be delegated; it is a question of how much or how little authority will be delegated to subordinates at different organizational levels.

Centralized Authority.   The extent to which authority is delegated determines the degree to which an organization is **centralized** or **decentralized.** Variations in the degree of delegated authority can range from the completely centralized organization (which in reality is not delegating) to the organization where authority has been delegated broadly to the lowest level. At the one extreme the chief executive is in close touch with all operations, makes all or most decisions, and gives all or most of the instructions. Little or no authority is delegated. Many small businesses operate along these lines. Of course, it is understandable that the owner of a small company may have no desire or may be in no position to delegate authority, especially at the beginning of the undertaking.

Limited Decentralized Authority.   There are many organizations in which authority has been delegated to a limited degree. In these organizations major policies and procedures are decided by the top manager; applications of policies and procedures in day-to-day operations and planning are delegated along with limited authority to first-line supervisors. This kind of arrangement often is found in medium-sized companies. It has the advantage of limiting the number of supervisors that the top manager must hire. Further, it can be advantageous in that the knowledge and good judgment that the top manager possesses can be applied rather quickly and directly. Hundreds of thousands of businesses in the United States are organized with such a limited degree of delegation of authority.

Broadly Decentralized Authority. At the other end of the spectrum are those organizations where authority has been delegated to the broadest possible extent and to all levels of management, including first-line supervision. More and more organizations, particularly large ones and others whose operations are complex or widely dispersed, are practicing broad decentralization.

In order to determine how decentralized an organization is, we must study what kind of authority has been delegated, how far down the organization it has been delegated, and how consistently it has been delegated. The criteria for delegation usually can be found in answers to these questions: "How significant a decision can be made by a manager?" and "How far down within the managerial hierarchy is the decision to be made?" The answers to these questions usually will indicate whether an organization's management has delegated authority to a limited or broad extent.

Although centralized authority or limited decentralized authority are logical in the early stages of an organization, a manager sooner or later will be faced with the problem of delegating more authority and decentralizing it. Decentralization becomes necessary when an organization finds itself so preoccupied with routine decision making that top managers do not find enough time to adequately perform their planning function or to maintain a long-range point of view. With the growth of an organization, usually there will be a gradual movement toward decentralization.

DELEGATION BY THE SUPERVISOR

Although few supervisors at the departmental level will have an opportunity or need to practice broad decentralization of formal authority, every supervisor must delegate a certain amount of authority to subordinates. This assumes, of course, that there are employees available who are capable and willing to accept the authority delegated to them. Yet many employees complain that their supervisors make all of the decisions in the department and that their supervisors constantly watch their work closely, because the supervisors do not trust them to carry out assignments. These types of complaints usually describe a supervisor who is unable or unwilling to delegate except to a minimal extent.

Reasons for Lack of Supervisory Delegation

A supervisor may be reluctant to delegate for several reasons—some valid, some not.

Shortage of Qualified Employees.   A lack of qualified or trained subordinates is often used by some supervisors as an excuse for not delegating authority. Actually, such supervisors feel that their employees are not capable of handling authority or are not willing to accept it. If these supervisors refuse to delegate, employees will have little opportunity to obtain the necessary experience and training that will improve their judgment and enable them to handle broadened assignments. Supervisors must always bear in mind that, unless they make a beginning somewhere, they probably will never have enough employees who will be capable and willing to accept more authority with commensurate responsibility.

Fear of Making Mistakes.   Some supervisors think it best to make most decisions themselves because, in the final analysis, they retain overall responsibility. Out of fear of mistakes, such supervisors are unwilling to delegate, and, as a result, they continue to overburden themselves. However, indecision and delay often are costlier than the mistakes they hoped to avoid by refusing to delegate any of their authority. Also, there is a likelihood that the supervisors may make mistakes by not drawing on employees for assistance in decision making.

The "Do It Myself" Mentality.   The old stereotype of a good supervisor was that of a boss who pitched in and worked alongside the employees, thus setting an example by personal effort. Even today, this type of supervision often occurs where a supervisor has been promoted through the ranks and for whom the supervisory position is a reward for hard work and technical competence. By being placed in a supervisory position without having been trained as a manager, this type of supervisor is faced with new problems that are difficult to comprehend. The supervisor therefore resorts to a pattern where he or she feels "secure" and "more comfortable" by working alongside the employees. Admittedly, there are occasions when this actually is needed as, for example, when the job to be performed is of a particularly difficult nature or when an emergency arises. Under these conditions the supervisor should be close to the job to offer help. Aside from emergencies and unusual situations, the supervisor should be carrying out the supervisory job, and the employees should be doing their assigned tasks. Normally, it is the supervisor's job not to do, but to get things done.

Frequently supervisors complain that, if they want something done right, they have to do it themselves. They believe that it is easier to do the job personally than to correct an employee's mistake. Or they may simply prefer to correct an employee's mistakes rather than to clearly explain what should have been done. Perhaps such supervisors even feel that they can do the job better than any of the employees, and chances are this may be true. But these attitudes interfere with a supervisor's prime responsibility to supervise others in order to get the job done. An employee who does the job almost as well will save the supervisor time for more important jobs—for innovative thinking, planning, and more delegating. Thus the effective supervisor strives to see to it that each employee, with each additional job, becomes more competent. After a period of time, the employee's performance on the job should be as good or better than what the supervisor would have done.

Benefits from Supervisory Delegation

Can supervisors realize benefits from delegation if they have only a small number of employees and if there is no real need to create separate groups or organizational subunits within a department? This is the kind of situation that many supervisors face. Is delegation in this type of working situation worth the trouble and risks that it entails? In general, the answer to this question is a strong yes.

The supervisor who relies on delegation expects employees to make more decisions on their own. This does not mean that the supervisor is not available for advice and judgment. It means that the supervisor encourages the employees to make many of their own decisions and to develop their self-confidence in doing so. This in turn should mean that the supervisor will have more time to concentrate on managing. Effective delegation should result in employees performing an increasing number of jobs and recommending solutions that are workable and contribute to good performance. As the supervisor's confidence in employees expands, their commitment to better performance should also grow. This may be a long, tedious process, and the degree of delegation may vary with each employee and with each department. But in most situations, a supervisor's goal should be one of delegating more authority to employees whenever feasible. This goal usually is in accordance with the goal of developing higher employee motivation and better job performance.

Of course, there are some supervisory areas that cannot be delegated. For example, it remains with the supervisor to formulate certain policies and objectives, to give general directions for the department or work unit, to appraise subordinates, to take necessary disciplinary action, and to promote employees. Aside from these types of supervisory management responsibilities, the employees should be doing most of the departmental work themselves.

GENERAL VERSUS AUTOCRATIC SUPERVISION

Most employees accept work as a normal part of life. In their jobs they seek satisfactions that wages alone cannot provide. Most employees probably would prefer to be their own bosses, or at least have a degree of freedom to make decisions that pertain to their own work. The question arises as to whether this is possible if an individual works for someone else. Can a degree of freedom be granted to employees if they are to contribute their share toward the achievement of organizational objectives? This is where the delegation of authority can help. The desire for freedom and being one's own boss can be enhanced by delegation, which in the daily routine essentially means giving directions in broad, general terms. It means that the supervisor, instead of watching every detail of the employees' activities, is primarily interested in the results they achieve and is willing to give them considerable latitude in deciding how to achieve these results.

General Supervision

The delegation process in the daily working situation can become a reality through an approach described as **general supervision.** This usually means that the supervisor sets the goals and discusses with subordinates the objectives to be accomplished. The supervisor also fixes the limits or constraints within which the work has to be done, but gives the employees considerable freedom to decide how to achieve their targets. In a more advanced form of general supervision, the supervisor may even encourage subordinates to establish their own approaches and objectives within the framework of the department's goals. If properly carried out, this can be one of the most positive approaches for increasing employee motivation.[3]

For example, an office supervisor may discuss with several employees the various projects and paperwork that must be completed by the end of the week. The supervisor will outline which items have top priority but will avoid stating exactly how the work is to be done or in what order. Thus the supervisor demonstrates confidence that the employees will complete the work on time and in the proper fashion. The employees are trusted to figure out how to allocate the available time accordingly.

Advantages of General Supervision

Several major advantages accompany the approach described as general supervision. These are:

1. *It allows the supervisor more time to be a manager.* General supervision frees supervisors from many details, which gives them time to plan, organize, and control. Further, this approach should give the supervisor more time to receive and assume additional authority and responsibility. By contrast, the supervisor who demonstrates close, detailed supervision and who tries to make almost every decision personally soon becomes exhausted physically and mentally. In addition, such a supervisor can irritate employees and make them less productive (see Figure 3–3).

---

[3]This is a version of "management by objectives," which is discussed in Chapters 4 and 7. General supervision is discussed again in Chapter 15.

Fig 3–3.
In general
supervision the
supervisor
discusses with
subordinates the
objectives to be
accomplished.

2. *It provides subordinates with a chance to develop their talents and abilities by making on-the-job decisions themselves.* At times the supervisor will have to be away from the department. By practicing general supervision, the supervisor can be more confident that employees will carry out the work and develop suitable approaches to making decisions on the job. It is difficult to instruct employees in decision making; they can learn it only by practice.

   Related to this advantage is the fact that a supervisor's decisions on work details may not be as good as the decisions made by the employees, who are closest to these details. Further, there is no guarantee that mistakes will not happen when the supervisor specifies all the details of every job. By getting practice in making decisions and using their own judgment, employees can become more independent and competent.

3. *It motivates subordinates to take pride in the results of their own decisions.* Most employees prefer to be on their own to some degree. Surveys have shown that employees appreciate the boss who shows them how to do a job and then trusts them enough to let them do it on their own. By participating in decision making, they feel that they have a better chance to advance to higher positions.

In summary, there is considerable evidence to conclude that general supervision usually is a more effective way to manage for supervisors, for employees, and for the organization as a whole. By pursuing a broad, general kind of supervision, many of the satisfactions that employees seek on the job—and which money alone does not provide—may be fulfilled. More important, general supervision is conducive to better work performance.

Autocratic Supervision

There are still many supervisors who believe that emphasis on formal authority, or **autocratic supervision,** is the best way to obtain results. A supervisor of this type uses pressure and close control in order to require people to work and may even threaten disciplinary action, including discharge, if they do not perform as ordered. An autocratic supervisor may even assume that most employees are lazy, that the primary reason they work is to earn money and benefits, that they work because they fear losing their jobs, and that they try to get away with doing as little as possible.[4] By harboring these assumptions, this type of supervisor feels a need for very close, autocratic supervision by telling the workers precisely what is to be done throughout the day without allowing them to use their own judgment. Further, such supervisors believe that they must be strong and that to delegate would be a sign of weakness.

However, the totally autocratic approach to supervision has lost the majority of its followers. This approach was perhaps acceptable in the early days of the Industrial Revolution or in Great Depression days when workers were close to economic ruin and would do anything in order to obtain food, clothing, and shelter. In recent decades employees have come to expect more from their jobs, and the "be strong" policy has become less effective. Most employees expect not only economic satisfactions in a job, but also other personal satisfactions—particularly when times are good and employment is not difficult to obtain. In addition, the educational process of our society has had a significant influence on attitudes. Many years ago, children were accustomed to strict obedience to their elders. Now schools and homes emphasize freedom and self-expression. Therefore, younger employees tend to resent autocratic supervision on the job. Further, the growth of labor unions and protective legislation have made it more difficult for supervisors to discipline or discharge employees for average performance.

Those who believe in the sheer weight of authority and the "be strong" form of supervision tend to discount the fact that workers may react in ways that were not intended by the supervisor. Employees who strongly resent autocratic supervision may become quite frustrated, rather than find satisfactions in their daily work. Such frustration can lead to arguments and other forms of discontent.

The excessive autocratic approach provides little incentive for employees to work harder than the minimum required in order to avoid punishment and discharge. Under such conditions and where employee antagonism toward autocratic supervision is severe, employees—even if they are not unionized—may engage in slowdowns, sabotage, and spoilage. Supervisors will likely react to such actions by watching the workers even more closely. This, in turn, encour-

---

[4]This is similar to a "Theory X" style of motivational assumptions, which is discussed in Chapter 4.

ages employees to try to "out-smart" management. Thus a vicious circle may begin, with new restraints being imposed by supervisors and new methods being devised by employees for evading them.

THE PROPER BALANCE OF DELEGATION

Although we have stressed the advantages of delegation as exemplified in general supervision, it must be recognized that the process of delegation is delicate. It is not easy for a supervisor to part with some authority and still be left with the responsibility for the performance and decisions made by workers. Proper delegation requires sound judgment and skill. The supervisor must weigh among "too much," "too little," and the right amount "happy medium" in order to delegate enough without losing control. There will be situations where supervisors will have to resort to their formal authority in order to attain the objectives of the department and to get the job done. Supervisors at times will have to make decisions that are distasteful to employees. Delegation does not mean that a supervisor should manage a department by consensus or by taking a vote on every issue.

How and when a supervisor should delegate depends on many factors. To a large degree, however, the answer is related considerably to understanding employee motivation and alternative leadership approaches that supervisors can implement. These will be discussed in the following chapter.

SUMMARY

Managerial authority is a necessary component of any manager's position, and delegating authority is the means of making the managerial process throughout the organization a reality. The formal way of looking at managerial authority is that it originates from the top and is delegated through a chain of command from the top executive down to the first-line supervisor. However, the acceptance theory of authority suggests that supervisors have authority only if and when their subordinates accept it.

In reality, an employee's choice between accepting or not accepting a supervisor's authority may be the choice between quitting the job and staying. But the degree of acceptance will affect the quality and quantity of the subordinate's work and the enthusiasm with which the employee performs the job.

The managerial process of delegation is made up of three components: assigning a job or duties, granting authority, and creating responsibility. All three are coextensive, and a change in one will of necessity cause a change in the other two. The question is not whether management will delegate authority; it is how much or how little authority will be delegated. If much authority is delegated to the first-line supervisors, then we speak of a decentralized organization. Among the major advantages to the supervisor who practices broad delegation are greater flexibility, better decisions, higher employee morale, and better job performance.

At the supervisory level, the practice of delegation usually takes the form of general supervision, which provides employees with considerable freedom in making certain decisions and in doing their jobs to meet departmental objectives. Some supervisors still believe that autocratic supervision is more likely to get results from employees than general supervision. There will be occasions when supervisors will have to fall back on the weight of their managerial authority. For the most part, however, these should be the exceptions, rather than the rule.

QUESTIONS FOR DISCUSSION

1. Define managerial authority. Discuss the following issues related to the concept of authority:
    a. The origin of formal authority.
    b. The acceptance theory of authority.
    c. Limits to a supervisor's authority.
2. What is meant by delegation of authority? Why is delegation of authority essential if an organization is to function and operate efficiently?
3. Define responsibility. Why are the concepts of responsibility, authority, and accountability closely interrelated? Why can a supervisor's personal responsibility not be delegated?
4. Define and discuss the three major components of the process of delegation.
5. Define the unity-of-command principle and the parity principle.
6. What are meant by the terms centralized and decentralized authority? How do organizations vary in terms of applying these concepts?
7. Why are many supervisors reluctant to delegate? What benefits typically accrue to a supervisor who learns how to delegate?
8. Define general supervision. Will this approach work with every employee? How can a supervisor know how and when to implement general supervision? Discuss.
9. Is autocratic supervision always inappropriate? Are there situations where a supervisor will have to rely on authority in order to receive proper employee performance? Discuss.
10. Discuss managerial authority and delegation in regard to attitudes among people, particularly young people, in a democratic society.

CHAPTER 4

Motivation and Supervisory Management Styles

CHAPTER OBJECTIVES

1. To develop an awareness of the primary determinants of human personality.
2. To understand employee motivation with particular reference to the hierarchy of human needs.
3. To discuss styles of supervisory management in conjunction with motivational theories and research findings.
4. To discuss specific supervisory approaches, especially participative management and management by objectives, which are designed to stimulate positive employee motivation, job satisfaction, and excellent work performance.

In our view, the primary management responsibility of most supervisors is the management of people. Of course, a supervisor must also manage resources other than people such as time, equipment, money, inventories, and space. All of these must be managed efficiently in order to achieve departmental and company objectives. But typically most of a supervisor's time and efforts will be devoted to the supervisory management of people. In Chapter 2, we defined management as getting things accomplished with and through people by guiding and motivating their efforts toward common objectives. This definition requires that supervisors understand employee motivation and develop approaches that are conducive to having employees motivated to work to the full extent of their capabilities.

Human beings constitute a resource that is quite different from any other resource the supervisor is asked to manage. In our society we place great value on the worth of human beings. Human beings have attitudes, values, and sentiments that significantly influence their behavior on the job. The feelings that people have toward their supervisors, their job environment, their personal problems, and numerous factors are often difficult to ascertain. Yet they have a tremendous impact on employee motivation and work performance.

The difficulty in assessing human feelings and attitudes is further complicated by the fact that every human being is a unique individual. Although at the start of the 1990s, an estimated $5\frac{1}{2}$ billion persons were living on the planet Earth—and by the year 2000, the world's population will have grown to over six billion people—no two human beings are exactly alike! This is because every individual is the product of many factors, and it is the unique combination of these factors that results in an individual human personality.

DETERMINANTS OF HUMAN PERSONALITY

The terms "human element" or "personality" are often used to describe the complex mix of knowledge, attitudes, and attributes that distinguish one person from all others. While there is far-from-complete agreement on the weight of each of these factors, there is general recognition that each is influential. A supervisor who is sensitive to the factors that shape workers as individual human beings usually is better able to understand them and thereby appeal to their needs and interests while attempting to guide them toward attainment of prescribed objectives.

Many people use the word personality to describe what they see and observe in another person. However, the real substance of human personality goes far beyond just a person's external behavior. The essence of an individual's personality includes the person's attitudes, values, and ways of interpreting the environment, as well as many internal and external influences that contribute to his or her behavior patterns. Countless books have been written about personality, and many studies have been made that help to explain why people are what they are. There are several major "schools" of personality study that can help us to comprehend the complexity of human beings. In this text, we briefly mention only the primary determinants of personality before we consider the more focused theories of employee motivation.

Physiological (Biological) Factors

A first major influence on human personality is a person's physiological (or biological) makeup. Such factors as sex, age, race, height, weight, and physique can be very important influences in a person's overall personality structure. Intelligence, which is at least partially inherited, is another. Most biological characteristics are apparent to others and may greatly affect the way in which a person is perceived. For example, a person who is tall is sometimes considered to possess more leadership abilities than a shorter person. One research study showed that tall male job applicants usually were offered greater starting salaries than were shorter male job applicants! While physiological characteristics alone should not be the basis for evaluating an employee's capabilities, they do exert considerable influence on an individual's personality as well as define certain physical abilities and limitations.

Early Childhood Influences (Childhood Determinism)

Many psychologists feel that the very early years of a person's life are crucial in the development of that individual. Some of them believe that early childhood is *the* most critical period of life that determines what a person actually becomes. Some writers refer to this concept as **childhood determinism,** which states that the manner in which a child is trained, shown affection, and disciplined will have a life-long influence on that person. Thus, an individual's ability to cope with problems and to work in harmony with others may be determined partly through the influences to which that individual was subjected as a child.

Environmental (Situational) Factors

Sociologists and social psychologists tend to emphasize the immediate situation or environment as being the most important determinant of adult personality. Such factors as education, income, employment, home, and many other experiences that confront an individual throughout life will influence or condition what that person is and eventually becomes. This is particularly true in terms of the immediate working environment. For example, the personality of the blue-collar worker performing routine, manual labor on an assembly line in a factory will be affected by this type of situation compared to the personality of a professional white-collar person who performs primarily mental work that involves thought and judgment.

Cultural (Societal) Values

The broader culture of society also influences personality. In America such values as competition, rewards for accomplishment, equal opportunities, and similar concepts are part of a democratic society. Individuals are educated, trained, and encouraged to think for themselves and to strive for the achievement of worthwhile goals. However, some cultural values are changing. For example, for many years the labor force in the United States was relatively homogeneous and the cultural values of the majority of workers tended to be similar in scope. In recent decades, however, the work force has become increasingly diversified, reflecting many different subcultures and subgroups. As the diversity of the work force has increased, so has the effect of different cultural norms and values on the workplace. In particular, certain values of ethnic, age, and minority groups may be quite different in comparison to the values of the majority of others. By recognizing and respecting the different cultural values and expectations of peoples, supervisors should become more adept in dealing effectively with others unlike themselves.

RECOGNIZING HUMAN DIFFERENCES AND SIMILARITIES

The many complexities of human personality have been only briefly discussed, because there are literally an infinite number of factors that influence personality and cause it to adapt and change over time. Every day of a person's life becomes part of that individual. Stating this another way, what a supervisor does in a work situation becomes part of the personalities of the people being supervised.

Every individual is the product of many influences and experiences, all of which are dynamic and changing in intensity. The importance of a specific influence depends on the individual and the situation at that time. Ideally, supervisors should attempt to know their employees so well that they could tailor their supervisory approaches to the uniqueness of each individual's personality. Realistically, this is generally impossible, because the demands made on supervisors are too many.

Fortunately, however, behavioral studies have demonstrated that people tend to be more alike than different in their basic motivational needs and reasons for behavior. If a supervisor learns to supervise and implement managerial techniques that emphasize the similarities rather than the differences among people, there is a better chance of achieving the type of motivation and performance desired. This does not mean that unique differences in people should be overlooked. Being aware of and sensitive to the unique needs and personality makeup of individual employees can make the difference in adapting general approaches by which a supervisor seeks to attain good performance. But a consistent supervisory approach based on similarities rather than individual differences is more likely to result in increased employee motivation and performance. A consistent approach also tends to draw the workers closer together and to instill in them a feeling of "belonging" to a team.

UNDERSTANDING MOTIVATION AND HUMAN BEHAVIOR

Too often motivation is viewed as something that one person can give to or do for another. Supervisors sometimes talk in terms of giving a worker a "shot" of motivation or of having to "motivate their employees." However, positive motivation of employees is not that easily accomplished, since human motivation really refers to an inner drive or an impulse. Motivation cannot be poured down another's throat or injected intravenously! Motivation, in the final analysis, comes from within a person. A person has been motivated when his or her desire to behave in a certain way has been stimulated.

Since employee motivation is crucial to organizational success, it is a subject about which there has been much research. The theories and ideas for understanding motivation to be considered in this text are fundamental in nature, and very much more has been written elsewhere. However, most explanations emphasize the similarities, rather than differences, in the needs of human beings.

The Hierarchy of Human Needs (Maslow)

Most psychologists who study human behavior and personality generally are convinced that all behavior of human beings is caused, goal-oriented, and motivated. Stating this another way, there is a reason for everything that a person does (assuming of course that the person is rational, sane, and not out of control, e.g., drunk). People constantly are striving to attain something that has meaning to them in terms of their own particular needs and in relation to how they see themselves and the environment in which they exist. Often we may not be directly aware of why we behave in a certain manner, but even then there are subconscious motives that govern the way we behave when confronted with certain situations.

One of the most widely accepted theories of human behavior is that people are motivated to satisfy certain well-defined and more or less predictable needs. A famous psychologist, Abraham H. Maslow, is credited with having formulated the concept of a **hierarchy (or priority) of human needs.**[1] Maslow maintained that these needs range from lower level needs to higher level needs in an ascending priority (see Figure 4–1). These needs actually overlap and are

---

[1]See Abraham H. Maslow, *Motivation and Personality* (2d ed.; New York: Harper & Row Publishers, Inc., 1970), Chapter 4. See also Stuart M. Klein and R. Richard Ritti, *Understanding Organizational Behavior* (2d ed.; Boston: Kent Publishing Company, 1984), pp. 251–261.

Fig 4–1.
Hierarchy of
human needs.

SELF-FULFILLMENT

SELF-RESPECT (ESTEEM)

SOCIAL (BELONGING)

SECURITY (SAFETY)

BIOLOGICAL (PHYSIOLOGICAL)

interrelated, and it is perhaps preferable to consider them as being along a continuum, rather than as being separate and distinct from each other.

Maslow's theory of a hierarchy of human needs implies that people for the most part attempt to satisfy these needs in the order in which they are arranged in the hierarchy. Until the lowest level or basic needs are reasonably satisfied, a person will not be motivated strongly by the other levels. As one level of needs becomes more-or-less satisfied, the individual then focuses on the next level which then becomes the stronger motivator of behavior. Maslow even suggested that once a lower level of needs was reasonably satisfied, that it no longer would motivate behavior, at least in the short term.

Physiological Needs. At the first level of human needs are the **physiological (or biological) needs.** These are needs that everyone has for food, shelter, rest, recreation, and other physical necessities. Virtually every employee views work as being a means for taking care of these fundamental needs. The paycheck enables a person to purchase the necessities vital to survival as well as the comforts of life.

Safety Needs. Once a person's physiological needs are reasonably satisfied, other needs become important. The **safety (or security) needs** are those we have to protect ourselves against danger and threat and to guard against the uncertainties of life. Most employees want some sense of security or control about their future. In order to satisfy such expectations, many employers offer a variety of supplementary benefits. For example, medical, retirement, hospitalization, disability, and life insurance plans seek to protect employees against various uncertainties and their possible serious consequences. Wage and benefit packages provided by companies to their employees usually are designed to satisfy physiological and safety needs and, at the same time, to be competitive in the labor market in attracting and retaining competent personnel.

Social Needs.   Some supervisors believe that positive employee motivation should be achieved if a company pays good wages and offers ample benefits. These supervisors tend to discount the importance of the higher level needs of human beings, beginning with the **social (or belongingness) needs.** These are needs that people have for personal attention, for being part of a group, and for being accepted and respected by their peers. Many studies have shown that group motivation can be a powerful influence on behavior of employees in a work situation, both in a negative or positive direction. For example, some employees may deliberately perform in a manner contrary to a supervisor's wishes in order to feel that they are an accepted part of an informal group. On the other hand, positive group motivation can be a strong influence in helping supervisors achieve above-average or exceptional performance from their people. The latter is more easily accomplished in some work settings than in others. Further, some employers even provide or support off-the-job social and athletic opportunities for their employees as a means of helping them satisfy their social needs and to build loyalty to the organization as a whole.

Esteem Needs.   Closely related to the belongingness needs are the **esteem (or self-respect, or ego)** needs. These are needs that everyone has for recognition, achievement, status, and a sense of accomplishment. They can be very powerful, since they relate to one's personal feelings of self-worth and importance. Unfortunately many jobs offer little opportunity for satisfaction of these needs. Often it is left to the supervisor to look for ways by which these intrinsic needs may be satisfied in more meaningful work experiences and personal relationships.

Self-Realization Needs.   At the highest level of human needs are the **self-realization (or self-fulfillment) needs.** These are the most personal or individualistic of human needs, which most people attempt to satisfy within the totality of their life experiences. These include the desire to fulfill one's capabilities and potentialities, and to be creative and occupied in doing what a person wants to do within the limits of his or her capacities. Presumably these highest level needs are not satisfied until a person reaches his or her own full potential. As such, these needs theoretically persist throughout a person's life and probably are incapable of ever being completely satisfied.

Here, too, many jobs frustrate rather than fulfill this level of human

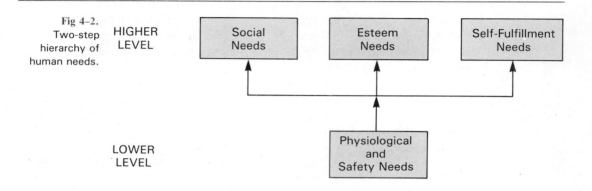

Fig 4–2.
Two-step
hierarchy of
human needs.

needs. For example, many factory and office jobs are routine and monotonous, and workers must seek self-fulfillment in pursuits off the job and in family relationships.

The Two-Step Hierarchy of Needs Model

While Maslow conceptualized a five-step hierarchy of human needs, other researchers maintain that there really are only two fundamental levels of human needs. According to the two-level model, physiological and security needs are at the lower level, while social, esteem, and self-fulfillment needs comprise the upper level. Only after the lower level needs (also called *lower order needs*) are reasonably satisfied do the upper level needs (also called *higher order needs*) become important in motivation and behavior.[2] Figure 4–2 illustrates the two-step hierarchy concept.

The two-step hierarchy suggests that there is no firm, stepped sequence among levels of human needs. Once lower level needs are relatively satisfied, any need in the upper level may then take priority. In other words, the sequence in which needs in the higher level emerge for individuals is not the same for everyone. For example, for many young people belongingness (social) needs take precedence over esteem needs, and this typically changes as young people mature and become working adults.

Regardless of which hierarchy of human needs concept is more correct, most experienced supervisors can identify with the two-step model. We tend to believe that there are more differences among people than Maslow's five-step hierarchy might appear to indicate. That is to say, while all people probably are first interested in satisfying their lower order needs, they may differ in the upper level needs they next seek to satisfy.

---

[2]See H. Joseph Reitz, *Behavior in Organizations* (3d ed.; Homewood, Illinois: R.D. Irwin, Inc., 1987), pp. 74–76.

Application of the Needs Hierarchy to Supervision

The theory or model of a hierarchy of human needs is generally accepted and recognized as being very useful, although the complexities of human nature are such that caution should be exercised in interpreting and applying this model in explanations of all human behavior.[3] Nevertheless, supervisors can utilize the model of a hierarchy of human needs as a framework to visualize the kinds of needs that people have and to assess their relative importance in understanding motivation. The supervisor's problem is to seek ways to translate this understanding of human needs into supervisory practices that will enable employees to find satisfaction of their needs on their jobs, while at the same time performing their work well.

We mentioned previously that many supervisors believe that motivation is something they do to get a response from their employees. However, the essence of motivation is what individuals themselves feel and do in relation to their own particular needs. Ultimately, all motivation is essentially self-motivation. Thus a good supervisor endeavors to supervise in such a manner that employees are motivated to perform well because they find good work performance satisfying to their own particular needs.

In today's economy, a majority of employees expect good wages and generous benefit plans. In such circumstances, the key to longer term, positive motivation of employees probably resides in better satisfying the higher level needs (social, esteem, and self-fulfillment) of individuals. Supervisors should recognize that just giving employees more money, better benefits, and better working conditions will not bring about excellent work performance. For many employees, these items may play a secondary role in their day-to-day motivation. In fact, much of the negative employee motivation that is widespread today takes place among highly paid and relatively secure employees, much to the consternation and dismay of their supervisors.

Negative Employee Motivation and Frustration

Actions or conditions that do not bring about the desired fulfillment of a person's needs will ultimately result in dissatisfaction and frustration. Thus when their needs are not satisfied on the job, many employees resort to behavior patterns that usually are detrimental to their job performance and to the organization. A typical approach for frustrated employees is to resign themselves to just getting by on the job. This means that they simply go through the motions and put in time without trying to perform in other than an average

---

[3]Michael Hitt, R. Dennis Middlemist, and Robert Mathis, *Management: Concepts and Effective Practice* (2d ed.; St. Paul, Minn.: West Publishing Company, 1986), pp. 316–317.

or marginal manner. They look for personal satisfactions off the job and are content to do just enough to draw a paycheck.

Another approach for negatively motivated employees is to adopt what has been called **detour behavior.** Such employees find things that constantly distract them from doing the job, and at times they even try to beat the system. They often are absent and tardy or break the rules as a way of trying to get back at situations which they find frustrating.

Still other employees who are dissatisfied adopt aggressive behavior, which ultimately may cause them to leave the job situation. Examples of aggressive behavior are poor attitudes, vandalism, theft, fighting, and temper outbursts. When the situation becomes intolerable for some employees, they quit or almost force their supervisors to fire them because of their unacceptable negative behavior.

Obviously, these types of reactions to job situations are undesirable and should be prevented. Costs of employee turnover, absenteeism, tardiness, poor performance, and other unsatisfactory conduct on the job can be extremely high to an organization. Rather than just accepting an employee's negative motivation and behavior, a supervisor should endeavor to help the employee to cope with frustrating situations by seeking sound solutions to problems and providing more opportunities for positive motivation. Of course, this is much easier to say than to accomplish in many situations.

SUPERVISORY MANAGEMENT STYLES

A continuous (and unresolved) question that always has confronted supervisors concerns the general approach, or style, that supervisors should utilize in order to achieve positive employee motivation. This age-old dilemma typically focuses on the degree to which supervisory approaches should be based on satisfying the lower level and the higher level needs of people. In a sense, this often becomes an issue of the degree to which supervisors should rely on their authority and position as compared with trying to utilize human relations practices that may provide greater opportunities for employee motivation.

Research and the literature concerning supervisory management styles is replete with many findings and some contradictions. Here, we review only a few of the significant research findings and concepts that prominent authorities have offered. Although their motivational and leadership ideas are not exactly identical, it should be apparent that they generally urge supervisors and managers toward a similar leadership style or direction.

McGregor's Theory X and Theory Y

A number of years ago, Douglas McGregor wrote an outstanding book entitled *The Human Side of Enterprise.* In this book McGregor noted that individual supervisory approaches were usually related to each supervisor's perceptions or beliefs concerning what people were all about. That is, each supervisor will manage employees according to his or her own attitudes and ideas about people, their needs, and their motivations. For purposes of comparison, McGregor stated that the extremes in contrasting attitudes among managers could be classified as **Theory X** and **Theory Y.**

The basic assumptions of Theory X and Theory Y as stated by McGregor are:[4]

Theory X

1. The average human being has an inherent dislike of work and will avoid it if possible.
2. Because of this characteristic dislike of work, most people must be coerced, controlled, directed, and threatened with punishment to get them to put forth adequate effort toward the achievement of organizational objectives.
3. The average human being prefers to be directed, wishes to avoid responsibility, has relatively little ambition, and wants security above all.

Theory Y

1. The expenditure of physical and mental effort in work is as natural as play or rest.
2. External control and the threat of punishment are not the only means of bringing about effort toward organizational objectives. A person will exercise self-direction and self-control in the service of objectives to which he or she is committed.
3. Commitment to objectives is a function of the rewards associated with their achievement.
4. The average human being learns, under proper conditions, not only to accept, but to seek responsibility.
5. The capacity to exercise a high degree of imagination, ingenuity, and creativity in the solution of organizational problems is widely, not narrowly, distributed in the population.
6. Under the conditions of modern industrial life, the intellectual potentialities of the average human being are only partially utilized.

Supervisors who are Theory X oriented have a rather limited view of employees' capabilities and motivation. They feel that employees must be strictly controlled, closely supervised, and motivated on the basis of money, discipline, and authority. Theory X supervisors believe that the key to employee

[4]Douglas McGregor, *The Human Side of Enterprise* (New York: McGraw-Hill Book Company, 1960), pp. 33–43 and 45–57. For additional insights into McGregor's contributions, see Allan R. Cohen, Stephen L. Fink, Herman Gadon, and Robin D. Willits (with the collaboration of Natasha Josefowitz), *Effective Behavior in Organizations* (Homewood, Illinois: Richard D. Irwin, Inc., 1984), pp. 186–188 and 245–247.

Fig 4–3.
The two
extremes of
managerial
approach are
typified by the
Theory X and
Theory Y
supervisors.

motivation is in the proper implementation of approaches designed to satisfy the lower level needs of people.

Theory Y supervisors, however, have a much higher opinion of employees' capabilities and possibilities. They feel that if the proper approaches and conditions can be implemented, employees will exercise self-direction and self-control toward the accomplishment of worthwhile objectives. They feel that management's objectives and activities should fit into the scheme of each employee's own particular set of needs. Therefore, Theory Y managers believe that the higher level needs of employees are more important in terms of each employee's own personality and self-development.

The two approaches described by McGregor represent extremes in supervisory styles and practices. Realistically, most supervisors are somewhere between Theory X and Theory Y. Neither of these approaches is actually wrong in and of itself, for the appropriateness of a given approach will depend on the needs of the individuals involved and the demands of the situation. In practice, supervisors may on occasion take an approach that is contrary to their usual or preferred one. For example, even the strongest Theory Y supervisor may revert to Theory X in a time of crisis, such as when the department is very shorthanded, when there is an equipment failure, when a serious disciplinary problem has occurred, or when a few employees need "firm" direction.

Advantages and Limitations of Theory X.   Supervisors who adopt the Theory X style usually find that in the short run a job typically will be accomplished faster. Since the questioning of orders and instructions is not encouraged, it may appear that the workers are competent and knowledgeable and that work groups are well-organized, efficient, and disciplined.

A major disadvantage of the Theory X approach is that there is little opportunity available for personal growth of employees. Since supervision is close and constant, employees are unlikely to develop initiative and independence. Further, many workers resent Theory X supervision, and this may breed negative motivation as discussed previously.

Advantages and Limitations of Theory Y.   An overriding advantage of Theory Y supervision is that individual growth is better facilitated. Since workers are given opportunities to assume some responsibility on their own and are encouraged to offer their ideas in accomplishing their tasks, it is possible for them to partially satisfy their higher level needs on the job.

Although the Theory Y approach is often viewed as a more positive and desirable approach for supervisors, it is not without some disadvantages. Theory Y in practice can be time-consuming, especially in the short run. Since personal development is emphasized, supervisors must become instructors and coaches if they are to assist their employees to move toward the simultaneous attainment of organizational and personal goals. Many supervisors find this to be more idealistic than practical, since some employees expect strong and firm direction from their supervisors.

The Managerial Grid®

Another approach to analyzing the leadership styles of managers and supervisors has been described by Robert R. Blake and Jane S. Mouton. They developed a Managerial Grid, which indicates five identifiable types of managerial leadership based on a supervisor's "concern for production" coupled with a supervisor's "concern for people." The Managerial Grid has a nine-unit scale on both the vertical and horizontal axes, as shown in Figure 4–4.

The five managerial styles identified by Blake and Mouton are as follows:

1. The *impoverished* (1,1) supervisor is more or less "withdrawn." This supervisor does little either to stimulate employees or to get work out but is primarily interested in getting by and surviving.
2. The *country club* (1,9) supervisor believes that by taking care of the human relations needs of people and by encouraging a friendly, happy work environment, the work will get done in some way.
3. The *authority-obedience,* or *task* (9,1) supervisor has primary concern for getting the work done. This supervisor is similar to those who follow Theory X. This supervisor emphasizes efficiency and authority and arranges the work in such a way to ensure that human elements interfere in a minimal fashion.
4. The *organization man,* or *middle-of-the-road bureaucratic* (5,5) supervisor is one who tries to balance demands for production against human factors,

Fig 4–4.
The Managerial
Grid.®

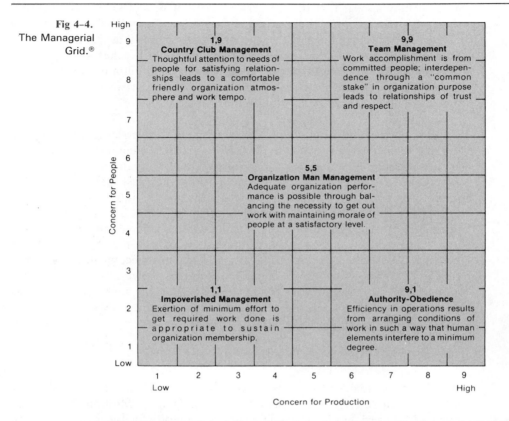

Concern for Production

SOURCE: Blake, Robert R., and Mouton, Jane Srygley. *The Managerial Grid III: The Key to Leadership Excellence* (Houston: Gulf Publishing Company, Copyright © 1985), p. 12. Reproduced by permission.

particularly those of employee morale. This type of supervisor is not wholly committed either to production or people. Often he or she adopts a political role of getting just enough work done to satisfy the boss but at the same time giving some attention to human needs.

5. The *team* (9,9) supervisor is very similar to one who follows the Theory Y style. The team supervisor has a high concern for both getting out the work and developing the capacities of people. This supervisor believes that the best organizational performance can come from people who are committed to the objectives of the organization and who see that their own needs can best be served by pursuing worthwhile organizational goals. The team supervisor has a high concern for bringing out the very best in people and helping them grow and develop in the organization.

Although they recognize that the (9,9) style of management may be difficult to implement in some work situations, Blake and Mouton advocate the (9,9), or "participation-centered teamwork" approach, as being applicable in any work environment. Blake and Mouton's research led them to conclude that this approach is the one most positively associated with high productivity, job satisfaction, and creativity of people involved. Further, they have found that (9,9) types of supervisors and managers tend to be evaluated favorably by their bosses and typically are advanced at a faster rate within their organizations than are those who utilize other managerial styles.[5]

Motivation-Hygiene Theory

Another theory that has had a significant impact on managerial thinking and practices in relation to employee motivation is the **motivation-hygiene theory,** sometimes called the **two factor theory** or the **dual factor theory,** developed (primarily) by Frederick Herzberg.[6] Herzberg's research has demonstrated that certain factors that managers and supervisors traditionally believe will motivate people serve primarily to mitigate their dissatisfactions, rather than to motivate them positively.

Herzberg and others have conducted numerous studies in which people were asked to describe events and circumstances that made them feel particularly good or bad about their jobs. Other questions were asked in order to determine the depth of their feelings, the duration for which these feelings persisted, and what types of situations made employees feel motivated or frustrated. These studies were made of employees in various companies and industries, including personnel at all levels and from different technical and job specialties. Interestingly, the general pattern of results was fairly consistent. It revealed a clear distinction between those factors that tend to motivate employees (motivation factors) and those factors that, while expected by workers, are not likely to motivate them positively (hygiene factors).

Motivation Factors.   Herzberg noted that the motivation factors are primarily related to the intrinsic nature of the job itself rather than to environmental matters. Among the most frequently identified motivation factors are the following:

---

[5]Robert R. Blake and Jane S. Mouton, *The Managerial Grid III* (Houston: Gulf Publishing Company, 1985), p. 13 and pp. 95–96.

[6]For a discussion of Herzberg's principal findings and recommendations, see Robert C. Dailey, *Understanding People in Organizations* (St. Paul, Minn.: West Publishing Company, 1988), pp. 70–72 and 163–165.

Opportunity for advancement;
Recognition of accomplishments;
Challenging work;
Responsibility for work;
Opportunity for growth.

Stating this another way, job factors that tend to motivate people positively are primarily related to their higher level needs and aspirations. Opportunities for advancement, greater responsibility, recognition, growth, achievement, and interesting work consistently are identified as the major factors that make work motivating and meaningful. Of course, the absence of these factors can be frustrating and nonmotivating to the individuals involved. These motivation factors are not easily measured in certain situations, and they may be difficult to find in certain types of jobs.

Hygiene Factors.   Also referred to as the *dissatisfiers,* hygiene factors reflect the environment in which the job is performed. Herzberg identified the following hygiene factors:

Working conditions;
Money, status, and security;
Interpersonal relationships;
Supervision;
Company policies and administration.

The circumstances that employees complained about the most included: poor company policies and administrative practices; lack of good supervision, both in a technical and human relations sense; poor working conditions; and inadequate wages and benefits. Herzberg concluded that these factors tend to dissatisfy rather than to motivate. Where these factors are negative or inadequate, employees will be unhappy and dissatisfied. Even where these items are adequate, they do not tend to motivate people strongly. This does not mean that hygiene factors are unimportant. They are very important, but they serve primarily as a foundation in achieving positive employee motivation.

Other Results Supporting Herzberg's Research.   Herzberg's findings have been supported or reinforced by other researchers. For example, M. Scott Myers has generally replicated Herzberg's results in a series of studies that primarily were conducted at the Texas Instruments Corporation.[7] Other studies have shown that some supervisory ideas are out of step with what workers themselves really want from a job. For example, in a large-scale survey conducted some years ago, several thousand employees were asked, "What do

---

[7]M. Scott Myers, *Every Employee a Manager* (New York: McGraw-Hill, 1970).

you want most from your job?'' and then, ''How would you rate these wants in order of importance?'' At a later time, their managers and supervisors were asked to rate these factors in the order in which they felt their employees would rank them. Among the employees, ''credit for work done'' and ''interesting, challenging work'' were rated as being the most important considerations to them. However, their supervisors and managers rated ''fair pay with increases'' and ''job security'' as being the primary concerns of their employees.[8] The difference in perceived priorities was obviously a considerable one.

It must be emphasized again that these types of findings should not be interpreted as saying that money, benefits, good working conditions, and the like are unimportant. These factors are extremely important, and companies must strive continuously to be competitive in these areas. However, these ''hygienic'' conditions often are taken for granted by employees, especially during periods when job opportunities are plentiful. Positive employee motivation today seems to be more related to the higher level needs of people. The supervisor who wants to obtain better performance is well advised to consider strategies that will contribute to the satisfaction of employees' social, esteem, and self-realization needs.

Expectancy Theory

Another interesting and practical way of looking at employee motivation is provided by **expectancy theory**.[9] This theory is based on the worker's perception of the relationship between effort, performance, and reward. According to expectancy theory, workers will be motivated to work harder if they believe that greater efforts on their part will actually result in improved performance and that such improved performance will then lead to rewards that are desirable to them. An expectancy theory model is illustrated in Figure 4–5.

Expectancy theory is based on worker perceptions and on relationships referred to as ''linkages.'' Employee motivation is dependent on the workers being able to perceive an ''effort-performance linkage'' as well as a ''performance-reward linkage.'' If an employee cannot recognize that such linkages clearly exist, he or she will not be highly motivated.

For example, if a carpenter must use inferior equipment and tools or if a computer operator has not received adequate training and instruction, it is unlikely that these persons will be able to perceive a relationship between their effort and performance. Instead they will conclude that no matter how much effort they expend, there will be no significant improvement in their job

[8]See *Action Guide to Motivating People* (Waterford, Connecticut: Bureau of Business Practice, 1978), pp. 12–13.

[9]For a discussion of a number of variations of the expectancy theory, see Robert P. Vecchio, *Organizational Behavior* (Chicago: The Dryden Press, 1988), pp. 180–183.

Fig 4–5.
The expectancy
theory.

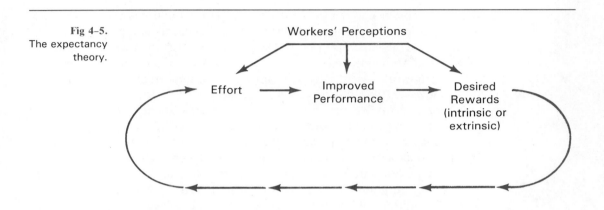

performance. Similarly, if a group of nurse's aides in a hospital perceive that their highly performing co-workers are not being rewarded any more than the average or even substandard performers, they will not believe that there is a per-formance–reward relationship either.

Yet, some managers and supervisors confidently assert that their compa-ny's reward system is one that reinforces and rewards high-quality work. Such an assertion, while sincere, is probably based on management's perception of the reward system. Consequently, little supervisory effort is made to verify whether the workers actually do view the reward system as management wishes for it to be viewed. Considering the widespread problems of motivating work-ers, it is apparent that supervisors and employees often do not view reward systems in the same way. For example, on his last day on the job, an assembly-line employee in a manufacturing plant participated in an exit interview. When the interviewer asked him why he was leaving, the worker said that he had become extremely frustrated waiting for work to come to his work station. The worker said that he became fed up with coming to work every day know-ing that, no matter how hard he would work, it would not be visible on the production chart.

It does not really matter how clearly supervisors view the relationship be-tween effort, performance, and rewards. If the workers cannot see the links, they might just as well not be there. Here is where supervisors should strive to show the employees that improved work performance will result in increased rewards. These may be extrinsic, in the form of additional pay, or intrinsic, such as a sense of accomplishment or some type of praise or recognition. Prob-ably the most important characteristic of a reward is that it is something a person desires.

Of course, a supervisor may have limited control over the rewards that are available. Union labor agreements and other pay and promotional systems typically are tied to seniority. Supervisors often complain that many employee wage increases are "automatic" with little relation to merit and job performance. But even in these types of situations, there are approaches available to supervisors that can yield motivational results.

SUPERVISORY APPROACHES FOR ATTAINING POSITIVE EMPLOYEE MOTIVATION

Having reviewed several prominent theories of employee motivation and management styles, the next question is: Which theories of motivation and supervisory management are the most meaningful? The answer depends on the individual employees involved, the situation, the supervisor, the nature of the organization, and many other complex factors. There are no simple "cookbook" rules that a supervisor can implement to achieve high motivation and excellent performance. Human beings are much too complex for any simple set of "do's" and "don'ts" for supervision. Although leadership skills can be learned and developed, it is well recognized that there are no formulas or checklists that will apply in all situations and with all people.

Certain behavioral science researchers have proposed various models and approaches, which have been described under the general headings of *contingency style leadership* or *situational management.* A discussion of these types of models and suggested approaches is beyond the scope and purpose of this text, since they can become rather complex and theoretical in orientation.[10] Essentially, these models emphasize that no one supervisory management style or approach is universally applicable and that the proper style or approach is contingent on numerous factors in any given situation. These include considerations involving the supervisor, the organization, the type of work, the subordinates involved, time pressures, and other factors. However, critics of contingency and situational type models contend that these models are inconclusive and may even lead supervisors to believe that they should not be consistent in supervisory management approaches with their people. Some skeptics have even gone so far as to contend that a contingency style of leadership is "no style" and one that is "consistently inconsistent."

We recognize that there are no absolutely definitive supervisory management approaches that can be prescribed for supervisors to follow for all types of employees, situations, and organizational constraints. Nevertheless, we are in agreement with a large body of other behavioral research and management literature, which holds that there are preferred ways of supervising and managing people that can result in better degrees of positive motivation and job

---

[10]For a discussion of several leading contingency style and situational management models, see John R. Schermerhorn, Jr., *Management for Productivity* (New York: John Wiley & Sons, Inc., 1984), pp. 315–327; or Ross A. Webber, Marilyn A. Morgan, & Paul C. Browne, *Management: Basic Elements of Managing Organizations* (3d ed.; Homewood Illinois: Richard D. Irwin, Inc., 1985), pp. 229–250.

performance. In general, these approaches are consistent with a Theory Y or (9,9) team, participative style. The premises and approaches suggested here also agree with what is known about people, their needs, and their motivations. There is widespread evidence that, when implemented sensibly and consistently, these approaches do work to influence employee motivation and job performance in a positive way. These approaches are further advocated throughout this book, particularly in Part 5.

Delegating Authority with Responsibility

As discussed at some length in the previous chapter, a sound principle of good management is that everyone in an organization should be given the authority necessary to carry out his or her assigned responsibilities and tasks. This principle is also an important approach by which supervisors can attempt to build positive motivation among employees. Wherever and whenever possible, supervisors should delegate as much authority as each employee needs to carry out his or her assignments. Many employees will be willing to accept (and perhaps even welcome) additional duties, challenges, and opportunities to contribute if the supervisor is willing to give them the necessary latitude and authority to carry out such duties. Yet, supervisors often are afraid to give employees additional authority, citing the following excuses:

> "I can do it better myself."
> "They'll just foul it up."
> "I'd rather do it myself."
> "They don't have the ability."
> "They'll make stupid decisions."

Because of their refusal or hesitance to delegate, some supervisors get bogged down in trivia and may be unable to pursue their own high-priority tasks. While there are some risks inherent in delegating, these are risks that must be balanced with the possibilities of attaining better employee motivation and job performance. Of course, a supervisor must exercise prudent judgment when determining which employees can handle additional responsibilities and authority.

Broadening the Scope and Importance of Each Job

Consistent with delegating authority with responsibility, there are ways to give employees new tasks and new work experiences by which the basic nature of the job may be broadened in scope and importance. Most employees tire of doing the same routine and monotonous chores day in and day out.

Job Rotation.   Rotating employees to perform various tasks within the department or work area on a periodic or scheduled basis is known as **job rotation.** This is something that most supervisors can implement, and it often is accompanied by higher levels of job performance and increased interest of employees in their duties. Job rotation not only helps to relieve employee boredom, but also enhances their job knowledge. Although job rotation involves essentially the same skill level, it may be perceived by some employees as job upgrading and training for promotion in the future. A major side benefit to the supervisor is that job rotation results in a more flexible work force, which can be advantageous during periods of employee absences, vacation, and the like. Further, job rotation should mean that both pleasant and unpopular tasks are shared by different employees and that the supervisor thus may avoid being criticized for being unfair in making work assignments.

Job Enlargement.   Another motivational strategy that has met with varying degrees of success is **job enlargement,** which means expanding an employee's job with a greater variety of tasks to perform. For example, tasks that were previously handled by several employees may be combined or consolidated within one or two enlarged jobs.

Some employees respond positively to job enlargement, which is reflected in their performance and in increased job satisfaction. In one furniture factory, for example, a number of very routine jobs were changed so that each job required five or six distinct operations. Employees were very supportive of the change. Such comments as, "My job seems more important now" and "My work is less monotonous now," were common reactions.

There can be problems in implementing job enlargement. Difficulties involved in restructuring work operations vary from one setting to another, and such changes can require a considerable amount of a supervisor's time and attention. Union work rules and job jurisdictional lines may limit the supervisor's authority to change job assignments. Further, attitudes toward the idea of job enlargement may present significant difficulties. Some employees, for example, object to the idea of being given expanded duties because they are content with their present jobs and pay. Usually they will not object if at least a small increase in pay comes with the enlarged job.

Job Enrichment.   An increasingly advocated motivational approach is **job enrichment,** which goes beyond job rotation and job enlargement in an effort to appeal to the higher level needs of employees. At the least, job enrichment can be accomplished by seeing to it that everyone in a department has a fair share of the challenging as well as the routine jobs. Unfortunately, many supervisors prefer to assign the difficult, challenging jobs only to their key or best employees and the dull jobs to the weaker or marginal employees. This can be defeating in the long run. It is preferable for the supervisor to try to provide opportunities for all or most employees to find challenging and interesting work experiences within the realistic framework of the department's operations and rules. Sometimes job enrichment can be accomplished by committee assignments, special problem-solving tasks, and other unusual job experiences that go beyond the routine performance of day-to-day work. In its most developed form, job enrichment may involve planning or restructuring jobs in such a way that employees are given greater latitude and direct control and responsibility for what they do.

A supervisor who attempts to implement job enrichment may be uncomfortable with it at first. Job enrichment may require a supervisor to relinquish certain prerogatives and to delegate some supervisory aspects of planning and decision making. But if job enrichment is sincerely practiced, usually subordinates over time assume an active role in making or participating in decisions about such matters as their job requirements and individual responsibilities. Job enrichment requires innovation on the part of supervisors. For example, one supervisor enriched the jobs of machine operators by giving them a greater role in scheduling work and devising their own work rules for the work group.

In a sense, job enrichment involves the employees' assumption of some of the supervisor's everyday responsibilities. The supervisor remains accountable, however, for the satisfactory fulfillment of these obligations. Therein lies a major risk inherent in job enrichment; yet despite the risk, job enrichment has been endorsed by many supervisors because it does work.

Due to the complexities of human behavior, there is no guarantee that job enrichment will solve all motivation problems. In some organizations any attempts at job enrichment will represent a radical departure from normal operating procedures. It may not be feasible technologically, or it may cost more than it will yield in tangible or intangible benefits. People may resist change because of the uncertainties which accompany job enrichment, and higher management may view a suggestion for it as an implied criticism of their present approach!

In summary, the differences among job enrichment, job enlargement, and job rotation are differences in degree. Each is an attempt to diversify the work and to make it more meaningful to employees. Job enrichment adds a vertical dimension or greater depth to the task, so that employees may be better able to satisfy their higher level needs through their work. Job enlargement emphasizes the horizontal dimension of the task since it gives employees more duties. Job rotation moves an employee from one job to another on a periodic basis with the intent of reducing boredom and increasing employee involvement and interest. These three motivational strategies are similar in the sense that each attempts to increase employee performance by improving job satisfaction.

Participative Management

One of the most effective ways to build a sense of employee pride, teamwork, and motivation is for the supervisor to seek advice, suggestions, and information from employees concerning ways in which work should be performed and

problems solved. This generally is known as **participative management.**[11]
Many studies in group behavior have shown that work groups indeed can help
the supervisor in improving decision making. This does not mean turning over
all decisions to employees; nor does it mean just making employees "think"
that they are participating in decisions. Rather, it means that the supervisor
should earnestly seek employees' opinions whenever possible and be willing to
be influenced by the suggestions and even criticisms they may offer. When
employees feel that they are part of a team and that they can have a realistic
influence on the decisions that are made, they are more likely to accept the
decisions and to seek new solutions to future problems. Further, supervisors
who utilize participative management in a proper way are aware of the importance of prompt feedback. They know that it is vital to respond fully to the
suggestions of a subordinate promptly, that is, as soon as possible after having
had sufficient time to consider them.

The major advantages of participative management are that decisions tend
to be of higher quality and that the employees are more supportive or willing
to accept the decisions. Among the disadvantages is the fact that this approach
can be time-consuming, and participation makes it easier for employees to
criticize; some supervisors find this threatening. On balance, however, participative management is widely recognized as an effective motivational strategy
whose advantages usually outweigh its disadvantages.

Some companies and organizations have found that formal suggestion systems can be a definite help in this direction. Suggestion systems provide monetary rewards to employees for suggestions that are received and accepted.[12]
The monetary reward is only part of the overall "compensation." Employees
like to have their suggestions heard and answered. To some employees, the
fact that a suggestion has been accepted may mean more to them in recognition than does the monetary award that is forthcoming.

Quality Circles and Quality of Work Life Programs

In recent years, many companies and organizations have adopted **quality circles (QC)** and **quality of work life (QWL)** programs both in unionized and
nonunionized situations. These types of programs or efforts often are known
by other terms, such as **employee involvement, labor–management participation teams,** and the like. By whatever name, they stem from a common emphasis on using participative management as an on-going, recognized activity.

---

[11]In Chapter 15, we discuss **consultative supervision,** which sometimes is used synony-
mously with participative management. For a large-scale review of the status of participative-type
programs in American industries, see "The Payoff from Teamwork," *Business Week,* (July 10,
1989), pp. 56–62.

[12]According to a 1988 survey, ideas from employees submitted under suggestion programs
saved companies $2.2 billion; employees received $160 million for their suggestions. See *Wall
Street Journal* (September 12, 1989), p. A1.

Fig 4–6.
A suggestion
system should
be genuine.

Quality circles (QC) usually involve some six to twelve employees and one or more supervisors—all from the same or similar work areas—who voluntarily meet on a regular basis to discuss production and quality problems in the department, plant, shop, or office. These groups try to identify job-related problems and develop feasible solutions to those problems, which then can be implemented realistically. Employees within a QC often come up with excellent ideas, and the QC also helps promote a flow of open two-way communication between employees and supervisors.

Much of the recent interest in quality circles has been influenced by so-called **Japanese-style management** practices, which have received much publicity. Japanese companies, for the most part, offer lifetime employment for their workers coupled with a major emphasis and commitment to involvement of employees in many production and quality decisions. Productivity and loyalty of Japanese workers to their firms have thrived under this system. William G. Ouchi has written extensively about Japanese-style management and has suggested what he calls a **Theory Z approach,** which would incorporate some of the Japanese ideas into American management practices. Theory Z suggestions, to a large extent, are based on Theory Y assumptions about people and are consistent with the practice of participative management and consultative supervision (which also is discussed in Chapter 15).[13]

---

[13]See William G. Ouchi, *Theory Z: How American Business Can Meet the Japanese Challenge* (Reading, Mass.: Addison-Wesley Publishing Company, 1981). However, not all quality-circle or similar efforts are always successful. For some disappointing results involving QC, see Berkeley Rice, ''Square Holes for Quality Circles,'' *Psychology Today* (February, 1984), p. 17.

Quality of work life (QWL) programs and efforts are even more ambitious in character than quality circles. The essence of QWL has been defined as:

The opportunity for employees at all levels in an organization to have substantial influence over their work environment by participating in decisions related to their work, thereby enhancing their self-esteem and satisfaction from their work.[14]

A comprehensive definition of QWL involving union-management environments was developed by the American Center for the Quality of Working Life as follows:

Quality of Work Life improvements are defined as any activity which seeks greater organizational effectiveness through the enhancement of human dignity and growth . . . a process through which the stakeholders in the organization—management, union(s), and employees—learn how to work together better . . . to determine for themselves what actions, changes, and improvements are desirable and workable in order to achieve the twin and simultaneous goals of an improved quality of life at work for all members of the organization, and greater effectiveness for both the company and the unions.[15]

A discussion of the many variations of QWL programs is beyond the scope of this text.[16] Suffice it to say that they involve ongoing, scheduled meetings between groups of managers, supervisors, employees and (where present) union officers in which problems, suggestions, criticisms, and the like are freely debated and discussed. The objective is to promote understanding and mutually desirable solutions and results. The long-term "payoff" is the desire to improve the competitive position of the firm and to make employees' jobs more secure and meaningful to them.[17] Obviously, any QWL effort must be based on a strong commitment to participative management as a way of organizational life.

---

[14]Paul D. Greenberg and Edward M. Glaser, *Some Issues in Joint Union-Management Quality of Worklife Improvement Efforts* (Kalamazoo, Mich.: W. E. Upjohn Institute for Employment Research, 1980), p. 11.

[15]Lee M. Ozley and Judith S. Ball, "Quality of Worklife: Initiating Successful Efforts in Labor-Management Organizations," *Personnel Administrator* (May, 1982), p. 27.

[16]For a comprehensive survey of QWL efforts, see "Labor-Management Cooperation: Recent Efforts and Results"—Readings from the *Monthly Labor Review,* published by the U.S. Department of Labor (LMSA Publication #6, BLS Bulletin #2153), December, 1982.

[17]Considerations along these lines played a major role in the 1935 negotiated agreement between company management and the United Auto Workers Union for the new General Motors "Saturn" plant in Tennessee. See "A New Labor Era May Dawn at GM's Saturn," *Business Week* (July 22, 1985), pp. 65–66.

Supervising with a Management by Objectives Emphasis

Another well-known motivational approach that has been widely adopted is called **management by objectives (MBO),** or **management by results.** Stated simply, it involves (a) having individual employees set or participate in setting their own performance targets within certain limits (rather than having the targets unilaterally set by supervisors or higher management); and (b) having employees initially appraise themselves in the context of their own objectives. Some companies have very elaborate MBO systems, which extend from top management all the way down to certain employees. Although this approach may not be practicable in some work situations (for example, on the assembly line), supervisors in most organizations can use it if they really are interested in trying to improve the motivation and performance of their people.

In brief, the MBO approach works as follows: Periodically, usually annually, the employee is asked to write down certain targets and objectives to be accomplished during the coming year. The employee's objectives must be within overall company and departmental objectives, and they must be stated in terms that are achievable and either measurable or verifiable. For example, a billing clerk might state objectives such as ''to reduce the number of errors on invoices by 10 percent''; ''to complete processing of all new order billings by the 15th of each month during the coming year''; or ''to develop a new filing system for late accounts by July 1.'' The supervisor and the employee then meet to discuss the objectives in order to decide which are feasible and to be agreed upon. An employee often will set objectives that are higher than what the supervisor initially would have set; the employee probably will be more committed to these objectives than if they had been ordered by the supervisor.

At the end of the period of time, the list of objectives is reviewed, and the employee is asked to rate his or her performance against the objectives. Here again, an interesting phenomenon usually develops. Typically, the employee will be more critical than the supervisor of the performance attained. The employee then is asked to restate or to list the objectives that should be accomplished in the next period. The entire process requires that the employee and the supervisor constantly communicate with each other, agree on mutually set objectives, and then evaluate performance in light of these objectives. Companies that have utilized MBO appropriately consider it to be a system of managing that is effective in stimulating employee motivation and job performance.

Of course, MBO will not work with everyone, and it is not a cure-all for supervisory problems. However, it does offer an approach by which certain aspects of planning and performance appraisal are placed on the employee rather than on the supervisor. This in itself should make it attractive to supervisors. In Chapter 7, we describe a step-by-step outline of the MBO process in greater detail.

SUMMARY

Prominent factors that interact to result in the personality development of each individual are the following: physiological makeup, early childhood experiences, the immediate and continuing environment through life, and cultural values. Among the infinite number of influences that become part of an employee's personality are the working environment and the supervisor's approach to management.

A supervisor should be sensitive to individual differences between people, and a supervisor should be even more aware of needs that tend to be similar among all human beings. Human behavior is caused, goal-oriented, and motivated, and motivation comes from within a person. Motivation and behavior stem from a hierarchy of human needs. According to Maslow, these needs in ascending order of importance are physiological, safety, social, esteem, and self-realization. Other researchers visualize a two-step hierarchy of needs in a more flexible relationship. Regardless of which needs hierarchy is more accurate, most supervisors can influence positive employee motivation if they place more reliance on supervisory approaches in connection with the higher level needs of their people.

The Theory X (authority-obedience or 9,1) supervisor believes primarily in emphasizing autocratic techniques, which relate to the lower level human needs. The Theory Y (team or 9,9) supervisor prefers to build motivation by appealing to the higher level needs.

Herzberg's motivation-hygiene research studies indicate that hygiene factors, such as money, management policies, working conditions, and certain aspects of supervision must be adequate, and attention to these factors is a necessary starting point. More important forces of positive employee motivation appear to lie in intrinsic factors, such as the employees' needs for achievement, opportunity for advancement, challenging work, promotion, growth, and recognition.

Expectancy theory suggests that employees will not be motivated unless they perceive a link between their efforts and performance and between their performance and rewards. Supervisors must clarify such relationships for the workers or strive to develop them.

Although contingency style leadership and situational management models recognize that no one supervisory management style is universally applicable, there are a number of approaches to supervisory management which are in harmony with modern theories of motivation. These include: delegation of authority with responsibility; job rotation, job enlargement, and job enrichment; participative management (including quality circles and quality of work life programs); and supervising with a management by objectives (MBO) emphasis. The supervisor must learn to implement different supervisory approaches as they are appropriate to different people and settings.

QUESTIONS FOR DISCUSSION

1. Why are human beings a type of resource different from any other that a supervisor must manage?
2. Discuss each of the major determinants of human personality. Which of these can be influenced or controlled to the greatest degree by the supervisor?

3. Evaluate Maslow's model of a hierarchy of human needs. Is this model realistic? Can it be of importance to the supervisor? Discuss.

4. Evaluate the concept of a two-step hierarchy of human needs. Is this model an improvement or just a refinement of Maslow's five-level hierarchy? Discuss.

5. What are the basic elements of Theory X and Theory Y? Should these theories be considered as ''right'' and ''wrong,'' and ''good'' and ''bad''? Why or why not? Is the Theory Y approach more appropriate for supervising employees today? Discuss.

6. Discuss the leadership styles described within the Managerial Grid. Compare the Managerial Grid with Theory X and Theory Y.

7. What are the major elements of Herzberg's motivation-hygiene theory? Discuss this theory in relation to the model of (a) Maslow's hierarchy of human needs, and (b) the two-step hierarchy of needs.

8. How can expectancy theory be useful to a supervisor's understanding of employee motivation?

9. What are the major contributions and criticisms of so-called contingency style leadership and situational management models?

10. Define and discuss each of the following approaches to supervision. Evaluate the degree of difficulty a supervisor might have in implementing these approaches in various circumstances.

    a. Delegating authority with responsibility.

    b. Job rotation, job enlargement, and job enrichment.

    c. Participative management, including quality circle and quality of work life programs.

    d. Supervising with a management by objectives (MBO) emphasis.

CHAPTER 5

Problem Solving and Decision Making in Supervision

CHAPTER OBJECTIVES

1. To emphasize the importance of problem-solving and decision-making skills in supervisory management.
2. To present the basic steps of the general decision-making process, which can be applied in most managerial decision situations.
3. To discuss approaches for both developing and evaluating alternatives as part of decision making, including ethical considerations.
4. To suggest criteria and factors by which supervisors can choose from available alternatives in order to make the "best" decision feasible.
5. To underscore the significance of decision making within the planning function of management.

All human activities involve problem solving and decision making. Everyone has problems at home, at work, and in social groupings for which decisions must be made. Thus decision making is a normal human requirement that begins in childhood and continues throughout life.

Similarly, when practicing supervisors are asked to state as briefly as possible what they do most of the time, many of them would reply that their job, as much as anything else, is "making decisions." Problem solving and decision making are at the core of all the major managerial functions. **Decision making** can be defined as the process of choosing a course of action to solve a particular problem; it involves selecting one alternative from a number of alternatives that have been considered.

Many of the problems that confront supervisors in their daily activities are recurring and familiar; for these problems most supervisors have developed routine answers. But when supervisors are confronted with new and unfamiliar problems, many of them find it difficult to decide on a course of action.

Managers and supervisors at all levels are constantly required to find solutions to problems that are caused by changing situations and unusual circumstances. Regardless of their managerial level, they should utilize a similar, logical, and systematic process of problem solving and decision making. Although decisions made at the executive level usually are of a wider scope and magnitude than decisions made at the supervisory level, the decision-making process fundamentally should be the same throughout the entire management hierarchy.

Of course, once a decision has been made, effective action is necessary. A good decision that no one implements is of little value. Getting effective action is not the problem with which we are concerned in this chapter. Here, we discuss the process that should lead to the "best" decision or solution before action is taken.

THE IMPORTANCE OF DECISION-MAKING SKILLS TO SUPERVISORS

A decision maker often is depicted as an executive with horn-rimmed glasses bent over some papers, with pen in hand, contemplating whether to sign on the dotted line. Or the image may be that of another manager in a meeting, raising an arm to vote a certain way. Both of these images have one point in common. They portray decision makers as persons at the moment of choice, as they are ready to choose an alternative that leads them from the crossroads. These simplified images do not reflect the long and tedious processes that should have taken place before the final moment of selecting one alternative over the others.

Decision making is an important skill for supervisors to possess. It is a skill that can be learned, just as the skills involved in playing tennis are learned. A good decision maker is basically a person with some natural intelligence who develops decision-making skills by learning, practice, and effort. By so doing, supervisors will learn how to make more thoughtful decisions and will improve their "batting average" in the quality of their decisions.

At the same time, supervisors should also be concerned that their employees learn to make their own decisions more effectively. A supervisor cannot make all the decisions necessary to run the department. Many daily decision-making activities of a department for which the supervisor is responsible are made by the employees who do the work. For example, various decisions concerning what materials to use, how a job is to be done, when it is to be done, and how to achieve coordination with other departments are decisions that employees often have to make without their supervisor. Therefore, the training of subordinates in the process of making decisions should be a high priority for all supervisors.

TYPES OF DECISIONS

Several decades ago, a prominent management decision-making theorist suggested that all decisions can be classified as either programmed or nonprogrammed. These types could be considered as being at two extremes, with many decisions falling somewhere between these extremes.[1]

Programmed Decisions

There are many daily problems that confront the supervisor which are not difficult to decide, because a more or less "pat answer" is available. These problems usually are routine or repetitive in nature, and fixed answers, methods, procedures, rules, and the like exist.

Decisions for these types of problems are called programmed decisions. **Programmed decisions** tend to be made when problems are repetitive, well-structured, and routine. The term "programmed" is descriptive in the same sense that it is used in computer programming—there is a specific procedure, or program, that can be applied to the problem at hand.

For example, if a purchasing agent has a number of similar buying decisions to make, he or she will develop specific inventory measurement procedures by which to handle them. In this way the purchasing agent can delegate much of the work to a clerical employee and still be confident that the decision will be made in an acceptable and routine manner. In Chapter 7 we discuss the

---

[1]Herbert A. Simon, *The New Science of Management Decision* (New York: Harper & Row, Publishers, 1960), p. 5. See also Harold Koontz and Heinz Weirich, *Management* (9th ed.; New York: McGraw-Hill Book Company, 1988), p. 143.

usefulness of policies, procedures, methods, rules, and standardized operating procedures, which are "standing plans" for making certain programmed decisions.

In recent years there has been widespread development in the programmed-decision area through the application of computers and operations research methods. For example, many companies utilize computers and data processing equipment to handle many problems that formerly required many employees to solve and decide.

Nonprogrammed Decisions

Nonprogrammed decisions occur when supervisors are confronted with a new or unusual problem where they must use their intelligent, adaptive problem-solving behavior. Such problems may be rare, unstructured, or unique, i.e., of an "ad hoc" nature.

Supervisors often face new or unusual situations for which there are no "pat answers" or previous guides for decision making. Or they may not know the full dimensions of a problem. While nonprogrammed decisions occur less frequently than programmed types, they tend to be more important, demanding, and strategic in nature. In nonprogrammed decision making, supervisors are called on to utilize good judgment, intuition, and creativity in attempting to solve the problem. Here supervisors should utilize a general decision-making process by which they can mentally approach such problems in a consistent and logical, but adaptable, pattern.[2] Our discussion to follow will primarily refer to problems of a nonprogrammed nature.

THE GENERAL DECISION-MAKING PROCESS

In making nonprogrammed managerial decisions, it is desirable for the supervisor to follow the suggested steps of the **general decision-making process.** First, the problem must be defined. Second, the problem must be analyzed, using available information. Third, after thorough analysis, alternative solutions should be developed. Only after these steps have been taken should the supervisor evaluate the alternatives and select the solution that appears to be the "best" or most feasible under the circumstances. The concluding step in this process is the follow-up and appraisal of the consequences of the decision.

---

[2]For a more thorough discussion of this approach, see Stephen Robbins, *Management: Concepts and Practices* (Englewood Cliffs, N.J.: Prentice-Hall, Inc., 1984), pp. 71–111; or Warren Plunkett and Raymond Attner, *Introduction to Management* (Boston: Wadsworth Publishing Company, 1983), pp. 146–165.

Step One: Define the Problem

It is common for supervisors to say, "I wish I had the answer" or "I wish I had the solution to this" or "I wish I knew what to do about this." These statements are indications that supervisors may be too preoccupied with looking for answers or solutions. Before seeking answers, the supervisor first should identify the real problem. The first step in decision making is to find out what the problem really is; only then should the supervisor work toward a solution or answer. It is an old axiom that nothing is as useless as the right answer to the wrong question.

Defining the problem is not an easy task in most cases. What appears to be the problem might at best be merely a symptom that shows on the surface. It usually is necessary to delve deeper in order to locate the real problem and to define it. For example, an office supervisor might believe that a problem of conflicting personalities exists within the department. Two employees are continually bickering and cannot get along together. After checking into this situation, the supervisor finds that the real problem is that she or he, as the supervisor, has never clearly outlined the functions and duties of each employee—where their duties begin and where they end. What appeared on the surface to be a problem of personality conflict was actually a problem caused by the supervisor. Only after the true nature of the problem has been recognized can the supervisor do something about it. The chances are good that once the areas of activities and responsibilities between the two employees are clarified, the friction will end.

Fig 5–1.
The effective supervisor usually follows the steps of the general decision-making process in their proper sequence.

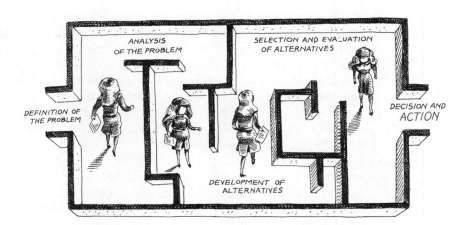

Defining a problem is, in most circumstances, a time-consuming task, but it is time well spent. A supervisor should not go any further in the process of decision making until the problem or problems relevant to the situation have been specifically determined.

Step Two: Analyze the Problem: Gather Facts and Information

After the problem—not just the symptoms—has been defined, the next (and sometimes more-or-less simultaneous) step is to analyze the problem. The supervisor begins by assembling facts and other pertinent information. This is sometimes viewed as being the first step in decision making; but until the real problem has been ascertained, the supervisor does not know what information is really needed. Only after having a clear understanding of the problem can the supervisor decide how important are certain data and what additional information should be sought. Being only human, a supervisor will find that personal opinion is likely to creep in somehow. This is particularly true when employees are involved in the problem. For example, if a problem involves one of the supervisor's "favorite" employees, the supervisor may be inclined to show this person greater consideration than if another, less-favored employee is involved. Therefore, great care and effort should be taken by the supervisor to be as impersonal and objective as possible in gathering and examining the information available.

Sometimes the supervisor does not know how far to go in searching for additional facts. A good practice to follow is to observe time and cost limitations that are reasonable with respect to the problem involved. This means gathering all the information that can be obtained without undue delay in time and without excessive costs.

Similarly, in the process of analysis the supervisor should try to think of intangible factors that may be involved and that can play a significant role. Some intangible factors are reputation, morale, discipline, and personal biases. It is quite difficult to be specific about these factors; nevertheless, they should be considered in the analysis of a problem. As a general rule, written and objective information is more reliable than mere opinions and hearsay evidence.

Step Three: Develop Alternatives

After the supervisor has defined and analyzed the problem, the next step is to search for and develop various alternative solutions. It should be an absolute rule for a supervisor to try to consider as many possible solutions as can reasonably be developed. The supervisor who makes a great effort to formulate many alternatives is less apt to overlook the best course of action. Or, stating this another way, *a decision will only be as good as is the "best" alternative that has been developed.*

Almost all problem situations have a number of alternatives, not just "either this or that." Alternative choices may not always be obvious, but it is the responsibility of supervisors to search for them. If supervisors do not do this, they are likely to fall into the "either/or" kind of thinking. Further, it is not enough for supervisors just to decide from among alternatives that have been suggested by employees, because there may be other alternatives that should be considered. Thus it is the job of supervisors to stretch their minds to develop additional alternatives, even in the most discouraging situations. None of the alternatives might be really desirable, but at least the supervisor can choose one that is most likely to be the "least undesirable" solution to the problem at hand.

For example, suppose that a plant manager has been ordered to make a 20 percent reduction in the plant's labor force because the firm is experiencing financing problems. After careful study, the plant manager develops the following feasible alternatives:

1. On a plantwide basis, lay off those workers with the least seniority, regardless of their jobs or performance, until the overall 20 percent reduction is reached.
2. On a departmental basis, lay off those workers with the least seniority until the overall 20 percent reduction is reached.
3. On a combined plantwide and departmental basis, lay off those workers with the least seniority, provided that there are enough qualified workers left in each department, until the overall 20 percent reduction is reached.
4. Without laying off any employee, develop a schedule of reduced work hours for every employee that would be equivalent to a 20 percent reduction.

Although none of these alternatives may be an ideal solution to this unpleasant situation, at least the plant manager has considered four alternatives before a choice and decision are made.

Brainstorming and Creative Problem Solving.   Where time is available, it may be possible for a supervisor to get together with a group of other supervisors or employees in a meeting to brainstorm solutions to a perplexing problem. A detailed discussion of brainstorming and creative problem solving is beyond the scope of this text.[3] Suffice it to say that the typical brainstorming approach is to have the supervisor present the problem and then to have participants in the group offer as many ideas and approaches as they can develop in the time available. It is understood that any idea—even those which may at first appear to be "wild" or unusual—will be given a chance to be heard.

---

[3]See James L. Gibson, John M. Ivancevich, and James H. Donnelly, Jr., *Organizations: Behavior, Structure, Processes* (5th ed.; Plano, Texas: Business Publications, Inc., 1985), pp. 82–85 and 583–587; or "Are You Creative?", *Business Week* (September 30, 1985), pp. 80–84.

Guidelines for Effective Brainstorming. Alex Osborn, an authority on creativity and the brainstorming approach, has suggested four major guidelines for effective brainstorming. These are:

1. *Defer all judgment of ideas.* During the brainstorming period, allow no criticism by anyone in the group. It is natural for people to suppress new ideas both consciously and unconsciously and this tendency must be avoided. Even if an idea at first seems impractical and useless, it should not be rejected by quick initial judgments, because such rejection could inhibit the free flow of more ideas.
2. *Seek quantity of ideas.* "Idea fluency" is the key to creative problem solving, and fluency means quantity. The premise here is that the greater the number of ideas, the greater the likelihood of "winners."
3. *Encourage "free wheeling."* Being creative calls for a free-flowing mental process in which all ideas, no matter how extreme, are welcome. Even the wildest idea may, on further analysis, have a germ of usefulness.
4. *"Hitchhike" on existing ideas.* Combining, adding to, and rearranging ideas often can produce new approaches that are superior to the original ideas. When creative thought processes slow or stop, review some of the ideas already produced and attempt to "hitchhike" on them with additions or revisions.[4]

Creative approaches and brainstorming meetings usually are not appropriate for programmed decisions. However, they are particularly adaptable to nonprogrammed decisions, especially if the problem is new, important, or strategic in dimension. Even the supervisor who takes time to mentally brainstorm a problem alone is likely to develop more alternatives for solving the problem than without doing so.

Ethical Considerations. Both in the development and evaluation of alternatives, it should be apparent that every alternative considered by a supervisor not only must be lawful but also should be acceptable within the company or organization's policies, procedures, and guidelines. In recent years, many firms have become very concerned that their managers, supervisors, and employees make ethical decisions, because they recognize that, in the long run, "good ethics is good business."[5] Consequently, many firms have developed

---

[4]Alex Osborn, *Applied Imagination* (New York: Charles Scribner & Sons, 1953), p. 84. See also Ramon Aldag and Timothy Stearns, *Management* (Cincinnati: South-Western Publishing Company, 1987), pp. 610–615.

[5]See Raymond L. Hilgert, "What Ever Happened to Ethics in Business and Business Schools?" *The Diary of Alpha Kappa Psi,* (Volume LXXIX, Number 1, April, 1989), pp. 4–7; John R. Schermerhorn, Jr., *Management for Productivity* (New York: John Wiley & Sons, Inc., 1984), pp. 656–685; or *Corporate Ethics: A Prime Business Asset,* a special report published by The Business Roundtable (New York, February, 1988).

handbooks, policies, and official statements that specify the ethical standards and practices expected.

In Chapter 7 we discuss corporate statements of goals and objectives, many of which include legal and ethical dimensions. Suffice it to say here that supervisors should always endeavor to make decisions that reflect the firm's ethical standards. If a supervisor believes that a particular alternative is not proper or might not be acceptable within the firm's ethical policies, the supervisor should consult with his or her boss—or with a staff specialist knowledgeable in the area—for guidance and suggestions concerning how to proceed. Figure 5–2 is an example of a policy guideline regarding expense accounts, which was developed for supervisors and sales representatives of a pharmaceutical firm whose customers are primarily doctors and hospital personnel.

Step Four: Evaluate the Alternatives

The ultimate purpose of decision making is to choose that specific course of action which will provide the greatest amount of wanted and the smallest amount of unwanted consequences. After developing alternatives, supervisors can mentally test each of them by imagining that each has already been put into effect. They should try to foresee the probable desirable and undesirable consequences of each alternative. By thinking the alternatives through and appraising their consequences, supervisors will be in a position to compare the desirability of the various choices.

Factors to Consider.   In making comparisons as to which alternative is most desirable, the supervisor should have in mind the degree of risk involved in each course of action. There is no such thing as a riskless decision; one alternative may simply involve less risk than the others.

The question of time may make one alternative preferable, particularly if there is a difference in how much time is available and how much time is required to carry out one alternative in comparison with another. The supervisor should also consider the facilities, records, tools, and other resources that are available. Also of critical importance is that different alternatives be judged in terms of economy of effort and resources. In other words, which action will give the greatest benefits and results for the least amount of costs and effort expended?

In those cases where one alternative clearly appears to provide a greater number of desirable consequences and fewer unwanted consequences than any other alternative, the decision of which alternative to choose is fairly easy. However, the best alternative is not always so obvious. It is conceivable that at certain times two or more alternatives may seem equally desirable. Here the choice may become a matter of personal preference. It is also possible that the supervisor may feel that no single alternative is significantly stronger than any

A WORD ABOUT ETHICS:
 We are given a very generous expense account. We can spend money as we deem necessary in our own individual territories. With this freedom, unfortunately, comes many choices. There are several rules that help when working with these decisions.

TREAT YOUR EXPENSE ACCOUNT AS IF IT WERE YOUR OWN!
 If it was coming right out of YOUR wallet, would you furnish lunch for that account?
 If it was your own PERSONAL check, would you contribute to your hospital's charity?

IF YOU HESITATE ABOUT A "FINANCIAL" DECISION, YOU SHOULD PROBABLY ASK YOUR MANAGER FOR ADVICE!
 If one of your accounts says, "If you'll contribute to our 'education fund,' we'll take your bid," should you write the check?
 If one of your doctors says, "If I could take my spouse to Tony's (the best restaurant in the city), I would remember to write you an order," should you give that physician a gift certificate?

 These examples seem a little absurd, but representatives run into decisions like these daily. For example, you do not want accounts to EXPECT food when you have an appointment. Always keep in mind that credibility and rapport are built slowly. There is no quick way to win over an account—not even with money! One important thing to remember is:

YEARS OF RAPPORT BUILDING CAN AND WILL BE DESTROYED BY JUST ONE EXAMPLE OF POOR JUDGMENT!

Fig 5–2. Policy guideline for supervisors and sales representatives of a pharmaceutical firm regarding expense accounts.

of the others. In this case, it might be advisable to combine the positive aspects of the better alternatives in an attempt to find a composite solution.

Unsatisfactory Alternatives.   Sometimes a supervisor is confronted with a situation in which none of the alternatives is satisfactory, and all of them have too many undesirable effects. Or the supervisor might feel that none of the alternatives will bring about the desired results. In such a case, the supervisor should begin again to think of new alternative solutions or perhaps even start all over again by attempting to redefine the problem at hand in some different way.

Moreover, a situation might arise where the undesirable consequences of all the alternatives appear to be so overwhelmingly unfavorable that the supervisor feels that the best available solution to the problem is to take no action at all. However, to do so may be self-deception, since taking no action will not necessarily solve the problem. Taking no action is as much a decision as is the decision to take a specific action, even though a supervisor may believe that an unpleasant choice has been avoided. The supervisor should mentally visualize the consequences that are likely to result from taking no action. Only if the consequences of no action are the most desirable should it be selected as the appropriate course.

Step Five: Select the "Best" Alternative

After developing and evaluating the alternatives, the supervisor must select that alternative which seems to be "the best." There are several criteria or factors on which the decision can be based. Among the most prominent are experience, intuition, advice from others, experimentation, and statistical and quantitative decision making.

Experience.   In making a selection from among various alternatives, the supervisor often will be influenced and guided by experience. Chances are that certain situations will recur, and the old saying that "experience is the best teacher" does apply to a certain extent. A supervisor often can decide wisely because of personal experience or the experience of some other manager. Knowledge gained from experience is a helpful guide, and its importance should not be underestimated. On the other hand, it is dangerous to follow experience blindly.

When looking to experience as a basis for choosing among alternatives, the supervisor should examine the situation and the conditions that prevailed at the time of the earlier decision. It may be that conditions still are practically identical to those which prevailed previously and that the decision should be similar to the one made on the previous occasion. More often than not, however, conditions will have changed considerably, and the underlying circumstances and assumptions are no longer the same. Therefore, the decision probably should not be identical to the earlier one.

Experience can be very helpful in the event that the supervisor is called on to substantiate his or her reasons for making a particular decision. In part this may be a defensive approach, but there is no excuse for following experience in and of itself. Experience must always be viewed with the future in mind. The underlying circumstances of the past, the present, and the future must be considered realistically if experience is to be of assistance in selecting from among alternatives.

Hunch and Intuition.   Supervisors will admit that at times they base their decisions on hunch and intuition. Some supervisors even appear to have an unusual ability to solve problems satisfactorily by quite subjective means. However, a deeper search usually will disclose that the ''intuition'' on which the supervisor appeared to have based a decision was really experience or knowledge that had been stored in the supervisor's memory. By recalling similar situations that occurred in the past, supervisors may better reach a decision even though they label it as ''having a hunch.''

Hunch or intuition may be particularly helpful in situations where all of the other alternatives available have been previously tried with poor or limited results. If the risks are not too great, a supervisor may choose a particular new alternative because of an ''intuitive feeling'' that a fresh approach might work and bring positive results. Even if the hunch does not work out well, the supervisor has tried something different. This can be remembered as part of the person's experience and be drawn upon in future decisions.

Advice from Others.   Although a supervisor cannot shift personal responsibility for making decisions in the department, the burden of decision making often can be eased by seeking the advice of others. The ideas and suggestions of employees, other supervisors, staff experts, technical authorities, and the supervisor's own boss can be of great help to the supervisor in weighing facts and information. Seeking advice does not mean avoiding a decision, since the supervisor still must choose whether to accept the advice of others. We discuss this in more detail in Chapter 12.

Experimentation.   In the scientific world, where many conclusions are based on tests in laboratories, experimentation is essential and accepted. In supervisory management, experimentation to see what happens often is too costly in terms of people, time, and money. There are some instances where a limited amount of testing and experimenting is advisable. For example, a supervisor may find it worthwhile to try several different locations for a new copy machine in the department to see which location is preferred by the employees and which is most convenient for the work flow. There are some instances where a certain amount of testing would be advisable in order to provide employees with an opportunity to try out new ideas or approaches—perhaps of their own design. In a motivational sense, experimentation may be quite valid; but in a supervisory position, experimentation can be a slow and relatively expensive method of reaching a decision.

Statistical and Quantitative Decision Making. During the past several decades, numerous techniques and models of quantitative decision making have received much attention in management literature and practice. Included among the techniques are linear programming, operations research, operations management, and statistical probability and simulation models. These tend to be sophisticated, mostly mathematical approaches in concept and design, often used in connection with computers.[6] They require the decision maker to quantify most of the information that is relevant to a particular decision. For many first-line supervisors, these quantitative decision-making techniques are rather remote.

With the increasing use of desktop computers, however, many firms are able to develop programs and information storage and retrieval systems that can be utilized by supervisors relatively easily for certain types of decisions, especially where historical and statistical databases are involved. For some types of problems, supervisors may be able to seek the help of mathematicians, engineers, statisticians, systems analysts, and computer specialists who might bring their tools to bear on appropriate and relevant problems and solutions. This can be an involved and costly procedure, and generally only a small portion of supervisory management decisions can be made primarily from statistical or quantitative models.

Step Six: Follow Up and Appraise the Results

After a decision has been made, specific actions are necessary in order to carry it out. Follow-up and appraisal of the outcome of a decision are actually part of the process of decision making.

Follow-up and appraisal of a decision can take many forms depending on the nature of the decision, timing, costs, standards expected, personnel, and other factors. For example, a minor production scheduling decision could easily be evaluated on the basis of a short written report or perhaps even by the supervisor's observation or a discussion with employees. However, a major decision involving the installation of complex new equipment will require close and time-consuming followup by the supervisor, technical employees, and higher management. This type of decision usually will require the supervisor to

---

[6]For a general overview of several approaches, see William Newman, E. Kirby Warren, and Andrew McGill *The Process of Management* (6th ed.; Englewood Cliffs, N.J.: Prentice-Hall, 1987), pp. 135–151; or Leslie Rue and Lloyd Byars, *Management: Theory and Application* (4th ed.; Homewood, Ill.: R.D. Irwin, Inc., 1986), pp. 168–187 and 532–595.

prepare numerous, detailed written reports of equipment performance under varying conditions, which will be compared closely with plans or expected standards for the equipment.

The important point to recognize is that the task of decision making is not really complete without some form of follow-up and appraisal of the actions taken. If the consequences have turned out well, then the supervisor can feel reasonably confident that the decision was sound.

If the follow-up and appraisal indicate that something has gone wrong or that the results have not been as anticipated, then the supervisor's decision-making process must begin all over again. This may even mean going back over each of the various steps of the decision-making process in detail. The supervisor's definition and analysis of the problem and the development of alternatives may have to be completely revised in view of new circumstances surrounding the problem. In other words, where follow-up and appraisal indicate that the problem has not been resolved properly, the supervisor will find it advisable to treat the situation as a brand new problem and go through the decision-making process from a completely fresh perspective.

DECISION MAKING WITHIN THE PLANNING FUNCTION

As stated before, every supervisor must make many decisions as he or she performs all of the managerial functions. Thus, decision making—like communication, which is the subject of the next chapter—is a pervasive aspect of supervisory management and a core skill of any effective supervisor.

At the same time, however, it should be recognized that effective decision making is particularly crucial as a supervisor carries out the planning function of management. As a supervisor plans, numerous choices from available alternatives have to be made, which will determine and guide the future direction of the department. As we have said before—and say again in later chapters—the planning function must come first in supervisory management. In this context, decision making is rightly viewed as being at the heart of all managerial planning.

SUMMARY

Decision making based on careful study of information and analysis of various courses of action available is still the most generally approved avenue of selection from among alternatives. Supervisors confront many decision situations, which can vary from the programmed type at the one extreme to the nonprogrammed type at the other. Decisions for routine, repetitive type problems are usually made easier by the use of policies, procedures, standard practices, and the like. However, decisions that involve unusual or unique problems require sound judgment and systematic thinking.

Better decisions are more likely to occur when supervisors follow the suggested steps of the general decision-making process. These are: (a) define the problem; (b) gather facts and information and analyze the problem; (c) develop many alternatives; (d) evaluate alternatives, thinking them through as if they had already been placed into action and considering their consequences; (e) choose the alternative that has the greatest amount of wanted and least amount of unwanted consequences; (f) follow up and appraise the decision.

In developing alternatives, supervisors should utilize brainstorming and creative thinking where these techniques are appropriate or applicable. Further, in the process of choice, a supervisor can be aided by personal experience or the experiences of other managers. Under certain circumstances, the supervisor may choose to use the advice of others or possibly experiment with several approaches.

QUESTIONS FOR DISCUSSION

1. Define managerial decision making. Does the process of managerial decision making vary depending on where a manager or supervisor is located in the managerial hierarchy? Discuss.
2. Distinguish between programmed and nonprogrammed types of decisions.
3. Review the steps of the decision-making process in their proper sequence. Why is proper definition of the problem perhaps the most important part of the decision-making process?
4. Identify the major elements of the brainstorming approach for developing alternatives in problem solving. Why will a decision be only as good as the best alternative that was considered?
5. Define and discuss the factors that a supervisor should consider in developing and evaluating alternatives in the decision-making process. To what degree should ethical policies be a consideration?
6. Discuss how a decision to take no action concerning a problem can be a valid approach, rather than an attempt to avoid an issue.
7. Evaluate each of the following as a criterion for selecting from among alternatives:
   a. Experience.
   b. Hunch and intuition.
   c. Advice from others.
   d. Experimentation.
   e. Statistical and quantitative decision making.
8. Discuss follow-up and appraisal as part of the decision-making process.
9. Why are the planning function of management and decision making closely related concepts?

CHAPTER 6

Communication: The Vital Link in Supervisory Management

CHAPTER OBJECTIVES

1. To emphasize the key role of effective communication in supervisory management.
2. To discuss the major channels of communication and the supervisor's role in understanding and dealing with the grapevine.
3. To discuss the means of communication available to the supervisor.
4. To identify major communication barriers and to suggest techniques for overcoming these barriers to make communication more effective.

Virtually every supervisor recognizes that the ability to communicate effectively is one of the keys to supervisory success. Communication is the process that links all of the managerial functions. There is no managerial function that a supervisor can fulfill without communicating. In managing their departments, supervisors must explain and discuss the arrangement of work. They must give directives, describe to all employees what is expected of them, and then speak to the employees regarding their performance. All of this requires communication.

A basic definition of **communication** is that it is a process of transmitting information and understanding from one person to another. Effective communication means that there is a successful transfer of information, meaning, and understanding from a sender to a receiver. In other words, communication is the process of imparting ideas and making oneself understood by others. While it is not necessary to have agreement, there must be a mutual understanding for the exchange of ideas or information to be successful.

THE NEED FOR EFFECTIVE COMMUNICATION

Most supervisors agree that many words and much information flow through and around them. With the advent of electronic forms of communication and other convenient means of information flow, it would seem that communication problems would be diminishing in many organizations. Yet, most supervisors still complain that communication difficulties remain as perhaps their most persistent problem and challenge. As one frustrated supervisor expressed herself: "There are more messages now being sent and received, but, frankly, I think we communicate with each other more poorly than ever before!"

Numerous studies have indicated that supervisors generally spend between 70 and 90 percent of their time sending and receiving information. Yet, it is apparent that effective communication does not take place in many exchanges. The mere activity of sending and receiving messages does not ensure that the supervisor is an effective communicator. Mutual understanding must also take place.

Because they are not good communicators, some supervisors do not achieve the desired results, despite the fact that they are competent, technically knowledgeable, and well-intentioned. They often are dismayed and their jobs hampered because the messages they send and receive become distorted. They may "lose touch" with their employees and, as a result, proper interpersonal relationships do not exist. Unfortunately many of these supervisors blame everything and everyone in the organization for shortcomings in communication, instead of trying to improve upon their own performance as communicators. The costs of poor communication are high—misunderstanding, waste, inefficiency, poor morale, ill feelings, confusion, and other negative consequences. Therefore, supervisors should make every effort to communicate effectively with their superiors and subordinates. Every supervisor has numerous opportunities to take small but significant steps wherever possible to become a more effective communicator.

Effective Communication Requires a Two-Way Exchange

Communication was defined as a process of transmitting information and understanding from one person to another. The significant point here is that communication always involves at least two people, a sender and a receiver. For example, a supervisor who is alone in a room and who verbally states a set of instructions does not communicate because there are no receivers present. While this is obvious, it may not be so obvious to a supervisor who sends out a letter. Once the letter has been mailed, the supervisor may be inclined to believe that communication has taken place. However, this supervisor has not really communicated until and unless the letter has been received and information and understanding have been transferred successfully to the receiver.

It cannot be emphasized too strongly that effective communication includes both information and understanding. A listener may hear a speaker because the listener has ears, but the listener may not understand what the speaker means. Understanding is a personal matter between people. If the idea received is the same in meaning as the one intended, then we can say that effective communication has taken place. But if the idea received by a listener or reader is not the one intended, then effective communication has not been accomplished. The sender merely has transmitted spoken or written words. Again, this does not mean that the sender and receiver must agree on a particular message or issue; it is possible to communicate and yet not agree.

Effective Communication Means Better Supervision

Some supervisors are much more effective as communicators than others. Usually these supervisors recognize that communication is vital, and they give it their major attention. Unfortunately many supervisors simply assume that they know how to communicate, and they do not work at developing their communication skills. Yet, a supervisor's effectiveness will depend greatly on the ability to transfer information and ideas to the employees so that the supervisor is understood and proper results are achieved. Employees cannot be expected to comply with directives unless they understand the meaning of the directives. Similarly, the supervisor must know how to receive information and understand the messages that are sent by employees, by fellow supervisors, and also by higher level managers. Fortunately, the skills of effective communication can be acquired and developed. By becoming a more effective communicator, a supervisor will become a more effective manager.

CHANNELS OF THE COMMUNICATION NETWORK

In every organization the communication network has two primary and equally important channels: the formal, or official, channels of communication and the informal channels, usually called the grapevine. Both types of channels carry messages from one person or group to another downward, upward, and horizontally in organizations.

Formal Channels

Formal communication channels are established primarily by the organizational structure. The vertical formal channels can be visualized by following the lines of authority from the top executive down through the organization to supervisors and employees.

Downward Communication. The concept of a downward formal channel of communication suggests that someone at the top issues a directive or disseminates some information, that managers at the next level in the hierarchy pass the communication along to their subordinates, and so on down the line. The downward direction is the most frequently used and relied upon channel utilized by higher management for communication. Downward communication helps to "tie" different levels together and is important for coordination. It is used by managers to start action by subordinates and to communicate directives, objectives, policies, procedures, and other information to them. Generally speaking, downward communication is mostly of an informative and directive nature and requires action on the part of subordinates. Downward communication from a supervisor involves giving instructions, explaining information and procedures, training employees, and communicating other types of activities designed to direct employees in performing their work.

Upward Communication. Upward is a second, but equally important, direction of communication in the official network. Supervisors who have managerial authority accept an obligation to keep their superiors informed. Similarly, employees should feel free to convey to supervisors their opinions and attitudes and to report on activities and actions related to their work. Managers and supervisors should encourage a free flow of upward communication. This is a vital means by which management can determine whether proper actions are taking place. A supervisor is the major link in encouraging these types of upward employee contributions.

Upward communication usually is of an informing and reporting nature, including questions, suggestions, complaints, and grievances. Supervisors should encourage and maintain upward communication among employees and give ample attention to the information transmitted. Supervisors must show that they "want the facts" and then must evaluate them properly and promptly. As discussed in Chapter 4, participative-type supervisors convey a genuine desire to obtain and use the ideas suggested and reported by employees. Lack of an effective upward communication channel throttles the natural desire of employees to communicate, can lead to their frustration, and may ultimately cause some employees to seek different outlets.

The supervisor's obligation for upward communication to his or her boss, especially when mistakes have occurred or serious problems have developed, are discussed again near the end of this chapter.

Horizontal Communication.   There is a third direction of formal communication that is essential for the efficient functioning of an organization. This is lateral, or horizontal, communication, which is concerned mainly with communication between departments or people at the same levels but in charge of different functions. In order to achieve coordination between various departments' functions, a free flow of horizontal communication is needed and should be encouraged.

Horizontal communication typically involves discussions and meetings in order to accomplish tasks that cross departmental lines. For example, a production manager may have to contact managers of the marketing and shipping departments in order to ascertain progress on a delivery schedule for a product. Or someone from the human resources department may have a meeting with a number of supervisors to discuss how a new medical-leave policy of the company is to be implemented at the departmental level. Still another example would be that of a maintenance department supervisor who calls an assembly-line supervisor to inquire when work should begin on overhauling a particular machine. Without effective horizontal communication, any organization would find it virtually impossible to coordinate specialized departmental efforts toward common goals.

Informal Channels—The Grapevine

Informal communication channels, commonly referred to as the **grapevine,** are a normal outgrowth of informal and casual groupings of people on the job, of their social interactions, and of their understandable desire to communicate with one another. Every organization has its grapevine. This should be regarded as a perfectly natural activity, since it fulfills the employees' desires to be "in the know" on the latest information. The grapevine offers members of an organization an outlet for their imaginations and an opportunity to express their apprehensions in the form of rumors. It has been categorized as a "network of spontaneous channels."

Understanding the Grapevine.   Although the grapevine is feared by many supervisors, it can offer considerable insight into what employees think and feel. An alert supervisor will acknowledge the grapevine's presence and try to utilize it to advantage if possible. The grapevine may carry some factual information, but most of the time it carries half-truths, rumors, private interpretations, suspicions, and other bits of distorted or inaccurate information. Even though the information spread by the grapevine is more often wrong than right, many employees have more faith and confidence in the grapevine than in what their supervisors tell them. In part, this reflects a rather natural human tendency to trust one's peers to a greater degree than to trust one's superiors, such as bosses or parents.

The grapevine has no definite patterns or stable membership. Its paths and behavior cannot be predicted, since the path followed yesterday is not necessarily the same as today or tomorrow. The vast majority of employees hear information through the grapevine, but some do not pass it along. Any person within an organization may become active in the grapevine on occasion, although some individuals tend to be more active than others. They feel that their prestige is enhanced by providing the latest news, and they do not hesitate to spread and change the news as to its "completeness" and "accuracy." The rumors they pass on serve in part as a release for their emotions, providing an opportunity to remain anonymous and say what they please without the danger of being held accountable.

At times, however, the grapevine does disseminate a certain amount of useful information (as contrasted to distortions, rumors, and half-truths). The grapevine sometimes helps clarify and supplement formal communications, and it often spreads information that could not be disseminated as well or as rapidly through official channels.

The Supervisor and the Grapevine. The supervisor should accept the fact that it is not possible to eliminate the grapevine. It is unrealistic to expect that all rumors can be stamped out, and the grapevine is certain to flourish in every organization. In order to cope with it, supervisors should tune in on the grapevine and learn what it is saying. They should determine who its leaders are and who is likely to spread the information.

Many departmental rumors begin in the wishful thinking stage of employees' anticipation. It is quite common that if employees want something badly enough, they may start passing the word along to each other. For instance, if secretaries want a raise, they may start the rumor that management will offer an across-the-board raise. Nobody knows for certain where or how it started, but the story spreads "like wildfire" since everyone wants to believe it. Of course, it is undesirable for the morale of a group to have their hopes built up in anticipation of something that will not happen. If such a story is spreading and the supervisor realizes it will lead to disappointment, the supervisor ought to move quickly to "debunk" it by presenting the facts. The best cure for rumors of this type is to expose the true facts to all the employees and to give a straight answer to all questions wherever possible.

Figure 6-1.
Most of the
time the
grapevine
carries bits of
distorted or
inaccurate
information.

Other frequent causes of rumors are uncertainty and fear. If business is slack and management is forced to lay off some employees, stories multiply quickly. During periods of insecurity and anxiety, the grapevine becomes more active than at other times. Often the rumors are far worse than what actually will happen. If the supervisor does not disclose the actual facts to the employees, they will make up their own "facts," which may be worse than reality. Thus much of the fear caused by uncertainty can be eliminated or reduced if the truth of what will happen is disclosed. Continuing rumors and uncertainty may be more demoralizing than even the saddest facts presented openly.

Rumors also start out of dislike, anger, or distrust. Here again, the best prescription is to state the facts openly and honestly. If the supervisor does not have all the information available, this should be frankly admitted to the employees and then every effort should be made to find out what the situation actually is so that it can be reported to them as soon as possible. One of the best ways to stop a rumor peddler is to expose the person and the untruthfulness of the statements. The supervisor should bear in mind that the receptiveness of a group of employees to the rumors of the grapevine is directly related to the quality of the supervisor's communications and leadership. If employees believe that their supervisor is concerned about them and will make every effort to keep them informed, they will tend to disregard rumors and look to the supervisor for proper answers to their questions.

As stated before, there is no way to eliminate the grapevine, even with the best efforts and use of all formal channels of communication. The supervisor, therefore, should listen to the grapevine and develop skills in dealing with it. For example, an alert supervisor might know that certain events will cause an

Figure 6–2.
Pictures, charts,
cartoons, and
symbols can be
effective visual
aids.

undue amount of anxiety. In this case, the supervisor should explain immediately why such events will take place. When emergencies occur, when changes are introduced, and when policies are modified, the supervisor should explain why and answer all employee questions as openly as possible. Otherwise, employees will make up their own explanations, and often these will be incorrect. There are situations, however, when a supervisor does not have the facts either. Here the supervisor should seek out the appropriate higher level manager to explain what is bothering the employees, to ask for specific instructions as to what information may be given, how much may be told, and when. Also, when anything happens that might cause rumors, it is helpful for supervisors to meet with their most reliable or "influential" employees to give them the real story and to guide their thinking. Then they can spread the facts before anyone else can spread the rumors.[1]

MEANS OF COMMUNICATION

The means of communication include words, visual media, gestures, and actions. Spoken and written words, of course, are by far the most important forms of human communication, but the power of visual media in conveying meaning and understanding to people should never be underestimated. Pic-

---

[1]For further discussion of informal channels of communication and the grapevine, see Robert A. Baron, *Behavior in Organizations* (2d ed; Boston: Allyn and Bacon, Inc., 1986), pp. 320–324.

tures, charts, cartoons, and symbols can be effective visual aids, and the supervisor should utilize them where appropriate. They are particularly effective if used in connection with well-chosen words to complete a message. Business enterprises make extensive use of visual aids to communicate understanding through blueprints, charts, drafts, models, posters, and other messages. Motion pictures and comic strips demonstrate the power of visual media in communicating.

Behavior Is Communication

It is sometimes overlooked by supervisors that their behavior as departmental managers on the job is an important form of communication to their subordinates. All of a supervisor's observable actions communicate something to employees, whether they are intended to do so or not. Gestures, a handshake, a shrug of the shoulder, a smile, even silence—all of these have meaning and may be interpreted differently by different people. For example, a supervisor's enthusiasm and erect posture can send out positive signals to the employees. Conversely, a frown on a supervisor's face may communicate more than ten minutes of oral discussion or a printed page.

A supervisor's inaction is a way of communication, just as unexplained action may communicate a meaning that was not intended. For example, a supervisor arranged to have some equipment removed from the production floor without telling the employees that the equipment was removed because it needed mechanical modifications. To the employees, who feared a threatened shutdown or move of the plant to another city, such unexplained action com-

Figure 6–3.
A supervisor's
observable
actions
communicate
thoughts or
feelings to
employees.

municated a meaning or a message that the supervisor had no intention whatsoever of sending.

Oral and Written Communication in Supervision

Of course, spoken and written words are the most widely used forms of communication in any organization. They also constitute a challenge and problem to every supervisor who wishes to communicate effectively. Words can be tricky. Instructions that mean one thing to one employee may have a different meaning to someone else. There is the old story about a maintenance supervisor who told a new worker, "Go out and paint the canopy in front of the building green." Upon checking on the job an hour later, the supervisor found that a wastecan had been painted bright green. The new employee had obviously interpreted the word canopy in a different manner than intended!

Since words are the essence of oral and written communication, supervisors should constantly exert effort to improve their skills in speaking, listening, writing, and reading. Although oral messages are most frequently used, a well-balanced communication system utilizes both written and oral media. First-line supervisors do not have as many occasions to use the written medium, since a high proportion of supervisory communication takes place by word of mouth.

Oral communication generally is superior to written communication, because it facilitates better understanding and takes less time. This is true both with telephone and face-to-face communication. At the departmental level, oral face-to-face discussion between a supervisor and the employees is the principal method of two-way communication. There is no form of written communication that can equal person-to-person (face-to-face) communication, and face-to-face communication is more effective than communication over the telephone, a public address system, or some form of electronic message. Employees like to see and hear the boss in person, and no written communication can be as effective as an interpersonal discussion or meeting. Another reason for the greater effectiveness of oral communication is that most people can express themselves more easily and completely by voice than by a letter or memo.

Probably the greatest single advantage of oral communication is that it can provide an immediate opportunity for determining whether effective communication has been accomplished between the sender and receiver. Although the response may be only an expression on the receiver's face, the sender can judge how the receiver is reacting to what is being said. Oral communication enables the sender to find out immediately what the receiver hears and does not hear. Oral communication enables the receiver to ask questions immediately if the meaning is not clear, and the sender can explain the message and clarify the meaning of certain words and problems raised by the communication. The manner and tone of the human voice can impart a message with meaning and shading that pages of written words cannot convey. Personal mannerisms and tone of voice create an atmosphere for communication, and responses are influenced accordingly.

The principal problem with oral communication is that usually there is no permanent record of it, and memories of speakers and listeners over time will blur the meaning of what was conveyed. This is why many supervisors find it advisable to follow up certain meetings and discussions with some type of letter, memorandum, or documentation in order to have a written basis for recalling what was spoken or discussed.

To reiterate, a supervisor must always remember that effective communication does not take place until and unless the meaning that is received by the listener is the same, or virtually the same, as that which the sender intended to send. Supervisors who are effective communicators know how to speak clearly and to be aware of the listener. They are sensitive to the many barriers to effective communication that can distort communication lines. They know how to overcome these barriers, how to "clear the pipelines." Such supervisors recognize that a speaker and a listener are unique individuals who live in different worlds and that there are many factors which can interfere and play havoc with messages that pass between them.

BARRIERS TO EFFECTIVE COMMUNICATION

Due to human differences and organizational conditions, there are many obstacles that distort messages between people. Most supervisors are familiar with misunderstandings, frictions, and inconveniences that develop when communication breaks down. These breakdowns not only are costly in terms of money but also create dilemmas that hurt teamwork and morale. Many supervisory human relations problems are traceable to faulty communication, since the way a supervisor communicates with subordinates constitutes the essence of their relationships.

Language and Vocabulary Differences

Words in themselves can be confusing, even though language is the principal vehicle used by people to communicate with each other. People at different levels or in different departments of an organization sometimes seem to speak in different "languages" although they are actually speaking English.[2] For

---

[2] The English language is estimated to contain some 750,000 words; but the vocabulary of the average person is only in the range of 20,000 to 40,000 words. English is now recognized as the world's primary international language; about 1 of every 7 people in the world have some knowledge of English. See "English: Out to Conquer the World," *U.S. News and World Report* (February 18, 1985), pp. 49–59.

Figure 6–4.
There are many
barriers to
effective
communication.

example, an accounting department supervisor may use specialized words, which may be meaningless when conversing with the plant manager. Similarly, if the plant manager uses highly technical engineering terms when conversing with the accounting supervisor, the latter will probably be quite confused. This is the communication problem known as **jargon,** or the tendency of people to use words that are peculiar to their particular background or specialty.

Another communication problem lies in the multiple meaning of words, also known as **semantics.** Words can and do mean different things to different people, particularly in the English language, which is one of the most difficult in the world. The way some words are used in sentences can cause people to interpret messages in a manner other than was intended. *Roget's Thesaurus,* which is a dictionary of synonyms, identifies the numerous meanings that commonly used words can have. For example, the word ''smart'' can be used in several ways. We speak of a ''smart'' person in the sense that a person is intelligent; a ''smart aleck'' is someone who is difficult to get along with; a person who dresses ''smartly'' is someone who dresses fashionably; and a ''smarting'' pain means a stinging or sharp pain. There are many other words that can be used in many different ways. Where a word can have multiple meanings, the meaning intended must be clarified, since listeners tend to interpret words based on their own orientations, ethnic, and cultural backgrounds.

There are instances where a frustrating conversation between a supervisor and employee ends with, ''We are not talking the same language,'' even though both have been conversing in English. In order to avoid such breakdowns, supervisors should strive to use the employees' language. That is, supervisors should use words to which the employees are accustomed and which they can understand. It is not a question of whether the employee *ought* to understand the words; the question is, *does* the employee understand? Therefore, supervisors should strive to use plain, direct words in brief, uncomplicated language. If necessary, they should restate messages in several ways to clarify the proper (semantic) meaning or context that was intended.[3]

Status and Position

The organization's structure, with its several levels in the managerial hierarchy, creates a number of status levels among members of the organization. **Status** refers to the attitudes that are held toward a position and its occupant by the members of the organization. There is a recognized status difference between an executive level and a supervisory level, and between supervisors and employees. Differences in status and position become apparent as one level tries to communicate with another. For example, a supervisor who tries to convey enthusiasm to an employee about higher production and profits for the company may find that the employee is indifferent to these types of company goals. The employee may be primarily concerned with achieving higher personal wages and security without having to exert extra effort. Thus the supervisor and the employee may represent different points of view merely by virtue of their positions in the company, and this may present a serious obstacle to understanding each other.

When employees listen to a message from the supervisor, several other factors become operative. The supervisor's words are evaluated in light of the employees' backgrounds and experiences. They also take into account the supervisor's personality and position. It is difficult for employees to separate the message from the feelings that they have about the supervisor who sends the messages. Therefore, the employees may add nonexistent motives to the message. For example, union members may be inclined to interpret a management statement in very uncomplimentary terms if they are convinced that management is trying to weaken and undermine the union. Such a mental block caused by status is another major impediment to understanding in the flow of communication.

Supervisors should be acutely aware that status and position influence feelings and prejudices and thus create potential barriers. Not only do subordinates evaluate a supervisor's words differently, but they also place importance

---

[3]Much concern has been expressed in recent years concerning the reading, writing, and speaking capabilities of many U.S. citizens. Some estimates place at 25 million persons (about 1 out of every 10) the number of people who are so-called functional illiterates. By this is meant that they are deficient in the basic language skills needed to function at a reasonable level on the job and in other areas of society.

on a supervisor's gestures, silence, smile, or other facial expressions. Here, too, the supervisor must be careful that such physical features are in harmony with the message to be conveyed.

Obstacles due to status and position similarly can distort the upward flow of communication, where subordinates are anxious to impress their superiors. Employees may conveniently and protectively screen certain information that is passed "up the line"; the employees tell the supervisor only what they think the latter "likes to hear" and omit or soften the unpleasant details. This is known as the problem of **filtering.** By the same token, some supervisors are anxious to cover up their own weaknesses when talking to a manager in a higher position. Supervisors often fail to pass on important information to their bosses because they believe that such information would reflect unfavorably on their own supervisory abilities. After two or three successive protective filterings of this sort, messages are likely to be terribly distorted.

Resistance to Change or New Ideas

Many people prefer things as they are, and they do not welcome changes in their working situation. If a message is intended to convey a change or new idea to employees—something that will upset or change their work assignments, positions, or part of their daily routine—the natural inclination is for the employees to resist or reject the message. It is normal for people to prefer that their existing environment remain in the status quo. Consequently, a message that will change this equilibrium may be greeted with suspicion. The employees' receiving apparatus works just like a screen, rejecting new ideas if they conflict with a currently comfortable situation.

In the same fashion, most listeners are likely to receive that portion of a message which confirms their present beliefs and will tend to ignore whatever conflicts with those beliefs. Sometimes beliefs are so fixed that the listeners do not hear anything at all. Even if they hear a statement, they will either reject it as false or will find a convenient way of twisting its meaning to fit their own mental perceptions.

Ultimately most receivers of a message usually hear what they wish to hear. If they are insecure, worried, or fearful in their positions, this barrier becomes even more difficult to overcome. Supervisors often are confronted with situations where their employees only "half listen" to what is being said. Employees become so busy and preoccupied with their own thoughts that they tend to give attention only to those ideas they want to hear and to select only those parts of the total message that they can use or accept. Those bits of information for which they do not care, or which are irreconcilable to their biases, are conveniently brushed aside, not heard at all, or easily explained away. A supervisor must be aware of these possibilities, particularly when a message intends to convey some change, a new directive, or anything else that may interfere with the normal routine or customary working environment.

Personality and Environmental Barriers

In addition to the barriers just discussed, there are others that arise from deep-rooted personal feelings, prejudice, and physical conditions. It may be employee indifference—the "don't care" attitude—that stands in the way of communication. A message gets through to the employee, but it is acted on only halfheartedly or not at all. Or there may be biases and stereotypes about age, race, sex, and other personality determinants.

To illustrate, a young, recent college graduate is assigned to work for an experienced office supervisor with many years of service and loyalty to the firm. The supervisor might believe that most young people are liberal, self-centered, and lacking in dedication to hard work. Consequently, the supervisor hears and evaluates everything the younger employee says with these notions in mind and has difficulty in relating to the younger employee. At the same time, the younger employee might feel that the older generation is stuffy, rigid, and resistant to change and new ideas. Thus the age gap between the employee and supervisor can easily lead to serious communication difficulties.

Since barriers to effective communication are numerous and diverse, supervisors should never assume that the messages they send will be received as they were intended. As a matter of fact, supervisors could well consider taking the attitude that most of the messages they send are likely to be distorted. If supervisors operate from this premise, they more likely will do everything within their power to overcome these barriers and to improve the chances for mutual understanding.

OVERCOMING BARRIERS TO EFFECTIVE COMMUNICATION

Most of the techniques and methods available for overcoming communication barriers are relatively easy and straightforward. Supervisors will recognize them as techniques that they sometimes utilize but that they do not utilize as frequently as they should. A supervisor once remarked to one of the authors, "Most of these are just common sense." The author's reply to this comment was simply, "Yes, but have you ever observed how uncommon common sense sometimes is?"

Preparation and Planning

A first major step toward becoming a better communicator is to avoid speaking or writing until the idea or message to be communicated has been thought through to the point that it is clear and firm in the sender's mind. Only if supervisors can express their ideas in an organized fashion can they hope for others to understand the ideas or instructions involved. Therefore, before communicating, supervisors should know what they want and should plan the sequence of steps necessary to attain their objectives.

For example, if a supervisor wants to make a job assignment, he or she should first analyze the job thoroughly so as to be able to describe and discuss it properly. Or if the supervisor is to explain the solution to a particular problem, the supervisor should study the problem until it is so clear in mind that little difficulty will be encountered in explaining the solution. Or when searching the facts, the supervisor should determine in advance what information is needed so that intelligent, pertinent, and precise questions can be asked. If a communication is to involve a disciplinary action, the supervisor should have sufficiently investigated the case and compiled all relevant information before issuing a reprimand or other penalty. In other words, communication should not begin until the supervisor knows what ought to be said in relation to what should be achieved.

Utilizing Feedback

Among the methods available to improve communication, feedback is by far the most important. **Feedback** means that communication becomes a two-way flow as a sender utilizes questions, discussion, signals, or clues in order to determine whether the receiver has understood the message. Merely asking the receiver, "Do you understand?" and receiving a "Yes" as an answer may not be enough feedback. More than this is usually required in order to make sure that a message was actually received as it was intended.

A simple way to do this is to observe the receiver and to judge that person's responses by nonverbal clues, such as an expression of bewilderment or understanding, the raising of an eyebrow, a frown, or the direction or movement of eyes. Of course, this kind of feedback is possible only in face-to-face communication, and this is one of the major advantages of this form of communication.

Perhaps the best feedback technique is for the sender to ask the receiver to restate or "play back" the information just received. This is much more satisfactory than merely asking whether the instructions are clear. If the receiver states the content of the message, then the sender will know what the receiver has heard and understood. At that time the receiver may ask additional questions and request comments, which the sender can provide immediately. This technique probably is the most direct and immediate approach to make certain that a message has been understood.

The feedback technique also is applicable when a supervisor is on the receiving end of a message from an employee or a higher level manager. In order to clear up possible misunderstandings, a supervisor can say: "Just to make sure I understand what you want, let me repeat in my own words that message you gave me." An employee or a boss will appreciate this initiative of a supervisor to improve the accuracy of communication.

The feedback technique just discussed is most applicable in face-to-face communication. When the supervisor is involved with written communication, feedback can be helpful, too. Before sending out a written message, the supervisor might have someone else—perhaps a colleague—read the message for comprehension. Most writing can be improved. It may be necessary to develop several drafts of a written message and have various people provide feedback as to which draft is the most clearly stated and readily interpreted.

Similarly, after sending out a memo or letter, it often is desirable for the supervisor to discuss the written correspondence over the telephone to make sure that the recipient of the memo or letter received and understood it. When a supervisor receives a written message from someone else, and if there is any doubt in the supervisor's mind about the meaning of the message, the supervisor should not hesitate to call or see the sender to discuss the message and clarify it as necessary.

Direct and Clear Language

Another sound approach for attaining effective communication is for the supervisor to use words that are understandable and as clear as possible. Long, technical, and complicated words should be avoided. The supervisor should use language that the receiver will be able to understand without difficulty. Jargon or "shop talk" should be used only if the receiver or listener is comfortable with it. The old, so-called K.I.S.S. approach is usually a good motto for a supervisor to remember: K.I.S.S. stands for "Keep It Short and Simple."

Calm Atmosphere

Tension, emotional stress, and anxiety were mentioned previously as being serious barriers to effective communication. If a supervisor tries to communicate with an employee who is visibly upset, chances for mutual understanding are minimal. It is much better to communicate when both parties are calm and not burdened by unusual tension or stress. One of the best ways for a supervisor to have the proper atmosphere for communicating or discussing a problem with an employee is to set an appointed time for a meeting in a quiet room or office. This usually enables both the supervisor and the employee to prepare themselves to discuss the problem at hand in a calm and unhurried fashion. Similarly, supervisors who want to discuss issues with their bosses may find it advantageous to arrange for appointments at times and places that are mutually conducive to having a good, uninterrupted discussion—as compared to a brief and tension-filled conversation in the plant or office.

Taking Time and Effort to Listen

Still another approach for overcoming barriers to communication is for both the sender and the receiver to take more time to listen, that is, to give the other person full opportunity to express what is on his or her mind. The supervisor who pays attention and listens to what an employee is saying learns more about the employee's values and attitudes toward the working environment. The supervisor may restate from time to time what has been expressed by asking the question, "Is this what you mean?" A supervisor should always patiently listen to what an employee has to say, even though it may seem unimportant. Intensive listening helps to reduce misunderstandings, and by listening the supervisor in turn will be better able to respond in ways that will be more appropriate to the concerns of the employee.

Part of the difficulty in listening is caused by the fact that the speed of thought is much faster than the speed of speech. It is estimated that (on average) people can listen at a rate of some 400 to 600 words per minute, but they can speak only at a rate of 200 to 300 words per minute. Thus it is easy for a listener to allow the mind to wander and daydream. When listening, a supervisor should make great effort to use the time lag between speech and thought to concentrate on what is being said. This can be done by listening for ideas, by summarizing in the mind what the speaker has said, by trying to read the thoughts behind the words, and by looking ahead toward what may be said. If the mind is concentrating on what the speaker is saying, listening efficiency can be improved. One of the worst things listeners can do is to sit with faked attention while their minds are on mental excursions.

The following are some practical "do's" and "don'ts" for learning to listen more effectively.

"Do's" for Listening:

1. Take time to listen, give the speaker your full attention, and hear the speaker out even though he or she is repetitious.
2. Withhold judgment until the speaker is finished; strive to locate the main ideas of the message.
3. Try to determine the word meanings within the context of the speaker's background; listen for what is being implied as well as what is being said.
4. Look (but don't stare) at the speaker most of the time; smile, nod, and give an encouraging sign when the speaker hesitates.
5. Ask questions at appropriate times to be sure that you understand the speaker's message.
6. Restate the speaker's idea at appropriate moments to make sure that you have it correctly.

"Don'ts" for Listening:

1. Avoid listening with only half an ear by "tuning out" the speaker and pretending that you are listening.
2. Don't unnecessarily interrupt the speaker or finish the speaker's statement because of impatience or of wanting to respond immediately.
3. Don't fidget or doodle while listening; don't let other distractions bother you and the speaker.

4. Don't confuse facts with opinions.
5. Don't show disapproval or insensitivity to the speaker's feelings.
6. Avoid responding until the speaker has said what he or she wants to say.

Repetition of Messages

It frequently is advisable for a supervisor to repeat a message several times, preferably using different words, phrases, or different approaches. The degree of repetition will depend largely on the content of the message and the experience and background of the employees or other persons involved in the communication. However, the supervisor should not be so repetitious that the message is ignored because it sounds too familiar or boring. In case of doubt, a degree of repetition probably is safer than none.

Reinforcing Words with Action

Supervisors who neglect to complement their words with appropriate and consistent actions will fail as communicators, regardless of how capable they are with words. Supervisors should be aware that they communicate much by what they do, that is, by their actions; and as the old but true cliché goes, actions speak louder than words. Therefore, one of the best ways to give meaning to messages is to act accordingly. If verbal announcements are backed up by action, the supervisor's credibility will be enhanced. However, if the supervisor says one thing but does another, sooner or later the employees will "listen" primarily to what the boss "does."

Figure 6–5. A supervisor communicates by actions as much as by words.

"Adult-to-Adult" Transactions

In recent years, much attention has been focused on principles of transactional analysis as a model for training supervisors and others in communication skills. Although a thorough discussion of *transactional analysis (TA)* is beyond the scope of this text,[4] suffice it to say that TA classifies human personality into three primary "ego states." The **parent** ego state uses words such as "should," "ought," "do," "don't," "must," etc., reflecting parental and authoritarian perspectives. The **child** ego state used words such as "can't," "won't," "don't want to," "I want," "why blame me," etc., which reflect somewhat immature perspectives. However, the **adult** ego state uses words such as "why," "what," "when," "where," "what are the alternatives," "Let's discuss," "Should we check it out," and so on. Thus when people communicate in words and ways designed to seek, give, and evaluate information and to look for desirable alternatives to solve problems, they are behaving as mature adults should be expected to behave.

Although transactional analysis training can take many forms, it usually seeks to encourage open communication on an "adult-to-adult" basis whenever possible. In supervision, the supervisor who sincerely and consistently considers his or her employees as fellow adults will tend to communicate with them accordingly. Adult-to-adult communication fosters more open and honest relationships and messages, which are conducive to mutual understanding and teamwork. Unfortunately, too many supervisors often communicate with their employees on a "parent-to-child" basis, and this tends to cause distortions and misunderstandings.

Good Supervisory Practices

In all of this, it should be apparent that the most effective communication will take place when people try to share common perspectives. If employees are on the team and want to do a good job—and if supervisors are clear in their objectives and are working toward improving the human relations atmosphere—there is a better chance of making the organizational climate conducive to effective communication. On the other hand, if the supervisor's relations with employees are characterized by hostility, tension, and other interpersonal barriers, effective communication is an impossibility. Good supervisory practices will not guarantee effective communication, but they are conducive for achieving it.

---

[4]For introductory principles of transactional analysis (TA), see Wendell L. French, Fremont E. Kast, and James Rosenzweig, *Understanding Human Behavior in Organizations* (New York: Harper & Row Publishers, 1985), pp. 161–163; or Robert P. Vecchio, *Organizational Behavior* (Chicago: The Dryden Press, 1988), pp. 426–429.

THE SUPERVISOR'S RESPONSIBILITY FOR UPWARD COMMUNICATION

All supervisors should understand that with their supervisory positions goes an important obligation to communicate upward. Supervisors are responsible not only for effective communication downward to employees but also for clear messages upward to keep the boss up-to-date and well-informed. Most supervisors will agree that it is often easier for them to "talk down" than to "speak up." This is particularly true if they have ever had to tell their boss that they did not meet a certain schedule due to poor planning or that they forgot to carry out an order. Nevertheless, it is a supervisory duty to advise the boss whenever there are significant developments and to do this as soon as possible either before or after such events occur. It is quite embarrassing to a boss to learn important news elsewhere; this can be interpreted to mean that the supervisor is not on top of his or her responsibilities. Thus supervisors have the duty to keep their superiors up to date, even if the information concerns errors that took place. Higher level managers need to have complete information, because they retain overall responsibility for organizational performance. Of course, this does not mean that supervisors need to pass upward every bit of trivial information. Rather, it means that supervisors should mentally place themselves in their bosses' position and consider what information their bosses need in order to perform their own jobs properly.

A supervisor's upward communication should be sent on time and in a form that will enable necessary action to be taken. Appropriate facts should be assembled and checked for objectivity before they are given to the boss. Of course, this may be quite difficult at times. A natural inclination is to "soften" the information a bit so that things will not look quite as bad in the boss's eyes as they actually are. Sooner or later the filtering will be discovered. When difficulties arise, it is best to tell the boss "what the score is," even if this means admitting mistakes. Higher management depends on the supervisor for reliable upward communication, just as the supervisor depends on his or her employees for upward information.

SUMMARY

The ability to communicate effectively is one of the most important qualities leading to supervisory success. Effective communication means that a successful transfer of information and understanding takes place between a sender and a receiver.

Formal channels of communication operate downward, upward, and horizontally. These communication channels primarily serve to link people and departments in order to accomplish organizational objectives. The formal network is supplemented by the informal network, or grapevine. The grapevine offers the supervisor possibilities for learning what subordinates think and feel. Much of the information carried by the grapevine will be distorted. The best way of dealing with the grapevine is for the supervisor to explain to employees why certain things are taking place, when changes are to be introduced, and how these events will affect the department.

Spoken and written words are the most important means of communication. Body language, gestures, and a person's behavior also communicate, often in more powerful ways than words themselves.

Among the many barriers to effective communication are differences in vocabulary and language; differences in status and positions; resistance to change; and other barriers that may reflect emotions, physical conditions, and various circumstances in the working environment. To overcome these barriers, supervisors should adequately prepare what they wish to communicate, and then use as many media as they think are necessary in order to have their messages sent, received, and properly understood. The greatest advantage of oral face-to-face communication is that it provides an immediate opportunity for feedback in order to determine whether mutual understanding has taken place. Feedback also can be utilized in written communication. In addition, supervisors should utilize direct and clear language; listen intently to what others say; bolster words with proper actions; and repeat and rephrase statements depending on the content of the message. In total, effective communication is more likely to take place when there has been good supervision, which promotes a positive human relations climate conducive to mutual understanding and teamwork.

A supervisor also has a duty to communicate upward to the boss. It is the supervisor's responsibility to forward information to higher management even in cases where this means admitting certain mistakes.

QUESTIONS FOR DISCUSSION

1. What is meant by effective communication? Why is mutual understanding at the heart of any definition of effective communication?
2. Why should communication always be considered a two-way process?
3. What are the major directions of formal communication channels?
4. How can the grapevine be both an asset and a problem to a supervisor?
5. Discuss the techniques by which a supervisor may effectively cope with the grapevine.
6. Discuss the various means of communication used in an organization. Why is the old cliché that "actions speak louder than words" applicable to the supervisory position?
7. What is the greatest single advantage of oral face-to-face communication? Why?
8. Analyze each of the following barriers to effective communication.
   a. Language and vocabulary differences.
   b. Status and position.
   c. Resistance to change or new ideas.
   d. Other barriers such as prejudices, physical conditions, and personal feelings.
9. Evaluate each of the following means to overcome communication barriers.
   a. Adequate preparation and planning.
   b. Feedback techniques.

       c. Direct and clear language.
       d. Calm atmosphere.
       e. Effective listening.
       f. Repetition of messages.
       g. Reinforcing words with actions.

10. What specific techniques can be utilized in order to improve a person's listening skills?

11. Discuss the communications aspects of transactional analysis. Why is the "adult-to-adult" relationship more conducive to better supervisor–employee communication?

12. Discuss the following statement: "Good supervisory practices and effective communication tend to go hand in hand."

13. Why is the supervisor's responsibility for upward communication to the boss an important obligation? Discuss.

CASE 1

The Socializing Supervisor

Tiffany Miles recently was promoted to the supervisory position in the Word Processing Department of a Savings and Loan Association. She had been chosen for this position by the Operations Manager, Roy Callahan, who felt that Tiffany Miles was the ideal candidate for the supervisory position. Miles had been hired some five years previously as a word processor, and she had accrued more seniority than any of the other employees (all women) in the department. Her job ratings had been superior, and she seemed to be well liked by her colleagues and others who knew her.

When Callahan told Miles that she was to become supervisor of the Word Processing Department, she asked him how she should handle the problem that her former fellow-employees now would be her "subordinates." Callahan told her not to be concerned about this and that her former associates would soon accept the transition. Callahan also told Miles that the company would send her to a supervisory management training program sponsored by a local financial services association "just as soon as time became available" for her to be sent to the program.

After several months, however, Callahn was getting the impression that Tiffany Miles was not making the adjustment to her position as supervisor of her department. Callahan particularly was concerned that he had observed Miles socializing with her employees during lunch breaks, coffee breaks, car pools, and the like. Callahan had received reports that Miles often socialized with several of her employees after work, including going on double-dates and parties arranged by these employees.

Further, Callahan had received a number of reports from supervisors of other departments that the word processing services were not being performed as efficiently as they should be. Several supervisors in the company told Callahan that the word processing department employees spent too much time away from their work in exceeding breaks, lunch periods, and the like. One supervisor even told Callahan that, "Since Miles became supervisor of word processing, there is little discipline in the department, and it's just a big social group which reluctantly does a little work."

Callahan realized that Tiffany Miles had not made a good adjustment to supervising employees in her department. He wondered how much of this was attributable to her lack of experience as a supervisor, and that her former colleagues might be taking advantage of her. At the same time, Callahan was concerned that Miles perhaps did not have the desire to disassociate herself from socializing and being a "buddy" to her employees. Callahan wondered what his next step should be.

CASE 2

Should a Supervisor Do the Work of the Employees?

Anita Matthews had worked in the Accounting and Data Processing Department of the Concord Community Bank for ten years. Recently she was promoted to the position of supervisor of a data-processing section that sends out bank statements to depositors. Due to an unusually large number of absences caused by a flu epidemic in the city, the department had fallen far behind in its scheduled operations. Many of the tabulating-equipment operators were absent because of illness. Since she used to do this work, Matthews decided to help in order to alleviate the situation. She spent between two and four hours a day operating one of the empty machines to help get the statements out. She did not neglect any of her supervisory duties to any extent. Of course, while she was running a machine, she was doing this and nothing else.

Art Roberts, Anita Matthews's superior, returned from an out-of-town trip and found her operating a machine and not in her office. Roberts had been looking for Matthews because he wanted to discuss some problems with her. He became very annoyed with her because of what she was doing, and he asked her into his office. He proceeded to give her a lecture, stating that it was a supervisor's job to get things done through and with people and that did not mean doing the work of the employees, even when a department was short-handed. Matthews, who listened patiently to Roberts's statement, pondered what her reply should be.

Long Hours for Supervisors

All supervisors of the Westside Manufacturing Company were employed with the understanding that they were expected to do everything within their capabilities to achieve the goals of the company and to get production out regardless of the hours they had to work. Supervisors were paid on a straight weekly salary basis. In addition, a certain percentage of the net profits were set aside for these supervisors each year and distributed among them as bonuses. For a number of years, these bonuses typically had amounted to several thousand dollars per supervisor. However, the amount of the bonuses had decreased in the last two years because of a general economic downturn. Expectations for the current year were not good, since the company was just about breaking even. The major reason for this was the depressed state of the economy, not a lack of employee productivity.

During the fall of the current year, the company received an unusually large number of orders. The work force put in one hour of overtime daily and worked on Saturdays, but even this did not alleviate the need for more output. The manufacturing manager informed the supervisors that the plant would have to work seven days a week. Supervisors, in turn, were to inform the employees that this seven-day schedule would be necessary for the next month.

The workers were delighted, since this meant double pay for Sunday work; therefore, all of them reported for work. However, five of the twenty supervisors did not show up on the first Sunday. In each case they phoned to explain their absence with various excuses. On the next Sunday seven supervisors were absent, although all the workers were on the job. The plant manager wondered what could and should be done about the supervisors' absences.

Who Needs Quality Circles?

Merrill Dawe, plant manager of a major food processing plant, had attended a meeting of a manufacturers' assocation in which he had been impressed by several presentations on quality circles (QCs) and labor-management participation teams. Dawe was convinced that such approaches would be very appropriate in his plant, since he felt they could help improve the employee relations climate and perhaps assist in improving productivity and reducing quality problems. Dawe decided to call a number of his supervisors along with the local union president and several of the plant's union shop stewards to his office to discuss his plans to implement quality circles. At a meeting in his office, Merrill Dawe outlined what he proposed to do. He said that he planned to have quality circle meetings on a periodic basis, perhaps once a month, in which various departmental employee groups and committees along with their supervisors would discuss production problems, quality problems, and any other problems that needed attention. Dawe emphasized that employees would be paid for the time they spent in these meetings and that any ideas, suggestions, and the like would be given open consideration and attention by supervision and higher management.

After listening patiently to Mr. Dawe's presentation, Jerry Bruno, the plant's local union president, responded as follows: "Mr. Dawe, our national and local union have heard about quality circles and efforts of this nature. In general, we're opposed to being part of them. We've heard that many companies simply use these as a way of trying to bypass the union contract and the contractual grievance procedure. We feel that quality circles are just another subterfuge to lull employees into thinking that management is concerned about them. Frankly, I'm skeptical that quality circles in this plant will be little more than a place where the workers will say what's on their minds, and then company managment will continue to ignore their concerns. Unless I'm convinced—and my fellow union representatives are convinced—that any quality circle in this plant will not be used to ignore the union and our labor agreement, we will not be willing to cooperate with you in this type of program."

Merrill Dawe pondered what his response should be to Jerry Bruno's comments and whether he should seriously attempt to implement a quality circle program.

CASE 5

Romance on the Assembly Line

Louise Nance had been working on the assembly line of the Jackson Manufacturing Company for about six months. During recent weeks, her supervisor, Ben Miller, noticed that her production had gone down to such an extent that she could not keep up with the pace, and she had caused serious delays. When Miller called this to her attention, Nance told him about the difficulties she was having at home. Her husband had recently left her without any explanation or cause. Miller replied that her personal affairs were of no interest to him and that he was concerned only with her work. He warned her that, unless her production improved, she would be separated from the company.

A few days thereafter, Ben Miller was promoted to a higher management position. His place was filled by Jack Armstrong, who had recently joined the company. Armstrong immediately took a liking to Louise Nance and started dating her. Although she told him about her marital difficulties, he kept seeing her. When she remarked to him one day that her car needed some repairs, he offered to see whether he could fix it for her.

On the following Saturday, Louise Nance's estranged husband appeared and found Jack Armstrong repairing her car, which was parked on the street in front of her apartment. The two men quickly got into a fight on the street, and police were called to separate them. The local newspapers carried a short report about the incident, mentioning the fact that Louise Nance and Jack Armstrong were employed at the Jackson Manufacturing Company.

A few days later, Jack Armstrong was called into the office of Kay McCaslin, the personnel director, who had read the newspaper reports. McCaslin advised Armstrong to stop seeing Louise Nance or he might be fired. McCaslin reminded Armstrong that informal company policy discouraged close fraternization between supervisors and employees, since this tended to weaken a supervisor's authority in dealing with employees. Further, publicity of this sort would undoubtedly hurt the company's image in the community. Armstrong replied that this was none of the company's business and that he could spend his time away from the plant any way he chose. He stated that a threat of discharge was totally improper, since his private life was his own and not subject to company regulations. Further, Nance's work record had improved under his supervision, and it was now about the same as the records of most of the other people on the line. Armstrong left the personnel director's office with the comment that he would continue to date Louise Nance, since they were very much in love.

Kay McCaslin wondered whether she should drop the matter or whether she should discuss it with higher management—including Ben Miller, who now was Jack Armstrong's superior.

CASE 6

Should the Foreman Have Authorized Overtime?

The foreman of the Shipping Department of the Zeltins Corporation, Tom Leeming, had been given strict instructions that all permissions for overtime had to come from his boss, the plant manager. In previous years the various department foremen had possessed the authority to have employees work overtime at time-and-a-half rates whenever they considered it absolutely necessary. The foremen generally had not taken advantage of this privilege. However, when a recent fiscal report showed a decline in profits and a substantial increase in labor costs, the company president issued directives stating that all overtime pertaining to manufacturing activities had to be approved by the plant manager. For certain other activities, the president's permission was needed.

Tom Leeming was now experiencing an increased work load. Due to some personnel absences, his Shipping Department was late in sending out important orders. As a matter of fact, he knew that these orders might be canceled by the customers if they were not shipped before the week was over. Since he was convinced that overtime work would help this situation, he tried to contact the plant manager. However, the plant manager was out of town at a convention and could not be reached. Leeming also had heard that some time ago a similar problem had occurred in the Maintenance Department and that the foreman in charge had authorized overtime without the necessary permission of the plant manager. Although the Maintenance Department foreman claimed that waiting for the plant manager's return the next day would have made the repair job more difficult and costly, he was seriously criticized and even disciplined for his unauthorized action.

Tom Leeming did not know what to do. If he authorized overtime, he would step beyond his area of authority. If he did not, some of the orders would not be shipped in time and would probably be canceled. He thought of contacting the president of the company, but the president also was out of town. So, Leeming decided to be on the safe side and did not ask his employees to work overtime. Some of the shipments, therefore, did not leave on time. Eventually, as he had feared, several of the orders were canceled by unhappy customers. He wondered what he should do if this situation occurred again.

CASE 7

The Troubled Technician Who Was in Serious Debt

As part of its main office, Centaur Electric Company had a Development Engineering Department. This department's work consisted of control and revision of old products and design of new products.

The chief development engineer and head of the department was Vincent Gabris. Assigned to Gabris were three development engineers and their technicians. In general, the development engineers did all the creative and design engineering work. The technicians worked closely with the engineers in mechanical and electrical testing, physical layouts, equipment and product plans, and on various other tasks as assigned.

The engineers scheduled the work of the technicians and were responsible for their training and performance. The engineers, however, did not determine the technicians' rate of pay. Development engineers were salaried, while technicians were paid hourly wages. In scheduling the work load of a technician, an engineer was responsible for the number of hours per day that the technician would work. However, Vincent Gabris often assigned projects to technicians;

Gabris was supposed to notify the development engineers when a technician was assigned to a different project or job.

The educational level of the engineers and the technicians differed by an average of about four years. Typically, development engineers had pursued graduate level studies beyond their bachelor of engineering degrees; none of the technicians had more than one year of college.

John Turner, a technician, had been working at Centaur for two years. He had no previous experience in this type of position. Turner had attended a local school of engineering for two semesters, had dropped out, and had gone to work as a factory laborer. On the basis of high scores on the firm's mechanical aptitude and intelligence tests, Turner was hired by Centaur for a technician's job. His training at Centaur was internal and informal in nature. Turner, age 28, was married, had two children, and his wife was expecting another. Barbara Kurton, an engineer, was Turner's current supervisor. Kurton considered Turner to be conscientious, task-oriented, and a "perfectionist" in his work; she also believed that he tried to learn and improve from his work experiences.

However, in recent months Kurton had detected a serious drop-off in Turner's output. He seemed to wander about the work area, doing little and complaining that he had too many bosses. It had been a particularly trying month, with considerable overtime work, so Kurton thought little about it. But when the problem persisted the next month, Kurton started to investigate. She talked with Turner and learned that he felt that too many people were making too many demands on him—often all at the same time. He said that he had tried to please everyone but that there wasn't enough time to work for all; this frustration was the cause of his lowered output. Kurton immediately set to work to alleviate the demands on Turner by asking everyone to channel all work requests for him through her. This, she felt, would give Turner the impression, at least, that he had a lighter work load, because she could assign priorities to the work given. It also could stabilize Turner's workload and ease the tension.

After putting this system into effect, Turner's workload did level out considerably, but his output nevertheless steadily dwindled. It eventually reached the point where Kurton felt that discharging Turner was justified. Hoping to avert this, she had several long talks with him. From these talks came the revelation that John Turner was tens of thousands of dollars in "short-term" debt. This included what he owed on his house-trailer and car. A problem with his car had "triggered" the conflict. When Turner had tried to sell the car, he found that he owed more on it than it was worth. With a new baby on the way, he was continually worried about the future and his money troubles. Kurton also learned that Turner had little understanding of financial matters or budgets.

Barbara Kurton pondered what she could do to help motivate this employee to return to his previous productive self or whether she should simply solve the problem by discharging him. She also wondered whether she should take the problem to her own boss, Vincent Gabris.

The Picnic Conversation

The annual picnic of the Collins Company was well attended as usual. It was a well-planned, day-long family affair for all the employees of the firm, giving them an opportunity to have an informal get-together. At the picnic, Charlene Knox, one of the factory supervisors, had a long chat with her boss, Jim Cross, the plant superintendent. They spoke about many things, including some work problems. Cross put great emphasis on the need for cutting production costs and a general "belt-tightening." He told Knox that he had already received a number of written suggestions and plans from some of the other supervisors. He highly praised their efforts as appropriate and helpful.

Three weeks after the picnic, Charlene Knox received a memo from her boss asking her why her "report in reference to cost-cutting had not yet arrived." At first she wondered what Jim Cross was referring to, and then she remembered their talk at the picnic. She realized that was the only time Cross had discussed with her the need to cut production costs! Knox pondered what her response should be.

PART 2

PLANNING

CHAPTER 7

Managerial Planning

CHAPTER OBJECTIVES

1. To emphasize the importance of planning as the first of the managerial functions.
2. To discuss the necessity of well-defined organizational goals and objectives, particularly as they relate to the supervisory level.
3. To discuss management by objectives (MBO) as a system of management and how it can be applied by supervisors.
4. To identify major types of standing plans and how these are helpful in supervisory decision making.
5. To discuss the principal types of single-use plans in which supervisors play an important role.

There is some disagreement among management scholars and practitioners concerning the number and designation of managerial functions. However, there is general consensus that the first and probably the most crucial of the managerial functions is that of planning.

MANAGEMENT FUNCTIONS BEGIN WITH PLANNING

Planning means to decide in advance what is to be done in the future. Planning logically precedes all other managerial functions, since every manager must project a framework and a course of action for the future before attempting to achieve desired results. For example, how could a supervisor organize the operations of a department without having a plan in mind? How could a supervisor effectively staff and direct employees without knowing which avenues to follow? How could a supervisor possibly control the activities of employees without having standards and objectives for comparison? Thus all of the other managerial functions depend on planning.

Planning is a managerial function that every supervisor must perform every day. It should not be a process used only at occasional intervals or when the supervisor is not too engrossed in daily chores. By planning, the supervisor realistically anticipates future problems and opportunities, analyzes them, anticipates the probable effects of various alternatives, and decides on the course of action that should lead to the most desirable results. Of course, plans alone do not bring about desired results. But without good planning, random activities eventually will prevail, producing confusion, inefficiency, and possibly even disruption.

All Managerial Levels Perform the Planning Function

Planning is the responsibility of every manager, whether the chairperson of the board, the president, a division manager, or the supervisor of a department. However, the importance and magnitude of a manager's plans will depend on the level at which they are performed. Planning at the top level is broader and more far-reaching than at the supervisory level. The top executive is concerned with overall operations of the enterprise and long-range planning for new facilities and equipment, new products and services, new markets, and major investments. At the supervisory level, the scope is narrower and more detailed. The supervisor usually is concerned with day-to-day plans for having departmental tasks accomplished, for example, meeting the production or service-order quotas for a particular day.

Although planning always involves looking to the future, an evaluation of what has happened in the past should be part of managerial planning. Every manager can learn to plan more effectively for the future by evaluating earlier plans and trying to benefit from past successes and failures.

In formulating plans, a supervisor may feel that certain aspects of planning call for specialized help, such as implementing employment policies, computer and accounting procedures, or technical know-how. In such areas, the supervisor should consult with specialists within the organization to help carry out the required planning responsibilities. For example, a supervisor will usually find that a human resource staff specialist will be willing to offer useful advice and suggestions concerning policies involving employees. A supervisor should utilize all of the available help within the organization in order to accomplish thorough and specific planning. This also means consulting with employees for their suggestions on how to proceed in certain situations. Employees like to be consulted, and their advice may be quite helpful to a supervisor in developing day-to-day plans for running the department. In the final analysis, however, it is each supervisor's personal responsibility to plan.

Planning Periods

For how long a period should a manager plan? Usually a distinction is made between long-range and short-range planning. The definitions of long-range and short-range planning will depend on the manager's level in the organizational hierarchy, the type of enterprise, and the kind of industry in which the organization is operating. Most managers, however, define **short-term planning** as that which covers a period of up to one year. **Long-term planning** goes beyond a year and may involve a span of three, five, or ten years or even more. In some firms, planning for one to five years is known as *intermediate planning*.

The supervisor's planning period usually will be of the short-range nature. Most of the time, a supervisor will plan for several months, one month, a week, or perhaps just for one day or a shift. Very short-range planning is involved, for example, in the scheduling of a production line or the scheduling of departmental employees in a retail store. There are some activities for which the supervisor can plan for several months in advance as, for example, the planning of preventive maintenance.

Supervisors on occasion will be involved in long-term planning. For example, a company may be considering a major expansion, or there may be a contemplated introduction of new equipment and technology brought about by competition and other developments. Supervisors may be asked for their opinions and suggestions about such long-range plans, and they will have to stay informed and be ready to adapt if and when these events occur.

For the most part, however, supervisors will give most of their attention to short-range planning. This means that a supervisor must take time to think through the nature and amount of work that is assigned to the department. Many supervisors prefer to do this at the end of a day—or at the end of a week—when they can "size up" what has been accomplished in order to formulate plans for the immediate future. This is the very least amount of planning that every supervisor has to do.

The Planning Process Through Managerial Levels

Figure 7–1 shows how the planning process might flow in a manufacturing company from top management down through the supervisory level. In order to coordinate the planning function throughout several management levels, there will be occasions when supervisors will give attention to long-term planning. As the need arises, middle management may discuss with supervisors the part they are to play in planning for the distant future. For example, supervisors may be informed of a contemplated expansion or addition of new facilities and be asked to make estimates of what their departments can contribute or what will be needed in order to achieve long-term results. Or supervisors might be asked to project the long-run trends of their particular activity, especially if it seems apparent that the activity will be affected by increasing mechanization, automation, or robotics.

Time and effort are required on the supervisor's part to make longer range plans, and more time will be needed to carry them out once they are made and approved. Long-range plans may indicate (a) that the need exists to reassign or retrain some of the employees, (b) that people with new skills have to be found and employed, or (c) that new procedures and new techniques are neces-

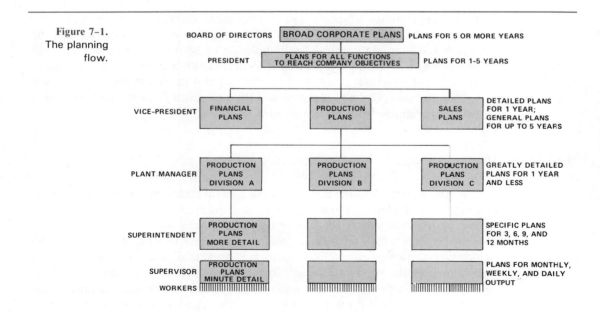

Figure 7–1. The planning flow.

BOARD OF DIRECTORS	BROAD CORPORATE PLANS	PLANS FOR 5 OR MORE YEARS	
PRESIDENT	PLANS FOR ALL FUNCTIONS TO REACH COMPANY OBJECTIVES	PLANS FOR 1-5 YEARS	
VICE-PRESIDENT	FINANCIAL PLANS / PRODUCTION PLANS / SALES PLANS	DETAILED PLANS FOR 1 YEAR; GENERAL PLANS FOR UP TO 5 YEARS	
PLANT MANAGER	PRODUCTION PLANS DIVISION A / PRODUCTION PLANS DIVISION B / PRODUCTION PLANS DIVISION C	GREATLY DETAILED PLANS FOR 1 YEAR AND LESS	
SUPERINTENDENT	PRODUCTION PLANS MORE DETAIL	SPECIFIC PLANS FOR 3, 6, 9, AND 12 MONTHS	
SUPERVISOR	PRODUCTION PLANS MINUTE DETAIL	PLANS FOR MONTHLY, WEEKLY, AND DAILY OUTPUT	
WORKERS			

sary due to changing market or competitive conditions. Thus from time to time every supervisor will participate in long-range planning.

Of course, short-range plans made by a supervisor should be integrated and coordinated with the long-range plans of higher management. Supervisors who are well informed about the long-range plans of the organization are in a better position to integrate their short-range plans with overall plans. All too often there is a gap between the knowledge of top management and what middle and supervisory levels of management are told about future plans. This often is justified by the claim that certain plans are confidential and cannot be divulged for security reasons. In reality, management practitioners know that very little can be kept secret indefinitely in most organizations.

Top-level, long-range plans should be communicated and fully explained to subordinate managers and supervisors as soon as possible so that they may be in a better position to formulate plans for their departments. By the same token, each supervisor should bear in mind that employees will be affected by plans that are made. Whenever possible, a supervisor should explain to employees in advance what is being planned for the department. The employees may be in a position to contribute helpful ideas and to begin preparing themselves for new skills that will be needed. At the very least, well-informed employees will appreciate the fact that they have not been kept "in the dark" or that they have not had to look to the grapevine for information about their future.

Better Planning Means Better Resource Utilization

Planning promotes efficiency and reduces waste and costs. By thorough planning, haphazard approaches can be minimized and duplication can be avoided. The minimum time for completion of activities can be planned and scheduled, and facilities can be used to optimum advantage. Even in a small department, the total investment in physical and human resources may be a substantial sum. Only by planning will the supervisor be able to achieve superior performance from employees and resources.

ORGANIZATIONAL GOALS AND OBJECTIVES

The first step in planning is to develop a general statement of goals and objectives that will identify the overall purposes and results toward which all plans and activities are directed. The setting of overall goals is a function of top management, which must define and communicate to all of its managers the primary purposes for which the business is organized. These overall goals usually include the production and distribution of products or services, obligations to the customer, being a good employer and responsible corporate citizen, a profit as a just reward for taking risks, research and development, and legal and ethical obligations. Figure 7–2 is a major company's statement of its overall corporate goals and objectives, which has been published and distributed to its employees and the general public.

Primary Goals (Objectives)

Although various organizations utilize different terminology,[1] the goals formulated for an organization as a whole usually are called **primary goals,** or **primary objectives,** in order to distinguish them from the goals established for divisions and departments. The primary objectives become the general framework for operations and lead to the formulation of more specific objectives for divisional and departmental managers and supervisors.

Supportive Objectives (Goals)

Each division or department in turn must clearly set forth its own objectives as guides for operations. Goals of the divisions or departments of an organization are usually called **supportive objectives, secondary objectives,** or **derivative goals.** By whatever name they are called, supportive objectives must be within the general framework of primary goals; they must contribute to the achievement of the organization's overall purposes. Supportive objectives sometimes have a contingency basis, that is, some may be dependent or contingent on the availability of certain resources or reflect changing priorities.

Supportive objectives usually are stated in terms that reflect the operations of the department or unit. For example, a maintenance department might have a number of objectives such as: "To keep production equipment functioning properly with minimum interruptions to production schedules" or "To provide necessary maintenance services for the entire physical plant." These types of objectives are more specific than the broadly stated primary objectives of a company, but obviously such supportive (or secondary) objectives are vital and necessary if the primary objectives are to be accomplished.

Whenever possible, supportive objectives should specify or emphasize actual targets that the supervisor and employees are to reach. It usually is desirable to have short-term objectives stated in measurable or verifiable terms, such as "To reduce overtime by 5 percent"; "To increase output per employee hour by 10 percent"; "To have monthly meetings with departmental employees"; and so on. This enables a supervisor to focus more clearly on targets that should be accomplished in a certain period of time. This approach is an

---

[1]Terminology is quite diverse and even confusing in this regard. Some companies define a "goal" as any long-run target, i.e., one that will take more than a year to achieve; an "objective" is a short-run target, i.e., one that will take less than a year to achieve. Other companies define these terms to mean exactly the opposite. We will use these terms interchangeably.

Fig. 7–2.
Statement of
corporate goals
and objectives.

XYZ Corporation

XYZ Corporation's existence is dependent on having the respect and support of four groups—its customers, employees, shareholders, and the public, which includes the citizens of each country in which we do business. For us to have a satisfactory future, we must continuously earn the support, respect, and approval of all four groups. This requires that XYZ:

For customers	Be a reliable preferred supplier of products and services.
For employees	Offer stability of employment, fairness in promotion, and opportunity for individual growth.
For shareholders	Offer both security of principal and competitive return through a combination of increased value of stock and dividends.
For the public	Conduct all of its business affairs not only in a legal manner but in a morally acceptable manner. XYZ must be a good neighbor.

XYZ's long-term corporate objectives and its interim goals must meet all of the obligations imposed by each of the four groups.

Corporate Objectives

1.	To achieve continuing long-term growth in earnings and a record of financial stability that attracts to XYZ the capital—equity and debt—required to support its growth.
2.	To concentrate our efforts in business and product areas in which XYZ can realistically expect to achieve a leadership position and in which leadership will be rewarded.
3.	To offer our products and services wherever in the world XYZ's operations can be consistent with its management principles and corporate benefits.
4.	To have a working environment in which each individual is treated with fairness that encourages and rewards excellence and stimulates maximum growth of the individual.
5.	To anticipate the needs of the future sufficiently well to develop the human talent necessary to remain and be a leader.
6.	To be a responsible corporate citizen.

essential part of management by objectives (MBO) programs, which have been implemented by many companies and organizations as a system for planning and attaining results.

MANAGEMENT BY OBJECTIVES—A SYSTEM FOR PARTICIPATIVE MANAGEMENT

Management by objectives (MBO), often known as "managing by results," has been described as an approach and system of management that brings together sound management and motivational principles designed to achieve excellent performance of individuals in an organization. George Odiorne, a leading proponent of MBO, has defined management by objectives as follows:

> In brief, the system of management by objectives can be described as a process whereby the superior and subordinate managers of an organization jointly identify its common goals, define each individual's major areas of responsibility in terms of the results expected, and use these measures as guides for operating the unit and assessing the contribution of each of its members.[2]

It should be apparent from this definition that MBO is a **management system,** that is, a total approach to management, which involves aspects of participative and consultative management. Management by objectives requires full commitment to the objectives of the organization, which must start at top management and permeate throughout all levels and key personnel of an organization. The emphasis is upon results, rather than upon techniques to achieve results.[3]

Why Use Management by Objectives?

There are many reasons why management by objectives approaches have been adopted by many companies and organizations. The following are among the most important. First of all, MBO is results-oriented. It is not permissive or weak management; it requires thorough planning, organization, controls, communication, and dedication to make it a way of behavior in an organization. Properly implemented, MBO helps to influence motivation and encour-

---

[2]George Odiorne, *MBO II: A System of Managerial Leadership for the 80's* (New York: Fearon Pitman Publishers, Inc., 1979), p. 53.

[3]For an expanded overview of MBO, see Louis E. Boone and David L. Kurtz, *Management* (3d ed.; New York: Random House, 1987), pp. 129–137. For a comprehensive book on MBO, see Dale D. McConkey, *How to Manage By Results* (4th ed.; New York: AMACOM, a Division of the American Management Association, 1983).

age commitment to results among those who are part of it. It provides a sound means for appraising performance of individuals by its emphasis on objective criteria, rather than vague personality characteristics. Further, it provides a more rational basis for sharing the rewards of an organization, particularly compensation and promotion based on merit.

Management by Objectives—A Step-by-Step Model

Any management by objectives system must be developed to meet the unique purposes and character of the organization. There is no such thing as a "pure" model or type that can be utilized for all situations and all places. The following, however, is a suggested step-by-step guideline, which might be applicable in most organizational situations.

Step 1—Top management must identify the major goals of the organization for the coming period; usually this is done at about the same time as is the preparation of the annual budget. Top management must determine the broad objectives for the coming period in such areas as sales, production levels, costs, profitability, employee development, and the like. Although corporate objectives may be broad in nature, the more specifically they are stated by top management, the better it is for communicating these goals throughout the organization. It is understood that these goals should be developed by top management in consultation with managers at the next level of management. When finalized, there should be a consensus that the goals are challenging, yet realistic and attainable within the established time frame.

Step 2—The next step, which in some respects must be done in conjunction with step 1, is to have each manager, supervisor, and key person review his or her job description or position guide. This means making sure that job responsibilities and authority are identified and understood. A thorough review of the organization structure will help to reveal "gray areas," where overlapping responsibilities need to be clarified.

Step 3—The crucial third step is for all managers, supervisors, and other key persons who have considerable latitude in determining their own performance, to develop their own specific objectives in relation to the broader organizational objectives. Each individual prepares a list of objectives—typically about six to ten—that should cover major results expected within their areas of responsibility. Objectives must be stated in terms that are either measurable or verifiable, that is, with a number, ratio, due date, or some other specific criterion for indicating accomplishment. It is important for supervisors to develop not only routine objectives for their normal areas of departmental responsibility but also to develop a number of objectives that will involve some elements of creativity and personal growth.

Step 4—A meeting must be arranged between each individual and his or her boss for a discussion of each list of objectives. At the supervisory level, the final statement of these should be "negotiated" to attain mutual agreement between boss and supervisor. Both parties should strive to agree on objectives that are challenging but realistic and attainable. Priorities must be established where appropriate.

Although it will not always happen, research results have shown that supervisors often will stipulate higher objectives than their bosses initially would have thought they were capable of attaining! Once the list of objectives is finalized, both the boss and the supervisor sign a copy, and this becomes the primary document on which the supervisor's performance will be judged.

Step 5—Time must be found for periodic review of progress being made toward accomplishment of the agreed-upon objectives. Some authorities suggest a quarterly review, during which objectives are compared with progress. During such reviews, objectives may be adjusted upward or downward as deemed appropriate.

Step 6—The "final" step is to review and compare results against objectives at the end of the period, usually a year.[4] A good approach is to have each individual do a self-evaluation of performance in terms of the objectives that were to be accomplished. Here, too, some supervisors will be more critical of their performances than if the boss had done the total appraisal independently.

There must then be a conference with the boss in which the performance of the individual is discussed. For supervisors, questions such as the following need to be addressed: What was the overall "batting average" of the supervisor? Were objectives accomplished (or not accomplished) due to the supervisor's performance or because of circumstances beyond anyone's control? What does the comparison of performance with objectives indicate about the supervisor's strengths and weaknesses? It is important to build on each individual's strengths and to seek ways by which areas of weakness can be mitigated or eliminated. Step 6 in reality starts the cycle all over again, since setting the next period's objectives will flow logically from the analysis of the results achieved in the previous period.

Most experts in the MBO field believe that salary adjustments should not be a part of the discussion described above as step 6. Of course, those who have performed well expect to be rewarded generously; those who fail to meet most of their objectives should expect less-favored treatment. It is thus desirable to have the salary discussion several weeks after the discussion concerning performance results. Done properly, salary adjustments should reinforce the total MBO program as a management system designed to reward favorably those who have contributed the most.

MBO Facilitates Better Planning and Coordination of Efforts

The foregoing was a brief outline of the format of management by objectives. There are other considerations that any management team should be aware of

---

[4]Regular performance appraisal and the appraisal interview are discussed in depth in Chapter 14.

before deciding to adopt an MBO program. It should not be looked upon as a panacea that will cure all management problems. But some aspects of MBO already exist in most companies and organizations of any appreciable size. Most managers, for example, have plans that revolve around production goals, sales targets, profit goals, cost containment, budgets, and the like. With or without MBO, effective higher level managers have long recognized the importance of delegating authority with responsibility to managers, supervisors, and other subordinates if goals and objectives are to be achieved. The advantage of a formal MBO system is that it ties together many plans, establishes priorities, and coordinates activities that otherwise might be overlooked or handled loosely in the stress of business operations. A sound MBO program encourages the contributions and commitment of people toward common goals and objectives.

There are pitfalls to be avoided, which are beyond the scope of this presentation. Moreover, implementation of an effective MBO program may take several years. However, organizations that utilize MBO believe that it is a desirable approach, which at the very least promotes better planning, and which usually brings about more effective management and motivation of people. Management by objectives—if properly applied—is a system of management that is suitable to most operations.

ADDITIONAL TYPES OF PLANS

After (or accompanying) the setting of major goals and objectives, all levels of management participate in the design and execution of numerous additional plans necessary for the attainment of desired objectives. Managers, from the chief executive officer down to the supervisor, must design and carry out a variety of plans that are necessary if an enterprise is to function and accomplish the desired results.

In general, such plans can be broadly classified as: (a) **standing** or **repeat use plans,** which can be used over and over as the need arises; and (b) **single-use plans,** which focus on a single purpose or specific undertaking.

STANDING PLANS

Much of a supervisor's day-to-day activities and decisions will be guided by the use of so-called standing, or repeat-use, plans. Although terminology varies, these types of plans typically are known as *policies, procedures, methods,* and *rules.* All of these should be designed to reinforce one another and should be directed toward the achievement of both primary and supportive objectives. Top management formulates most major standing plans, and each departmental supervisor formulates the necessary subsidiary standing plans.

Policies

Policies are probably the standing plans mentioned and used most frequently. A **policy** can be defined as a general or broad guide to thinking. Corporate policies are usually statements that channel the thinking of managers and define the limits within which supervisors must stay as they make decisions.

Effective policies promote consistency of decision making throughout an enterprise. Once policies are set, managers find it easier to delegate authority, since the decisions a subordinate supervisor makes will be guided by the boundaries of policies. Policies enable the supervisor to arrive at about the same decision that the boss would make or, at least, to be within acceptable parameters. While policies should be considered as guides for thinking, they do permit supervisors to use judgment in making decisions, so long as their decisions fall within the limitations of the policy.

For example, most companies have policies covering vacations with pay based on seniority. Depending on an employee's length of service with the company, an employees is entitled to one week, two weeks, three weeks, or more of vacation. All the supervisor has to do is ascertain an employee's years of service with the company in order to determine the length of that employee's vacation. However, the supervisor may have to develop a workable plan within the department concerning when each employee may take a vacation. The supervisor is likely to decide that the employee with the most seniority has first choice, the employee with the next highest seniority has second choice, and so on down the line. Further, the supervisor may limit the number of employees who can be on vacation at one time. In other words, the supervisor develops a departmental policy within the framework of the broader company policy. Figure 7-3 is a statement from an insurance company employee policy manual regarding flextime work scheduling. Figure 7-4 is a statement from a hospital employee handbook concerning rest periods. Both of these illustrate the importance of supervisory decisions in carrying out these types of policies.

Origin of Policies.   Rarely are policies developed just by chance. Most major policies are originated by top management, since policy making is one of its important responsibilities. Top management must develop and establish overall policies, which are required to guide the thinking of subordinate managers so that organizational objectives can be achieved. Broad policies become the guides for various policies that are developed within divisions and departments. Departmental policies as established by supervisors must complement and coincide with the broader policies of the company as originated by top management.

In addition, there are certain policies that are imposed on an organization by external forces such as government, labor unions, trade groups, accrediting associations, and the like. The word "imposed" indicates compliance with an

Work Week
Your normal work week is 38 hours and 45 minutes—7 hours and 45 minutes per day, Monday through Friday.

The normal work day begins at 8:15 a.m. and ends at 5:00 p.m. However under our "flextime" program, you may be given the choice, when possible, of working one of the following schedules:

      7:00 a.m.—3:45 p.m.
      7:15 a.m.—4:00 p.m.
      7:30 a.m.—4:15 p.m.
      7:45 a.m.—4:30 p.m.
      8:00 a.m.—4:45 p.m.
      8:15 a.m.—5:00 p.m.
      8:30 a.m.—5:15 p.m.
      8:45 a.m.—5:30 p.m.
      9:00 a.m.—5:45 p.m.

We think you will like having the opportunity of choosing a work schedule which best suits your personal needs. Your supervisor will tell you which options are available in your department.

Many of our employees are required by law to have their work time recorded on time cards. If you are in this category, your supervisor keeps a weekly record showing time lost during the week and any overtime that was worked. You and the supervisor will review and sign the time card at the end of each week to show that both of you agree with the information recorded.

outside force that cannot be avoided. For example, in order to be accredited, schools, universities, hospitals, and other institutions must comply with regulations issued by the appropriate accrediting agency. Government regulations concerning minimum wages, pay for overtime work, and hiring of people without regard to race, age, and sex automatically become part of an organization's policies. Any policy imposed in such a manner on the organization is known as an externally imposed policy, and is one with which everyone in the organization has to comply.

Rest Periods

I.   You will be granted rest periods according to the length of your tour of duty.

    A.   If you work at least eight hours in a day, you may be granted two fifteen minute rest periods, one near the middle of the first half of the workshift and one near the middle of the second half of the shift.

    B.   If you work at least four hours but less than eight hours, you may be granted one fifteen minute rest period, to be taken near the middle of your shift.

II.   Rest periods are planned and scheduled by your supervisor and may be rescinded should patient care or the efficiency of the department be jeopardized.

III.   You are not to leave your department for a rest period without the approval of your supervisor.

IV.   Rest periods are not to be taken at the beginning or end of the shift nor can they be added to the meal period.

    A.   If you go to the cafeteria during your rest period, there is no objection to your eating as long as you are mindful of the allotted fifteen minutes available to you.

    B.   You are entitled to one serving of coffee or tea in the cafeteria at no charge during each of your rest periods. You will be expected to pay for these items at all other times.

V.   You may not forego rest periods in order to shorten your daily tour of duty.

VI.   A department is never to be left unmanned during its normal hours of operation. Your supervisor keeps this in mind in scheduling your rest periods.

VII.   Disciplinary action will result from abuses of the rest period privilege.

Written Policy Statements Are Preferable.   Since policies are vital guides to decision making, it is essential that policies be explicitly stated and communicated to those in the organization who are affected by them. Although there is no guarantee that policies always will be completely followed or understood, it is desirable that most policies be written. Of course, few organizations have all of their policies in written form, and some have few or no written policies, either because they simply never get around to writing them down or because they would rather not state policies publicly. However, the benefits derived from clearly stated written policies usually far outweigh the disadvantages.

At times it may be difficult to put certain policies in "black and white," but the benefits usually are well worth the time and effort spent in doing so. The mere process of writing policies will require a manager to "think through" the issues more clearly and consistently. Supervisors can refer to a written policy as often as they wish. The wording of a written policy cannot be changed by word of mouth because, if there is any doubt, the written policy can be consulted. Further, a written policy is available to supervisors who are new in the organization so that they can quickly acquaint themselves with that organization's policies. As time goes on, every policy should be reviewed periodically and revised or discarded if conditions or circumstances warrant it.

Supervisory (Departmental) Policies.   Normally a supervisor will have to issue policies infrequently. Of course, if a department is large and if several subunits exist within the department, the supervisor may find it appropriate to issue and write departmental policies.[5] But for the most part, instead of writing policies the supervisor will be called on to apply existing policies in making decisions. That is, most of the time it is the supervisor's role to interpret, apply, and explain the meaning of new and existing policies. Since supervisors will be guided by policies in many daily decisions, they must know and understand the policies and learn how to interpret and apply them.

There are occasions when the supervisor may experience a situation for which no policy exists or seems applicable. For example, suppose an employee asks a supervisor for a six-week leave of absence for personal reasons. To make an appropriate decision, the supervisor should be guided by a policy so that a decision in this matter will be in accord with other decisions regarding leaves of absence. However, the supervisor finds out that higher management has never issued a formal policy to cover such a leave request. In this case, the supervisor needs a general guide and should ask the boss to issue a policy—a guide for thinking—to be applied in this case, as well as in the future if a leave of absence of this type again is requested. It is not likely that many such instances will happen, since top management usually has covered the major areas where policies are needed.

---

[5]For example, this would be the case for the nursing services department in most hospitals.

Procedures

Procedures, like policies, are repeat-use plans for achieving objectives. Procedures are derived from policies, but they are more specific. Procedures essentially are guides to action, not guides to thinking. **Procedures** define a chronological sequence of acts that are to be performed and specify a route of actions that will take subordinates toward their objectives. Procedures aim for consistency by defining steps that are to be taken and the order or sequence they are to follow.

For example, a company may have a policy that requires supervisors to use the staff personnel department in the preliminary steps of hiring. This policy may contain several guidelines designed to meet nondiscriminatory hiring goals. In order to carry out this policy, management develops a procedure governing the selection process. For example, the procedures to be followed by a supervisor who wants to hire a word processor for an office position might include filling out a requisition form, specifying the job requirements, interviewing and testing potential candidates, and other such actions. Thus the procedure lists in more detail exactly what a supervisor must do or not do in order to comply with the company's hiring policies. Supervisors in other departments must follow the same procedure.

At the department level, the supervisor often must develop procedures to determine how work is to be done. If a supervisor is fortunate and has only highly skilled employees to direct, they could be depended on to a great extent to select efficient paths of performance. But this is not too common, and most employees will look to the supervisor for instructions on how to proceed.

One of the advantages of well-defined procedures is that the process of preparing a procedure necessitates an analysis and study of work to be done. Another advantage is that once a procedure is established, it furthers greater promotes a predictable outcome. Procedures also provide the supervisor a encourages a predictable outcome. Procedures also provide the supervisor a standard for appraising work done by employees. In order to realize these advantages, a supervisor should devote considerable time and effort to devising departmental procedures. Procedures should be developed to cover virtually all phases of operations such as work operations and work flow, scheduling, and personnel assignments.

Methods

A method is also a standing plan for action but it is even more detailed than a procedure. Whereas a procedure shows a series of steps to be taken, a method is concerned with a single operation—one particular step. A **method** indicates exactly how one particular step is to be performed. For example, a departmental procedure may specify the chronological path and routing of work in the assembly of various components of a product. At each subassembly point, there should exist a stated method for the work to be performed at each step in the total process.

For most jobs, there usually exists a "best method," that is, the most appropriate way for a job to be performed under existing technology and circumstances. Again, if a supervisor could rely on skilled workers, they might develop or know the "best method" without having to be told. For the most part, it is necessary for the supervisor or someone in management to design the most efficient method for getting the job done under the circumstances. Much time should be spent in devising methods, since proper methods have all the advantages of procedures as cited previously. In devising methods, the supervisor may utilize the know-how of a methods engineer or a motion-and-time-study person, if such individuals are available in the organization. These are specialists who have been trained in industrial engineering techniques to study jobs systematically with the objective of making jobs more efficient. Where such specialists are not available, the supervisor's experience should be sufficient to design work methods that will be appropriate for the department.

In some activities of an organization there will be little need for a supervisor to be overly concerned with devising procedures and methods, because employees already have been trained in *standard methods* or *standard procedures*. For example, journeyman machinists are exposed to many years of schooling and training during which great emphasis is placed on proper procedures and methods of performing certain tasks. Similarly, in the supervision of a department where highly skilled or professional employees work, the supervisor's main concern will be to see to it that generally approved procedures and methods are carried out in professionally accepted ways. However, most supervisors will have employees who are not well trained and for whom procedures and methods must be established.

Rules

A rule is different from a policy, procedure, or method, although it is also a standing plan that has been devised in order to attain objectives. A rule is not the same as a policy, because it does not provide a guide to thinking, nor does it leave discretion to the parties involved. A rule is related to a procedure insofar as it is a guide to action and states what must or must not be done. However, it is not a procedure because it does not provide for a time sequence or set of steps. A **rule** is a regulating principle or directive that must be consistently applied and enforced. When a rule is a specific guide for the behavior of employees in a department, the supervisor must follow it appropriately without deviating from it wherever the rule applies. For example, "No possession or consumption of alcoholic beverages on company premises" is commonly on the list of organizational rules. It means exactly what it says, and there are to be no exceptions to the rule.

There will be occasions when supervisors have to devise their own rules or see to it that the rules defined by higher management are obeyed. For example, rules concerning employee meal periods usually specify a certain amount of time that employees may be away from their jobs for meals. Usually these rules are developed by higher management, but often a supervisor will have to formulate departmental rules concerning the actual scheduling of meal periods. Regardless of who develops the rules, it is each supervisor's duty to apply and enforce all rules uniformly as they relate to each area of responsibility.

SINGLE-USE PLANS

As discussed in the preceding sections, policies, procedures, methods, and rules are known as repeat-use, or standing, plans, because they are followed each time a given situation is encountered. Unless changed or modified, repeat-use plans are used again and again. In contrast to repeat-use plans are those plans that are no longer needed or are "used up" once the objective is accomplished or the time period of applicability is over. These are known as **single-use** or **single-purpose plans.** Single-use plans include budgets, programs, and projects. Major budgets, programs, and projects are usually the primary concern of higher management, but supervisors also play a role in developing and implementing single-use plans at the departmental level.

Budgets

Although budgets are generally thought of as being part of the managerial controlling function, a budget is first and foremost a plan. A **budget** is a plan that expresses anticipated results in numerical terms, such as dollars and cents, employee hours, sales figures, or units to be produced. It serves as a plan for a stated period of time—usually one year. All budgets eventually are translated into monetary terms, and an overall financial budget is developed for the entire firm or enterprise. After the stated period is over, the budget expires. It has served its usefulness and is no longer valid. This is why a budget is a single-use plan.

As a statement of expected results, a budget is associated with control. However, the preparation and making of a budget is planning, and this again is part of every manager's responsibilities. Since a budget is expressed in numerical terms, it has the advantage of being specific rather than general. There is a considerable difference between just making general forecasts and attaching numerical values to specific plans. The figures that the supervisor finds in a budget are actual plans, which become standards to be achieved.

The Supervisor's Role in Budgeting. Since supervisors have to function under a budget, they should have a part in its preparation.

Most people resent arbitrary orders, so it is desirable that budget figures and allowances be determined with the participation of those who are responsible for executing the budget. In order to assure participation in the budget-making process, it is desirable that supervisors participate in what commonly is called "grass roots budgeting." What this means is that supervisors should have the opportunity either to propose detailed budgets for their departments, or at least to participate actively in discussions with higher level managers before final departmental budgets are established. Supervisors, of course, will have to substantiate their budget proposals in discussions with their bosses and possibly with the financial manager when the final budgets are being set.

Supervisors usually will be more committed to budgets if they have had a role in formulating them. Further, supervisors are usually closest to the realistic needs of the department. This should not be construed to mean that the requests of the supervisor should or always will prevail. A supervisor's budget will not be accepted by the boss who thinks that the supervisor's plans are inadequate, incorrect, or overstated. No plan or budget should ever be accepted without careful study and analysis by both the supervisor and higher management. Differences between budget needs and estimates should be carefully discussed and resolved.

There are numerous types of budgets in which supervisors can play a part. For example, supervisors may be responsible for designing budgets in which they plan the work hours to be used for certain jobs within their departments. Supervisors may be asked to prepare budgets for materials and supplies, wages, utility expenses, and other departmental expenditures. If budgets are drawn up with the participation of supervisors, then it is more likely that they will comply with the budgets than if the budgets are handed down unilaterally by higher management.

Budget Review. Most organizations have interim reviews, such as monthly or quarterly, when the budget is compared to actual results. This is why a budget is also a control device. If feasible and necessary, the budget is revised in order to adjust to current results and revised forecasts. This topic is discussed further in Chapter 20.

Supervisors should carefully study and analyze significant variations from the budget to determine where and why certain plans went wrong, what and where adjustments need to be made, and what the revised budget should reflect, including new factors and any changes in the department. When an annual budget is about to expire, it becomes a guideline for preparing next year's budget. Thus the planning process continues from one budget period to the next in a closely related pattern.[6]

---

[6]This assumes that the enterprise practices traditional budgeting and not "zero-base budgeting," which is discussed in Chapter 20.

Programs and Projects

A **program** can be defined as a single-use set of plans for a specific major undertaking within the organization's overall goals and objectives. A major program may have its own policies, procedures, budgets, and the like. The program may extend over several years in order to be accomplished. Examples of major programs would be the expansion of a manufacturing plant or adding new facilities in a hospital. Such expansion programs usually involve myriad plans, such as architectural, new equipment or technology, financing, recruitment of employees, and publicity plans, all of which are part of the overall program. Once the expansion program is completed, the plans utilized for that program will not be used again. Thus a program is a single-use plan.

Although supervisors may play a role in organizational programs, they typically are more involved in planning projects. A **project** may be part of an overall program; it is an undertaking that can be planned and fulfilled as a distinct entity, usually within a relatively short period of time. For example, the preparation of a publicity brochure by the public relations department to acquaint the public with new facilities as part of a hospital expansion program could be called a project. Arranging the necessary construction financing for the building expansion would be another project. Although connected with a major program, these projects can be handled separately by individuals designed to implement them.

An example of a project at the supervisory level would be the design of a new inventory control system by a warehouse supervisor. Another example would be a research project conducted by a marketing department supervisor to determine the effectiveness of a series of television advertisements. Projects such as these are a constant part of the ongoing activities at the departmental level. The ability to plan and carry out projects is another component of every supervisor's managerial effectiveness.

SUMMARY

Planning is the managerial function that determines what is to be done in the future. It is a function of every manager from the top executive to the supervisor of each department. Planning helps facilitate utilization of resources and ensure economy of performance. The period of time of supervisory planning usually is of a much shorter duration than the period covered by top-level management planning.

Setting objectives is the first step in planning. Although the overall goals and objectives are determined by top management, there are many supportive objectives that must be clarified by the supervisor and that must be in accordance with the primary objectives of the undertaking. Management by objectives (MBO) is an approach that promotes coordinated planning and emphasizes achievement of results.

In order to attain objectives, standing plans must be devised. Policies are guides to thinking, and many or most of them originate with higher management. The supervisor's concern with policies primarily is one of interpreting, applying, and staying within them when making decisions for the department. In addition, the supervisor will be called on to design and follow procedures, methods, and rules, which essentially are guides for action. Supervisors should participate in establishing budgets, which are single-use plans expressed in numerical terms. A budget serves as a control device that enables the supervisor to compare results achieved during the budget period against the budget plan. Supervisors at times play a role in organizational programs and projects, which are single-use plans designed to accomplish specific undertakings on a one-time basis.

QUESTIONS FOR DISCUSSION

1. Define the concept of planning. Why is planning primarily a mental activity rather than a ''doing'' type of function?
2. Distinguish between long-range planning and short-range planning. Relate these concepts to the planning period for top-level managers as compared with the planning period for first-line supervisors.
3. Discuss how supervisors may have occasion to become involved in long-range planning.
4. Why is a statement of goals and objectives the first step in planning? Discuss the meaning of primary objectives as compared with supportive objectives.
5. Why has management by objectives (MBO) been categorized as a ''system to emphasize results''?
6. Review the step-by-step model for management by objectives presented in the text. Discuss which of these steps is/are most crucial if MBO is to be successfully implemented.
7. What is a policy? Why is it desirable that important policies be in written form?
8. Define and distinguish between each of the following:
    a. Procedure.
    b. Method.
    c. Standard procedures (standard methods).
    d. Rules.
9. Why is a budget both a plan and a control device? Why is a budget an excellent example of a single-use plan?
10. Discuss the supervisor's role in the normal budgeting process.
11. Discuss why supervisors are more likely to be involved in the planning of projects rather than major programs.

CHAPTER 8

Supervisory Planning and Time Management

Chapter Objectives

1. To emphasize the importance of and the major considerations involved in forecasting and planning at the supervisory level.
2. To discuss a number of tactical, or political, strategies available to supervisors in their planning.
3. To discuss major areas of supervisory planning for the effective and safe use of material and human resources.
4. To emphasize the importance of time management and to suggest techniques for supervisors to plan better use of their own time.
5. To suggest that good time management means better control of stress in the supervisor's job.

The survival and success of any organization depend in large measure on the skills of all of its managers to forecast and prepare for the future. Planning, as discussed previously, means deciding in advance what needs to be done, and thus managers must make certain assumptions about the future even if it is fraught with uncertainties.

Obviously, top executives must forecast the future in a more general and far-reaching manner than the supervisor. In order to predict the overall outlook of things to come, top management will be greatly concerned about the competitive and general economic climate in which the organization will operate during future years. Government fiscal, taxing, and spending policies and their impact on the economy will be considered. Assumptions will have to be made concerning possible future laws that could affect the organization's activities and environment. Demographic changes, resource availability and costs, and many other social, political, financial, and economic problems that influence business operations must be anticipated in top management's planning. However, our concern in this chapter is with planning at the supervisory level, where day-to-day planning is less likely to involve such global dimensions.

SUPERVISORY FORECASTING

Although they overlap to a certain degree, some distinction exists between planning and forecasting. Forecasts are an attempt to predict the future, but they do not spell out what actions to take. Forecasts are more like "building stones" on which plans are to be based. This means a supervisor has to look into the future and make forecasts in order to establish sound, realistic plans for the department.

Supervisory Concerns in Forecasting

Every supervisor has the responsibility to try to forecast the future of the departmental functions and their relationship to the organization. In particular, supervisors should be familiar with recent developments in technology relative to their fields, and be willing to estimate what the future holds in this respect. The supervisor can keep current by attending trade association meetings and exhibits and by reading journals and other appropriate literature. To some extent, assistance can be sought from suppliers making new equipment that could be used in the department. Because technology is progressing so rapidly, in a number of years a department's technological functions may be significantly different from what they are now. This may involve a trend toward a reduction or simplification of those functions; or those functions may be projected to grow, become more sophisticated, and take on greater prominence. The supervisor's technological projections should include some ideas about what types of equipment will be used in the department in both the short term and long term, and how such equipment will influence production, work flow, space allocations, material requirements, and other related factors. A supervisor may even need to explore the possibility and benefits of leasing versus buying new equipment.

Next, the supervisor must be prepared to forecast changes in employment needs and the types of employees who will be working in the department. The supervisor may foresee a need for better or differently educated or more highly skilled employees, or a need for employees who possess skills that previously have never been required or known in the department or anywhere else in the organization. Conversely, it could be that due to a projected increase in mechanization or computer systems, fewer or less-skilled employees can be utilized to perform departmental jobs.

In addition, the supervisor should have some familiarity with patterns of wages, benefits, and other costs that are likely to occur in the future. For example, it may be that a piece rate (or incentive) wage payment scheme that currently is in place should not be retained in the future and should be replaced by a salary payment plan.

Conceivably, it might appear to the supervisor that the department will diminish in importance or become obsolete due to new discoveries or new methods. Although this is not a pleasant thought, if it is looming on the horizon, it is better for the supervisor to recognize it early than to be confronted with such an event without being prepared for it. If obsolescence is threatening, the supervisor should inform higher management accordingly. Management usually is willing to find a new position for any supervisor who is so farsighted, since such a supervisor is recognized as being too valuable to lose. That person can be just as capable of supervising another department, perhaps one that heretofore has not existed. In other words, farsighted supervisors who have the courage to suggest that their departments might eventually be eliminated will themselves probably survive and prosper!

Only by making forecasts for the future will supervisors be able to clarify in their own minds the directions in which their departments must proceed. By forecasting, supervisors are in a position to formulate definite plans for implementation when and if the forecasted events occur.

Forecasting Means Readiness for Change

All forecasts contain certain assumptions, approximations, and estimates. At best, forecasting is an art and not an exact science. Forecasting accuracy, however, increases with supervisory experience. As time goes on, making estimates about the future becomes a normal activity. Supervisors should exchange forecasts, consult and check with each other, and share information whenever available. By so doing, a supervisor's forecasts should tend to become more accurate. Even if some of the anticipated events do not occur or do not materialize exactly as anticipated, it still is better to have forecast them than to risk being confronted with unanticipated major changes and their consequences.

Having made needed forecasts, supervisors usually are in a better position to ready their minds and departments to incorporate changes as they are needed. Although this may sound like a formidable task for supervisors, all that really is required is to be alert to possible changes and trends. It is not uncommon for supervisors to review their years of work and, with hindsight, lament that they did not take seriously certain trends that had been visible in earlier times. If supervisors constantly estimate and anticipate the future, they will be more ready to implement changes that are necessary when those events do occur.

SUPERVISORY PLANNING: TACTICS AND STRATEGIES

Before making specific plans for the future, supervisors should also consider a number of tactical (or political) types of strategies that may be crucial to a future plan. Supervisors should realize that they do not plan in a vacuum, nor can their plans be implemented in a vacuum. Plans will have an impact on others, and bring reactions from other supervisors, subordinates, the boss, and top management. Further, implementation is critical to the success of a plan. A well-implemented average plan may be superior to a poorly implemented excellent plan. Therefore, effective planning should take into account certain tactical considerations and strategies, which can help make a plan successful.

A supervisor should choose that tactic or combination of strategies best suited for the problem at hand. A few of the most commonly employed strategies will be suggested here, although they may not always be applicable or recommended. A supervisor's choice and the application of these or other approaches will depend on the people involved, the situation, the urgency of the objective, the means available, and a number of other factors. By thinking through the tactic or strategy that is most likely to be appropriate for a particular plan, a supervisor will be in a much better position to make a plan become a reality and to minimize negative reactions.

Timing Alternatives

Timing is a critical and essential factor in all planning. Thus a supervisor may choose the planning strategy, *strike while the iron is hot*. This strategy advocates prompt action when the situation and time for action are advantageous. For example, this strategy might be employed when a supervisor finds that many orders in the department have been delayed and perhaps a number of customers have been irritated and have complained because their orders have fallen behind schedule. The supervisor may then ask for more employees, more equipment, or other resources that are deemed necessary for the department over the long run.

On the other hand, the supervisor may decide to invoke the *time is a great healer* approach. This is not an endorsement of procrastination; but often it is advisable for the supervisor to move slowly in a difficult situation, because some things take care of themselves after a short while. This is also referred to as the *wait and see* strategy, which suggests that it may be better to move a bit more cautiously than to propose a major change under duress or in a crisis. For example, the introduction of a new, computerized customer checkout system in supermarkets typically causes numerous initial complaints from customers and employees. However, store managers of supermarkets have found that, with careful planning, ample communication, patience, and time, most of the initial complaints are mitigated. People eventually become accustomed to and accept the computerized system as an improvement in service.

Target Dates and Deadlines

The amount of time allotted for planning does set a constraint on a supervisor. Under the *do the best you can in the time available* strategy, a supervisor may request the boss to impose some time limits. Without any time limitation, a supervisor may either give a plan little attention or waste much time in search of a "perfect" plan. Either extreme is undesirable. Given a time constraint of two days, for example, a supervisor will have to develop a plan that is the most feasible within the time limits. The practicality of this approach was illustrated by the response one supervisor gave her boss, who asked her if the plan she submitted for a new budgeting procedure was the best possible one. She replied, "No, it is not. But it is the best recommendation I could make given the time available to me." Deadlines do serve to motivate supervisors to accomplish the planning task.

Responses to Organizational Change

When major organizational changes are involved in plans, the supervisor may choose the strategy of the *mass concentrated offensive*. This strategy advocates quick, radical, or complete action in order to make an immediate, favorable showing. For example, an office supervisor may believe that the performance of the office could be significantly improved by consolidating all word processing and other support services in a centralized location. To accomplish this plan, the supervisor may decide to make the change all at once in order to overcome potential opposition and to accomplish the objectives quickly.

On the other hand, the supervisor may prefer to use a different strategy, known as *get a foot in the door*. This tactic advocates that it may be better to propose or institute only a part of the planned change at the beginning, especially if it is of such magnitude that its total acceptance would be doubtful. In choosing this strategy, the same office supervisor might consolidate only part of the word processing and other services at a centralized location on a trial basis to see how it works out, before changing the entire office procedure.

Gaining Reciprocity

Sometimes a plan may advocate changes that could come about more easily if supervisors of other departments would participate in the plan and its implementation. A supervisor may find it advisable to have allies in order to promote the change by seeking *strength in unity*. For example, if a supervisor hopes to gain a budget increase for needed new departmental furniture, it may be expedient to have other supervisors join in making similar requests to higher management. This involves the strategy: *You scratch my back and I will scratch yours*. This tactic of reciprocity is well known in political circles and in the activities of sales representatives and purchasing agents. It simply means to return a favor for a favor. Reciprocity also is helpful in building more cooperative relationships among supervisors in carrying out other day-to-day obligations.

SUPERVISORY PLANNING FOR USE OF RESOURCES

Because supervisors are especially concerned with day-to-day and week-to-week planning at the department level, they must plan for the best utilization of all the resources at their disposal.[1] These resources include both physical and human resources.

Utilization of Tools, Machinery, and Equipment

Supervisors must plan for efficient utilization of the department's tools, machinery, and equipment, all of which frequently represent a substantial investment. Tools, equipment, and machinery that are poorly maintained or not efficient for the jobs to be done not only constitute a source of operating problems but also adversely affect employees' morale. A supervisor will not always have the most desirable or advanced equipment to work with; but the available equipment, when adapted and properly maintained, usually is sufficient to do the job. Therefore at the very minimum, supervisors should first determine whether employees are using available tools and equipment properly. Many times when employees complain about poor equipment, investiga-

---

[1]A number of studies have suggested that about one third of a supervisor's planning concerns events that will occur the same day and that about 40 percent of a supervisor's planning concerns events that are expected to take place a week later and beyond.

tion reveals that the equipment was operated incorrectly. Thus supervisors should periodically check and observe the employees using the equipment and ask them whether the equipment serves their purposes or needs improvement.

It also is the responsibility of the supervisor to work closely with the maintenance department in planning for periodic maintenance of tools, equipment, and machinery. Poorly maintained equipment may be blamed on the maintenance department in some cases, but the supervisor must share in the blame if he or she has not planned or scheduled needed maintenance with that department. In many plants it has been observed that the maintenance group can do only as good a job as other departments will "allow" them to do.

On occasion, the supervisor may decide that replacements ought to be sought for certain tools, machinery, or equipment in the department. This means that the supervisor must develop a plan to dispose of inefficient tools and equipment and submit this plan to a higher level manager and perhaps the director of purchasing. When should a change of tools, machinery, or equipment take place? Supervisors should review trade journals, listen to what salespeople have to say about new products, read literature which is circulated by distributors and associations, and generally keep up with developments in the field. A stronger argument can be advanced to higher management if the supervisor has thoroughly studied the alternatives available and is prepared to make a recommendation based on several bids and models that have been considered. This may include the question of whether new equipment should be bought or leased and the pros and cons of doing so. Facts, rather than emotional arguments, are more likely to be persuasive in bringing about a decision favorable to the supervisor's position.

Even though a supervisor has recommended a change that is supported with well-documented reasons, higher management may turn it down on the basis that it is not economically feasible to replace the equipment at present. Although disappointed, the supervisor should support the decision that has been made and live with it. However, the supervisor should not hesitate to point out at any appropriate time the potential hazards, both in production and in morale, of failing to replace the equipment in question.

In the long run, a supervisor's plans for replacement of equipment or additional new equipment probably will be accepted in some form. However, even when such requests are curtailed, the supervisor still will be recognized as a manager who was on top of the job by planning for better equipment use in the department.

Improvement in Work Procedures and Methods

Supervisors often are so close to the job and under such pressure that they believe that prevailing work methods are satisfactory and not much can be done about them. However, each supervisor should periodically look at departmental operations as a stranger coming into the department for the first time might view them. By looking at each operation with a detached point of view, the supervisor can determine answers to questions such as: (a) Is each operation really necessary? (b) What is the reason for each operation? (c) Can one operation be combined with another? (d) Are the steps performed in the best sequence? (e) Are there any avoidable delays? (f) Is there unnecessary waste?

Methods improvement generally means any change in the way the department currently is doing something that will represent a possible increase in production, lowering of costs, or improvement in the quality of a product or service. Improvement in work procedures, methods, and processes usually makes the job of the supervisor easier. Besides personally looking for ways in which operations can be improved, the supervisor should solicit ideas from employees. Employees often know their jobs better than anyone else in the organization. Alternatively, the supervisor may be able to enlist the help of a specialist, such as a methods or industrial engineer or a systems analyst, if this type of person is available within the organization.

When studying areas for methods improvement, a supervisor should concentrate on situations where large numbers of employees are assigned; where costs per unit are exceptionally high; or where scrap figures, waste, or injury reports appear to be out of line. A good reason for concentrating on such areas for methods improvement is that it will be less difficult for a supervisor to convince both employees and higher management that recommended changes will bring about considerable improvement, savings, or other benefits.

Safe Work Environment

Most managers and supervisors recognize that a safe work environment is one of their major responsibilities, since this is essential for the welfare and productivity of people. Safety statistics have long indicated that employees themselves cause accidents more often than do faulty tools and equipment, because of carelessness, poor attitudes, inadequate training, and a host of other reasons. Yet the supervisor shares a major responsibility, both ethically and legally, to do everything possible to see to it that the safest possible work environment is maintained. Of course, there are some job categories that by their very nature are more hazardous than others. For example, supervisors in mining, construction, and heavy manufacturing have major problems in working to reduce the potential for serious injuries and fatalities. By contrast, supervisors in the generally comfortable surroundings of an office usually do not have to worry about major injuries. Nevertheless, the potential for accidents exists in any situation, if employees are not fully trained and constantly admonished to follow safe work habits.

Observance of OSHA and Other Safety Regulations. Since the passage of the Occupational Safety and Health Act of 1970 (OSHA), many supervisors have been expected to devote major attention to reducing and preventing injuries and accidents on the job. OSHA has had a significant impact on the scope and administration of safety programs in many organizations. It has expanded the responsibility of the supervisor in planning for and bringing about a safer job environment.

The Occupational Safety and Health Act is a very complicated law.[2] Supervisors should make certain that they have a general understanding of all safety rulings and requirements that are associated with the law as it affects departmental operations. Many companies will have someone in management—typically in the human resources, safety, industrial engineering, or risk management departments—who is familiar with the technical requirements of OSHA, as well as any other laws, court rulings, and perhaps industry-mandated safety regulations that must be observed. Supervisors must plan to meet with safety managers, as well as with employees, union leaders, and even with government officials if necessary, in order to do everything possible to maintain compliance with all safety regulations.

Safety Committees and Safety Programs.   Many supervisors find it advisable to form employee safety committees which are sometimes jointly sponsored by both management and the union(s). The purpose of a safety committee is to assist the supervisor in developing safer work areas and in enforcing safety regulations. The supervisor and safety committee can plan for periodic meetings and projects to communicate to employees the importance of safe work habits and attitudes. Wherever possible, specific duties should be assigned to each safety committee member rather than allowing safety committee meetings to degenerate into low-level "shoot the bull" or gripe sessions.

Although a safety committee can be helpful and influential, the supervisor's constant attention to safety is mandatory if a safe work environment is to be maintained. Statistics show that well over three fourths of all accidents on the job are caused primarily by human failure. This means that the supervisor must emphasize safe work habits in daily instructions to employees and make sure that all equipment in the department is used properly and has ample protective devices. It is desirable for the supervisor to plan meetings throughout the year to emphasize safety themes. Supervisors will find that employees and higher management usually are willing to give major assistance in developing a strong safety program. A good safety record in any department does not happen just by wishing. Safety requires planning, effort, and follow-through. It goes almost without saying that accidents and injuries cause human suffer-

---

[2]For an introductory overview of OSHA, see William Holley and Kenneth Jennings, *The Labor Relations Process* (3d ed.; Chicago: The Dryden Press, 1988), pp. 450–453. For a discussion of safety programs in conjunction with legal requirements, see Robert Reber, Jerry Wallin, and David Duhon, "Safety Programs that Work," *Personnel Administrator* (September, 1989), pp. 66–69.

Fig. 8–1.
People are the
most common
cause of
accidents.

ing and financial hardship both to individuals and the organization, and every effort must be made by supervisors to prevent accidents before they happen.

A commonly held half-truth is that a safety program is the responsibility of the safety department or the safety engineers. However, without the full support of supervisors and diligent supervisory surveillance of employee work practices in every department, almost any safety program will be unsuccessful.

Efficient Use of Space

Supervisors must also plan for the allocation and utilization of space. This means that they should determine whether too much or too little space is assigned to the department and whether the space is used efficiently. Here, too, a supervisor may solicit industrial engineering help, if available.

In planning for use of space, a floor layout chart can be drawn and analyzed to determine whether there is sufficient space for the work to be performed and whether the space allocated has been laid out appropriately. If the chart indicates the need for additional space, a request for such should be placed before higher management with a thorough analysis of how current space is being allocated. Chances are that every supervisor has to compete with other departments, which also would like to have more space. Unless a supervisor's planning has been done thoroughly, the request for additional space has little chance of being granted. Even if the request is denied, the plans a supervisor has assembled will not have been prepared in vain. In all probability these will alert the supervisor to some of the conditions under which employees are working and where improvements might be feasible.

Use and Security of Materials, Supplies, and Merchandise

Another supervisory responsibility is to plan for the appropriate use, conservation, and security of materials, supplies, and merchandise. In most departments the quantity of materials and supplies used and maintained in inventory is substantial. Even if each single item represents only a small value, the aggregate of items adds up to sizable amounts in the total budget. Many employees do not realize the significance of the amount of money involved in materials and supplies, and often they are careless in this respect. The supervisor should constantly remind them that the economical use of supplies ultimately is to their own advantage. The supervisor should impress on employees that whatever is wasted cannot be used to raise wages or to improve working conditions.

A major problem in recent years has been the loss and theft of materials, supplies, merchandise, and other company property often carried out by employees themselves.[3] Supervisors must ascertain that adequate and ample security precautions are taken to discourage individuals from theft and to make it very difficult for items to be lost or stolen. For example, many departmental items can be kept under lock and key, with someone assigned the responsibility for distributing supplies only to those who have proper identification or authorization. If the company has its own security force, the supervisor should meet with security personnel to plan and implement security devices and procedures that are suited to the department. Or a supervisor may even request such assistance from local police or a private security agency.

A supervisor's plans and programs for utilization and security of materials, supplies, and merchandise will not eliminate all waste and loss. But such planning usually will reduce waste and loss, and it will tend to promote a more efficient and conscientious work atmosphere among employees.

Employee Work Schedules

To plan effective work schedules for employees, supervisors should operate from the premise that most employees are willing to turn in a fair day's work. Supervisors should not expect all employees to work continuously at top speed. Rather, they should establish a work schedule based on an estimate of what constitutes a fair (rather than a maximum) output. Allowances must be made for fatigue, unavoidable delays, personal needs, and a certain amount of unproductive time during the workday.

Some supervisors may be able to plan employee time with the help of a specialist, such as a motion and time analyst. Even without such help, most

---

[3]Statistically, such losses in U.S. businesses have been estimated in recent years to be some 15–20 billion dollars annually. One survey even suggested that for every $1.00 of merchandise lost to shoplifters, employees stole $15.00 of merchandise from their own companies!

supervisors have a good idea as to what they can expect, and they are capable of planning reasonable performance requirements, which their employees will accept as fair. Such estimates are based on normal rather than abnormal conditions. In this regard it may not be advisable for a supervisor to schedule a department to operate at 100 percent capacity, because this would not leave any room for emergencies or changes in priorities and deadlines that crop up from time to time. Some flexibility is invariably needed to operate, and thus only short periods of 100 percent capacity should be scheduled. Further, several rest periods usually are a regular part of employee work scheduling.

Overtime and Absences.   On occasion, supervisors will find it necessary to plan for overtime, although overtime should be considered primarily as an exception or emergency. As a general rule, supervisors should anticipate a downturn of between 5 and 10 percent in productivity from employees when they work overtime. If a supervisor finds that excessive overtime is regularly required, then alternative methods of doing the work should be found or additional employees should be scheduled or hired.

Supervisors must also plan for employee absences. Of course, a supervisor cannot plan for every instance when an employee will be absent because of sickness, injury, or personal conflict. However, a supervisor can plan for holidays, vacations, temporary layoffs, turnover, and other types of leaves or predictable absenteeism. Plans for absences that can be anticipated and managed must be made in order to ensure the smooth functioning of the department.

Flexible and Part-time Work Schedules.   In recent years, many companies and organizations have adopted variations of flexible work scheduling for their employees. The underlying concept is that employees are given an opportunity to choose—within certain limits—the hours they would like to work. Flexible work schedule plans are quite diverse. In some companies, employees have the option to choose a four-day workweek—usually a four-day, ten-hour-per-day arrangement. Other companies have made it possible for employees to select different starting and ending times within a five-day workweek. Government agencies have adopted flexible work schedules in numerous places. It is quite likely that "flextime" work arrangements will become more commonplace, particularly in office operations and in other work situations where employees' work is not closely interdependent or interrelated to other employees or departments.

Flexible working schedules do create additional planning problems for supervisory management. Supervisors have found that flexible work schedules create problems in maintaining coverage of all work stations or job positions, and that it may be difficult to exercise supervisory control at certain times of the workday. Nevertheless, supervisors who must cope with flexible work schedules learn to adapt within their departments and in their relations with other departments. In some situations, supervisors may be in charge of different work groups on different days and at different times of the day as a result of flexible work scheduling. This, in turn, necessitates that supervisors on different shifts and in different departments closely plan and coordinate their activities in such a way as to achieve overall effectiveness.

Additionally, there are many companies that utilize numerous part-time employees. Retailers, service establishments, and health-care centers, in particular, often have large components of part-time help. Here, too, the scheduling of part-time employees requires considerable advance planning in order to match the needs of the department or business operation with the hours that the part-time persons will be available.

"Flextime" or part-time work arrangements must be carefully developed and monitored, if they are to be advantageous to both employees and management. Most studies of "flextime" plans have concluded that employees generally appreciate the opportunity to select their work schedule, and that flexible work schedules usually are associated with modest improvements in absenteeism rates, tardiness rates, retention, morale, and productivity.[4]

Full Utilization of Human Resources

In all of this, it should be recognized that a supervisor's employees usually are the enterprise's most important resources; planning for their full utilization always should be uppermost in every supervisor's mind. Full utilization of the work force means getting the best out of them, not necessarily the most. It means making plans for recruiting, selecting, and training employees; searching for better ways to group activities; training employees in proper and safe use of the materials associated with their jobs; supervising employees with an understanding of the complexities of human needs and motivation; communicating effectively with employees; appraising their performance; giving recognition, promoting the deserving, adequately compensating and rewarding them; and, if need be, taking just and fair disciplinary actions. All of these considerations are ongoing aspects of a supervisor's plans for the full utilization of his or her human resources.

In essence, the supervisor who plans for the full utilization of the work force will be in a better position to achieve a situation wherein employees more willingly contribute their efforts toward the achievement of departmental objectives. Planning for the full utilization of employees is at the core of professional supervision. It is mentioned here again only briefly, since most chapters of this text are concerned in some way with this primary objective of supervisory management.

---

[4]See Raymond L. Hilgert and John R. Hundley III, "Supervision: The Weak Link in Flexible Work Scheduling?" *The Personnel Administrator* (January, 1975), pp., 24–26; or J. Carroll Swart, "Clerical Workers on Flexitime: A Survey of Three Industries," *Personnel* (April, 1985), pp. 40–44.

TIME MANAGEMENT

To this point, we have emphasized the need for thorough supervisory planning for optimum use of physical and human resources. Another very important resource that affects all other resources is the supervisor's own time.[5] The old saying that "time is money" applies with equal relevance both to the supervisor's own time and to employees' time. A supervisor's time is a major resource that must be expended carefully. All supervisors have experienced days that were so full of demands that they began to feel as though they could never take care of all the matters that needed attention. The days and weeks were too short; the supervisors would have liked to "buy" or get additional time somewhere. However, the supply of time is inflexible, and it cannot be renewed or stored. If supervisors want more time, they must "make" it themselves.

Most supervisors would welcome even a modest increase in the effectiveness with which they work—say, 5 to 10 percent. Given the many demands on them, supervisors who have a system and a plan for managing their time are far more likely to be effective than supervisors who approach each day haphazardly. Although some supervisors insist that they need more time, what they really need is better use of the time they already have.

Some supervisors put in extremely long days but they still are not on top of their jobs. Perhaps they erroneously equate long hours with devotion and effectiveness. Many times just the reverse is true. Such supervisors need to examine what effort is put into the hours worked and with what results, rather than looking only at the number of hours they've worked as a sign of their dedication. The key is to gain control over the working day rather than to be controlled by it. Time management, too, starts with careful planning.

Managing Time Means Managing Stress

In recent years much has been written and discussed about stress and its impact on people in all walks of life. Stress is often looked upon as being bad, but it also happens that stress can at times serve a purposeful role in influencing what a person does. Any full discussion of coping with or managing stress would be beyond the scope of this text, since the causes of stress are many-

---

[5]Excellent books on time management are: R. Alec Mackenzie, *The Time Trap* (New York: AMACOM, 1972); Alan Lakein, *How To Get Control of Your Time and Your Life* (New York: New American Library, 1974); Merrill Douglass and Donna Douglas, *Manage Your Time, Manage Your Work, Manage Yourself* (New York: AMACOM, a Division of the American Management Association, 1985); and R. Alec Mackenzie, *The Time Trap:* The New Version of the 20-Year Classic on Time Management (New York: AMACOM, 1990).

Fig. 8–2.
Managing time
means
managing
stress.

faceted and the forms it takes are physiological, behavioral, and psychological in nature.[6]

Briefly, however, it is well recognized that much stress is directly related to the ability one has to cope with various time and other pressures. **External stressors** are those that stem from pressures of the job, family, and environmental conditions. The supervisory position by its very nature is a pressure-prone position, since (as we discussed in Chapter 2) supervisors are "in the middle" of many demands from bosses, employees, and fellow supervisors. **Internal stressors** are those that supervisors and others place on themselves; being ambitious, diligent, competitive, and aggressive in nature are some of the frequently mentioned internal pressures that can induce stress.

Many courses and seminars are offered to suggest ways by which people can better learn to cope with the pressures that induce stress. Typically, however, the suggested remedy is better time management, or as it has been succinctly stated, "Managing stress means managing time. The two are so intertwined that controlling one can only help the other."[7] By better time management, a supervisor learns to prioritize duties and tasks, which in turn enables the supervisor to accomplish more of what he or she really needs and

---

[6]A recommended source book is Joe E. Yates, *Managing Stress: A Businessperson's Guide* (New York: AMACOM, 1980). See also Phillip Hunsaker and Curtis Cook, *Managing Organizational Behavior* (Reading, Mass.: Addison-Wesley Publishing Company, 1986), pp. 230–263.

[7]From Randall S. Schuler, "Managing Stress Means Managing Time," *Personnel Journal* (December, 1979), pp. 22–25.

wants to get done. Virtually by definition, better time management means more accomplishment and reduced stress and frustration.

Classifying Duties with a Time-Use Chart

A first step toward better time management is for the supervisor to "get a handle" on how he or she currently is utilizing time. Although many procedures have been suggested for gathering information on time utilization, in essence what first is required is a *time-use chart*, or *time inventory*. Supervisors should first examine how and where they currently are spending their time, before they can begin to attack pockets of inefficiency and ineffectiveness.

Prior to constructing such a chart or time inventory, the supervisor should identify his or her primary job duties and daily activities and classify them as: (a) routine duties, (b) regular duties, (c) special duties, and (d) innovative duties.[8] **Routine duties** are minor tasks that are done daily, but which make a limited contribution to the objectives of the department. Such work includes answering the telephone, reviewing the mail, informal chatting with others, clean-up, and the like. Some of these tasks usually could and should be assigned to subordinates. **Regular duties** constitute the supervisory work most directly related to accomplishing the objectives of the department. Regular duties primarily involve the day-to-day activities and tasks that the supervisor personally must do and that are the essential components of a supervisor's responsibilities. Examples of these are giving directives, checking performance, writing up reports, counseling employees, updating job descriptions, training new employees, and reviewing departmental operating procedures. The term *supervisory duties* could be used here as a synonym for "regular duties." **Special duties or assignments** consist of meetings, committee work, and special projects, which may or may not be directly related to the department. **Innovative duties** are essentially creative-thinking and improvement oriented; for example, they involve looking at new or improved work methods, finding better ways to communicate with employees, etc.

Supervisors who are effective at managing their time do find time, or "make time," for the innovative part of their job. Indeed, it is the innovative supervisor who usually stands out and who is most often noticed and given favorable attention by higher management. This, of course, should not imply that a supervisor ought to work on innovative duties to the neglect of the other duties." **Special duties or assignments** consist of meetings, committee work, supervisory time should be spent on their regular supervisory duties; about 15

---

[8]The supervisor may wish to add another classification to cover time spent handling "emergencies." Of course, it is difficult to anticipate or predict an emergency and the time necessary to correct an emergency situation.

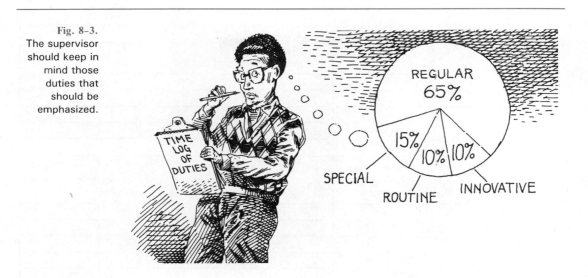

Fig. 8–3. The supervisor should keep in mind those duties that should be emphasized.

percent on special duties; approximately 10 percent on routine duties; and the remaining 10 percent on innovative, or creative-type, duties. These percentages, of course, are only suggested approximations; supervisors themselves must judge what are the appropriate proportions for their particular departmental situations. One thing is clear, however: if a supervisor does not plan carefully, routine and special duties have a way of crowding out the time needed for regular and innovative duties.

A time-use chart, or time inventory, mentioned earlier is a useful technique for gathering information about how a supervisor currently is spending time. Figure 8–4 is an example of a time-use chart. The supervisor can start out by constructing a chart similar to Figure 8–4. Duties should be classified under the major categories discussed previously, i.e., routine, regular, special, and innovative. Then, the supervisor should decide what is the desirable amount of time that normally should be allocated to duties under each category and correspondingly set goals for each day. Once these steps are taken, the supervisor should keep an on-going record of time that actually was spent on various duties. After a week or two of recording daily how time is actually spent, the supervisor should bring together the time-use sheets and total the amount of time spent in each of the categories. These totals should be compared with the original estimates or goals. The supervisor is then in a position to evaluate the use of his or her time. With rare exceptions, the supervisor will be in for some surprises!

From an analysis of the actual times versus the goals or estimates, a supervisor can determine whether appropriate amounts of time are being spent on various duties. For example, are there regular duties that are not getting done

Fig. 8–4.
Time-use chart.

Goals for the Day	Estimated Time (in hours and fractions of hours)	Percentage (calculate)
Routine		
Regular		
Special		
Innovative		

Actual Time Use (Do not record for lunch period)	Routine	Regular	Special	Innovative
	(Record the time spent in hours and fractions of hours)			
8:00–9:00				
9:01–10:00				
10:01–11:00				
11:01–12:00				
12:01–1:00				
1:01–2:00				
2:01–3:00				
3:01–4:00				
4:01–5:00				
Totals				
Calculated Percentages				

Evaluation of Effectiveness _____

because too much time is devoted to routine duties or special projects? Are there some tasks that could be eliminated altogether? Is there sufficient time for innovative work and planning? Answers to these and similar questions give the supervisor a better "feel" for what she or he ought to be working on, rather than simply tackling the problems that happen to come up first or seem most pleasant to work on at the moment.

Delegation and Setting Priorities

Invariably, supervisors will discover time wasters that have interfered with and hampered their ability to work on important things in their department. Such time wasters as random activities, too much time on the telephone, too much time visiting or being visited, procrastination, unnecessary meetings, a lack of delegation, and others, may be revealed by a time inventory. The discovery and recognition of time wasters represent only one step. It is important that the supervisor begin immediately to attack these old habits and build desirable ones.

Of course, supervisory problems crop up continuously, often without an apparent sequence of priority or importance. Therefore, supervisors must discipline themselves to "sort and grade"—that is, to decide between those matters that they must handle personally and those that can be assigned to someone else. For every task delegated—particularly routine duties—supervisors gain time for more important matters, such as regular and innovative duties. Doing this may be worthwhile even if supervisors have to spend extra time training an employee in a particular task. Supervisors then should plan the remaining available time so that it is allocated properly among the duties that they alone must perform. They will again have to classify these duties according to which are the most and the least urgent.[9]

A supervisor who does not establish a priority of duties will be inclined to pay equal attention to all matters at hand. This type of supervisor will tend to handle each problem in the order it happens, and, consequently, the most important matters may not receive the attention they truly deserve. By establishing priorities, time is planned so that the most important things will have sufficient space on the schedule. However, supervisors should leave some flexibility in their schedules, because not every event that occurs can be anticipated. Emergencies and changing priorities do occur, and supervisors must attend to these. Flexibility will permit supervisors to take care of unanticipated problems without significantly disrupting their schedule of priorities that should be accomplished.

Basic Tools of Time Management

In essence, effective time utilization requires mental discipline. This means that the supervisor should assign priorities to duties and stop trying to do everything brought to his or her attention. Once such a mental attitude is fixed and maintained, the supervisor can better use a number of common and handy tools as aids in managing their time.

At the very least, every supervisor should use a *pocket or desk calendar* to note every day those items that need major attention such as appointments, meetings, reports and discussions. By scheduling such activities as far in ad-

---

[9]The "Pareto Principle," so-named after a famous nineteenth century Italian economist, is that many people (because they fail to set priorities) spend most of their time on minor, unimportant tasks. For some supervisors, it has been estimated that they spend 80 percent of their time on duties that contribute to only 20 percent of the total job results.

vance as practicable and noting them on their calendar, chances are far better that a supervisor will not overlook them.

Another effective tool for time utilization is the *weekly planning sheet* (or, if preferred, a *monthly planning sheet*). Typically a planning sheet for a week is prepared at the end of the previous week. The planning sheet shows the days of the week divided into mornings and afternoons and lists the items to be accomplished (see Figure 8–5). At a glance the supervisor can visually check what is planned for each morning and afternoon. As each task is accomplished, it is circled. Those tasks that have been delayed must be rescheduled for another time. Those tasks that are planned but not accomplished during the week (they are still uncircled) should be rescheduled for the following week. Such a record indicates how much of the original plan was carried out, and it provides information concerning where the supervisor's time was spent.

Still another basic tool that many supervisors find helpful is the so-called *to-do list*, which can be used in conjunction with a desk calendar or weekly

Fig. 8–5.
The weekly
planning sheet.

MONDAY 9/22	TUESDAY 9/23	WEDNESDAY 9/24	THURSDAY 9/25	FRIDAY 9/26
AM Monthly Safety Committee meeting	AM Discuss with Human Resources Director interpretation of changes in mendical benefits Policy.	AM Talk to Engineering about Preventive Maintenance Plan	AM Turn in scrap report for last month	AM Attend Management Seminar
PM Discuss direct labor cost figures with Comtroller	PM Work on budget for next six months	PM	PM Check absentee, turnover, and accident rates	PM Meeting with Union Grievance Commitee to discuss unresolved grievances

planning sheet. This is essentially an ongoing listing of things to do—both major and minor—to which a supervisor can make reference as each day progresses. As an item is accomplished, it is crossed off the list. Here, too, a supervisor must prioritize all items on the list, and schedule and perform important tasks first before doing the minor items. Many supervisors find that the best time to review and "reprioritize" their to-do lists is at the beginning of their workday, or at the end of their workday before they leave for home.

There are other tools and handy "tricks of the trade" that supervisors can implement to accomplish better time management. Regardless of what tools supervisors decide to use, it is their responsibility to plan and manage their time for each day and week, and to have a system for recording those tasks that were planned and those that were accomplished.

Time for Creative and Innovative Thinking

Every supervisor needs to leave some time open for creative and innovative thinking. Although a boss's evaluation of a supervisor will depend primarily on how effectively the department functions, a boss also will appraise a supervisor for innovative changes, new ideas, and progressive suggestions. Unless supervisors set some time aside for thinking about constructive improvements, they will find themselves bogged down with routine work and "putting out fires."

One technique that some supervisors find helpful in this regard is to develop a list of improvement projects or innovative ideas and to write these down on a special desk pad or wall chart. This list becomes a constant visual reminder of items that the supervisor would like to accomplish when time becomes available. When there are lulls in a day, or during slack periods, the supervisor can then decide which of the innovative items on the list should be tackled. Interestingly, the mere thought of having such a list can be a major stimulus or incentive to attempt an improvement project which otherwise might not be attempted. When the improvement project is done, it is a good feeling to cross the item off the list and to mark it as accomplished!

SUMMARY

Supervisory planning must be approached with future conditions in mind. General forecasts are made by top management, and supervisors narrow these to forecasts for their departments' particular activities. Supervisors must relate all general forecasts to the activities of their departments and make relevant plans accordingly.

Supervisors who realistically try to anticipate the likelihood of certain events will be in a better position to prepare for them. In so doing, they should be concerned with the effects that their planning may have on other members of the organization. At times, supervisors may resort to various strategies that can be helpful in having plans accepted and carried out by higher management or other supervisors.

Supervisory planning typically focuses on short-term operational matters. Specifically, supervisors must plan for the full utilization of all resources they have at their disposal, such as tools, machinery, and equipment; work procedures and methods; safety; space; materials, supplies, and merchandise; and employee time.

Additionally, supervisors must plan and manage their own time if they are to be effective. Supervisors need to analyze and plan their schedules so as to maximize their time on regular and innovative duties and to minimize through delegation and setting priorities their time on routine and other low-priority tasks.

QUESTIONS FOR DISCUSSION

1. Discuss the relationship of forecasting at the top management level with forecasting at the supervisory level.
2. What are some of the most important concerns that a supervisor should consider in making departmental forecasts?
3. Why is forecasting more of an art than an exact science?
4. Evaluate each of the following tactical, or political, strategies that can be used in a supervisor's planning function. Then identify guidelines a supervisor should use in choosing which strategy (or combination thereof) to use in planning.
   a. "Strike while the iron is hot."
   b. "Time is a great healer" or "wait and see."
   c. "Do the best you can in the time available."
   d. "Mass concentrated offensive."
   e. "Get a foot in the door."
   f. "Strength in unity."
   g. "You scratch my back and I will scratch yours."
5. Discuss and evaluate the supervisor's planning responsibility for: tools, machinery, and equipment; work procedures and methods.
6. Why has safety planning received more supervisory emphasis in recent years? Outline several steps that supervisors can take in planning for a safer work environment.
7. What techniques should a supervisor utilize in order to plan for better use and security of space, materials, supplies, and merchandise?
8. Discuss the major considerations that supervisors should keep in mind when planning employee work schedules. Discuss the pros and cons of flexible and part-time work scheduling.
9. Analyze and evaluate the following statement: "Planning for the full utilization of employees is at the core of professional supervision."
10. Why is the supervisor's time a major resource that must be managed carefully?
11. Evaluate the statement, "Managing time means managing stress."
12. Define each of the following types of supervisory duties in connection with a time inventory or time-use chart:
    a. Routine duties.
    b. Regular duties.
    c. Special duties.
    d. Innovative duties.

Should a supervisor also plan a certain amount of time to be allocated for "emergency duties"? Discuss.
13.   Discuss general and specific approaches that supervisors can utilize in order to plan their own time more effectively.

CASE 9

A Shortage of Policies

The Montclair Manufacturing Company produced a wide array of electronic gauges and employed about 250 people. Chuck Adams, the factory superintendent, was eating his lunch in the company cafeteria with Bill Whitaker and Gerry Parker, two supervisors on the assembly line; Mary Stoebeck, the purchasing agent; and Werner Koff, one of the district sales managers. Their conversation centered around a common complaint, namely, that the company had few written policies or guidelines and that this lack caused them unnecessary concern and discomfort when they had to make decisions. Adams deplored the fact that some employees ate their lunches at the workbench, and he felt that there should be a policy forbidding this practice. Whitaker and Parker mentioned the need for a policy on granting employees leaves of absence. Stoebeck stated that she needed a clear policy that would specify how to obtain bids from prospective suppliers. Koff was concerned that top management had not bothered to issue a policy about whether salespeople should wear informal sportswear or conventional business attire when making calls. In addition to these specific concerns, there were numerous other complaints, which obviously reflected a feeling of dissatisfaction among the company's managers.

The group generally concluded that the best way to attack this problem would be to confront the president of the company, Jay Montclair, with these questions and to ask him to define policies in these and other areas. While they were deliberating this, Abe Murphy, the assistant to the president, joined them at lunch and listened to much of the conversation. Murphy asked, "Are these really matters for the president to decide, or should you supervisors be making these types of decisions for your own departments?"

CASE 10

Interpreting Funeral-Leave Policy

Joan Sutherland supervised a unit of 15 nurses who worked on the evening shift at a large hospital located in a midwestern city. She had recently been promoted to the position of supervisor after having worked as a registered nurse in another unit in the hospital for three years.

One day Sutherland received a telephone call from one of her subordinates, a licensed practical nurse named Betty Sherman who had been employed at the hospital for about four years. It was obvious from Sherman's voice that she was upset; she had difficulty in speaking without crying. She said, "My Aunt Frances passed away last night. She was my foster mother who helped raise me for several years during my teens, after my parents separated and my mother remarried. I will need several days off in order to attend the funeral. Aunt Frances lived in a small town about 50 miles away from here, and the rest of the family will be gathering there this afternoon."

Joan Sutherland replied, "I'm terribly sorry that you had this death in your family. Let me check the policy manual to see what you are entitled to." Quickly, she opened the policy manual to the section marked "Death in Family." The section read as follows:

> In the event of death in your immediate family (spouse, child, parent, brother, sister, father-in-law, mother-in-law), if you are a permanent employee, you will be granted an excused absence with pay of up to 3½ successive days following the death.

Joan Sutherland said, "I'm not sure whether this policy provides time off for the death of a foster parent. I'll call the human resources department to see if they have a ruling. Let me call you right back." With that she dialed the human resources department office, but she was informed by a secretary that the director of human resources would be out of town until the following week. The secretary did not know whether the hospital provided for funeral-leave benefits to employees who lost a foster parent.

As Joan Sutherland hung up the telephone, she wondered what she should say to Betty Sherman.

CASE 11

Objections to Free Coffee and Beverages

Art Erickson was the Administrative Office Manager of the Southern Oil Company; he was in charge of about 75 office employees. There were 10 departments within the office, and each was headed by a supervisor. This made for an average span of supervision of approximately 6 to 10 employees, although two departments handling routine work had 15 employees.

It had been customary for employees to go out of the building to a nearby restaurant for their morning and afternoon breaks. These breaks were so timed that only some of the employees were gone at any one time. Although 20 minutes had been allocated for this, employees usually were absent from their desks for about 30 minutes.

Erickson was about to send a suggestion to his boss, the vice-president of operations, to replace these outside breaks by sending a "coffee cart" twice a day through the departments. The company would provide coffee and other beverages free. Although this would entail some expense, the company would save money by having employees served at their desks instead of their being away for about 30 minutes.

Before submitting this recommendation for approval, Erickson thought he should discuss it with the 10 supervisors in his office. Much to his surprise, the offer for free coffee and beverages served from the "coffee cart" was not greeted by them with enthusiasm but rather with severe criticism and misgivings. Some of the major objections were that this would prevent the supervisors and employees from getting together informally. Further, this would remove their chance to speak with personnel from other departments, with whom they often discussed company problems as well as personal matters. The supervisors felt that these outside breaks offered an important channel of communication, the loss of which would hurt the smooth functioning of the office.

After meeting with his supervisors, Art Erickson pondered what he should do next.

The Violator of the No-Smoking-in-the-Washroom Rule

"Tom, we're going to have to fire Charlie Fiedler. He's been goofing off, and I've had all of it I can take. Let's get him out of here," said Mike Walling over the telephone to Tom Keel, the director of human resources of the Giles Manufacturing Company.

"But Mike, I thought you rated Charlie Fiedler as one of your bright young guys who might be an apprentice toolmaker in a couple of years," responded Keel.

"Well, he seemed to be a good man for awhile; but ever since we got rid of those old lathes and I've had him on bench work, he's gone totally sour, and now he's a real troublemaker," retorted Mike Walling.

"Okay, Mike, but I'd like to talk to him," said Keel. "What's the specific reason for the discharge?"

Walling responded, "Well, you can put it on the record that I found him smoking in the washroom three times. He was warned twice and I just caught him the third time. Management has insisted that we enforce that no-smoking-in-the-washroom rule, and Charlie's the worst offender. I know he didn't like it when we took him off the lathes. We put in two high-speed machines and got rid of five old ones. Others had seniority. There wasn't anything to do with Charlie but put him on bench work, and ever since he's been goofing off."

"Send him up to me, Mike," said Keel. "I'll tell him you're letting him go for breaking rules."

Tom Keel first reviewed Charlie Fiedler's employment record and noticed that he had been with the company for about three years. Fiedler was 24 years old, a high school graduate, and had been married for approximately six months. During his employment with the company, he had received five pay increases and "superior" ratings on three appraisal reviews. After his last two reviews, his record had been marked "promotable" by his foreman, Mike Walling.

Within a few minutes Charlie Fiedler was in the human resources office and seemed to be anxious to speak with Tom Keel. As soon as he was seated at Tom's desk he blurted out, "Is Mike going to fire me?"

"Well, Charlie," said Tom, "he's not exactly pleased with your work at this moment, and he says he thinks you ought to be discharged from the machine shop. Tell me, just what is your trouble with Mike?"

Fiedler: *Things are terrible in the shop now. I used to think Mike was a great guy. He's an expert on every machine in the shop and he taught me a lot, but now I'm convinced he's a slave-driver. All he wants is work, work, work—its impossible to please him. I've worked on drill presses, punch presses and small lathes, and when I was full time on bonus jobs I had no trouble. But this lousy bench work is getting me down. You're always shifted from one job to another—and you can't make standard on any of them. And then three or four bosses are always coming around telling me what to do, and Mike's the worst of the lot.*

Keel: *Didn't you expect a different kind of work when you were moved from the lathes to the benches?*

Fiedler: *Oh, that was a terrible deal. It must have been three months ago. I had been on lathes for a long time. In fact, I even told my wife that I had the best job in the world. I used to make thirty dollars a week or more bonus. But I never knew Mike was going to get rid of the old lathes and get in those high-speed jobs. He never said a word to me about it, and then one Monday morning I come to work and find a dispatcher's table where my lathe should have been. When I tried to find my machine, he says, "You knew we were going to get rid of those old lathes. You're supposed to go over and work on the benches today." I've been doing this lousy bench work ever since.*

Keel: *But Charlie, didn't you realize that all of the old equipment throughout the shop is being replaced with new machinery?*

Fiedler: *Oh, I knew there were a lot of changes, but I never really thought it would put me out of machine work.*

Keel: *Well, Mike says the specific reason for letting you go is because you are always violating the "no smoking" rule.*

Fiedler: *Mr. Keel, that rule is a big joke. Everyone goes into the washroom and has a smoke. There's no other place to go except outside the building, and we can't do that except on breaks or lunch hour. Anytime Mike wants to get someone in trouble he waits until they've gone in the washroom and then nine times out of ten he can go in and catch them smoking. Sure, he caught me a couple of times. It's the way Mike does things—he's really sneaky and I never realized it until lately. I really like the company, but I guess I ought to quit my job because Mike has it in for me now.*

Keel: *Don't you work for a supervisor who reports to Mike? What do you think of him?*

Fiedler: *Yes, Bill Simpson supposedly is in charge of bench work. He's okay, but he doesn't have much to say. I guess you think there are seven or eight supervisors on the floor, but they only do "set-up" work. Simpson is just a "straw boss" who does whatever Mike tells him to do. There are a hundred and fifty people in the shop and everyone takes orders from Mike. I guess I'm washed up around here so I might as well tell you—that man is just another Hitler.*

For several minutes, Tom Keel listened patiently to Charlie Fiedler's criticism of his foreman, Mike Walling. Keel realized that at one stage Fiedler's past performance had been extremely good and wondered whether something could be done to retain his services for the company. Keel concluded the interview by asking Fiedler to leave the plant and to return for another interview the following morning at ten o'clock.

CASE 13

The Busy Manager

Paul Jackson, president of the Laclede Manufacturing Company, arrived at his desk and found a stack of papers on it, although he remembered that he had cleared everything away before he left at eight o'clock the previous night. He asked his secretary what these papers contained. She informed him that they had arrived in the mail late yesterday afternoon and that they were requisitions and letters for authorization from the Texas plant. Since she had read them, he asked her to tell him briefly what each request contained. He thought he could save time by doing this. The discussion went as follows:

Secretary: *Request for approval for the purchase of five acres of land adjoining the Ft. Worth plant amounting to $175,000, as discussed while you were in Ft. Worth the last time.*

Jackson: *Okay, I'll sign it.*

Secretary: *Request for approval to purchase an additional computer and printer for word processing, $4,700.*

Jackson: *I know nothing about this. Please inquire why it is needed and who is supposed to get it.*

Secretary: *Requisition for a new sign at the entrance of the plant costing $700.*

Jackson: *Okay, I'll sign it.*

Secretary: *Request for approval to place an ad amounting to $80 as a contribution to the local Police Circus.*

Jackson: *Why not! I'll approve.*

Secretary: *Requisition to contribute $1,000 to the company's bowling league expenses.*

Jackson: *Absolutely not. Get some more information on this.*

Secretary: *This needs your approval, also. Some of the offices need painting, and the contractor's estimate is $2,200. (Jackson didn't answer, but put his signature on this paper.)*

Secretary: *Request for approval of the purchase of stationery and factory work tickets, totaling $450. (Again, Jackson signed the paper without comment.)*

On and on it went. After more than an hour, Paul Jackson was finished with these requisitions, and all the other incoming mail from the morning was placed on his desk. As he started to read, he received numerous telephone calls. He was informed that five people were waiting in the anteroom to discuss some matters with him. While he was still reading the mail, his secretary informed him that the plant superintendent had an important problem on the factory floor and asked that he come to the plant at once. Jackson immediately left his desk and returned after half an hour, wondering to himself why the superintendent could not have solved the problem on his own. All day, things were piled up regardless of how many decisions he made and how many problems he solved.

On his way home late in the afternoon, Paul Jackson asked himself, "Why do I seem to be so terribly busy and yet, when the day is over, I don't know where all the hours have gone? The day passes all too quickly, and too little is accomplished. And there are so many people who think that being the president of a company is a soft job."

PART 3

ORGANIZING

CHAPTER 9

Principles of Organizing

Chapter Objectives

1. To identify the organizing function of management as a process of designing the structural framework and establishing authority relationships.
2. To define and discuss important principles of organizing, such as unity of command and span of supervision, and their application in supervisory management.
3. To describe the process of departmentation and alternative approaches for grouping activities.
4. To explain the meaning of line, staff, and functional authority in organizations.
5. To discuss and analyze major types of organizational structures.

As one of the five major functions of management at all levels, the organizing function requires that every manager be concerned with building, developing, and maintaining working relationships that will bring about achievement of the organization's objectives. Although organizations may have a variety of objectives and may operate in many kinds of environments, the fundamental principles (or concepts) of organizing are universal.

A manager's **organizing** function consists of designing a structural framework, that is, grouping activities and assigning them into distinctive areas (e.g., departments, units, services, teams) so that activities can be executed as planned. Organizing includes establishment of formal authority and responsibility relationships among the various activities and departments. In order to make such a structure possible, management must delegate authority throughout the organization and establish and clarify authority relationships among the departments.

Organizing should mean that management designs the structural framework and establishes authority relationships based on sound principles and organizational concepts, such as delegation of authority, unity of command, span of supervision, division of work, departmentation, and line and staff authority.

Organizing the overall activities of the enterprise is the responsibility of the chief executive. However, eventually it becomes the responsibility of supervisors to organize the departments over which they have been placed in charge. Therefore, it is necessary for supervisors to understand what it means to organize. Although the range and magnitude of problems associated with the organizing function will be of broader dimensions at higher managerial levels than for supervisors, the principles to be applied are the same.

THE PRINCIPLE OF UNITY OF COMMAND

The chief executive of an organization must group the activities of the organization into divisions, departments, services, teams, or units, and assign duties accordingly. Managers and supervisors are placed in charge of divisions and departments, and their authority relationships are defined. This means that supervisors must know exactly who are their bosses and who are their subordinates. To arrange authority relationships in this fashion, management normally should follow the principle of unity of command (previously discussed in Chapter 3). **Unity of command** means that there is only one person in each organizational unit who has the direct authority to make certain decisions appropriate to the position. It means that each employee has only one immediate supervisor, that is, only one boss to whom the employee is directly accountable.

THE PRINCIPLE OF SPAN OF SUPERVISION

The establishment of departments and the creation of several managerial levels are not ends in themselves; actually, they are the source of numerous difficulties. Departments are expensive; they can involve large cost outlays because they must be staffed by supervisors and employees. Further, as more departments and levels are created, additional problems may be encountered in communication and coordination. Therefore, there must be valid reasons for creating levels and departments. The reasons are associated with the **span of supervision** principle, which succinctly stated means that there is an upper limit to the number of subordinates a supervisor can effectively manage. Often this principle is called **span of management, span of managerial responsibility, span of authority,** or **span of control.** It is preferable to use the term span of management or span of supervision, since these definitions are most meaningful.

Practicing supervisors know that they can effectively supervise only a certain number of employees. Because no one can manage an unlimited number of people, top management must organize divisions and departments as separate areas of activities over which middle-level managers and supervisors are placed in charge. Authority is delegated to the middle managers, who in turn redelegate authority to supervisors, who in turn will supervise the employees. If a manager could supervise a hundred or more employees effectively, each of the one hundred subordinates would report directly to that manager and their different activities would not have to be grouped into departments. Of course, such a wide span of management is impossible.

Fig. 9–1
A manager can effectively supervise only a certain number of subordinates.

The principle that a manager can effectively supervise a limited number of subordinates is virtually as old as mankind.[1] However, it is not possible to state a definite figure as to how many subordinates a manager should have. It is only correct to say that there is some upper limit to this number. In many industrial concerns, the top executive will have from three to eight subordinate managers. But the span of supervision usually increases the farther down a person is within the managerial hierarchy. It is not unusual to find a span of supervision of from 15 to 25 employees at the first level of supervision.

Factors Influencing the Span of Supervision

The number of subordinates that can be effectively supervised by one person depends on a number of factors, such as the abilities of the supervisor, the types and amounts of staff assistance available, the employees' capabilities, the kinds of activities being performed within the space or physical layout, and the degree of objective standards in place.

Supervisory Abilities.   Among the most significant factors that influence the span of supervision are the training, experience, and know-how that the supervisor has acquired—in other words, the competence of the supervisor. Obviously, some supervisors are capable of handling more employees than others. Some are better acquainted with good management principles, have had more experience, and basically are better managers. For example, what the supervisor does during the time available is of major importance. More time is taken by the supervisor who must make individual decisions on every departmental problem as compared to the supervisor who has established policies, procedures, and rules that simplify decision making as routine problems arise. Comprehensive planning can reduce the number of decisions the supervisor has to make and hence increase the potential span of supervision. Thus the number of employees a supervisor can effectively supervise depends to some degree on the quality of the supervisor's managerial competence.

Specialized Staff Assistance.   Another factor on which the span of supervision depends is the availability of help from specialists within the organization. If numerous staff experts are available to provide specialized advice and service, then the span of supervision can be wider. For example, when a human resources department services and assists supervisors in recruiting, selecting, and training employees, supervisors will have more time and energy available for their departments. But if supervisors themselves are obligated to do all or most of these activities, then they cannot devote that portion of time to other-

---

[1]See Exodus, Chapter 18, in the Bible for the story of Moses and Jethro. Jethro has been referred to as the ''World's First Management and Organizational Consultant.''

wise managing their departments. Therefore, the amount and quality of staff assistance available will influence the span of supervision.

Employee Abilities.   How broad a span a supervisor can handle also depends on the abilities and makeup of employees in the department. The greater the capacities for self-direction by employees, the broader will be the span that is feasible. Here, of course, the training and experience of subordinates are important. For example, the span of management could be greater with fully qualified mechanics than with inexperienced mechanics. However, the factor of employee competence may be offset to some degree by the nature of the activities being performed.

Nature and Complexity of Activities.   The amount, nature, complexity, and predictability of activities influence the span of management. The simpler, routine, and more uniform the work activities, the greater can be the number of persons managed by one supervisor. If the tasks to be performed are repetitious, the span may be as broad as 25, 30, or even more employees. If the activities are varied, interdependent, or of significant consequence, the span might have to be as small as three or five. In those departments that are engaged in relatively unpredictable activities—for example, nurses in an intensive care unit in a hospital—the span will tend to be narrow. In those departments that are concerned with more or less stable activities—such as an assembly line or a word processing center—the span of supervision can be broader.

Objective Performance Standards.   Still another factor influencing the span of supervision is whether a department has ample, objective standards for guiding and measuring employee performance. If each employee knows exactly what standards are expected—for example, a certain number of units of production of a specified quality each day—the supervisor will not need to have frequent discussions with employees about performance. Thus good standards support a broader span of supervision.

Balancing the Factors

As stated previously, there is no set figure to identify the number of subordinates a supervisor can manage effectively. The principle of span of supervision (or span of management) indicates only that an upper limit exists. In most situations there must be a balancing of the factors just discussed to arrive at an appropriate span of supervision for each departmental supervisor. Such a balancing of factors for the most part is the responsibility of higher management.

Relationship Between Managerial Levels and Span of Supervision

If a higher level manager concludes that the span of supervision for a certain activity or department is too broad, he or she may decide to divide the span into two or three groups and place someone in charge of each group. By narrowing the span to a smaller number of employees, the manager creates another organizational level because a supervisor or lead person has to be placed over each of the smaller groups.[2] Other things being equal, what happens is that the narrower the span of management becomes, the more managerial levels have to be introduced into organizational design. This may not be desirable, since more levels are costly and also complicate communication and control. Thus there is an apparent trade-off between the width of the span and the number of levels. The managerial problem is: Which is more advisable, a broad span of supervision with few levels, or a narrower span with more levels? (See Figure 9–2.) This is an important question, which often confronts higher management. A first-line supervisor normally does not directly confront this question, but supervisors should understand how it influences the design and structure of their organizations.

DEPARTMENTATION

How an organization structure is designed will be determined largely by the familiar and age-old principles of **division of work** and **specialization**. By these are meant that jobs can be divided into smaller components, specialized tasks, and functions in order to achieve greater efficiency and output. The expansion of knowledge and technology, and advances in all fields of endeavor, have brought more and more specialized employees and diversified units into most organizations of any appreciable size. Thus division of work and specialization continue to influence the design of organizational structures and various kinds of authority relationships.

Departmentation is the process of grouping the many and varied activities into distinct organizational units, usually known as departments. A **department** is a designated area of certain activities over which a manager or supervisor has accepted responsibility and has been granted authority. Terminology used by organizations is quite varied: a department in one may be called a division, an office, a service, a unit, or some other term in another. Most organizations have departments of some sort, since division of work and specialization are conducive to efficiency and better results.

---

[2]A lead person, or working supervisor, typically is not considered to be part of management, especially in unionized firms. Nevertheless, these individuals do perform most of the managerial functions, although they usually do not possess full authority or the right to discipline employees.

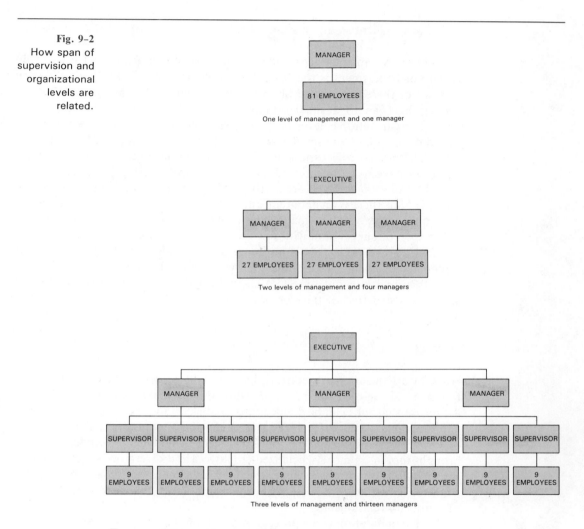

Fig. 9–2
How span of
supervision and
organizational
levels are
related.

MANAGER

81 EMPLOYEES

One level of management and one manager

EXECUTIVE

MANAGER   MANAGER   MANAGER

27 EMPLOYEES   27 EMPLOYEES   27 EMPLOYEES

Two levels of management and four managers

EXECUTIVE

MANAGER   MANAGER   MANAGER

SUPERVISOR SUPERVISOR SUPERVISOR SUPERVISOR SUPERVISOR SUPERVISOR SUPERVISOR SUPERVISOR SUPERVISOR

9 EMPLOYEES 9 EMPLOYEES 9 EMPLOYEES 9 EMPLOYEES 9 EMPLOYEES 9 EMPLOYEES 9 EMPLOYEES 9 EMPLOYEES 9 EMPLOYEES

Three levels of management and thirteen managers

Types of Departmentation

Whereas major departments of an organization are established by top management, supervisors primarily are concerned with activities within their own
areas. Nevertheless, from time to time supervisors will be confronted with the
need to departmentalize within their areas, and they should be familiar with
the alternatives available for grouping activities. These are the same options
available to top-level managers when they define the major departments; usually this is done according to function, products or services, territory, customer, process and equipment, or time.

   Functional Departmentation.   The most widely used type of departmentation is to group activities by function—the jobs to be done. This is the first

guiding thought in the establishment of most departments within businesses and all other organizations. Consistent with the idea of specialization and division of work, activities that are alike or similar are placed together in one department and under a single chain of command. For example, typing and stenographic services may be grouped together into a clerical department or word processing center; sales activities into a sales department; production work into a production department; or inspection activities into a quality control department; and so on. As an enterprise undertakes additional activities, these new activities—for the most part—are simply added to the already existing departments.

Functional departmentation is a method that has been and still is successful in most organizations. It is a basic method that makes good sense, since it is a natural and logical way of arranging activities of any enterprise. Grouping departments along functional lines takes advantage of occupational specialization by placing together jobs and tasks that are performed by people with the same kinds of training, experience, equipment, and facilities. Each supervisor is responsible primarily for one type of operation on which his or her energy and expertise can be concentrated. Functional departmentation also facilitates coordination, since a supervisor is placed in charge of one type or area of activity. It is easier to achieve coordination this way than to have the same functions performed in different departments.

Product or Service Departmentation.   Many companies utilize product or service departmentation. To departmentalize on a product basis means to establish each major product (or group of closely related products) in a product line as a relatively independent unit within the overall framework of the enterprise. For example, a food products company may choose to divide its operations into a frozen food department, a dairy products department, a produce department, and the like. Product departmentation can also be a useful guide for grouping activities in service businesses. For example, most banks have separate departments for commercial loans, installment loans, savings accounts, and checking accounts. Many home maintenance firms have separate departments for carpentry, heating, and air-conditioning services.

Geographic (Territorial, Locational) Departmentation.   Another way to departmentalize is by geographical considerations. This type of departmentation is important for organizations with physically dispersed activities. Large-scale enterprises often have divisions by territories, states, and cities. Increasingly, many companies also have international divisions. Where units of an organization are physically dispersed or where functions are to be performed in different locations—even different buildings—geographic departmentation may be desirable. Locational considerations may be significant even if all activities are performed in one building but on different floors. An advantage of territorial departmentation is that decision-making authority can be placed close to where the work is being done.

Customer Departmentation. Many organizations find it advisable to group activities based on customer considerations. The paramount concern here is to service the differing needs and characteristics of different customers. For example, a university that offers evening programs in addition to day programs attempts to comply with the requests and special needs of part-time and full-time students. Companies may have special departments to handle the particular requirements of wholesale and retail customers. Major department stores may attempt to reach different segments of the buying public, such as customers for a "bargain basement" or lower priced division at the one extreme and an exclusive high-priced fashion division at the other extreme. Many hospitals have a separate unit for outpatient services.

Process and Equipment Departmentation. Activities also can be grouped according to the process involved or equipment used. Since a certain amount of training and expertise is required to handle complicated processes and operate complex equipment, activities that involve the use of specialized equipment may be grouped into a separate department. This type of departmentation often is similar to functional departmentation. For example, in a machine-shop department, specialized equipment is used, but only certain functions are performed; both function and equipment become closely allied. A data processing department utilizing a main-frame computer may serve the processing requirements of any number of operations and departmental needs throughout an organization.

Time Departmentation. Another way to departmentalize is to group activities according to the period of time during which work is performed. Many organizations are engaged in round-the-clock operations and departmentalize on the basis of time by having work shifts. Activities are departmentalized by time (day, afternoon, night shift), although the work operations of all the shifts for the most part may be the same. Here, too, there may be an overlap in the departmentation process. Where time is a partial basis for departmentation, it is likely that other factors will be involved. For example, a maintenance division—based on function and services—may be further departmentalized by shifts, e.g., the maintenance night shift. Shift departmentation can create organizational questions of how self-contained each shift should be and what relationships should exist between regular day-shift supervisors and the off-shift supervisors.

Mixed Departmentation. In order to achieve the most effective structure, a supervisor may have to apply several types of departmentation at the same time. This is referred to as **mixed departmentation**. For example, there may be an inventory control clerk (functional) of the third floor (geographic) on the night shift (time). In practice, many organizations have a composite departmental structure involving functional departmentation, geographic departmentation, and other types. All of these alternatives may be available to supervisors in order to facilitate the grouping of activities in their departments.

There are some departments in which additional subgroupings are not needed. But supervisors of departments of considerable size may find it necessary to divide various jobs and skills into different groups under a lead person or foreman, who in turn will report to the supervisor. Whatever structure is chosen, the purpose of departmentation is not to have a beautiful, well-drawn organization chart. The purpose is to have a sound departmental structure that will best achieve the objectives of the department and the entire organization.

Making Work Assignments

The problem of how and to whom to assign work is a much more frequent problem to a supervisor than is the problem of how to organize departments. This problem always involves differences of opinion. Nevertheless, the assignment of work should be justifiable and explainable on the basis of good management, rather than on personal likes and dislikes or hunch and intuition. The supervisor will be subject to pressures from different directions. There will be those employees who are willing or who want to assume more work, and there will be those who feel that they should not be burdened with additional duties. It is one of the supervisor's most important responsibilities to assign work so that everybody has a fair share and so that all employees do their parts equitably and satisfactorily.

Supervisors often are inclined to assign heavier and more difficult tasks

Fig. 9–3. The assignment of work should be justifiable and explainable on the basis of good management.

to the capable employees who are most experienced. However, in the long run it is advantageous to train and develop the less experienced employees so that they, too, learn to perform the difficult jobs. If too much reliance is placed on one or a few persons, a department will be weakened if the top performers are absent, are promoted, or if they should leave the enterprise.[3] It is desirable to have a sufficient number of employees available who have been well trained and who have flexible skills. One way to develop a flexible work force is to assign certain employees to different jobs within the department on a temporary basis as, for example, during vacation periods or employee absences. In this way there will usually be someone available to take over any job if the need arises. As has been emphasized previously, a supervisor's problems of assigning departmental work will be negligible if the supervisor consistently attempts to utilize the strengths and experience of all employees available.

AUTHORITY RELATIONSHIPS AND ORGANIZATIONAL STRUCTURES

The second major component of the organizing function is the establishing and clarifying of authority relationships among and within the departments. In Chapter 3, we discussed the meaning and substance of managerial authority and the process of delegation. Now we are at the point of discussing how authority relationships are established by most organizations, which, to begin with, means an understanding of line and staff organization—the most commonly used arrangement.

Line and Staff as Authority Relationships

In many large organizations it is common to speak of the sales staff, the human resources (personnel) staff, the nursing staff, the administrative staff, and other staff designations. In such a context, the word staff is used to identify groups of people or departments who are engaged primarily in one activity or several related activities or jobs. However, in most books and other writings about formal organizational structure, the meaning of the word staff is quite different. In this text—consistent with other management literature—*the terms line, staff, and functional represent different types of authority relationships within an organization.*

Much has been written and said about line and staff, and few aspects of management have evoked as much debate as these concepts. Yet it is also true that many of the difficulties and frictions encountered by supervisors are due

---

[3]This is a major component of the *principle of organizational stability,* which advocates that no organization should become overly dependent on one or several key ''indispensable'' individuals, whose absence or departure would seriously disrupt the organization.

to line and staff problems. Misconceptions and lack of understanding of what constitutes line and staff can be the source of confrontation, personality conflicts, disunity, duplication of effort, waste, and lost efficiency.

All supervisors should know whether they are part of the organization in a line or in a staff capacity, and what these words imply in terms of their positions and in relation to other departments. Supervisors should consult their job descriptions or organizational manuals. If necessary, they should ask higher level managers for clarification, because it is top management that confers line or staff authority on a department.

In previous chapters, we referred to managerial authority as an essential component of the managerial job, and defined it as the legitimate managerial right to direct the activities of subordinates. Technically this is line authority, and at this point it is necessary to add to and clarify further the meaning of authority.

Line Organization Structure

In every organization there is a vertical, direct line of authority, which can be traced from the chief executive down to the first level of supervision. **Line authority** (also referred to as **scalar authority**) provides the ultimate right to direct others and to require them to conform to decisions, policies, rules, and objectives. Line authority enables directives to be issued and followed through a chain of command. A primary purpose of line authority is to make the organization work.

Some organizations consist entirely of line authority arrangements (see Figure 9–4). Usually these organizations are fairly small in size, both in operations and in number of employees. A **line-type organization structure** enables managers to know exactly to whom they can give directives and whose orders they have to carry out. There is visible unity of command, which can be traced in a direct line (or chain) of authority relationships. A line-type organization structure has the advantage that results can be achieved more quickly. It particularly is appropriate for organizations that are small in size, such as a sole proprietorship.

Line-and-Staff Organization Structure

As time passes and as organizations grow, activities become more specialized and complicated; hardly a manager can be found who could be expected to adequately and expertly direct subordinates in all phases of operations without some assistance. Line managers, in order to perform their managerial functions, usually need the assistance of specialists who have been granted staff authority for their staff positions. **Staff authority** is the right and duty to provide counsel, advice, support, and service in regard to policies, procedures, technical issues, problems, and the like; these areas have been assigned to cer-

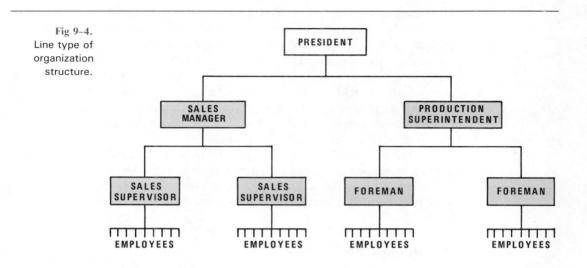

Fig 9–4.
Line type of
organization
structure.

tain specialists because of their position or specialized knowledge. Persons who hold staff positions do not issue orders or commands except within their own staff departments. Rather, it is the function of staff personnel to assist other members of the organization whenever the need arises for specialized help. Staff authority is not inferior to line authority; it is of a different nature. The objectives of staff groups ultimately are the same as those of the line departments, namely, the achievement of overall organizational objectives.

As stated previously, supervisors should know whether their departments are to operate within the organization in a line or staff capacity. This enables supervisors to understand their obligations and relationships to other members of the organization. Staff department supervisors primarily provide guidance, counsel, advice, and service in their specialty to those who request it. Typically they also have the responsibility to see to it (or monitor) that certain policies and procedures are being carried out by line departments. However, staff department supervisors do not have the direct authority to order line personnel to conform to policies and procedures; they can only persuade, counsel, and advise. Line department supervisors can accept the staff person's advice, alter it, or reject it; but since the staff person is usually the expert in the field, line supervisors for the most part are likely to accept, follow, and even welcome the advice of the staff person.

Within a particular department, it does not matter whether it is a line or staff department. Supervisors are line managers with direct authority over the employees in their departments, regardless of whether their departments serve the organization in a staff or in a line capacity.

It is common in many business organizations to find that certain depart-

Fig 9–5.
Line-and-staff
type of
organization
structure.

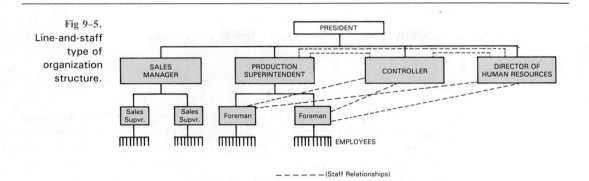

— — — — —(Staff Relationships)

ments, such as human resources (personnel), legal, or accounting, are considered to be staff. (See Figure 9–5.) However, it should not be assumed that these departments are always staff. As stated before, line and staff are characteristics of authority relationships and not necessarily of functions. Nor is a title indicative in recognizing line or staff. For example, in industrial organizations it is common to find a vice-president of production, a vice-president of sales, a vice-president of human resources, and so on. Merely looking at an organization chart is not sufficient to identify staff relationships, because most positions on a chart are shown only as small rectangular boxes.

In most organizations the director of human resources and the human resources department operate in a staff capacity.[4] The human resources department exists to provide advice and service to all departments concerning personnel matters, such as: recruit, screen, and test applicants; maintain personnel records; provide for wage and salary administration; advise line managers on problems of discipline and required fair employment practices; and provide other services and assistance. If line supervisors have difficult personnel problems, the human resources department is available for assistance. Staff managers in the human resources department are qualified to furnish advice and current information, since this is their background and specialty. Most staff managers prefer to offer suggestions to line supervisors, who in turn must decide whether to accept, alter, or reject those suggestions. If a line supervisor feels that a suggestion of the human resources manager is not feasible, the supervisor will make his or her own decision. But in most situations the staff manager's advice will be accepted, since staff individuals are considered to be experts on problems in their areas. Thus staff authority lies primarily in knowledge and expertise in dealing with special problems. Staff persons

---

[4]Often this department is called the *Personnel Department*, or some other name. We use the terms "human resources department" and "personnel department" somewhat interchangeably. Relationships between department (line) supervisors and human resources department staff are discussed extensively in Chapter 12.

"sell" their ideas based on the authority derived from their expertise, but they cannot (at least theoretically) "tell." If a suggestion of the staff person is carried out, it is carried out as a line directive under the name and responsibility of the line supervisor, not that of the staff person.

Functional Authority

Generally speaking, it is correct to state that in a line-and-staff organization, staff managers provide counsel and advice to line managers but do not have the right to give them direct orders.[5] This arrangement maintains the principle of unity of command. However, there is an exception to this generalization, namely, through the use of functional authority.

Functional authority is a special right given by higher management to certain staff persons to give directives to other members of the organization about certain matters based on the staff person's extensive knowledge, expertise, or position in a specialized field. For example, assume that a company president of a unionized firm is concerned that the grievance procedures of the labor agreement should be interpreted consistently and uniformly. Therefore, the president decides to confer sole authority to the labor relations director for the final settlement of grievances—a function that otherwise might belong to line managers. The labor relations director is part of the human resources department, which is a staff department. By giving sole authority for the final adjustment of grievances to the labor relations director, top management confers authority for this function to someone who ordinarily would not hold this authority. Now the labor relations director has this authority, and it no longer belongs to the line supervisors. This is an example of functional authority which sometimes is called **functional staff authority**.

Another example of functional staff authority is the common case where a human resources department is given full authority to maintain legal compliance with wage and hour laws, equal employment opportunity laws, and the like.[6] The decisions of line supervisors in these matters must conform to the orders and stipulations of the human resources department.

The use of functional staff authority does violate the principle of unity of command, since it introduces a second source of authority for certain matters. But in some situations functional authority is advantageous because it facilitates a more effective use of staff specialists. It is up to top management to

---

[5]When an organizational policy or procedure requires a supervisor to consult with a staff person before making a certain type of decision, this is known as following the *principle of compulsory staff advice* (or *compulsory staff service*). The supervisor still presumably may accept or reject the staff person's advice, unless it is a situation involving *functional staff authority* as described in this section.

[6]In a large company, the human resources department itself may rely on advice it receives from the company's legal department or from a corporate attorney.

weigh the advantages and disadvantages of granting functional authority to staff specialists before it is conferred.[7]

Matrix Organization Structure

In many organizations the complexities of operations and the need to coordinate activities of numerous departments have contributed to the development of the **matrix type** of organizational structure. The matrix form of organization is also called **project structure, product management structure**, or **grid**, among other designations. The matrix arrangement is "superimposed" on the line–staff organization, and it adds horizontal dimensions to the normal vertical (top-down) orientation of the organization structure.

During recent years, many so-called high-tech companies have resorted to project (matrix) structures in order to focus special talents on specific projects for given times. Project structure enables management to undertake several or numerous projects simultaneously, some of which may be of relatively short duration. Each project is assigned to a project manager who manages the project from inception to completion. Employees from functional areas or departments are assigned to work on each project as needed, either on a part-time or full-time basis.

Although the degree of complexity of matrix structure will vary depending upon a number of considerations, a basic matrix form might resemble the chart shown in Figure 9–6. This chart illustrates how some managers have been given responsibility for specific projects within the firm, while departmental supervisors primarily have the responsibility for supervising employees within their regular departments. The type of arrangement shown in Figure 9–6 might apply to an engineering or architectural firm. The project managers (A and B) are responsible for coordinating activities necessary for engineering and completion of designated projects. The project managers, however, must work closely with the departmental supervisors of Functions X, Y, and Z. The employees who work in these departments report directly (functionally) to the departmental supervisors, but their services are utilized under the authority and responsibility of the project managers to whom they are assigned for varying periods of time.

There are several problems associated with the matrix organizational structure. The most frequent problem is the question of direct accountability. Like functional staff authority, the matrix structure violates the principle of unity of command, since departmental employees are accountable to both a departmental supervisor and a project manager. Other problems involve priorities of scheduling for individual employees who are assigned to work on sev-

---

[7]Because functional authority may be an extension of staff authority conferred upon certain staff specialists, in practice it may be difficult to clearly distinguish between these authority arrangements in some situations.

Fig. 9–6.
Basic matrix
(project) type
organization
structure.

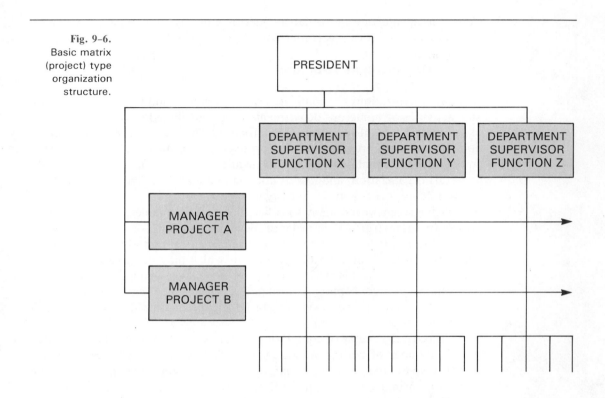

Fig. 9–7.
A disadvantage
of the matrix
form of
organization is
that it does
violate the
principle of
unity of
command.

eral projects. These problems can be avoided, or at least minimized, by proper planning and clarification of authority relationships by the top executive prior to the start of a project.

Despite such problems, the matrix structure is widely used because organizations find it advantageous. The success of a matrix arrangement depends primarily on the willingness of both the project managers and the departmental supervisors to coordinate various activities and responsibilities in working toward completion of each project. Such coordination is vital in the scheduling of work, and it is imperative in the performance appraisal of employees. Employees must recognize that they remain directly accountable to their departmental supervisor, who will rely to a great extent on the project managers' evaluations of the employees' work when the departmental supervisor conducts the annual performance appraisal and salary review. This is discussed at length in Chapter 14.

SUMMARY

The organizing function of management means to design a structural framework, that is, to group and assign activities to distinctive areas so as to achieve the desired objectives. Organizing includes establishing authority relationships between managers and departments. An organizational structure normally should adhere to the principle of unity of command. In assigning the number of employees reporting to one supervisor, the principle of span of supervision also should be observed. The actual span of supervision will be determined by factors such as the competence of the supervisor, the previous training and experience of subordinates, and the amount of and nature of work to be performed. Other things being equal, the smaller the span of supervision, the more levels of management will be needed; the broader the span of supervision, the fewer levels will be required.

The most widely used basis of departmentation is to group activities according to functions. Besides departmentation by function, it is possible to departmentalize along geographic lines, by product or service, by customer, by process and equipment, or by time. Rather than designing new departments within a division, the supervisor most often will be faced with the task of assigning activities and employees within an existing department in order to provide an optimum arrangement.

Every supervisor is attached to an organization either in a line or in a staff capacity. Within their own departments, all supervisors are line managers, regardless of whether they are running a line department or a staff department. If a person is in a staff capacity, his or her normal role is to furnish counsel, guidance, advice, and service in a specialized field. In the usual line–staff structure, a line supervisor may accept or reject the staff's advice; the use of functional staff authority creates an exception to this rule. Where a staff person has been granted functional authority over a specialized area, line supervisors are not free to reject the advice or orders that this person may give.

Most large organizations have a considerable number of staff people whose specialized knowledge and skills are employed to aid others in doing a better job. Further, a matrix (project) type of organization utilizes certain managers to concentrate on coordinating activities surrounding a particular product, project, or service, while having the line supervisors manage the employees in regular departments.

QUESTIONS FOR DISCUSSION

1. Define the managerial organizing function.
2. What is meant by unity of command? Is this principle realistic in today's large, complex organizations?
3. Define the span of supervision principle. What are some of the major factors that influence a supervisor's span of supervision?
4. Explain the trade-off between the number of levels of management and the span of supervision. How does this problem typically affect a first-line supervisor?
5. Define departmentation. Why is the functional approach the most widely adopted approach to departmentation? Discuss other approaches to departmentation and how these often overlap in nature.
6. Why does fair assignment of work activities involve both quantity and quality of work?
7. What are the basic differences between a line type of organization and a line-and-staff type of organization?
8. Discuss the functions of staff personnel. Does the relationship between a line supervisor and a staff person (from whom the line supervisor seeks advice or counsel) violate the concept of unity of command? Why or why not?
9. Identify the departments in organizations that are most likely to be in a staff capacity. Can you tell from looking at an organizational chart or from a person's title whether that individual is line or staff? Why or why not?
10. Discuss the concept of functional authority. Give several examples of how organizations have used this concept. Does the use of functional authority (or functional staff authority) violate the principle of unity of command? Discuss.
11. Does the matrix organization violate the unity-of-command principle? Discuss. What are the advantages of the matrix structure?

CHAPTER 10

Organizing at the Supervisory Level

CHAPTER OBJECTIVES

1. To emphasize the importance of delegating and decentralizing authority at the departmental level and consider when recentralizing is necessary.
2. To discuss the advisability of developing supervisory understudies.
3. To suggest how a supervisor should plan for an "ideal" departmental structure and work toward this objective.
4. To define and discuss certain organizational tools that are useful in supervisory organizing efforts.
5. To discuss the impact that informal organization and informal group leaders can exert on the supervisory position.

Most departmental supervisors will not be involved in major decisions concerning the design of the overall organizational structure of their firms. Supervisors primarily will be concerned with the organizing function within the framework of their departmental responsibilities and the authority delegated to them by higher management. That is, supervisors often will become greatly involved in decisions that must be made about the structure of their own departments. Before we discuss special considerations for organizing at the supervisory level, it is appropriate to review the importance of delegating and decentralizing authority and also to discuss the occasional need for recentralizing.

DELEGATING, DECENTRALIZING, AND RECENTRALIZING

In Chapter 3 we emphasized that the supervisor's leverage and the "energy flow" of an organization was the delegation of authority (commensurate with responsibility). If no authority has been delegated, one can hardly speak of an organization. From an organizational point of view, it is not a question of whether authority is delegated; rather, it is a question of how much and in what forms authority has been delegated to subordinates at different levels. The extent to which authority has been delegated determines the degree to which an organization is **decentralized.**

If delegation of authority is to be effective, a sincere desire and effort to delegate must permeate the entire management team. Top management must believe in and practice delegation of authority. Yet even though top management may intend it, the desired degree of decentralization may not be achieved. Somewhere along the line there may be an authority "hoarder" who refuses to delegate further.

Achieving Decentralization

There are several ways to achieve the desired degree of decentralization. Some companies make great efforts to indoctrinate their entire management team in the philosophy of decentralization. Managers are made to understand that by carefully delegating authority they neither lose status nor absolve themselves of their responsibilities. One way to accomplish decentralization is to organize so that each manager has a fairly large number of subordinate supervisors. By stretching the span of supervision, the manager has little choice but to delegate authority. Another means that some companies use is to establish a policy that a manager cannot be promoted if he or she has not developed subordinates who can take over their positions. With this policy in mind, the manager is expected to delegate authority and to develop junior supervisors who are prepared to assume additional responsibilities. Where this is the case, a manager usually sees the wisdom of delegating as much authority as possible.

When Recentralization is Necessary

From time to time, top management will take a look at its organizational structure—checking, questioning, and appraising whether it is sound. There may be a need for changes due to technological advances, changes in the environment, changes in the enterprise itself, and for other reasons. Reorganization may be needed to overcome perceived shortcomings. Consequently, management may decide to realign, "tighten up," or recentralize. Management may feel that it has lost control over certain activities, perhaps because established controls were not effective. **Recentralization** (also called realignment or reorganization) is the act of revoking delegated authority in connection with realigning functions and duties. For example, in recent years many companies have centralized their budgetary and financial departments in order to have better financial control over operations that previously might have been highly decentralized. A periodic review of the amount of delegated authority is both advisable and necessary in any organization. This also applies to any authority that the supervisor has delegated to employees.

Whenever recentralization takes place, there are apt to be tensions and resistance among members of the organization whose authority is lessened. Feelings of discouragement, mistrust, suspicion, and insecurity will be common. If these feelings are to be eased, higher management should explain thoroughly to subordinate managers the reasons and rationale for the recentralization. Similarly, if a supervisor decides to revoke certain authority that has been delegated to an employee, the supervisor should discuss the reasons for this decision with the employee, as well as with others who may be affected. Generally speaking, recentralization is a difficult process. Prudent and careful decentralization of authority in the first place is the best prevention to avoid circumstances which call for recentralization.

DEVELOPING UNDERSTUDIES AS A WAY OF DELEGATING

In Chapter 3 we discussed a supervisor's delegation of authority in the daily working situation. We emphasized the manner in which a supervisor exercised authority. We suggested that general supervision is an approach that tends to place employees on their own as much as possible; it is usually a better way to use supervisory authority than the close and autocratic exercise of power.[1] In this chapter, however, our concern is with the supervisor's delegation of authority as a means of building an organizational structure within the department, even to the point that if the supervisor is away or removed from the scene, operations go on in an orderly fashion.

---

[1] Introduced in Chapter 3, general supervision is discussed further in Chapter 15.

The Need for an Understudy

In many situations the number of employees within a supervisor's department will be rather small, and the supervisor may wonder whether it is really necessary to delegate authority. Regardless of the size of the department, however, every supervisor needs someone who can be relied on to run the department if the supervisor should have to leave either temporarily or for any length of time. This person is called an **understudy,** an **assistant,** a **backstop,** or some other designation. It is a serious weakness if there is no one in a department who can take over when the supervisor has to be away from the job for sickness or other reasons. Further, as mentioned before, a supervisor personally may miss a promotion if no one is capable of taking over the department. Sooner or later, every supervisor needs an understudy.

There are several advantages that supervisors will discover if they decide to select, train, and develop understudies. Training understudies usually forces supervisors to formulate a much clearer view of their own duties, departmental operations, and ways to arrange jobs more efficiently. Additionally, the supervisor will learn more effective ways of delegating authority to subordinates.

Selecting an Understudy

The first step in developing an understudy is to select the right person for the position.[2] The supervisor usually knows which of the employees are more capable than the others. The individual selected preferably should be someone to whom other employees turn in case of questions—a person who is regarded by fellow workers as a leader. This employee should be an individual who: knows how to do the job and handle problems as they arise; who does not get into arguments; and who is respected by other employees. A potential understudy should have demonstrated good judgment in carrying out assignments and in approaching, analyzing, and solving problems. This person should be interested in developing himself or herself for a better position. Without ambition to advance, even the best training will not achieve the desired results. Additionally, this employee must have shown dependability and a willingness to accept responsibility. Even though he or she has not had the opportunity to display all of these qualities, whatever latent attributes exist usually will be discovered during the training and development process.

If the supervisor has two or three equally good employees as potential understudies in the department, it may be desirable to train all of them on a comparable basis. This provides the supervisor with even more backup leader-

---

[2]In this section we assume that the supervisor is not restricted in choosing an understudy, as might be the case in a unionized firm with strict seniority criteria. The terminology varies, but typically the understudy is also called a ''lead person,'' ''working supervisor,'' ''foreman,'' ''supervisory assistant,'' or other names.

Fig 10-1.
Every supervisor
needs an
understudy.

ship in the department. It also gives the supervisor more information and greater opportunities to observe potential understudies in action until a final selection is made.

Developing the Understudy

Although the word *training* frequently is used to denote the educational process for a supervisory understudy, it is not a totally fitting term. Rather, it should be a matter of developing or "bringing along" an employee—an experience of *self-development* on the understudy's part. Understudies must indicate their eagerness to develop themselves and have the initiative to be self-starters. Bringing understudies to the point where they can assume considerable authority may be a slow and tedious process, but it is worth the effort.

Since no two people are alike, no exact procedures or time schedules can be outlined that will work in every case. However, there are some common guidelines and steps in the development process that seem to work well in most situations. Gradually supervisors should bring understudies in on the detailed workings of the department. For example, supervisors should show them departmental reports and explain where, when, and how information is provided. Supervisors should tell the understudies why such reports are necessary and what is done with them. Supervisors should introduce the understudies to other supervisors, staff members, and personnel with whom they must associate, and have them contact these people as time goes on. It is advisable to permit understudies to attend supervisory meetings after they have had a chance to learn general aspects of the supervisory job. Supervisors should show them how the work of each department is related to that of other departments. As daily problems arise, supervisors should encourage the understudies to try to solve some of them on their own. As understudies develop their own solutions, supervisors will have a chance to see how they analyze situations and approach decision making. Supervisors can teach the understudies the steps of decision making, pointing out guidelines to be followed and pitfalls to be avoided (as discussed in Chapter 5).

In time, supervisors should give the understudies certain areas or activities for which they will be responsible; in other words, understudies should gradually be delegated more duties and commensurate authority. This relationship requires an atmosphere of confidence and trust, with the supervisor recognized by the understudy as a *coach* and *mentor*—and *friend*. In an eagerness to develop understudies as rapidly as possible, supervisors should not overload them or pass on problems that are beyond their capabilities; it may take some time for understudies to be able to handle problems of magnitude. Further, supervisors must be aware that sooner or later the understudies will expect some tangible rewards to compensate for the additional duties.

This process may take much effort and many supervisory hours, weeks, and months. It is conceivable that at about the time that the understudy can be of major help, he or she may be transferred to another job outside of the supervisor's department. This may be discouraging for the moment, but the supervisor can be confident that higher management will appreciate the supervisor's efforts and success in the development of a competent understudy. Further, the supervisor's part in the development or advancement of an employee is one of the most satisfying personal feelings that a supervisor can experience.

Encouraging Reluctant Subordinates

The development of an understudy and delegation of authority involve a two-sided relationship. Although the supervisor may be ready and willing to delegate authority, a subordinate may be reluctant to accept it. Some employees are unsure of themselves and feel that they may not be able to tackle the job. Or they fear having additional responsibilities that may add to the burden of their daily work. Some employees do not want to move up since they are reluctant to leave what they consider to be the security of their peer group—for example, if they are part of a labor union. If a supervisor merely tells a potential understudy to have more self-confidence, or "pull yourself together," this will have little effect. However, the supervisor can contribute to a potential understudy's self-confidence by carefully coaching and training the person to undertake additional and more difficult assignments. It often happens that employees who have a high sense of responsibility are inclined to underrate themselves. Yet these may be the very employees who will develop into excellent understudies if they are encouraged and assisted to accept the challenge.

A potential understudy's reluctance to accept additional authority and

Fig 10–2.
Although the
supervisor may
be ready and
willing to
delegate
authority, a
subordinate may
be reluctant to
accept it.

broadened assignments can be mitigated by the supervisor's continual coaching. In order to delegate effectively, a personal relationship must develop between the supervisor and the understudy. This often will be a growing and shifting relationship, which becomes more meaningful with the passage of time. At some point, the understudy should be able to take over the complete supervision of the department. When that happens, the supervisor truly will have "organized a department" that will carry on even if he or she should leave the position.

The same process will hold true if only one understudy is developed, or if the size of the department should warrant a number of assistants. Of course, with increased responsibilities, there should be adequate positive incentives provided for supervisory assistants such as pay increases, appropriate titles, recognized status within the organization, and other rewards of a tangible or intangible nature.

PLANNING THE "IDEAL" DEPARTMENTAL STRUCTURE

Although some supervisors will have an opportunity to design an organizational structure for a totally new department, most supervisors are placed in charge of existing departments. In either case, all supervisors should think of and conceptualize an "ideal" organizational structure, which could be defined as that structure which the supervisor believes is most desirable for the achievement of the department's objectives. It is not essential that the supervisor's plans for the department appear beautiful on paper or that the organization chart look symmetrical and well-balanced. Nor should an "ideal" structure be thought of as being in the distant future. Rather, it should be considered as a goal or standard by which the supervisor can assess the present organizational arrangement and which should serve as a guide for rearrangements and for long-range plans for the department.

The supervisor should plan the departmental structure on the basis of sound organizational principles, not around personalities. If the organization is planned primarily to accommodate current or available individuals, existing shortcomings probably will be perpetuated. If a department is structured around personalities, serious problems can occur when key employees are promoted or resign. But if the departmental organization is planned on the basis of the necessary activities and functions to be performed, then an appropriate search for qualified personnel can be undertaken. For example, if a supervisor relies heavily on one or two key employees who are "jacks of all trades," the supervisor may find that the department is disrupted if one or both of these employees leave. Conversely, if a number of weak employees do not carry their share of the total load, the supervisor may find that too many employees are assigned to certain activities because the supervisor has tried to compensate for poorly performing individuals. Therefore, an organizational structure must be designed that will best serve the objectives of the department. Then the available employees should be matched with the functions to be performed.

This is easier said than done. It frequently happens, particularly in smaller departments, that available employees do not fit well in the planned "ideal" structure. In most situations the supervisor will be placed in charge of an existing department without having had the chance to decide its structure or to choose the employees. In these circumstances the supervisor can gradually adjust to the capacities of the available employees. Then, as time goes on, the supervisor can make changes that will move the department closer and closer to an "ideal" organizational structure in the future.

ORGANIZATIONAL TOOLS AND THEIR APPLICATION

Considerable misunderstanding often occurs because some managers, supervisors, and employees do not understand how their positions and responsibilities "fit in" with the positions and responsibilities of other personnel. To reduce some of this confusion, supervisors can be aided considerably by the application of organization charts and manuals, job descriptions, and job specifications. These tools are helpful in clarifying the organization's structure, and they can assist supervisors in understanding their positions and the relationships between various departments throughout the enterprise. The obligation to prepare a firm's overall organization chart and manual rests with top management. However, supervisors themselves will usually need to develop all or some of these tools for their departments and also to keep them up to date.

Organization Charts

Organization charts are a means of graphically portraying organizational relationships. An organization chart primarily depicts managerial and supervisory positions as rectangular boxes.[3] Each box represents one position, and the boxes are usually interconnected to show the grouping of activities that make up a department, division, or section. By studying the position of boxes in their scalar (vertical) relationships, anyone can readily determine who reports to whom. Although different types of organization charts are used, the vast majority are vertically constructed and show levels of organization arranged in the shape of a top-down pyramid (see Figure 10–3).

A supervisor will gain a number of advantages from establishing and maintaining an organization chart of the department. It requires, first of all, a careful study and analysis of the departmental structure. Preparing the chart might reveal duplication of efforts or inconsistencies in certain functions or activities. A chart may enable the supervisor to spot where dual reporting relationships exist (that is, where one employee is reporting to two supervisors) or where there are overlapping positions. The chart may also suggest whether the span of supervision is too wide or too narrow.

Organization charts are a convenient way to acquaint new employees with the structure of the department and the entire enterprise. It is natural for most employees to have an interest in knowing where they stand and where their supervisor stands relative to higher management. Of course, there are limitations to charts, especially if they are not kept up to date. It is imperative that all changes be recorded promptly, since failure to do so makes the chart as outdated and useless as last week's newspaper. It also should be noted that organization charts primarily show formal authority relationships and do not show the informal organization, which we discuss later in this chapter.

Organization Manuals

The organization manual is another helpful tool, because it provides in comprehensive written form the decisions that have been made about a company's organizational structure. Not every company will have an organization manual, but most firms of appreciable size do. Typically the **organization manual** defines the scope of authority and responsibility of managerial positions and

---

[3]Some organization charts use lines, circles, or other artistic designs rather than boxes to depict organizational positions.

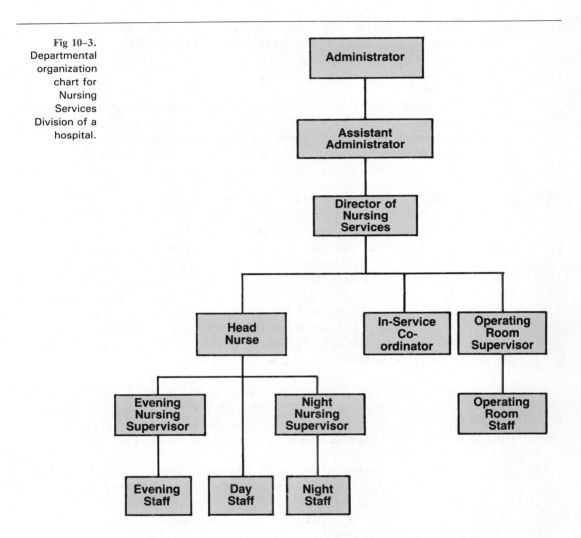

Fig 10–3.
Departmental
organization
chart for
Nursing
Services
Division of a
hospital.

the formal channels for obtaining decisions or information. A manual is vital to supervisors, since it specifies the responsibilities of each supervisory position and how each position is related to other positions within the organization. The manual may outline the purposes and functions of the organization and of each department, and explain how relationships within the organization contribute to accomplishing the objectives. The manual may also contain major policies and procedures, particularly those relating to personnel. Every supervisor should be thoroughly familiar with the contents of the organization manual, especially with those phases that most affect their own departmental operations.

Job Descriptions and Job Specifications

Job descriptions often are included in an organization manual. **Job descriptions,** also known as **position descriptions,** identify the principal elements, functions, and duties, and the scope of authority and responsibility, involved in each job. Some job descriptions are very brief; others are quite lengthy. Job descriptions often are based substantially on information obtained from employees who actually perform the jobs and from their supervisors as they perceive the jobs to exist or as they should exist.[4]

In practice, there is some overlap in the use of the terms "job description" and "job specification." Generally speaking, job descriptions describe the functional duties of a position, whereas **job specifications** refer to the human qualities—personal specifications—that are necessary to perform the job adequately. Many organization manuals include the job specification as part of each job description (see Figure 10–4).

If a department does not have job descriptions and job specifications for existing jobs, or if new jobs are to be created, the supervisor should see to it that they are developed and written up. If help is needed, the supervisor should ask the human resources department, which usually has the necessary experience and know-how to facilitate this task.

INFORMAL ORGANIZATION

Every enterprise will be affected by a social subsystem known as the **informal organization** (sometimes referred to as the "invisible organization"). The informal organization reflects the spontaneous efforts of individuals and groups to influence the conditions of their environment. Whenever people work together, social relationships and informal work groups inevitably will come into being.[5] Informal organization develops when people are in frequent contact with each other, although their relationships are not necessarily a part of formal organizational arrangements. Their contacts may be a part of or incidental to their jobs, or they may primarily stem from personal preferences and desires to be accepted as a member of a group.

At the heart of informal organization are people and their relationships, whereas the formal organization primarily represents the organization's structure and the flow of authority. Supervisors can create and rescind formal orga-

---

[4]Further discussion on the development of job descriptions is presented in Chapter 12. For supervisory and other managerial positions, many firms prefer to use such terms as *position guide* or *position description,* rather than job description, in identifying the responsibilities of these positions.

[5]Informal work groups also are discussed in Chapter 16.

Fig 10–4.
Job description
and
specification
for a custodian.

```
                          AJAX CORPORATION

                    JOB DESCRIPTION AND SPECIFICATION


     Title  Custodian                     Promotional line:
                                               Custodian
     Salary Range  $xxx - xxx monthly          Maintenance Repairer


     FUNCTION OF THE JOB:
        Under direct supervision to perform duties involving cleaning and upkeep of buildings.

     CHARACTERISTIC DUTIES AND RESPONSIBILITIES:

        1.  Clean plant facilities and offices as regularly assigned.
        2.  Clean restrooms and halls as regularly assigned.
        3.  Wax floors as needed.
        4.  Dispose of trash as accumulated.
        5.  Empty waste cans and cigarette urns in regularly assigned area.
        6.  Perform related duties as assigned.










     SUPERVISION RECEIVED:

        Oral and written instructions are received from designated supervisor.




     SUPERVISION GIVEN:

        None.

     MINIMUM ACCEPTABLE QUALIFICATIONS:

        Good physical condition.
        8th grade education.
        Ability to work and get along with people.
```

nizations that they have designed; they cannot eliminate an informal organization, since they did not establish it.

Informal groups come into existence in order to satisfy needs and desires of their members that the formal organization apparently does not satisfy. Informal organization particularly satisfies the members' social needs by providing for recognition, close personal contacts, status, companionship, and other aspects of emotional satisfaction. Groups also offer other benefits to their members, such as protection, security, and support; they further provide convenient access to the informal communications network or grapevine (discussed in Chapter 6). Information through the grapevine provides a channel of communication and facilitates the members' desires to know what is going on. Further, informal organization influences the behavior of individuals within the group. For example, an informal group may exert pressure on individuals to conform to certain standards of performance agreed upon by the majority of the group. This phenomenon may occur in any department or at any level in the organization.

The Informal Organization and the Supervisor

At times the informal organization may make the job of the supervisor either easier or more difficult. Because of their mutual interdependence, the attitudes, behavior, and customs of informal work groups affect the formal organization. Every organization operates in part through informal work groups, which can exert either a constructive or negative force on the operations and accomplishments of a department.

Numerous research studies have demonstrated that informal groups can influence employees to either strive for high work performance targets or restrict production; to either cooperate with supervisors or make life miserable for them, even to the point of having them removed. Supervisors must be aware that informal groups can be very strong and can even shape the behavior of employees to an extent that interferes with supervision. Pressures from informal groups can frustrate the supervisor in getting the results that higher management expects the supervisor to achieve.

A supervisor who would like for the informal organization to play a positive role first of all must be willing to accept and understand it. Such an attitude will encourage the supervisor to group employees so that those most likely to comprise harmonious teams will be working together on the same assignments. Further, the supervisor should avoid activities that would unnecessarily threaten or disrupt those informal groups whose interests and behavior patterns are supportive of the department's overall objectives. Conversely, if an informal group is influencing employees in a negative direction to the extent that there is a serious threat to the department's functioning, a supervisor may have to take action (for example, redistributing work assignments or adjusting work schedules).

Supervising and Informal Work Group Leaders. Most informal work groups develop their own leadership. An informal leader may be recognized or chosen by the group, or may just somehow assume the reins of leadership by being a spokesperson for the group. Work group leaders play significant roles in both the formal and informal organizations; without their cooperation, the supervisor may have difficulties or even be unable to control the performance of the department. A sensitive supervisor, therefore, will make every effort to gain the cooperation and goodwill of informal leaders of different groups, and will involve their aid and cooperation in furthering departmental objectives. If properly approached, an informal leader can be helpful to the supervisor, especially as a channel of communication. An informal leader may even be a viable candidate as the supervisor's understudy, if that person would accept such a position. However, it is questionable whether this person can still function as an informal leader once he or she has been designated as an understudy.

Instead of viewing informal leaders as "ringleaders," supervisors should consider them as employees who have influence and who are "in the know," and then try to work with them. For example, in an effort to build good relations with informal leaders, a supervisor periodically may provide information to them before anyone else or ask their advice on certain problems. However, the supervisor must be careful to avoid having informal leaders lose status within their groups, because the leaders' close association with the supervisor certainly is being observed and could be interpreted negatively by employees. Similarly, the supervisor should not extend unwarranted favors to informal leaders as this could undermine their leadership roles. Rather, the supervisor should look for subtle approaches to have informal groups and their leaders dovetail their special interests and endeavors to be supportive of the department's activities.

SUMMARY

Decentralization of authority is not achieved easily, because some managers and supervisors are unwilling to delegate to subordinates. Nevertheless, delegation and broad decentralization are necessary if effective organizations are to be developed.

At the departmental level, supervisory delegation can be fostered through the selection, training, and development of understudies. Unless the supervisor develops someone to be an understudy and grants authority to this person, the department may be hampered seriously if the supervisor has to leave the scene.

In designing the organizational framework of a department, the supervisor should conceptualize an ideal arrangement based on the assumption that all required and qualified employees would be available. Since there are seldom people available with the exact qualifications desired, employees who are available must be fitted into the structure, deviating from the "ideal" where necessary.

A number of organizational tools are helpful to the supervisor in the organizing function. The organization chart shows a graphic picture of organizational relationships. Organization manuals usually contain statements of objectives, policies, job descriptions, and job specifications and identify relationships of various positions for the total organization.

The informal organization is closely related to and yet apart from the formal organization. It can have either a constructive or a negative influence on employee performance. In order to make positive use of the informal organization, supervisors should become familiar with the workings of the informal organization and its leaders and should determine how to enlist their cooperation in order to further departmental objectives.

QUESTIONS FOR DISCUSSION

1. Why are delegation of authority and decentralization highly interrelated concepts? Is it proper to say that delegation of authority is necessary in order to have an organization? Discuss.

2. Why does top management sometimes resort to recentralization? Will a supervisor have occasions to revoke authority (i.e., recentralize)? Discuss.

3. What are the major steps and issues involved in the selection and development of an understudy at the supervisory level?

4. Why do some employees resist opportunities to accept an understudy assignment? What can the supervisor do in order to encourage capable employees to seek advancement within the organization?

5. Discuss the issues involved in the question of whether a supervisor should organize on an ''ideal'' basis or on a ''real'' basis.

6. Define and discuss the application of the following organizational tools at the supervisory level:
   a. Organizational charts.
   b. Organizational manuals.
   c. Job descriptions.
   d. Job specifications.

7. What is meant by informal organization? How does the informal organization affect the formal organization? Discuss approaches by which the supervisor may foster cooperation with informal groups and their leaders.

CHAPTER 11

Meetings, Committees, and Conference Leadership

CHAPTER OBJECTIVES

1. To emphasize the purposes, benefits, and limitations of meetings.
2. To identify major types of committees and suggest guidelines in determining the composition and size of a committee.
3. To discuss the major considerations involved in having committees perform effectively, with emphasis on the chairperson's role in problem-solving meetings.

The increasing size and specialization within most organizations make communication and managerial coordination difficult and, at the same time, more urgent. To facilitate coordination, from time to time committees must be formed and meetings must be held. Without committees and meetings, it would be virtually impossible for many organizations to operate. Of course, there are other ways to supply individuals with information that they need to perform their jobs and to receive their ideas and opinions. However, holding a meeting is often the most effective way to achieve these objectives.

A **committee** can be broadly defined as a group of people who meet and function collectively by working together for various reasons. For purposes of brevity, we use this term to include other designations, such as **commission, team, task force, board,** and the like.

Supervisors should be familiar with the workings of meetings and committees, because frequently they will be members of a committee and participate in meetings. Further, supervisors themselves will chair and conduct meetings and thus need to develop their abilities to lead a meeting, a skill we refer to as **conference leadership.**[1]

TYPES OF MEETINGS

Most group meetings may be described as being either informational, discussional, or decisional in nature. In the **informational meeting** the group leader does most of the talking in order to present information and facts. For example, a supervisor may call a meeting to announce a new job scheduling system as a substitute for posting a notice or speaking to each employee separately. Such a meeting enables everyone in the department to be notified at the same time. It also provides employees with a chance to ask questions about the meaning and consequences of the announcement. However, questions from the employees are confined to a clarification of the supervisor's remarks.

In a **discussional meeting,** the group leader encourages the participation of group members in order to secure their ideas and opinions. For example, instead of asking employees individually for their suggestions on how to solve a problem, the supervisor could call a meeting for the same purpose. A number of suggestions may be offered and discussed in the meeting. Typically, the implementation of an idea that was suggested and discussed will receive more employee support, since they have participated in considering the problem.

A **decisional meeting** takes place when a discussional group has been delegated authority to make decisions on a particular problem. Just as a supervisor

---

[1]For a comprehensive source on conducting meetings, see Donald L. Kirkpatrick, *How to Plan and Conduct Productive Business Meetings* (2d Ed.; New York: AMACOM, a division of American Management Association, 1986); or Milo O. Frank, *How to Run a Successful Meeting in Half the Time* (New York: Simon and Schuster, 1989).

can delegate authority to an individual employee to make a decision, a supervisor can call a meeting and delegate authority to a group. For example, if a group of maintenance employees in a plant complains about the allocation of overtime and asks the supervisor to make a decision, the supervisor might prefer that the employees themselves find a solution. Perhaps the supervisor does not care what decision is made as long as the time allotted for overtime is not exceeded. If the majority of the group itself makes a decision, the solution probably will be more acceptable to the employees. Even if the group's solution is not the very best, it may be better for the supervisor to have an adequate solution that is implemented by the group than to impose a supervisory decision that meets with their resistance or grudges.

A supervisor may not be concerned with the detailed solution of a problem as long as the solution remains within certain limits. Such limits must be clearly stated when the problem is submitted to a group for a decision. For example, if the group is to decide on the allocation of overtime, the number of hours that are available must be stated. Also, it may be necessary for the supervisor to point out that no one should work for more than a certain number of hours a day, and so forth. When feasible, it is desirable to let the group decide for themselves what should be done within stated guidelines.

Benefits from Meetings

A group of individuals exchanging information, opinions, and experiences usually will develop a better solution to a problem than could any one person who thinks through a problem alone. People bring to a meeting a range of experiences, backgrounds, and abilities, which rarely would be available if the same subject had been assigned to one person alone. Many problems are so complicated that one person could not possibly have all the knowledge, background, and experience needed to arrive at proper solutions. An open interchange of ideas can stimulate and clarify thinking. Solutions or recommendations that a group reaches will tend to be better than those that any single member of the group would have selected.

Group deliberation also can be of major help in promoting coordination. Suggestions from members of a group are more likely to be carried out with greater willingness than suggestions that come from only one person. When people have participated in the formulation of a plan, they tend to be more motivated toward its implementation than if they have not been consulted. It matters less how much they have actually contributed to the plan, so long as they were part of the meeting. Thus group meetings are advantageous in promoting coordination, cooperation, and motivation.

Limitations of Meetings

Despite its beneficial nature, the meeting device often is abused. A common complaint of supervisors is that there are too many meetings in their organiza-

Fig 11-1.
It is difficult to criticize the individual members of a group meeting since each member can hide behind the responsibility of the total group.

tions. Another such complaint is that many meetings are too time-consuming. This latter complaint usually surfaces when each person at a meeting wants to have a major say and uses up a great amount of time in order to convince the others of his or her particular points of view.

Another shortcoming of meetings is the concept of divided responsibility. When a matter is assigned to a group for deliberation, responsibility does not weigh as heavily on the individual members as it does when the matter is assigned to one person. The problem becomes everybody's responsibility, which in reality means it is nobody's responsibility! Although the group leader technically is responsible for the action or inaction of the group, this person can hardly be held accountable for the group's decision. Similarly, it is difficult to criticize the group as a whole or its individual members, if each member can hide behind the responsibility of the total group. This thinning out of responsibility is natural, and there is no way to avoid it when a problem is referred to a committee for a decision.

Still another possible shortcoming is the phenomenon of what has been called "groupthink." This occurs when the group's desire for consensus becomes paramount over its desire to reach the best possible decision. Deliberations become dominated by efforts to avoid conflict among the group, and therefore individuals do not express dissenting views that might be helpful in realistically appraising alternative choices of action.[2]

The supervisory problem is to weigh the many advantages emanating from group deliberation against the shortcomings of holding a meeting. Fortunately

---

[2]See Irving L. Janis, *Groupthink: Psychological Studies of Policy Decisions and Fiascoes* (2d ed.; Boston: Houghton-Mifflin Company, 1982).

the advantages usually exceed the disadvantages. If group members are carefully selected and if meetings are led and managed well, most meetings will become a vital contributing part of any organization.

COMMITTEES: TYPES, COMPOSITION, AND SIZE

As stated previously, we use the term **committee** to cover various designations of groups of people who are assigned to meet and work together for the purpose of discussing designated problems, responsibilities, or tasks. Members of a committee normally have other full-time jobs, and their committee work is an additional duty or corollary assignment.

Permanent (Standing) Committees

A **permanent (or standing) committee** usually has an official, even permanent place in an organization. Its members are appointed by someone in higher management—or they are elected or nominated in some fashion—to deal with certain recurring issues or problems. Members of a standing committee are expected to serve either for a stated period of time or indefinitely. Usually they are drawn from various departments and represent supervisors, employees, and specialist personnel. Some common examples of permanent standing committees are a plant's safety committee, a university's affirmative-action monitoring committee, an employees' credit union committee, and the like.

Temporary (Ad Hoc) Committees

A **temporary (or ad hoc) committee** is a group that meets only for a certain time period and usually for a limited, specific purpose. When the work of the temporary committee is finished, the group usually is disbanded. Ad hoc committees can serve to discuss almost any type of organizational issue that comes up and which is not already assigned to a permanent committee. Many of the group meetings that supervisors conduct within their own departments and with other departmental supervisors are of an ad hoc nature.

Membership and Size of a Committee

The membership (or composition) of a committee usually is important to its success. If the subject matter to be deliberated or decided is of sufficient magnitude, the committee should bring together representatives of the relevant interest groups. If specialists from different departments are to be brought together, interested parties should have adequate representation in order to have balanced group deliberation. This encourages departmental personnel to

Fig 11–2.
The committee
will be less
effective if
interest groups
are not properly
represented.

feel that their interests will be heard and considered. Although this consideration is important, the manager or supervisor who is appointing the committee should not carry it to extremes. It is more important to have capable members serve on a committee than just to have representatives from every conceivable faction that may be affected. Individuals selected should be able to express and defend their opinions, but they also should be open to other points of view. Further, it is advisable that they be "independent" of each other (e.g., not in a direct authority–reporting relationship).

No definite figure can be stated concerning the optimum size of a committee. Some authorities have suggested that up to a dozen or so members is near the upper limit for effectiveness. In any event, a committee should be large enough to provide for broad sources of information and thorough group deliberation. However, it should not be so large that it will be unwieldy and cumbersome. If the nature of the subject under consideration is such that a very large committee is needed, then it may become necessary to form subcommittees. For example, a large managerial committee formed to discuss a major project consisting of manufacturing and marketing a new product may find it advantageous to divide into subcommittees. The subcommittees meet separately to consider detailed aspects of the project, such as design, production, advertising, and distribution. After the subcommittees have deliberated, the committee meets as a whole to hear reports from each of the subcommittees and then proceeds accordingly.

The question of committee composition usually does not exist if the meeting covers just the employees of a supervisor's department. The employees in the department establish the nature of "the committee" that will participate in a departmental meeting.

PROBLEM-SOLVING MEETINGS AND CONFERENCE LEADERSHIP

For the most part, meetings should be called only when necessary. If a matter can be handled by a telephone call or personal discussion, there is no need to call a conference. If a manager or supervisor decides that a meeting is necessary, then the subject to be deliberated should be communicated to the committee members, and the committee's role should be delineated and clarified. That is, members should be informed concerning the task of the committee, and the kind and degree of its authority should be specified. This means that it must be clear whether the committee is to serve in an informational, discussional, or decisional capacity. If it is to be a temporary committee, members should be selected appropriately, and their numbers should be reasonable. However, as previously mentioned, more important than the number of committee members are their qualifications and their willingness to tackle the problems at hand.

A committee meeting or conference may not be successful if the goals of the meeting are too numerous and difficult to achieve. Generally, the goals of a **problem-solving meeting**[3] should be: (a) to come up with the best possible or feasible solution to the problem under consideration; (b) to do this with unanimity or a majority consensus; and (c) to accomplish this in a short period of time. This can be an arduous task, but it is not insurmountable.

The Chairperson and Committee Teamwork

The success of any committee meeting will depend largely on **conference leadership,** that is, the group leader's abilities and skills in leading and guiding a meeting toward its stated goals. For purposes of brevity, the term **chairperson** is used to define a conference or committee leader, who is either formally or informally appointed. In many situations supervisors will serve as chairpersons, especially in meetings held with their own departmental employees.

A chairperson should recognize that members of a committee bring to a meeting unique points of view and behavior patterns. It is human nature for committee members to think first of how a topic, issue, or proposal will affect

---

[3]We use this term to include both discussional and decisional types of meetings, that is, where a group is asked to grapple with a problem or problems and may or may not have delegated authority to implement solutions. In this regard, when a problem is assigned to a committee to make a decision and carry it out, the committee has been given line authority. However, if the charge to the committee is only to deliberate, debate, advise, and make recommendations, then the committee acts in a staff capacity.

them, their jobs, their departments, and their own working environment. These thoughts can easily lead to friction. The chairperson should approach the members in such a way as to fuse individual viewpoints and positions so that sooner or later teamwork will develop.

A frequent observation about committees is that the problems on the conference table are not as difficult to deal with as the people around the table. Individuals at a meeting often react toward each other more than they do to issues or ideas. For instance, whatever Mr. Jones suggests might be rejected because he talks too much. Ms. Smith might be someone who tends to oppose whatever the group is for. Mrs. Brown might be that committee member who keeps her mouth shut most of the time. Patience and skill on the chairperson's part can reduce such difficulties, so that committee members eventually start concentrating on the content of the meeting and the issues involved and not just on the individuals around the table. For a meeting to be successful, the chairperson should encourage committee members to set aside personalities and outside allegiances and to work as a team to deliberate and arrive at a solution to the problems at hand.

Conducting Meetings: The Role of the Chairperson

The role of a chairperson is a demanding one. As stated before, the goal of a problem-solving meeting is to develop a good solution with as much unanimity as can be gained in a short period of time. However, the quality of a group's decision may depend in part on the amount of time that is used. A hasty meeting may not produce the most desirable solution. On the other hand, most

Fig 11–3. The autocratic chairperson may have difficulty in getting committee members to participate.

meetings should be under a time limit. If a meeting drags on too long, conference members become bored and frustrated. It is the chairperson's role to offer members a chance to participate fully and to voice suggestions and opinions. The chairperson may have to use persuasion to convince a minority to go along with the decision of the majority. On other occasions the chairperson will have to persuade the majority to make concessions to the minority. This takes time, and it may result in a compromise that does not necessarily represent the optimum solution, but at least it becomes an acceptable one.

Variations in the chairperson's role can run anywhere from the one extreme of a dominating autocratic person to the other extreme of the very permissive, overly democratic leader. At times, it will be necessary for a normally democratic chairperson to use tight control over a meeting; at other times only the loosest control will be needed.

The Chairperson's Personal Opinions.   A chairperson generally should strive to assist committee members in reaching their own decisions by stimulating and encouraging them to offer and consider different ideas and alternatives. If the chairperson expresses too many personal views, conference members may hesitate to disagree. This is especially true if the conference leader is the boss or part of top management. Yet there are occasions where it would be unwise and unrealistic for the chairperson not to express any views. He or she may possess relevant factual information or sound opinions, and the value of the group's deliberations would be lessened if these were left unknown to committee members.

On the whole, therefore, it is desirable for a conference leader to express opinions, but at the same time he or she must clearly state that those opinions are open to constructive criticisms and suggestions of the group. Silence on the part of a chairperson, especially when the chairperson is the boss or the highest ranking member of the group, may be interpreted to mean that the chairperson cannot make decisions or does not want to do so for fear of assuming responsibility. Thus the chairperson must use good judgment in determining when and to what extent personal opinions are relevant or needed.

Committee Structure.   If committee members are mature and well motivated, formality may not be necessary. Normally, however, committees need some stable structure and the leadership of a formally elected or appointed chairperson, who is responsible for keeping the meeting moving with orderly discussion directed toward an efficient conclusion. Here, too, sensitive judgment on the chairperson's part is required to maintain an appropriate balance of formal structure with the necessary amount of informality that encourages active participation by all committee members.

The Agenda.   A useful technique for keeping a meeting from wandering off into time-consuming discussion of irrelevant matters is a well-prepared agenda. Before the meeting, the chairperson should outline the overall meeting plan with an agenda. Topics to be discussed should be listed in sequence, and it may even be advisable to include a tentative time limit as to approximately how long the meeting will last. The chairperson may even have in mind a general timetable for discussing each item on the agenda, although this should be for the chairperson's guidance only and not be controlling in conducting the meeting. The actual agenda should be distributed in ample time for members to prepare themselves for the meeting.

Although an agenda outlines the meeting plan, it must not be so rigid that there is no means for adjusting it. The chairperson should plan and apply the agenda with a degree of flexibility, so that if a particular subject requires more attention than originally anticipated, time allocated to other topics can be adjusted. Although staying close to an agenda will help reduce irrelevant discussion, the chairperson must not be too quick to rule people out of order. What seems trivial to the chairperson may be important to some of the members. As a matter of fact, some irrelevant discussion actually may contribute to a more relaxed atmosphere and relieve tension which sometimes develops.

Since it is the chairperson's role to keep the meeting moving toward its goals, he or she should pause periodically during the meeting to consult the agenda and remind the group what has been accomplished and what remains to be discussed. Astute conference leaders learn to sense when the opportune time has arrived to summarize one point and move on to the next item on the agenda. If experience tells them that their meetings have a tendency to run overtime, it might be advisable to schedule them shortly before the lunch break or just before quitting time. This tends to speed up meetings, since participants seem to run out of pointless arguments around those hours of the day!

Encouraging Full Participation.   After a few introductory remarks and social pleasantries, the chairperson should make an initial statement of the matter(s) to be discussed. All members of the meeting should be encouraged to participate in the discussion and to bring out those aspects and information that are important to them. There are usually some members at a meeting who talk too much and others who do not talk enough. One of the chairperson's most important roles is to encourage the latter to speak up and to keep those who talk too much from doing so. This does not mean that all members of a meeting must participate equally. There will be some who know more about a given subject than others, and some will have stronger feelings about an issue than others. The chairperson should strive to stimulate as much overall participation as practicable.

The chairperson's general attitude is of crucial importance. Initially everyone's contribution should be accepted without judgment, and everyone should feel free to participate. The chairperson may have to ask controversial questions in order to get discussion and participation started. This is sometimes done by asking provocative, open-ended questions that ask who, what, why, where, and when. Questions that can be answered with a simple "yes" or "no" should be avoided. Another technique is to start at one side of the conference table and ask each member in turn to express his or her thoughts on the problem. Although this approach "forces" everyone to participate, it discourages spontaneous participation and allows the rest of the group to sit back and wait until called on. Further, this approach may cause some individuals to take a stand on an issue before they are really mentally prepared to do so.

A chairperson may be so anxious to have everyone say something that there is considerable aimless discussion just for discussion's sake. The chairperson should observe the facial expressions of different members for clues as to whether someone has an idea but is reluctant to speak up. This is particularly important when one or several talkative members of the group dominate the meeting, while other participants have to struggle to contribute their comments. There are several techniques the chairperson can use to cope with the member who talks too much. After the talkative member has had sufficient opportunity to express opinions, the chairperson can conveniently overlook that person and not recognize him or her again, calling on other conference members to speak. Or the chairperson may ask the talkative member to please keep any additional remarks brief so that others may contribute. Most of the time, however, other members of the meeting will find subtle ways of "censoring" those who have too much to say.

If a meeting is made up of a large number of participants, it may be advisable to divide it into smaller groups, commonly known as "buzz sessions." Each of the small subgroups reports back to the overall meeting after a specified period of time. This is similar to the subcommittee approach mentioned previously, and it encourages those who hesitate to say anything in a larger group to be more comfortable and willing to participate and offer their opinions.

Guiding the Group to a Decision.   Once a problem is identified and is generally understood by members of the group, the relevant facts should be presented in a logical, organized manner. After the facts have been discussed and evaluated, the next appropriate step for the group is to suggest alternative solutions for the problem at hand. From this point, the chairperson should guide the group through the remaining steps of the decision-making process, as outlined in Chapter 5.

A chairperson should always realize that the "best" solution will only be as good as is the "best" alternative considered. Accordingly, the chairperson should strive to make certain that no realistic solution is overlooked, and conference members should be urged to propose as many alternatives as they can develop. The next step is to evaluate alternative solutions and to discuss the advantages and disadvantages of each proposal. Discussion eventually will narrow down to several alternatives on which general agreement can be reached. It then may be advisable to eliminate all other alternatives by unanimous consent. Those alternatives that remain should be evaluated thoroughly in order to arrive at a solution.

The chairperson may have to play the role of a "mediator," or "conciliator," by working out or proposing an overall solution that would be acceptable to most members of the group, possibly even convincing some members that their opinions are not as persuasive as others. Preferably, the final solution will be a synthesis of the desirable outcomes of the few remaining alternatives. By a process of integration, the most important points are incorporated into the most desirable solution. The chairperson also has the sensitive job of helping those holding minority viewpoints to "save face." It is easier to achieve this if the final decision can incorporate something of each person's ideas so that everyone has a partial victory. Of course, this can be a long and tedious process, and there is also a possibility that a compromise may not result in the strongest solution.

It may happen that the chairperson will be confronted by a group that is hostile to virtually every proposal. In such a situation, it is necessary to find out what is bothering the group, to bring their opposition into the open, and to discuss it frankly and objectively. When confronted with a new idea, committee members often will concentrate on the objectionable features rather than on the desirable results that may be gained. Objections thus have to be clarified and discussed. If open discussion does not reduce the real and unwarranted fears and objections, it may be appropriate to adjourn the meeting and to try again at some later time.

Taking a Vote.   A chairperson often is confronted with the problem of whether a vote should be taken. Although voting is a democratic way to make decisions, at times voting actually may accentuate differences among members of a group. Once individuals publicly commit themselves to a position, it becomes difficult for them to change their minds and yet save face. Further, if they are members of the losing minority, they cannot be expected to carry out the majority decision with great enthusiasm. Therefore, wherever possible, it is better not to take an early formal vote but to work toward unanimous or near-unanimous agreement.

Obviously a major disadvantage of working toward total agreement is that such a process can take a long time, and unanimity may cause serious delay. Also, for the price of unanimity, the solution may be reduced to a common denominator that is not as ingenious, bold, or imaginative as it would have been otherwise. Whether the chairperson should seek unanimity in a solution will depend on the situation and the magnitude of the problem.

The skilled chairperson usually can sense the feeling of the meeting. A remark such as, "It seems to me that the consensus of the group is that 'such and such' is our solution," may be appropriate. This type of summary statement can avoid the taking of a formal vote. If this is not possible, a vote should be taken in order to reach a decision. In a small group, a show of hands

Fig 11–4.
If open discussion does not reduce the fears and objections of a hostile group, it may be advisable to adjourn the meeting.

I SUGGEST WE ADJOURN.

or secret written ballot is adequate for the voting procedure. For large group meetings, the observance of parliamentary voting procedures (such as *Robert's Rules of Order*) can save time and keep the meeting from becoming unwieldy and disorderly. The form of the voting procedure may be less important than whether the participants understand the issue involved, believe that a fair hearing has been held in the meeting, and are ready to vote.

Importance of Follow Up. As a general rule, the chairperson should see to it that a written summary or a copy of the minutes of the meeting is provided to every member of the committee. This is a useful device to review what actually took place or what was decided at the meeting. For certain decisions, the summary or minutes of the meeting may serve as a permanent policy guideline for future situations involving similar problems. If some matters are left undecided, the summary or minutes can provide a review of the alternatives that were discussed and help to crystalize thinking of the participants who attended. It may even be advisable to use this opportunity to announce when the group will next meet to take up undecided problems and to consider new issues.

SUMMARY

Supervisors will be involved in meetings and committees either as members, organizers, or chairpersons. Meetings usually are called to disseminate information or to discuss or solve problems.

Group deliberations often produce more satisfactory and acceptable conclusions than those that might be reached by an individual. Major complaints about meetings are that there are too many of them, they are time-consuming, and they divide responsibility.

The function of standing committees is to deal with recurring problems or issues. Ad hoc or temporary committees usually are appointed to serve for a limited time and for a specific task.

In selecting the membership of a committee, the most interested parties to the issues at hand should be represented. These should be persons who are capable of presenting their views and of integrating their opinions with those of other members. The size of a committee should be large enough to permit thorough deliberations, but not so large as to make it cumbersome.

The success of any committee's deliberations depends largely on effective conference leadership. For problem-solving meetings, the chairperson's task is to obtain an optimal solution in a minimal amount of time with the greatest amount of unanimity. The chairperson constantly is faced with the problem of either running the meeting too tightly or too loosely. If control is lacking, members of the meeting may experience feelings of aimlessness and confusion. Thus the chairperson should strive for intensive group participation that has just enough structure to arrive at an effective and efficient conclusion.

QUESTIONS FOR DISCUSSION

1. Discuss the distinctions between (a) an informational meeting, (b) a discussional meeting, and (c) a decisional meeting. Are these distinctions always clear?
2. Is it advisable for a supervisor to delegate authority to a group of employees? If so, in what form? Discuss. If a supervisor delegates decision-making authority to a group, can he or she escape accountability for the decision that is reached? Why or why not?
3. Discuss and evaluate the benefits and limitations of a group discussion of problems requiring a departmental decision. Why is the lack of fixed responsibility both an advantage and disadvantage of referring problems to a group?
4. Is the supervisory complaint that "there are too many meetings and they take up too much time" a valid complaint? How should meetings be viewed by the supervisor in relationship to his or her managerial role?
5. Define and discuss the major differences between a standing committee and an ad hoc committee. Give several examples (other than those given in the text) of each type of committee in various types of organizations.
6. What are some of the major factors to be considered in deciding on the composition of a committee? Is there an "optimum size" committee? Discuss.
7. Discuss and evaluate each of the following in reference to problem-solving meetings, committee operations, and conference leadership:
   a. The usual goals of a problem-solving meeting.
   b. Personalities of the group members.
   c. Whether the chairperson should express opinions in a meeting; if so, how.
   d. A flexible or inflexible agenda.

   e.   Achieving participation from all conference members.
   f.   Discussion of alternatives in the group decision-making process.
   g.   Whether to take a vote on an issue.
   h.   The need for follow-up after adjournment of a meeting.
8.   Why is the ability to hold, lead, or participate in meetings an important skill to be developed by a supervisor?

CASE 14

Turnover on the Third Floor

The following were employed in various positions at Grove Hospital and are the main characters in this case:

Edna Drombowski, associate administrator;
John Davis, director of personnel;
Jean Murphy, director of nursing services;
Georgia Yamada, supervisor of the third floor;
Heather McGuire, a newly hired nurse.

John Davis had been working at his new job for about a week when Jean Murphy came to see him. Murphy explained that she needed more registered nurses on the third floor, since that floor was presently understaffed and three more nurses had just submitted their resignations. She added that she hoped he would do a better job of hiring nurses to fill vacancies than the previous personnel director. Davis said that he would take care of the matter.

Realizing that the problem might be more than just a matter of hiring additional nurses, John Davis started checking the personnel records of nurses on the third floor. To his surprise he found that the third floor had a much higher turnover rate for registered nurses than any other floor in the hospital. In fact, only one nurse currently working on the third floor had been at the hospital for over a year. Davis therefore decided that it was time to see Edna Drombowski about the problem. After explaining the problem to Drombowski, Davis called Jean Murphy in. The three of them agreed to investigate the third floor to see if any clues to the turnover problem might be discovered.

A week later Drombowski called a meeting to see what progress had been made on the investigation. Murphy reported that she had met with Georgia Yamada to discuss the problem. According to Murphy, it was Yamada's opinion—with which Drombowski concurred—that the high turnover rate on the third floor probably was a matter of coincidence. Yamada indicated that no real problems existed except for the constant lack of nurses, which was the major irritant to people working on the third floor. Yamada said that the work got done and that the type and number of nurses' complaints on the third floor were no different from that on other floors.

John Davis then gave his report, but his findings were quite different from Murphy's. First, he had examined the personnel records of all nurses to see if different patterns existed on the third floor with regard to age, race, marital status, number and age of children, previous experience, and length of employment. Since he could not find any differences, Davis had concluded that the general hiring practices could not be blamed for the high turnover on the third floor.

John Davis had then decided to examine all the exit interviews involving nurses on the third floor that had been conducted within the last year to see if these would shed any light on the problem. Although a variety of reasons had been given for leaving the hospital, he noticed that rarely did any of the exit interviews include a reason that was under the hospital's control. Most of the reasons concerned outside factors, such as pregnancy, husband leaving the community, going back to school, no baby sitter available, etc. Since the past exit interviews, which had been conducted by the previous personnel director, did not seem to reveal the true reasons for leaving, Davis decided to conduct exit interviews with the three nurses who were about to quit the third floor.

The results of the three exit interviews comprised the major and most informative portion of John Davis's report. By some skillful probing, he discovered the real reasons why the three nurses were quitting Grove Hospital and learned what they felt were major problems on the third floor. These nurses explained that, until about ten months ago, the third floor had a full-time evening nurse and a full-time night nurse. This meant that the nurses who worked days (the majority of nurses on the floor) were seldom required to rotate to the evening or night shifts. When they rotated, it was usually only once or twice a month. Then, when the two full-time nurses quit due to outside factors, they were not replaced by full-time evening and night nurses. As a result, the day-shift nurses started rotating to the other shifts on a much more regular basis. This upset them. Furthermore, the increased rotation led to other scheduling problems, such as working an evening shift and then doubling back to the day shift the next morning. Because the third floor was short-handed, the nurses often did not get off work in the evening until midnight or later. And returning to work before seven o'clock the next morning put a real strain on them.

Another major problem as seen by the three nurses was the lack of clear lines of authority on the third floor. The two head nurses who assisted Georgia Yamada on the third floor had quit three months ago but had not yet been formally replaced. It was rumored that recently hired Heather McGuire was eventually going to be one of the head nurses, although Yamada had made no mention of it to the other nurses. Since McGuire often assumed the duties of a head nurse, the other nurses on the floor were perplexed. They didn't know whether they should assume that McGuire had the authority of a head nurse or whether they should receive their instructions from Yamada only.

Finally, the problem of being short-handed was not minor in the eyes of the three nurses. They felt that they could not do their jobs properly since they spent most of their time on routine tasks, such as passing medication, carrying out physicians' orders, charting, etc. Often they found themselves brushing off conversation with their patients because they had so much to do. They were quite dissatisfied since their expectations of their roles as nurses were not being met.

After hearing all these reports, Edna Drombowski, John Davis, and Jean Murphy agreed that they had a real problem on their hands. They decided to meet a week later to discuss possible solutions.

CASE 15

The Hardworking Controller

Walter Grant, controller of the Rollings Paint Company, started with the company 20 years ago. He began as a "one-person accounting department" and now had eight employees in his department. He was a most loyal and hardworking supervisor, who preferred to do as many things as possible by himself instead of assigning more duties to subordinates.

In recent years, however, numerous complaints about the Accounting Department becoming more and more "bogged down" were being lodged by various supervisors. Delays in getting up-to-date figures were increasing, and there also were a greater number of errors in payroll checks and in other clerical areas.

Sam Rollings, the president of the firm, felt that much of the problem in the Accounting Department centered on Walter Grant. Rollings occasionally urged Grant to assign more duties to subordinates and to delegate authority to them. Rollings also tried to impress on Grant the need for new procedures and the importance of listening to new ideas from subordinates, but somehow Grant did not get the message and was doing nothing to change. In the meantime, things in the Accounting Department kept getting worse, and Rollings was considering what steps to take. He was reluctant to fire Grant, who was 60 years old and a close, personal friend.

CASE 16

The Interfering Secretary

Lee Darst was vice-president of manufacturing at the Coyle Chemical Company. He had direct line authority over Ed McCane, the plant superintendent; Charles Evans, the chief engineer; Diane Purcell, the purchasing agent; Ron

Weaver, supervisor of maintenance; and Carol Shiften, supervisor of the shipping department.

Three years ago, Lee Darst hired Bernice Billings as a secretary. Billings was a diligent, capable, and efficient worker. She quickly won the admiration and confidence of her boss. Darst felt fortunate to have such a capable secretary, since Billings willingly assumed numerous duties that allowed him to devote more time to his broad responsibility over the five departments. At times Darst's supervisors received written instructions in the form of memos that clearly originated with Billings, but which came to them with Darst's initials. Billings also took it upon herself from time to time to give oral directives to Darst's subordinates. For example, several times she went to the plant superintendent, Ed McCane, and gave him instructions concerning plant scheduling problems. At times she went directly to the production floor and asked various employees of the department to rush orders along or made other requests of this sort, without seeing McCane first. She often told maintenance employees to do various projects, which, she said, "Mr. Darst would like you to do." Similar occurrences took place in the Shipping Department, where she frequently left instructions for special treatment of some customers' orders.

In most of these situations, Lee Darst was not aware that Bernice Billings had taken it upon herself to communicate directly with subordinates in order to expedite solutions to problems that had come to her attention. Some individuals grumbled that these directives should have come from either Darst or the appropriate departmental supervisor. In most cases, however, everyone concerned realized that Billings had the best interests of the company in mind, and they normally complied with her requests.

However, as time went on, the supervisors began to feel that Bernice Billings was interfering more than she was helping to expedite problems. In several instances some of the employees on the production floor did not check with Ed McCane but went directly to Billings for instructions. Similar incidents took place in other departments. One day, over a cup of coffee, Ed McCane, Carol Shiften, and Ron Weaver angrily poured out their concerns to each other. At the outset, they had looked upon Billings favorably, but now they considered her to be a disturbing and disrupting factor who was undermining their supervisory positions.

CASE 17

Trick or Treat?

The Customer Relations Department of a midwestern utility employed about 100 people whose primary function was to answer customer telephone complaints, problems, and inquiries. The department did not have face-to-face contact with the customers. It was open 24 hours a day, every day; during peak hours, some 65–70 employees worked in the department.

One October 30, which happened to be the day before Halloween, a group of 12 day-shift female employees decided to "dress up" as "ladies of the evening" for Halloween. None of the employees consulted her supervisors or the department manager. The next day—Halloween—the group appeared in full dress, including ribbons, extra makeup, and leather miniskirts. When several of the supervisors and the department manager noticed the women, they gave no indication of a negative response. In fact, two of the supervisors laughed at the group's attire and commended them on their originality. Most of the group's co-workers thought that the attire was humorous, although a few employees said that the costumes depicting "hookers" was "a bit much!"

Approximately an hour after the women had reported for work, one of the supervisors, Sheila Brookings, went into the department manager's office. Brookings was visibly upset; she said that she was outraged at the costumes, and she demanded that the employees be sent home for the day without pay. Brookings commented that in all her 15 years as a supervisor, "I've never been so offended as I am today!" Angrily Brookings continued, "This is a business, not a place for partying. Further, I find their dress to be personally offensive to me and my religious values!"

The department manager, George Crampton, knew that this would be one of the busiest days of the year in the department and that he could not afford to send some 15–20% of his staff home and still give proper, prompt service to customers. Crampton also considered the fact that none of the women in the group had ever been a serious disciplinary problem. Crampton pondered what if any action should be taken against the employees and how he should respond to Brookings. Crampton knew that if he suspended or disciplined the employees, many of the office employees would become extremely upset. Crampton feared that he might find the total office disrupted if he took disciplinary action; at the same time, he also felt that he had to be very sensitive in responding to Brookings's complaint.

CASE 18

Sanders Supermarkets (#32): Why Have Another Meeting?

Sanders Supermarkets operated over 50 stores in a major metropolitan area. In an attempt to improve its market share, the company embarked on a new program in regard to the merchandising and pricing of meat products. A company-wide meeting of all district managers and store supervisors was held.

At the meeting the company president stressed the important points of the new meat program, one of which was that each store supervisor should have a store meeting to explain the program to all the store's employees.

On a follow-up later that same week, Dick Barton, district manager, went into Store #32 to evaluate the progress of the program. Dan Rolan was its store supervisor. The following dialogue took place:

District Manager: *Dan, I just walked the store and talked with your Bakery, Deli, and Meat Department heads. It seems that there wasn't a store meeting here this week. Why not?*

Store Supervisor: *I didn't think we needed to have another meeting. I did talk to each and every one of my department heads about the new meat program, if that's what you're referring to.*

District Manager: *That's exactly what I was referring to. You know that you were told by the president to have a meeting in the store. Also, you received a bulletin from the Sales Department explaining the new program, didn't you? And at the bottom of the first page, it said, "Have a store meeting."*

Store Supervisor: *Dick, do you expect me to have a store meeting every time the Sales Department writes that on a bulletin? If so, then I'll probably be having a store meeting every other day. When will I find time to manage this store? Besides, how long should such a meeting take? I've never had any training or instructions about holding meetings. Most of the meetings I have with my employees in the store seem to accomplish very little other than to waste my time and theirs.*

District Manager: *Oh, come now, Dan, it doesn't take any special training to hold meetings. And what are you saying? Do you really mean that "Have a store meeting" appears on quite a few company bulletins?*

Store Supervisor: *Absolutely, and not only that, Dick. What about all the company mail I receive daily that I have to read? Usually in the middle of the page it says "All Stores Except—." Do you realize just how much store mail comes in every day? And the bad part is that most company bulletins either don't apply to my store or are so redundant that they put me to sleep.*

District Manager: *Okay, Dan, but why didn't you complain about this before, if it's a problem?*

Store Supervisor: *Frankly, I didn't think it would make any difference if I did complain. There are too many people in our organization who think that communication means just writing memos and having more meetings, even if they're not needed.*

District Manager: *Well, at any rate, I want you to have a store meeting on the meat program right away. I don't want my boss raising hell with me that one of my stores didn't follow through on his instructions.*

Store Supervisor: *Okay, I'll have the meeting, but I think it will be a waste of time. My employees already are well-informed on this program.*

District Manager: *Dan, I understand your feelings, but we all have to follow orders. It seems to me that our discussion today has highlighted several problems. Think about them, and when I see you again in a few days perhaps we can discuss what we can do to attack them.*

PART 4

STAFFING

CHAPTER 12

The Staffing Function and the Human Resources Department

CHAPTER OBJECTIVES

1. To discuss the managerial staffing function with emphasis at the supervisory level.
2. To understand relationships between the human resources department and line supervisors by tracing historic and current patterns of personnel functions.
3. To identify major equal employment opportunity laws and regulations and their impact on employment policies and decisions.
4. To emphasize the importance of maintaining supervisory accountability for staffing decisions.
5. To discuss how supervisors perform the staffing function through the use of job descriptions, job specifications, and careful hiring decisions.

The managerial **staffing** function includes the selection, placement, orientation, training, development, and compensation of employees. These activities are part of every supervisor's responsibilities, although much help and support are usually provided by staff specialists. The supervisory staffing function also includes the evaluation and performance appraisal of employees according to their efforts and abilities. Further, supervisors play a role in determining how employees are to be rewarded on the basis of their work performance.

Not every company has a human resources (personnel) department. Very small companies, for example, usually do not need or cannot afford to have specialized staff personnel. As a company grows in size, it is likely that at some point top management will recognize the need to hire a human resources director and staff specialists to assist in carrying out the staffing function. In U.S. corporations, currently about one human resources staff person is employed for every 100 employees on the payroll.[1] The role and size of the typical human resources department have expanded considerably in recent decades.

THE PERSONNEL DEPARTMENT IS NOW THE HUMAN RESOURCES DEPARTMENT

In the discussion to follow, we assume that the enterprise has a **human resources department** within its organizational structure and that it is a staff department as defined in Chapter 9. In some organizations this department is called the **personnel department,** the **industrial relations division,** the **employee relations section,** or by some other name.

During the 1970s and 1980s, a majority of U.S. corporations adopted the designation of human resources department for a variety of reasons. Regardless of its official name, the usefulness and effectiveness of any human resources department will depend on its ability to develop close working relationships with line supervisors. The quality of these line–staff relationships will, in turn, depend on how clearly top management has defined the scope of activities and authority of the human resources department.

Before discussing ways to achieve effective relationships between the human resources department and line supervisors, it is helpful to review both the historic roles of the department and current patterns by which the staffing function is carried out by line supervisors with the help of the human resources department. In order to provide a bit of "historic flavor" in this discussion, we use the term personnel department in the historical overview section that follows, and we use the term human resources department when we discuss evolving and current patterns.

---

[1]"ASPA–BNS Survey No. 53, Personnel Activities, Budgets, and Staffs: 1988–1989," *Bulletin to Management* (Washington, D.C.: The Bureau of National Affairs, Inc., June 22, 1989), p. 1.

Personnel Departments: Historic Review

Early Origins.   During the early years of the twentieth century, many personnel departments began as record-keeping departments. Typically, early personnel departments were responsible for maintaining employment records of a firm's employees. These records included letters and forms pertaining to employment applications and hiring, job positions held by employees, dates of job changes and promotions, wage and salary changes, leaves of absence granted, disciplinary penalties imposed, and other types of employment information.

Even today, maintenance of employee records is of great importance because of emphasis on nondiscriminatory employment, pension and insurance programs, seniority provisions, and promotion and development policies. If employee records were not maintained in a centralized location, every supervisor would have to maintain these records for his or her department. This would be cumbersome and time-consuming for supervisors and also would interfere with their daily departmental chores. Thus most supervisors, both historically and currently, have been content to have a staff department perform these support services. Besides, some supervisors do not possess skills to perform clerical duties adequately.

Impact of Labor Unions.   As time went on, particularly during the 1920s, many managers in industry felt that employees would be more content and productive if management made efforts to provide expanded employee services, such as cafeterias, better personal facilities, company athletic teams, company stores, and other benefits. Since the activities involved in providing

Fig 12–1.
The usefulness of the human resources staff will depend on its ability to develop close working relationships with line supervisors.

such services hardly fit into normal line operating departments, they were usually assigned to the personnel department. Although providing these services was a bit paternalistic in nature, top management thought that such efforts might make employees happier and less resentful of the then-existing working conditions and environment. This perception lasted for a relatively short period of time.

During the 1930s, 1940s, and 1950s, another shift in emphasis took place with the tremendous increase of labor unions. Because of strikes, grievances, and negotiations, personnel departments were expected to take direct charge of virtually all employee and union relations. Personnel departments often assumed major responsibility for hiring and disciplining employees, as well as handling labor problems. At that time top management believed that most employee and union questions could be handled best by personnel specialists, so that line supervisors would be free to concentrate on their jobs. Unfortunately this type of thinking by top management led to another serious problem.

Reduced Status of Supervisors.   As the duties and powers of the personnel department increased during the 1930s to the 1950s, the supervisor's status as a manager was diluted. This was because the personnel department often dominated the hiring, rewarding, and promoting of employees within the organization. Even disciplinary measures primarily were directed by the personnel staff. As a result, many employees no longer looked to their line supervisor as their real ''boss.'' This situation demoralized many supervisors, who felt it was impossible for them to be effective leaders within their departments. They justifiably contended that they could not run their departments without having the right or influence to select, hire, discipline, and reward. Under these conditions it is understandable that many employees did not view their line supervisors as being managers with authority, even though the supervisors were responsible for departmental operations. Eventually this situation led to a confused state of affairs in many organizations. Top management began to realize that a clearer demarcation between the personnel department's functions in a staff capacity and the supervisor's position as a departmental manager was necessary.

HUMAN RESOURCES DEPARTMENTS: EVOLVING AND CURRENT ROLES

Balancing the Roles and Authority

Along with the gradual adoption of the name human resources department over the last several decades, most organizations have recognized and have tried to achieve a proper balance of influence and authority between line supervisors and human resources staff.

It is now well understood and essential that line supervisors and human resources staff must work together, because their activities are vital and interdependent. Further, their primary roles and areas of authority should not be permitted to shift substantially. The human resources department should primarily focus on advising and assisting line supervisors who request or need their help in certain areas. At the same time, line supervisors should take full advantage of the department's expert advice and assistance, while supervising their departments within the framework of the organization's personnel policies and procedures and any union contract that may exist. As a first step in this direction, supervisors should have a major role in defining employee qualifications and describing job positions for their own departments.

Assistance in Recruitment and Selection.   When supervisors have certain positions open in their departments, they normally will request the human resources department to recruit qualified applicants from available labor markets. The human resources department usually knows where to look in order to find qualified applicants. The recruitment tasks are performed by informing the community and by advertising, with care being taken to develop a favorable image of the organization as an employer. Often this may involve a combination of efforts, such as planned community relations efforts, advertising programs, and tapping sources of potential employees, such as high schools, training institutions, and colleges. To select from among job seekers, usually the human resources department will have applicants fill out an employment application form and conduct preliminary interviews to determine whether the applicants' qualifications match the requirements for positions available. The department also makes reference checks of the applicants' previous employment and background. For certain positions the department may administer one or more tests in order to determine whether applicants have the necessary skills and aptitudes. This may mean conducting statistical studies of tests that are used to determine whether they validly predict how an employee will perform on the job.[2] Eventually, applicants who do not have the required qualifications are screened out. Those candidates who do have the qualifications are referred to the supervisor of the department where the job is open.

Supervisors Interview and Decide.   After the human resources department has screened and selected qualified applicants for a job opening, the departmental supervisor normally is given an opportunity to interview each candidate before any decision is made. It is highly desirable that the supervisor

---

[2]For information on employment testing, the following sources are suggested: Dale S. Beach, *Personnel: The Management of People at Work* (5th ed.; New York: Macmillan Publishing Co. Inc., 1985), pp. 148–163; or Richard D. Arvey and Robert H. Faley, *Fairness in Selecting Employees* (2d ed.; Reading, Mass.: Addison-Wesley Publishing Company, 1988), pp. 121–212.

Fig 12–2. The human resources department makes the necessary reference checks of previous employment and past records of applicants.

should make—or at least have the most say in making—the final decision to hire any candidate(s) for jobs within his or her department. Of course, the supervisor must follow the same guidelines and policies used by the human resources department to ensure that any selection decision is nondiscriminatory. There may be occasions when the supervisor will have to compromise because of affirmative action or other programs that are mandated by com-

Fig 12–3. A supervisor may not have "complete" hiring authority.

pany directives. But, in general, the supervisor is the person who should make the decision to hire or not to hire. If the supervisor does not have the "final" hiring authority, his or her employees will tend to believe that it is the human resources department that actually controls the supervisor's employment decisions.

After the applicants are hired, the supervisor assigns them to their jobs, and it is the supervisor's responsibility to decide how to use their skills in order to get departmental work accomplished. Even though the human resources department may have provided new employees with a general orientation about the company, its benefits, and overall rules and policies, the supervisor is responsible to introduce them to requirements and details of the job, departmental rules, and the like. Similarly, general training programs may be taught by staff training specialists, but it is the supervisor who must provide instructions and training on the job. It is the supervisor's duty to follow up, check, and appraise each employee's performance. If necessary, it is the supervisor's duty to take disciplinary measures and perhaps even to initiate the discharge of those employees who do not meet performance standards.

Compliance with Equal Employment Opportunity and Other Laws. Probably the most pervasive influence that currently affects the staffing function is a mass of government laws and regulations. Human resources departments have assumed the primary obligation to make sure that their firms' employment policies and practices comply with federal, state, and local equal employment opportunity laws. These laws prohibit employment procedures that discriminate against applicants and employees on the basis of race, creed, sex, color, religion, or national origin. Nor can age be used as a criterion in employment decisions involving individuals who are beyond the age of 40 (except in several limited circumstances).

Under affirmative-action programs, some companies give hiring preferences to minority persons and women who have the qualifications or potential to fill available positions. Also, there are laws that require companies to have preferential hiring and affirmative action programs for handicapped individuals and veterans. Table 12–1 is a partial list of the major laws on equal employment opportunity and the agencies that enforce them.

Additionally, the Immigration Reform and Control Act of 1986 (IRCA) requires employers to make reasonable efforts to ascertain that anyone whom they hire is a citizen of the United States, or has a legal residency or permit if he or she is not a citizen.[3]

---

[3]The Immigration Reform and Control Act (IRCA) of 1986 (Public Law 99–603) places a major responsibility on virtually all employers to determine whether anyone that an employer hires is a citizen or has a valid immigration or work-permit status before being employed. Penalties and fines can be imposed on employers who do not meet the requirements of this law. Employers must certify each new employee's legal status within twenty-four hours of hiring that person,

Table 12–1. Laws and regulations affecting equal employment opportunity.

It is understandable why supervisors are confused by the laws, executive orders, regulations, and guidelines which they may have heard or read about. The following is a partial overview of the framework of laws, regulations, and enforcement agencies which govern staffing policies and decisions of an employer concerning equal employment opportunity.

Subject	Law	Enforcement Agency
Race	*Title VII of the Civil Rights Act of 1964	EEOC
Sex	*Title VII of the Civil Rights Act of 1964	EEOC
	Equal Pay Act of 1963	EEOC
Color	*Title VII of the Civil Rights Act of 1964	EEOC
Religion	*Title VII of the Civil Rights Act of 1964	EEOC
National origin	*Title VII of the Civil Rights Act of 1964	EEOC
Age (protection for those beyond 40 years old)	Age Discrimination in Employment Act of 1967, as amended in 1978 and 1986.	EEOC
Handicapped persons	**Rehabilitation Act of 1973	U.S. Department of Labor
Vietnam-Era veteran	The Vietnam-Era Veteran Readjustment Assistance Act of 1974	U.S. Department of Labor
Some of the above	State and local legislation	State and local commissions
All of the above as incorporated in affirmative-action programs	Various Executive Orders, principally E.O. 11246 and Revised Order No. 4, which regulate government contractors and subcontractors	Office of Federal Contract Compliance, U.S. Department of Labor

*As amended by the Equal Employment Opportunity Act of 1972 and the Pregnancy Discrimination Act of 1978. EEOC stands for Equal Employment Opportunity Commission.

**At the time of writing of this text, legislation was pending in the U.S. Congress which would further extend legal requirements for employment of the handicapped.

using such items as birth certificates, drivers' licenses, work permits, passports, and so forth, to make a good-faith effort to comply. Employers must complete and file a special form that requires the employer to indicate that the employer has examined documents provided by the employee and that such documents appear to be genuine. See William B. Werther, Jr., and Keith Davis, *Human Resources and Personnel Management* (3rd ed.; New York: McGraw-Hill Book Company, 1989), pp. 66–67 and p. 181.

A full discussion of equal employment opportunity and other employment laws is beyond the scope of this book.[4] Our concern is to focus primarily on how supervisors are affected by legal considerations in performing their managerial staffing function. This concern is discussed further in Chapter 13; then in Chapter 17 we discuss how supervisors need to give special consideration to "protected" categories of people who are covered by equal employment opportunity laws.

Human Resources Staff Advice and Supervisory Decisions

Because of many complexities and employee problems that continually arise, supervisors often will consult with human resources department staff for assistance, information, and advice. At times, without even realizing it, supervisors may unnecessarily concede much of their authority and responsibility to that department.

The following example illustrates how blurred the distinction can become between a staff department's function of providing advice and the supervisor's decision-making responsibility. An office supervisor wants to recommend a salary increase for a word processor and inquires of the staff salary administrator in the human resources department about the current "going rate" for word processors. If the salary administrator states that the average current market rate in the community for experienced word processors is $1,600 per month, he or she is simply providing information without injecting an opinion. However, if the salary administrator states that raising the word processor's salary to the rate of $1,600 per month might be inequitable and cause problems among other experienced employees who are making less than that amount, the salary administrator is providing information *and* advice. By selecting facts and phrasing comments carefully, the salary administrator may sway the supervisor's decision one way or the other. For example, the administrator may even suggest raising the word processor's monthly salary by a certain amount and making salary adjustments for other positions. Thus without even being consciously aware of it, the supervisor may allow information to become advice and advice to become a decision. This happens not because the staff person desires to reduce the supervisor's authority, but because the supervisor has willingly encouraged this type of staff influence.

Of course, in this example, it probably would be quite appropriate for the supervisor to accept the salary administrator's advice. Whenever the human resources staff has the expertise and knowledge that are directly relevant to a

---

[4]For a comprehensive discussion on equal employment opportunity compliance, see David P. Twomey, *A Concise Guide to Employment Law* (Cincinnati: South-Western Publishing Company, 1986).

decision, supervisors are well advised to accept and follow such advice and recommendations.

Maintaining Supervisory Accountability.   Some supervisors readily welcome the human resources staff's willingness to "make" certain decisions for them, so that they will not have to solve difficult employee problems in their own departments. These supervisors reason that their own departmental tasks are more important than dealing with issues that the human resources staff can handle just as well or better than the supervisors. Other supervisors may accept the staff's decision because if the decision later proves to be wrong or undesirable, they can say, "It wasn't my choice; human resources made the decision—not me!" For these supervisors it is a pleasant relief to rely on the staff's advice and consider it a decision. However, in so doing, these supervisors "pass the buck" to the human resources department in the hope of avoiding their own accountability for the outcome of the decision.

Occasionally supervisors may find it convenient to "pass the buck" to staff, but such an approach eventually can backfire. For example, many supervisors have said that they would like to give their employees a wage increase or a certain benefit, but that "they" (the human resources department) will not let them do so. This statement may be expedient for the moment, but it can lead to an erosion of a supervisor's respect and authority. Similarly, a supervisor may see a need to discipline an employee, but accepts the advice of the director of human resources not to do so. If in the future this employee's performance leads to additional difficulties for the supervisor, he or she may feel inclined to shrug off the responsibility by proclaiming that, "I wanted to fire the employee long ago, but the director of human resources told me not to do so." Again, such disclaiming of responsibility can only foster undesirable reactions both within and beyond the supervisor's department.

Although it is understandable why some supervisors are reluctant to reject a staff person's advice, they should recognize that a staff person may see only a part of the entire picture. The director of human resources is not responsible for the performance of a supervisor's department. Usually there are many unique factors that are better known and better understood by each departmental supervisor than by anyone else.

If a supervisor permits the human resources department staff to "make" major employee-related supervisory decisions, the supervisor's relationship with his or her employees sooner or later will be weakened. Employees will believe that it is human resources, not the supervisor, that has the real power to control or influence their jobs. By words and actions, supervisors must show clearly that they are responsible for departmental staffing decisions and that they are accountable for such decisions. Further, even though they follow the human resources staff's advice, they as supervisors remain accountable for the outcomes of their departmental decisions and actions. Supervisors must always demonstrate that they are managers who are in charge of their departments.

SUPERVISORY STAFFING CONSIDERATIONS

The managerial staffing function is an ongoing process for the supervisor; it is not something that is done only when a department is first established. It is more realistic to think of staffing in the typical situation where a supervisor is placed in charge of an existing department. Although a nucleus of employees exists, employee changes take place due to separations from the work force, changes in operations, growth, or other reasons. Since supervisors are dependent on employees for results, supervisors must make certain that there are sufficient well-trained employees available to fill various positions.

Determining the Need for Employees

A continuous aspect of the supervisory staffing function is that of assessing and determining the need for employees in the department, both number and kind. If a supervisor has designed the structure of the department, there should be an organization chart or manual in which functions and jobs are depicted in their formal relationships. If the supervisor takes over an existing department, he or she should become thoroughly familiar with existing departmental jobs and functions, and consult the organization chart or manual if one is available. For example, the supervisor of a maintenance department may find that there are groups of painters, electricians, carpenters, and other employees with different skills. The supervisor should study each of these skills to determine how many positions there are or should be, and in what relation they should be working together. The supervisor may have to compromise by adjusting a preferred arrangement to existing realities, or by combining several positions into one if there is not enough work for one employee to perform a single function. By carefully studying the organization of the department, the supervisor can reasonably determine how many and what employee skills are needed to accomplish the various work assignments.

Developing Job Descriptions

A subsequent or companion step is to match the jobs available with individuals. This usually is done with the aid of **job descriptions,** which indicate the duties and responsibilities involved in each job. A supervisor may find existing job descriptions available; if they are not available for existing jobs, they can be developed with the assistance of higher management or human resources staff. Similarly, if a new job is created, the supervisor should decide on the

Table 12-2.   How to develop housekeeping job descriptions.

The following steps are suggested for the preparation of housekeeping job descriptions:

Step 1. Prepare a questionnaire to be sent to housekeeping employees and their supervisors, asking them to list what they feel are the major functions and subfunctions that must be performed to do their job effectively.

Step 2. Have several higher-level managers who are interested in housekeeping list what functions they feel should and should not be performed by housekeepers.

Step 3. Find out from others in the organization what they believe should be and should not be the functions of a housekeeper.

Step 4. Tabulate the results of each of the three sources given above.

Step 5. Reconcile the differences of the above three viewpoints with the objectives of your organization, and prepare a detailed list of activities to be performed.

Step 6. Classify activities as major and minor activities.

Step 7. Determine what each housekeeper needs to know what qualifications are necessary to perform designated activities, and specifically why each activity is to be performed.

Step 8. Submit the results of Steps 5 to 7 to a committee of housekeepers and supervisors for their discussion and recommendations. At this point you may find that you have been asking employees to do more than could possibly be accomplished reasonably. Revise and finalize the job description and job specification as appropriate.

Step 9. Periodically — at least annually — review and revise the job description, following the eight steps listed above, when you feel that changes in products, equipment, the economic climate, or service demands necessitate a change in the job to be performed.

*This approach was developed in a hospital setting to be performed primarily by the personnel director in cooperation with the director of housekeeping services and supervisors in the housekeeping departments.

duties and responsibilities of the job, and eventually develop an appropriate job description.

The supervisor may find it helpful to ask departmental employees to write down the tasks and assignments that they perform during a given time period, say, a day or a week. This will provide the supervisor with considerable information from which to develop the content of a job description. Although the final form of the job description may be written by a staff person, it is the supervisor's responsibility to determine what actually goes into it.

Table 12-2 is a step-by-step approach to developing job descriptions for a housekeeping services division, which was developed by an assistant administrator and the personnel director of a hospital. The steps suggested would be adaptable to many other types of jobs. Table 12-2 also combines the development of a job description with that of a job specification.[5]

It is advisable for a supervisor periodically (at least annually) to compare

---

[5]See Figure 10-4 for a sample job description and job specification for a custodian.

each job description with what each employee does. As job descriptions become outdated, they may no longer fit the actual contents of the jobs and should be corrected. The supervisor may find that some of the duties assigned to a job no longer belong to it, have been deleted, or should be assigned elsewhere.

Developing Job Specifications

When the content of each job has been determined, or reevaluated, a supervisor next should identify the knowledge and skills that are required of employees who are to perform each job category. A written statement of required knowledge, skills, and attributes is referred to as a **job specification**.[6]

For most jobs, there are certain things an employee should know in order to perform a job adequately. For example, it may be necessary for a drafter to be able to read blueprints and be familiar with college-level algebra. A job specification for this position that simply says that "a knowledge of mathematics is required" would be poorly stated. The word mathematics could imply only an ability to handle basic arithmetic, which would be much less than is expected. The more clearly the required job knowledge is described, the easier it will be to find the persons who possess it.

For other jobs, individuals must possess certain skills in addition to previous education or job knowledge. For example, job specifications for administrative assistants or word processors usually indicate the typing speeds required. Here, too, the supervisor is usually in the best position to describe what skills are wanted, but the supervisor should avoid the temptation to ask for higher skill levels than are necessary. One way to avoid requiring unnecessarily high knowledge and job skills is to periodically check the job specification with the qualifications of employees who are doing the same or similar kinds of work. For example, investigation may reveal that a high school education is not essential for a certain job. Or the supervisor may discover that it is not realistic (or legal) to employ only young men to perform heavy-duty warehouse work, when an older man or a woman in good physical condition can do this work. As mentioned previously, equal employment opportunity laws and rulings require that job specifications be job related and must not discriminate against certain categories of people. A supervisor who does not understand the ramifications of nondiscriminatory employment policies should consult the human resources department for clarification and guidance. In fact, many human resources departments have assumed much of the responsibility for writing job specifications because of concerns about compliance with such laws and regulations.

---

[6]The term "job specification" is not universally utilized. Many firms prefer to use the term *job qualifications,* or some other similar designation.

Supervisors should realize that if job requirements are set unrealistically high, the task of finding people to meet these specifications becomes more difficult and costly. Further, if requirements are set too high and if people are hired who have abilities much higher than a job demands, it is likely that these employees will prove to be troublesome, because they become bored when their capacities are quite underutilized. By the same token, it is just as ill-advised to ask for less than is necessary. An employee without sufficient knowledge or skill will probably not be satisfactory. Most of these difficulties can be minimized if the supervisor diligently analyzes each job's content and then realistically and clearly specifies the knowledge and skills required.

Job descriptions and job specifications usually are maintained and monitored by the human resources staff as well as by the supervisor. Thus when there is a need to fill a departmental job, all the supervisor should have to do is to notify the human resources department concerning the job that is open. The human resources department will recruit suitable applicants to fill the position, and will screen out those applicants who do not have the knowledge, skills, or other requirements. Those applicants who best meet all of the requirements will be referred to the supervisor for an interview and the final decision as to acceptance or rejection.

Determining How Many to Hire

Supervisors are not frequently confronted with a situation in which large numbers of employees for the department have to be hired at the same time. This situation occurs when a new department is created or when a major expansion takes place. The more usual pattern involves the hiring of one or several employees as the need arises. Of course, some supervisors constantly request additional employees, because they feel pressured to get their work done on time. In many cases, however, a supervisor's problems are not solved by getting more help. As a matter of fact, the situation may become worse; instead of problems being reduced, new problems are encountered due to inefficiencies that accompany overstaffing.

Normally a supervisor will need to hire a replacement when a regular employee leaves the enterprise by resignation, dismissal, retirement, or for some other reason. There is little question then that the job must be filled. However, if major changes in the technological nature of the position have taken place or are anticipated, a replacement may not be needed.

There are other situations in which additional employees have to be hired. For example, if new functions are to be added to the department and no one in the department possesses the required job knowledge and skills, it may be necessary to go into the labor market and recruit new employees. Sometimes a supervisor will ask for additional help, because the work load has increased substantially and the department is under extreme pressure. Before requesting additional help, however, the supervisor should make certain that the employees currently in the department are being utilized fully and that any additional help is absolutely necessary and within the budget.

SUMMARY

The staffing function of management includes hiring, training, evaluating, developing, and compensating employees. In fulfilling departmental responsibilities for staffing, the supervisor can be aided substantially by services of the human resources department. Usually, the human resources department serves the organization in a staff capacity, and its purpose is to counsel, advise, and service line departments. Although the role and scope of the human resources department have changed and grown over the years, it generally is recognized that there must be a balance of influence and authority between line supervisors and human resources staff in staffing policies and decisions. The pervasive presence of equal employment opportunity laws and regulations has resulted in the human resources department assuming much of the responsibility to ensure that an organization's employment policies and practices comply with these laws.

Sometimes the human resources department may be willing to take primary responsibility for hiring, policy interpretation, writing job descriptions, and the like. Supervisors should not release these staffing areas totally to human resources, although at times it might seem expedient to do so. A supervisor remains accountable for decisions, even when the advice of human resources staff has been relied on.

Job descriptions and job specifications, in conjunction with other organizational tools, assist the supervisor to ascertain the numbers and types of employees necessary to fill various jobs. In ongoing staffing activities, the supervisor should utilize the services of the human resources department when appropriate, especially in decisions involving the selection of employees where laws and policies must be followed.

QUESTIONS FOR DISCUSSION

1. Why should staffing be considered as a major managerial function of supervision? Many supervisors believe that staffing primarily is the responsibility of the human resources department. Are there valid reasons for their feelings in this regard?

2. Discuss how personnel departments evolved historically in American business. Discuss how these historic patterns have left some problems in present-day line-staff relationships between supervisors and the human resources department.

3. What are some of the major activities of the human resources department that can assist the line supervisor in the staffing function? What should be the primary responsibility of human resources staff and of line supervisors for various employment and other staffing activities? Is there a clear dividing line of responsibility? Discuss.

4. Define some of the major laws and regulations that govern equal employment opportunity. Why have many companies and organizations assigned to the hu-

man resources department the primary responsibility for making sure that their employment policies and practices are in compliance?

5. How have equal employment opportunity laws and affirmative-action programs made it more complicated for supervisors in sharing responsibility with the human resources department for the hiring of employees? Discuss.

6. Why should line supervisors neither automatically accept the advice of a human resources staff person nor permit this department to make most staffing decisions for them?

7. What is meant by a job description and a job specification? How are they interrelated and useful in staffing decisions?

8. Outline some of the steps a supervisor might take in order to develop departmental job descriptions and job specifications.

9. What criteria should a supervisor examine before requesting more employees? Discuss.

CHAPTER 13

Selection, Orientation, Training, and Development

CHAPTER OBJECTIVES

1. To discuss directive and nondirective interviewing, with emphasis on their application in the employee selection interview.
2. To outline and discuss essential elements of employee selection interviewing at the supervisory level.
3. To identify major equal employment opportunity concerns and guidelines that must be observed in the employee selection process.
4. To suggest a number of factors that supervisors should consider in appraising job applicants and in reaching a selection decision.
5. To emphasize the supervisor's role in initial job orientation and continued training and development of employees.
6. To discuss the importance of training and career development for supervisors themselves.

After the preliminary screening of job applicants by the human resources department, it usually is the supervisor's responsibility to meet the suitable applicants, interview them, and select those who are best qualified for the jobs that are vacant. This is a critical decision point for both applicants and the supervisor. It requires the supervisor to match each applicant's experience and abilities with the demands of the job, the strain of working conditions, and the rewards it offers. It further requires that the selection decision be based on valid employment considerations and that it not violate laws or regulations that cover employment decisions.

EMPLOYEE SELECTION

For supervisors, the most frequently used selection device—and often the most important part of the selection process—is the **employee selection interview.**[1] It is difficult to make an accurate appraisal of someone's strengths and potential during and after a brief interview. If there are several applicants for a position, the supervisor must ascertain which individual is most qualified and acceptable among those referred to him or her for the interview. This means trying to determine which individual is most likely to best perform on the job and also to stay with the company in the long run.

Interviewing is much more than a technique; it is an art that can and must be learned by every supervisor. Although our focus in this chapter will be on the employee selection interview, over time every supervisor will conduct or be involved in other types of interviews that occur during the normal course of events. Among these are: appraisal and counseling interviews; interviews regarding complaints and grievances; interviews regarding disciplinary measures or discharge; and exit interviews when employees voluntarily quit. The basic approaches and techniques, however, are generally common to all interviewing situations.

Basic Approaches to Interviewing

In general, there are two basic interviewing approaches for any type of interview: *directive* and *nondirective*. These approaches are classified primarily according to the amount of structure imposed on the interview by the interviewer.

---

[1] This interview is also known as the preemployment interview, the preliminary employment interview, and by other similar designations. For a general discussion of interviewing techniques, see Auren Uris, *88 Mistakes Interviewers Make—and How to Avoid Them* (New York: AMACOM, 1988).

Fig 13–1. If there are several applicants for a position, the supervisor must ascertain which individual is most acceptable.

Directive Interview. In a **directive interview** the interviewer guides the course of the discussion with a predetermined outline and objectives in mind. This approach is sometimes called a **patterned** or **structured interview.** The development and use of an outline helps the interviewer to ask specific questions to cover each planned topic on which information is wanted. It also allows the interviewer to question and expand on related areas. For example, if a supervisor asks about the applicant's previous work experience, the applicant next may be asked to explain what he or she liked and did not like about previous jobs. The supervisor guides and controls the interview but does not make it a rigid, impersonal experience.

Nondirective Interview. The purpose or strategy of a **nondirective interview** is to encourage interviewees to talk freely and in depth, stimulating the discussion by asking broad, open-ended questions. This approach is most frequently used in problem-solving or counseling interviews and in interviews concerning complaints and grievances. When troubled employees are allowed to express their feelings openly and fully, this type of interview has a certain therapeutic value. Talking about a problem gives an employee a chance to gain insight into it. The interviewer hopes that the employee himself or herself will arrive at some kind of answer or course of action that might solve the problem. An essential element of a nondirective interview is that the employee is permitted to talk through the situation without being criticized or interrupted by the supervisor.

Nondirective interviews generally are more difficult and time consuming to conduct than are directive interviews. They require that interviewers give concentrated and continuous attention to what is being said. Interviewers must exert self-control and hide their own ideas and emotions during nondirective interviews. This means to avoid expressing approval or disapproval even though the interviewee may request it.

Blending Directive and Nondirective Approaches.   Ultimately, the purpose of any interview is to promote mutual understanding. Interviewing is an experience in human relations that should bring the interviewer and interviewee to understand each other better through open and full communication.

In an employee selection interview, the directive approach most often is used, since a supervisor finds it convenient to obtain information by asking a job applicant direct questions. However, at times supervisors should strive to blend both directive and nondirective techniques in order to obtain additional information that might be helpful in reaching a decision. By asking a number of open-ended questions in conjunction with directive questions, the supervisor may gain deeper insights that could make the difference in choosing which applicant to hire. For example, some open-ended questions are: "How do you feel about working overtime?" or "Have you any work-shift preferences in relation to your personal situation?" or "Tell me about your longer term goals if you are hired for this job." Such questions encourage the applicant to reveal motives, attitudes, or facts that might not or cannot be ascertained from other sources.

Preparation for an Employee Selection Interview

Since the purpose of an employee selection interview is to collect information and arrive at a decision concerning a job applicant, careful preparation on the part of the interviewing supervisor is required. The supervisor must know what information is needed from the applicant, how to get this information, and how to interpret the information that is obtained.

As stated earlier, the directive interview is the most common approach used in selecting employees. Although most supervisors are left to devise their own questions, there are also many organizations that have forms and procedures which they provide for the guidance of supervisors in selection interviewing. For example, some companies require supervisors to fill out a detailed form on all applicants who are interviewed. Others use a standard patterned interview form which more or less limits a supervisor to asking only those questions that are included on the form. These interview forms sometimes are used in order to prevent supervisors from asking questions that might be considered discriminatory and thus in violation of government laws and regulations. Therefore, an initial consideration in preparing for an employee selection interview is for the supervisor to know what can and should not be asked of job applicants during the interview.

Influence of Equal Employment Opportunity Laws. Prior to the 1960s, a relatively loose and unplanned approach to employee selection interviews was used in many organizations. However, the passage of federal and other laws on equal employment opportunity has placed restrictions on the questions that employers ask job applicants.

The most overriding principle to follow in employee selection interviews is to ask job-related questions. Questions about topics not related to the person's ability to perform the job for which he or she has applied should be avoided. For example, asking an applicant for a welding job about previous welding job experience would be directly job-related. However, asking this applicant about owning or renting a home is of questionable purpose. Employee selection procedures also must ensure that "legally protected groups" such as minorities and women are treated fairly.[2] Information that would have an adverse effect, or negative impact, on protected groups can be used only if it is directly job-related. For example, the question "Who cares for your children?" is potentially discriminatory, because traditionally it has adversely affected women more than men.

Table 13–1 contains a list of some of the most common areas of legal and potentially legal inquiry. The guidelines in Table 13–1 apply to all phases and criteria used in the selection process. Application forms, tests, interviews, reference checks, and physical examinations must all be nondiscriminatory and deal essentially with job-related requirements.

To determine whether a selection criterion is appropriate and complies with the law, one consultant firm has suggested the OUCH test.[3] OUCH is a four-letter acronym that represents the following:

O—Objective
U—Uniform in Application
C—Consistent in Effect
H—Has Job Relatedness

A selection criterion is *objective* if it systematically measures an attribute without being distorted by personal feelings. Examples of objective criteria include typing-test scores, number of years of education, degrees, length of service in previous positions, etc. On the other hand, examples of subjective

---

[2]In Chapter 17, special situations concerning "legally protected" categories of persons are further identified and discussed.

[3]This concept was part of a training program developed by Jagerson Associates, Inc., for the Life Office Management Association.

Table 13-1. Areas of illegal or potentially illegal inquiry in application forms and employment interviews applicable at the time of publication of this text.

Subject of Inquiry	Illegal or Potentially Illegal Questions
Applicant's name	1. Maiden name 2. Original name (if legally changed)
Civil and family status	1. Is applicant single, married, divorced, etc. 2. Number and ages of applicant's children 3. Child-care arrangements 4. Is applicant pregnant or does she contemplate pregnancy
Address	Foreign addresses which would indicate applicant's national origin
Age	*Before hiring,* any requests for birth certificate, baptismal certificate, or statement of age
Birthplace (national origin)	1. Birthplace of applicant 2. Birthplace of applicant's spouse, if any, and parents 3. Lineage, ancestry, nationality
Race or color	Any question that would indicate applicant's race or color
Citizenship*	1. Country of citizenship if not U.S. 2. Does applicant intend to become a U.S. citizen 3. Citizenship of spouse, if any, and of parents
Photographs	Any request for applicant's photograph
Religion	1. Religious denomination or customs 2. Pastor's recommendation or reference 3. Identification of employee's religious affiliation may not be made
Arrests and convictions	Numbers and kinds of arrests experienced
Education	1. Nationality, race, or religious affiliation of schools attended 2. Mother tongue, or how foreign language skills were acquired
Organizations	Is applicant a member of any association other than unions and/or professional or trade organizations
Military experience	1. Type of discharge from the U.S. Armed Forces 2. Did applicant have military experience with governments other than the U.S.
Relatives	Names and/or addresses of any relatives

*However, the Immigration Reform and Control Act of 1986 requires that employers determine that anyone whom they hire is a U.S. citizen or has a legal residency status.

criteria include a supervisor's general impression about a person's interest in a job, or feelings that a person is "sharp."

A selection criterion is *uniform in application* if it is consistently applied to all job candidates. Asking different interview questions of male and female applicants would not be uniform in application.

A selection criterion is *consistent in effect* if it has the same proportional impact on protected groups as it does on others. For example, criteria like possessing a high school diploma or living in a certain area of town may be objective and uniformly applied to all job candidates, but they could screen out proportionately more members of minority groups. When a selection criterion is not consistent in effect, the burden of proof is on the employer to demonstrate that it is job-related.

A selection criterion *has job relatedness* if it can be demonstrated that it is necessary in performing the job. For example, in most cases it would be extremely difficult to prove that a selection criterion like marital status is job-related. Job-related criteria should stress skills required to perform the job.

Supervisors may not always understand the reasons for some of the requirements and restrictions imposed on them by the equal employment opportunity policies of their organizations. Therefore, they should not hesitate to consult with specialists in the human resources department for explanations and guidance in this regard.

Reviewing the Applicant's Background.   Before interviewing a job applicant, the supervisor should review all available background information that has been gathered by the human resources (or employment) office. By studying whatever is available, the supervisor can develop in advance a mental impression of the general qualifications of the job applicant. The **application form,** such as that shown in Figure 13–2, will supply data and facts concerning the applicant's schooling, experience, and other items that may be relevant. Today, of course, the available information from application forms is somewhat more limited than was true in the past, because of the legal concerns discussed earlier.

When studying the completed application form, the supervisor should always keep in mind the job for which the applicant will be interviewed. If further questions are suggested after studying the completed application form, the supervisor should write them down so that they will not be forgotten. For example, if an applicant for an engineering position shows a gap of a year in employment history, the supervisor should plan to ask the applicant about this gap and why it occurred.

A supervisor should also review the results of any employment tests that may have been taken by the applicants. Human resources departments often administer skill and aptitude tests as part of their normal procedures to screen out applicants who may be unqualified for certain types of jobs. The human resources department must be able to document that these tests are valid, job-

Fig 13–2.
An application
form (front)

ATLAS CORPORATION

APPLICATION for EMPLOYMENT

NAME: _____   DATE: _____

ADDRESS: _____   PHONE: _____

_____   S.S. #: _____

DESIRED POSITION: _____   SALARY REQUIREMENT: _____

REFERRED BY: _____   DATE AVAILABLE: _____

ARE YOU ELIGIBLE TO WORK IN THE UNITED STATES? _____ (Yes/No) (If hired, you will be required to provide employment eligibility verification.)

ARE YOU AVAILABLE TO WORK OVERTIME WHEN NECESSARY?:   Weekdays: _____ (Yes/No) Weekends: _____ (Yes/No)

WERE YOU PREVIOUSLY EMPLOYED BY ATLAS?: _____   WHEN/POSITION: _____

PRESENT EMPLOYER: _____   PHONE: _____

ADDRESS: _____   PRESENT SALARY: _____

_____   START DATE: _____

TITLE/RESPONSIBILITIES: _____

MAY WE CONTACT YOUR PRESENT EMPLOYER?: _____ (Yes/No)   SUPERVISOR: _____

EDUCATION	NAME AND LOCATION OF SCHOOL / COLLEGE	NO. YEARS COMPLETED	GRADUATED (Yes/No)	MAJOR STUDIES / DEGREE
HIGH SCHOOL				
COLLEGE				
OTHER				

HONORS: _____

ACTIVITIES: _____

SKILLS: Typing: _____ wpm   Shorthand: _____ wpm   Dictating Machine: _____ (Yes/No)

Word Processor:(Model) _____   Other Skills: _____

_____

Equal Opportunity Employer

Fig 13–2.
An application
form (back)

PAST EMPLOYMENT: (List your previous employers, the most recent first. Exclude present employer as referenced on other side.)				
NAME OF EMPLOYER ADDRESS PHONE NO. SUPERVISOR	EMPLOYMENT DATES		TITLE/DESCRIPTION OF MAJOR RESPONSIBILITIES	REASON FOR LEAVING
	FROM MO/YR	TO MO/YR		
Former Employer: _____ Address: _____ Phone: _____ Supervisor: _____ _____		Ending Salary $ _____		
Former Employer: _____ Address: _____ Phone: _____ Supervisor: _____ _____		Ending Salary $ _____		
Former Employer: _____ Address: _____ Phone: _____ Supervisor: _____ _____		Ending Salary $ _____		

I hereby certify that the facts set forth in the above Application for Employment are true and correct. I understand that, if employed, false statements on this Application shall be considered sufficient cause for dismissal. I certify that I am eligible to work in the United States and if employed, I will provide documentation. Unless otherwise indicated above, you are hereby authorized to contact my former employers for information concerning my employment, character, ability, and experience.

DATE: _____   SIGNATURE: _____

related, and nondiscriminatory. This typically involves studies and statistical analyses by staff specialists—procedures that normally are beyond the scope of a supervisor's concern. Those applicants whose test scores and other credentials appear to be acceptable are referred to the departmental supervisor for further interviewing. It is essential, however, for a supervisor to understand what a test score represents and how meaningful it is in predicting an applicant's job performance. By consulting human resources department staff, a supervisor should become more familiar with the tests that are used and learn to interpret the meaning of test scores.

An additional source that may be available is **reference information.** For the most part, information obtained from personal sources such as friends or character references will be quite positively slanted, because applicants tend to list only persons who will give them good references. Information from previous employers usually is more useful and relevant. However, because of emerging personal privacy regulations and potential damage claims, an employment background investigation is best conducted by staff department specialists. If possible, job references should be obtained in writing, should deal with job-related areas, and should be gathered with the knowledge and permission of the applicants. After getting and reviewing all available background information, the supervisor should be able to identify those areas in which little or no information is available and those areas that require expansion or clarification.

Preparing Key Questions. As part of preparation for the interview, the supervisor should develop a list of questions, which may include both directive and nondirective components. Preferably, the supervisor should develop a list of key questions—perhaps six to ten—that are vital to the selection decision and are job-related. It is important that all applicants be asked the same core set of key questions, so that responses can be compared and evaluated. For example, the supervisor may want technical information about an applicant's previous work experience, why the applicant left a previous employer, and whether the applicant can work alternative shift schedules and overtime without difficulty. By planning to ask such questions in advance, the supervisor can devote more attention to listening to and observing the applicant, instead of having to think about what else should be asked. A thoroughly prepared plan for the employment interview is well worth the time spent on it.

Conducive Physical Setting. Privacy and some degree of comfort are requirements for a good interview setting. If a private room to conduct an interview is not available, then the supervisor should at least create an atmosphere of semiprivacy by speaking to an applicant in a place where other employees are not within hearing distance. This much privacy, at the very least, is a necessity.

Conducting the Employee Selection Interview[4]

The employee selection interview is not just a one-way questioning process, since the applicant also will want to know more about the company and the potential job. The interview should enable the job seeker to learn enough to help decide whether he or she should accept the position if it is offered. The supervisor must conduct the interview professionally by opening the interview effectively, explaining the job requirements, and using good questioning and note-taking techniques.

Opening the Interview.   The experience of applying for a job often is one of stress and tension for an applicant. It is to the supervisor's advantage to relieve this tension.

Some supervisors try to create a feeling of informality by starting the interview with social conversation about the weather, the heavy city traffic, the World Series, or some other topic of broad interest. The supervisor may offer a cup of coffee or make some social gesture that appears appropriate. Such an informal opening can be helpful in reducing an applicant's tensions or fears. However, if this approach is used, it should be brief; then the discussion should move quickly to job-related matters.

The supervisor should avoid excessive informal conversation, because studies of employee selection interviews have revealed that frequently an interviewer makes a favorable or unfavorable decision after the first five minutes of the interview. If the first ten minutes are spent discussing items not related to the job, then the supervisor may be making a selection decision based primarily on irrelevant information.

Many supervisors begin the employee selection interview with a "door opener." This is a question that is nonthreatening and is easily answered by the applicant, but it also contains job-related information that the supervisor might need. An example of a common "door opener" is: "How did you learn about this job opening?"

Explaining the Job.   During the interview, the supervisor should discuss details of the job, working conditions, wages, benefits, and other factors that are relevant. In so doing, the supervisor should describe the situation realistically. Because of eagerness to make a job look as attractive as possible, the supervisor may be tempted to describe conditions in better terms than they actually are. For example, a supervisor could "oversell" a job by telling the applicant in glowing terms about what really is available only for exceptional

---

[4]For an expanded discussion of the employee selection interview, see Gary Dessler, *Personnel Management* (4th ed.; Englewood Cliffs, N.J.: Prentice-Hall, Inc., 1988), pp. 204–225.

employees. If the applicant is hired and turns out to be an average worker, this could lead to disappointment and frustration.

Effective Questioning. Even though the supervisor will have some knowledge of the applicant's background from the completed application form and from information that the applicant volunteers, the need still exists to determine the applicant's specific qualifications and "fit" for the job opening. Questions that ask the applicant to repeat the same information already on the application form should be avoided. Instead, questions should be rephrased to probe for additional details. For example, the question "What was your last job?" is likely to be answered on the application form. This question could be expanded as follows: "As a programmer at Acme Company, with what type of computer system did you work?"

Some questions that may not appear to be directly job-related nevertheless may be appropriate. For example, it may be important to know what an individual considers to be an acceptable income level. Salary limits of a position for which an applicant is interested may make it impossible for that person to meet existing financial obligations. This could force the individual to seek an additional part-time job to supplement income, thus taking away some energy from the primary job. Or in order to meet immediate financial needs, the applicant might accept a low-paying position where he or she would be unhappy and continue to look for a higher paying position with another firm. Problems of this nature, although not directly connected with job requirements, are relevant to the work situation and may be part of a selection decision.

A supervisor must use judgment and tact when questioning applicants. The supervisor should avoid "trick" or "leading" questions such as, "Do you daydream frequently?" or "Do you have difficulty getting along with other people?" Questions such as these are sometimes used by interviewers in order to see how an applicant responds to difficult personal questions. However, these questions may antagonize the applicant. By no means should the supervisor out of curiosity pry into an applicant's personal affairs which are irrelevant or removed from the work situation.

Taking Notes. In their efforts to make better selection decisions, many supervisors take notes during or immediately after the interview. Having written information is especially important if a supervisor interviews a number of applicants. For example, trying to remember what each of five applicants said during their interviews, and exactly who said what, is virtually impossible.

To take notes effectively, the supervisor should avoid writing while an applicant is answering a question. Instead, the supervisor should jot down brief summaries of responses after the applicant has finished talking. This is more courteous and useful. Although a supervisor does not have to take notes on everything said in the interview, key facts that might aid in choosing one applicant over the others should be noted.

Avoiding Pitfalls in Selection Interviewing and Evaluation

The chief problem in employee selection usually lies in interpreting the applicant's background, personal history, and other pertinent information. As normal human beings, supervisors are unable to eliminate their personal preferences and prejudices, but supervisors should face up to their own personal biases and make efforts to avoid or control them.

Supervisors should particularly avoid making "snap" judgments during interviews with job applicants. Although it is difficult not to form an early impression, a supervisor should complete an interview before making any decision and should strive to avoid the numerous pitfalls that can occur both during or after an interview.

Halo Effect.   One of the most common pitfalls is known as the halo effect. This means basing one's overall impression of an individual on only a part of the total information and using this limited impression as a primary influence in rating all the other factors. This may work either favorably or unfavorably,[5] but in either event it is improper. For example, a supervisor may judge a male applicant with a full beard on the basis of a general dislike for bearded men, rather than on what the applicant has to say. Or the supervisor may base an overall evaluation of an applicant on a single factor—the person's ability to communicate fluently. Just because an applicant is articulate does not mean that all other qualifications are excellent. A glance at current employees in the department should remind the supervisor that some very competent employees have comparatively limited verbal skills.

Overgeneralization.   Another common pitfall is overgeneralization. A supervisor should not assume that when an applicant responds in a certain manner during an interview, the individual will behave correspondingly the same way in all other situations. For example, there may be a special reason why the applicant answers a question in a rather evasive manner. It would be wrong to conclude from evasiveness in answering one question that the applicant is underhanded and not trustworthy. Or an applicant may be dressed in rather old or worn clothing and may not present a neat appearance. A supervisor should not generalize from this that the applicant will be sloppy and disinterested in good work habits and work performance. Unfortunately many supervisors are apt to generalize too quickly.

---

[5]When it occurs in an unfavorable direction, this is sometimes called the "horns effect." Thus selective biasing in evaluating people has been collectively referred to as "the halo and the horns dilemma."

Comparison with Current Employees. Sometimes a supervisor may judge an applicant by comparison with others who currently are working in the department. The supervisor may feel that any applicant who is considerably different from most current employees is undesirable. This kind of thinking can be detrimental, since it tends to breed uniformity and conformity; carried to the extreme, it could contribute to mediocrity. This should not be interpreted to mean that the supervisor should deliberately look for "oddballs," who obviously would not fit into the department. But just because an individual does not exactly fit into the same pattern or mold of other employees is no reason to conclude that the person would not make a suitable or excellent employee.

Excessive Qualifications.   In an eagerness to get the best talent available, a supervisor may look for qualifications that far exceed the requirements of the job. Although an applicant should be qualified, there is no need to expect qualifications far in excess of actual job requirements. In fact, overqualified applicants may make poor employees, because they often become frustrated in a job that is not sufficiently challenging to them. They also may spread dissatisfaction among co-workers, either by visibly showing unhappiness in the work situation or by demonstrating a superior attitude.

Closing the Interview

At the conclusion of the employee selection interview, the supervisor likely will have a choice among several alternatives—ranging from hiring the applicant,

Fig 13–3.
An overqualified applicant usually makes a poor employee.

deferring the decision to hire until later, or rejecting the applicant. Obviously most applicants are eager to know which of these actions a supervisor will take.

What a supervisor decides will be guided by the policies and procedures of the organization. Some supervisors will have authority to make selection decisions solely on their own; others will be required to check with either their boss or the human resources department. Still others may have only the authority to recommend which applicant is to be hired. For purposes of brevity, we assume in the discussion to follow that the supervisor has the authority to make the final selection decision. Under these circumstances, then, the supervisor can decide to hire an applicant on the spot. All the supervisor has to do is to tell the applicant when to report for work and to provide any additional instructions that are pertinent.

If the supervisor wishes to defer a decision until several other candidates for the job have been interviewed, the supervisor should inform the applicant that he or she will be notified later. The supervisor should indicate a time limit within which the decision will be made. However, it is not fair to use this tactic to dismiss an applicant so as to avoid the unpleasant task of telling the applicant that he or she is not acceptable. By telling the applicant that a decision is being deferred, the supervisor gives the applicant false hope. While waiting for the supervisor's decision, the applicant might not apply for another job and thus let some other opportunities slip by. Therefore, if the supervisor has made the decision not to hire this person, he or she should be told in a tactful way. For example, some supervisors deem it best to turn down the job seeker in a general way without stating specific reasons. This is often accomplished by merely saying that there was not a sufficient "match" between the needs of the job and the qualifications of the applicant.

The supervisor should keep in mind that an employment interview is an excellent opportunity to build a good reputation for the employer. The applicant realizes that other candidates probably have applied for the job and that not everyone can be selected. The last contact an applicant may ever have with the organization is with the supervisor during the employment interview. Therefore, even if the applicant should not get the job, the supervisor should recognize that the way the interview was handled will make either a good or a negative impression, sometimes a permanent one. An applicant should leave the interview, regardless of its outcome, feeling that he or she has been treated fairly and courteously. It is every supervisor's managerial duty to build as much goodwill for the organization as possible, since it is in a company's self-interest to maintain a good image.

The Hiring Decision

The decision to hire can be quite challenging when the supervisor has interviewed several applicants and all of them appear to be qualified for the available job. There are no definite guidelines that a supervisor always can utilize to select the best-suited individual from among qualified candidates. At times, certain information will be learned from the application forms, tests, and interviews that will indicate to the supervisor which of the applicants should be hired. There will be other times when available information is not convincing or perhaps is even conflicting. For example, it may be that an applicant's aptitude test score for a sales job is relatively low, but the person has favorably impressed the supervisor in the interview by showing an enthusiastic interest in the job and a selling career.

Here is where supervisory judgment and experience come into play. The supervisor must always remember to select employees who are most likely to contribute to good departmental performance. The supervisor may consult with human resources staff for their observations and evaluations, but in the final analysis, it should be the supervisor's responsibility to choose. By carefully analyzing all of the information available and by keeping in mind previous successes and failures in selecting other employees in the department based on similar information, the supervisor should be able to select those applicants who are most likely to succeed.

Of course, the decision to hire or not to hire always involves uncertainties. There are no exact ways to predict how individuals will perform until they actually are placed on the job. However, the supervisor who approaches and carries out the hiring decision in a thorough, careful, and professional manner more likely will consistently select those applicants who will become excellent employees.

Documentation.   In recent years, many supervisors have been asked by higher management and human resources staff to document the reasons for their hiring decisions from among applicants who were interviewed. Documentation is necessary to ensure that a supervisor's decision to accept or reject an applicant is based on job-related factors and is not discriminatory. At times, a supervisor's hiring decision will be challenged; the supervisor must be able to justify that decision, or risk being reversed by higher management. Similarly, supervisors sometimes will be strongly encouraged by higher management or human resources staff to give preferential hiring considerations to minority or female applicants, especially if the company is actively seeking such employees. Some supervisors resent this type of pressure, but they should recognize that the company may be obligated under various laws to meet certain hiring goals. In general, if a supervisor has followed the approaches suggested in this chapter, he or she should be able to distinguish the most qualified people from among the applicants available and also be prepared to justify their employment selection.

Temporary Placements.   Occasionally it happens that an applicant is not qualified or is overly qualified for a certain job, but he or she would be suitable for another position. A supervisor might wish to attract a desirable applicant by offering temporary placement in any job that is available. For example, the supervisor might offer a qualified word processor a position as a file clerk at a certain rate of pay, with a promise to transfer him to a word processor position at a higher rate of pay when such a position becomes available.

However, temporary placement frequently causes misunderstanding and problems, since it usually is frustrating for someone to "mark time" in a lower level job hoping for the better job to open up. Such strain causes dissatisfaction after a certain length of time, and this dissatisfaction may be communicated to other employees within the work group. Further, if an employee is placed on a temporary job for which the person is overqualified, he or she may receive special treatment from the supervisor which in turn is likely to create resentment among other workers. If the expected position does not open up, the employee will be left in an unsatisfactory job. Therefore, generally speaking, temporary placements are ill-advised and should be avoided.

ORIENTATION OF NEW EMPLOYEES

When new employees report for work the first day, the manner in which they are welcomed by the supervisor and the way they are introduced to other employees in the department may have a lasting effect on their future performance. Many studies have indicated that the first days on the job for most new employees are disturbing and anxious. They typically feel like strangers in new surroundings and with other people whom they have just met. It is the supervisor's responsibility to make the transition as smooth as possible and to guide and assist new employees in the desired directions. This initial phase is called *orientation.*[6]

There are several approaches that a supervisor can use in departmental orientation of new employees. The supervisor may choose personally to escort the new employees around the entire department, showing them equipment and facilities and introducing them to other employees. Or the supervisor may prefer to assign new employees to an experienced, capable employee and have this person do all of the orienting, perhaps including "breaking-in" new employees on how to perform their jobs.

Using a Checklist

A useful technique for a supervisor to ensure that new employees are well-oriented is to make use of a checklist. When developing an **orientation checklist,** the supervisor should strive to identify all the things that a new employee ought to know. Without some type of checklist, a supervisor is apt to skip some important item that will be needed by the new employee. Figure 13–4

---

[6]For an expanded discussion of employee orientation, see Wayne Cascio, *Managing Human Resources* (New York: McGraw-Hill Book Company, 1986), pp. 213–223.

shows an orientation checklist prepared by a personnel department for use by supervisors in an insurance company.

Discussing the Organization

It usually is a good idea for the supervisor to sit down with new employees on the first day in some quiet area and to discuss the department, the company, and its policies and regulations. In some companies the human resources de-

Fig 13–4. Orientation checklist of an insurance company.

☐ Welcome the new employee. When the new employee arrives, go to the reception area and greet the person cordially. On the new employee's first day, try to make him or her feel at ease.

☐ Show the workplace. Briefly describe the group's work.

☐ Introduce to co-workers.

☐ Tour of company. This can be done by one of your experienced employees. Show the coat closet, cafeteria, time clock, restroom facilities, and the other departments which will be pertinent to the new employee's job.

☐ Personnel Department. After a tour of the company take the new employee to the Personnel Department to fill out the necessary employment papers.

☐ Explain the telephone system. Take the new employee to the reception area where a switchboard operator will explain the telephone system.

☐ Make sure your new employee understands the following:
   • Use of the time clock
   • Starting and stopping times
   • Proper work clothes
   • Parking facilities
   • Lunch period and break period
   • Rate of pay and how it is figured
   • Overtime pay
   • Pay deductions
   • What to do about errors in paycheck
   • Probation period of 30 days
   • Job evaluation
   • Reporting of absences

☐ Remind employee to come to you for information and assistance.

partment will provide booklets or pamphlets that give much general information about the company, including corporate benefits, policies, and procedures. There may even be a formal class or conference in which new employees are provided with this type of information, and perhaps they will be conducted on a tour of the company's premises and facilities.

A common mistake made by some supervisors when orienting new employees is to give them too much information on the first day. Presenting too many items in a very short period of time may result in what is called **information overload.** A new employee is not likely to remember many details if they are all presented in the first two hours of the first day. Consequently, it is desirable for the supervisor to spread different aspects of orientation over a new employee's first few days or weeks. Also, the supervisor should schedule a review session several weeks later to discuss any problems or questions the new employee might have.

Being Supportive

More important than the actual techniques used in orienting new employees are the attitudes and behavior of the supervisor. If a supervisor conveys to new employees a sincerity in trying to make the transition period a pleasurable experience, and tells employees that they should not hesitate to ask questions and how to get help when problems arise, this in itself will be much appreciated by the new employees and will smooth the early days on the job. If it would be helpful, the supervisor might request human resources staff assistance to develop more formal orientation procedures for the department. But it remains the supervisor's responsibility to assist each new employee to quickly become an accepted member of the departmental work team and a contributing, productive employee.

TRAINING AND DEVELOPMENT

In most job situations, new employees require both generalized and specific training. If skilled workers are hired, the primary training need may be in the area of company and departmental methods and procedures. If unskilled or semiskilled workers are hired, specific job skills will have to be taught in order to make the workers productive within a short period of time. Methods of formal training utilized in organizations are varied and dependent on the unique circumstances involved in each situation. Regardless, at the departmental level, training and developing employees by helping them improve their aptitudes, skills, and abilities to perform both current and future jobs is another continual responsibility of the supervisor.[7]

---

[7] For an expanded discussion of employee training and development, see John M. Ivancevich and William F. Glueck, *Foundations of Personnel—Human Resources Management* (4th ed.; Homewood, Illinois: BPI-Irwin, 1989), pp. 530–551.

On-the-Job Training

Most training at the departmental level takes the form of on-the-job training. The supervisor may prefer personally to do as much of the training as time will permit; this has the advantage of helping the supervisor get to know the new employees while they are being trained in the proper methods and standards of performing the job. If the supervisor does not have time to do the training himself or herself, then the training should be performed by one of the best current employees. The supervisor should give the training task only to those experienced employees who enjoy this additional assignment and who are qualified to do so. Further, the supervisor should make periodic follow-up visits to see how each new employee is progressing.

Off-the-Job Training

There usually are numerous options for training new as well as existing employees, which are conducted outside of the immediate work area. Some of these may be coordinated, taught, or handled by human resources staff or training departments. Where there are skilled crafts involving, for example, electricians, machinists, or toolmakers, a formal apprenticeship training program may be developed and established. Usually this includes having the employee being away from the job for formal schooling while working part-time on the job in the department.

There also may be courses and programs offered within the company during working hours or outside of working hours. For example, safety training meetings and seminars are commonly scheduled during working hours for supervisors and employees alike. The extent and scope of a company's training program usually are developed by higher management and administered through the human resources or training departments of the organization.

Ongoing Development of Employees

Employee development involves the need for supervisors to assess the skills and potential of employees so that they can perform better both now and in the future. If a supervisor believes that an area of training is needed, which cannot be provided at the departmental level, the supervisor should go to a higher level manager or to the human resources department to see what can be arranged, or whether there are existing courses outside the company to meet departmental training needs.

Many companies have **tuition-aid programs** to help employees further their education. A supervisor should be aware of available course offerings at nearby educational institutions, and encourage employees to take advantage of all the educational avenues open to them. Unfortunately some supervisors do not like to have their employees away from the job to take educational courses, or expending their energies on scholastic efforts. These supervisors should recognize that learning experiences usually help employees develop knowledge, abilities, and skills that should improve their performance and prepare them for more demanding responsibilities.

Supervisory Training and Career Development

The need for training and development is not limited to departmental employees. Every supervisor should recognize the need for personal training and development in order to avoid obsolescence or status-quo thinking. Taking academic courses and attending seminars are even more important for supervisors than for departmental employees. By expanding their own perspectives, supervisors more likely will be in a frame of mind to encourage employees to improve their knowledge and abilities and to keep up-to-date.

Most supervisors likely will attend a number of supervisory management training and development programs, as well as courses in technical aspects of company and departmental operations. Supervisors may find it advantageous to belong to one or more professional or technical associations, whose members meet periodically to discuss problems and topics of current interest and to share common experiences. Further, supervisors are well advised to subscribe to a number of technical and managerial journals or publications and to find time to read and digest articles of professional interest.

For the long run, supervisors also should give some thought to their own career development. The ambitious supervisor will find it helpful to formulate some type of **career plan,** by which the supervisor writes down definite targets or goals to which he or she would like to progress during the next five to ten

Fig 13–5. Career planning sheet used by a major chemical firm.

Performance Appraisal (Managerial)   Page 3

CAREER PLANNING

This sheet is for your use in making known your career goals and the training and experience you feel you need to achieve them.

You may list the training needs from the company's own program, or programs offered by schools and colleges in the area.

You may feel you have an interest or a need to gain plant, marketing, or some other type experience.

These notes should be made so that you and your supervisor may discuss them and formulate plans around them.

In summary, it is your plan with suggestions from your boss on how you may best achieve your career goals.

years. Such a career plan includes both a preferred pattern of future assignments and job positions, and a listing of educational and training activities that will be needed as part of such career progression.

Some companies expect their supervisors to periodically indicate their personal training and development needs and objectives on an official company form. This particularly is so if the company uses management by objectives (MBO)—or some version of MBO as discussed in Chapter 7. For example, Figure 13–5 is a page from a major chemical company's MBO-type appraisal form, by which this company strongly encourages its managerial personnel to make known their career goals.

Of course, it is impossible for anyone to predict or control the future. Many supervisors find that their careers in management often are influenced more by unpredictable, even random happenings than by carefully anticipated strategies that they have charted. Nevertheless, realistic career planning by a supervisor can be a positive aspect of a supervisor's own program of self-development, which should prepare a supervisor for additional responsibilities regardless of how far a supervisor advances beyond his or her current position and within or outside the organization.[8]

SUMMARY

Supervisors play a vital role in selecting, orienting, and training employees. Supervisors are most likely to be involved in employee selection interviews, although they will also need to develop interviewing skills for other situations. Two basic interview approaches are the directive and nondirective techniques. The employee selection interview primarily is a directive interview, although it may contain elements of nondirective interviewing. However, nondirective interviewing tends to be more frequently used in problem situations and employee counseling.

It is vital for a supervisor to thoroughly prepare for the selection interview situation. A supervisor should be aware of equal employment opportunity concerns and guidelines that are applicable. Job-related questions that foster nondiscriminatory treatment should be used. All selection criteria should be objective, uniform in application, consistent in effect, and job-related. Before conducting the interview, the supervisor should review the applicant's application form, test scores, and other background materials that may be available. By having a list of key questions to ask, the supervisor should be able to cover the most important areas where more information is wanted.

The supervisor may open the employee selection interview by using an approach that will reduce tension, such as by asking a question that is easily answered. The

---

[8]For an expanded discussion of career development, see Arthur W. Sherman, Jr., George W. Bohlander, and Herbert J. Chruden, *Managing Human Resources* (8th ed.; Cincinnati: South-Western Publishing Co., 1988), pp. 222–249.

supervisor should explain the job, use effective questioning techniques, and take appropriate notes.

When evaluating an applicant, the supervisor should avoid such common pitfalls as the halo effect, overgeneralization, comparing the applicant only with current employees, and looking for qualifications that far exceed the requirements of the job. At the conclusion of the interview, the supervisor should remember that the applicant is entitled to a decision just as soon as possible. The supervisor should strive to have the applicant leave with a good impression of fair and courteous treatment. Temporary job placements generally are to be avoided, since they usually prove to be difficult for both the new employee and the organization.

The proper orientation and training of new employees are also supervisory responsibilities of high priority. Training is a continual process, which requires major supervisory attention in cooperation with human resources staff or the training department. Additionally, supervisors must recognize the need for their own training and development, and they should utilize whatever opportunities for continuing education that may be available to them. Supervisors should also consider having a career plan to help them chart and monitor their long-term career progression.

QUESTIONS FOR DISCUSSION

1. Discuss the differences between a directive interview and a nondirective interview. Does the employee selection interview tend to be directive or nondirective in nature, or both? Why?
2. What are the primary steps a supervisor should follow in preparing for an employee selection interview?
3. How have equal employment opportunity laws and regulations affected the questions and information that can be solicited from a job applicant? What guidelines can be utilized to determine whether an interview question or other selection criteria are legal?
4. Discuss how adequate supervisory preparation for an employee selection interview can be crucial to the interview's success.
5. Discuss each of the following considerations in conducting an employee selection interview:
   a. Opening the interview.
   b. Explaining the job.
   c. Using effective questioning techniques.
   d. Taking notes.
   e. Concluding the interview.
6. Identify several pitfalls that supervisors may encounter in evaluating job applicants, both during and after an interview.
7. Why is the employee selection interview important from a public relations standpoint? What role does deferring a selection decision play in this regard?
8. What guidelines can be suggested to a supervisor in order to improve decision making when hiring job applicants?
9. Why are supervisors and many employers now required to document why they did or did not hire applicants they have interviewed?

10. Is temporary job placement a desirable practice in reaching an employment decision? Why or why not?
11. How is orientation of a new employee related to future performance? Discuss approaches that a supervisor may take in orienting a new employee.
12. Why is on-the-job training most likely to be the type of training utilized at the departmental level? Enumerate other approaches for training and development that may be available.
13. Discuss the need for supervisors to have their own personal training and development programs. Is a long-term career plan for a supervisor more likely to aid a supervisor in career progression, or be a source of frustration and disappointment? Discuss.

CHAPTER 14

Performance Appraisal, Promotion, and Compensation

CHAPTER OBJECTIVES

1. To discuss the importance and advantages of a formal performance appraisal system.
2. To present concepts and techniques in using employee performance appraisal forms and conducting a sound appraisal interview.
3. To suggest how a supervisor's decisions on promoting employees should consider a realistic balance between their seniority and their merit and ability.
4. To discuss the supervisor's important, although limited, role in employee compensation, including benefits.

From the time that employees begin their employment with a firm, the supervisor is responsible for evaluation of their job performance. Of course, day-to-day feedback is needed to improve employee performance and to provide the appropriate incentives. But, further, most organizations require that supervisors formally appraise their employees periodically; these evaluations become part of an employee's permanent employment record and play an important role in supervisory decisions that involve promoting, transferring, and compensating employees.

EMPLOYEE PERFORMANCE APPRAISAL

Many supervisors underestimate the importance of evaluation of employee performance. It is sometimes a difficult, distasteful, and time-consuming task, and therefore the supervisor may approach the evaluation process in an indifferent or routine manner. This can be self-defeating in both the short and long run. Supervisors must approach this aspect of their responsibilities as another of the many significant requirements of good supervision.

Appraisal of employee performance is, of course, a daily, ongoing aspect of the supervisor's job. Our focus in this chapter is on how employee appraisal is accomplished through a formal system—usually called **performance appraisal, employee evaluation, employee rating** or **merit rating.** The purpose of formal performance appraisal is to evaluate, summarize, and document in understandable and objective terms the performance, experience, and qualities of employees as compared with their abilities and job requirements. This is done by taking into consideration factors such as dependability, output, housekeeping, judgment, safety, initiative, and the like, based on observation of an employee over a certain period of time.

Advantages of a Formal Appraisal System

A formal appraisal or evaluation system requires the supervisor to consider carefully and systematically factors such as those just cited, and it should reduce the personal biases that a supervisor may have toward individual employees. It forces the supervisor to observe and scrutinize the work of employees from the point of view of how well they are performing and what can be done to improve their performance. An employee's poor performance and a failure to improve may be due in part to the supervisor's own inadequate supervision. Thus a formal appraisal system also provides clues to the supervisor's own performance and may suggest where the supervisor needs to change and improve.

A formal appraisal system serves another important purpose. Employees have the right to know how well they are doing and what they can do to improve. Most employees want to know what their supervisors think of their work, and this desire to know how they stand can stem from different reasons. For example, some employees may realize that they are doing a relatively poor job, but they hope that the supervisor is not too critical and they are anxious to be assured in this direction. Other employees, feeling that they are doing an outstanding job, want to make certain that the supervisor recognizes and appreciates their services.

Regular formal appraisals can be an important incentive, particularly to employees of a large organization. Many employees feel that due to the size of the organization and the great amount of job specialization, individual employees and their contributions are forgotten and lost. Formal, scheduled appraisals provide employees with some assurance that they are not overlooked, and that the supervisor and the organization do know and care about them.

Additionally, formal appraisals usually become part of an employee's permanent employment record. These appraisals serve as documents that are likely to be reviewed and even relied on in future decisions concerning an employee's promotion, compensation, disciplinary action, and even termination.

The Supervisor's Responsibility for Performance Appraisal

A performance appraisal should be made by the employee's immediate supervisor, who—with rare exceptions—knows more about the employee's performance than anyone else in the organization.[1] Formal appraisal of all employees should be made by the supervisor at least once a year, which normally is considered long enough to develop a reasonably accurate record of the employee's performance and short enough to provide current, useful information. However, if an employee has just started or if the employee has been transferred to a new and perhaps more responsible position, it is advisable to make an appraisal within three to six months. In the case of a new employee, the supervisor may have to make an appraisal in conjunction with the employee's probationary status; this usually determines whether the employee will be retained as a regular employee. In some organizations, appraisals are made according to the dates when each employee started; in others, appraisals are made once or twice a year on fixed dates.

As stated before, performance evaluation should be a normal part of the day-to-day relationship between a supervisor and employees. The supervisor who frequently communicates with employees concerning how they are doing will find that the annual appraisal primarily will be a matter of reviewing much of what has been discussed during the year. Nevertheless, periodic scheduled appraisals assure the employee that whatever improvement has been made is

---

[1] There are some situations where a ''consensus'' or ''pooled'' type of appraisal may be done by a group of supervisors—for example, where an employee works for several supervisors because of rotating work-shift schedules, a matrix organizational structure, or for other reasons. This requires that all of the supervisors involved have adequate knowledge of the performance of the employee being rated. The employee's direct supervisor usually remains responsible for completing the appraisal form and conducting the appraisal interview.

appreciated and that the employee may be rewarded for it. As time goes on, periodic appraisals become an important influence on employee motivation and morale. Appraisals reaffirm the supervisor's genuine interest in employees and in their development and future. Most employees would rather be told how they are doing, even if it involves some criticism, than to be left "in the dark" by their supervisor.

Typically a formal employee performance appraisal by a supervisor involves: (1) completing a written appraisal form; and (2) conducting an appraisal interview.

Completing a Written Appraisal.   In order to facilitate the appraisal process and make it more uniform, most organizations use performance appraisal forms. These forms identify and list various elements for appraisal in objective terms; they are known as **performance rating, merit rating,** or **performance evaluation** forms. For most supervisors, the first step in performance appraisal is to fill out these rating forms, which usually are provided and prepared by the human resources department, perhaps in response to supervisors' suggestions.

There are numerous types of forms for the evaluation of employees. Most forms include factors that serve as criteria for measuring job performance, skills and abilities, and personality. The following are some of the factors that most frequently are included on employee performance rating forms:

- Quantity of work.
- Quality of performance.
- Absenteeism.
- Tardiness.
- Amount of supervision required.
- Attitude.
- Conduct.
- Cooperation.
- Job knowledge.
- Safety.
- Housekeeping.
- Judgment.
- Adaptability.
- Initiative.
- Ability to work with others.

For each of these factors, the supervisor may be provided with a number of choices or degrees of achievement to be filled in. Some appraisal forms use a series of descriptive sentences, phrases, or adjectives to assist the supervisor in understanding how to judge or evaluate the rating factors. Many forms are of a "check-the-box" type, which is helpful to the appraiser and tends to make it somewhat easier and less time-consuming to complete the appraisal form.

Figures 14–1 and 14–2 are examples of appraisal forms typically used in

Fig 14–1.
A ''check-the-
box'' type of
performance
appraisal form.

SANDERS SUPERMARKETS

EMPLOYEE APPRAISAL FORMS

Employee's Name: _____

Occupation: _____

The following general definitions apply to each factor rated below.

SATISFACTORY: The employee's performance with respect to a factor meets the full job requirements as the job is defined at the time of rating. A satisfactory rating means good performance. **THIS IS THE BASIC STANDARD FOR RATING ANY FACTOR BELOW.**

FAIR: The employee's performance with respect to a factor is below the requirements for the job and must improve to be satisfactory.

VERY GOOD: The employee's performance with respect to a factor is beyond the requirements for satisfactory performance for the job.

UNSATISFACTORY: The employee's performance with respect to a factor is deficient enough to justify release from present job unless improvement is made.

EXCEPTIONAL: The employee's performance with respect to a factor is extraordinary, approaching the best possible for the job.

RATE ON FACTORS BELOW	UNSATISFACTORY	FAIR	SATISFACTORY	VERY GOOD	EXCEPTIONAL
EFFECTIVENESS IN DEALING WITH PEOPLE: Extent to which employee cooperates with, and effectively influences those with whom he comes in contact.	Relations too ineffective to retain in job without improvement.	Somewhat less effective than required by job.	Maintains effective working relations with others.	Ability superior to normal job requirements.	Extraordinary. Beyond that which present job can fully utilize.
PERSONAL EFFICIENCY: Speed and effectiveness in performing duties not delegated to subordinates.	Efficiency too poor to retain in job without improvement.	Efficiency below job requirements in some respects.	Personal efficiency fully satisfies job requirements.	Superior efficiency.	Extraordinary degree of personal efficiency.
JOB KNOWLEDGE: Extent of job information and understanding possessed by employee.	Knowledge inadequate to retain in job without improvement.	Lacks some required knowledge.	Knowledge fully satisfies job requirements.	Very well informed on all phases of work.	Extraordinary. Beyond scope which present job can fully utilize.
JUDGMENT: Extent to which decisions and actions are based on sound reasoning and weighing of outcome.	Judgment too poor to retain in job without improvement.	Decisions not entirely adequate to meet demands of job.	Makes good decisions in various situations arising in job.	Superior in determining correct decisions and actions.	Extraordinary. Beyond that which present job can fully utilize.
INITIATIVE: Extent to which employee is a ''self-starter'' in attaining objectives of job.	Lacks sufficient initiative to retain in job without improvement.	Lacks initiative in some respects.	Exercises full amount of initiative required by the job.	Exercises initiative beyond job requirements.	Extraordinary. Beyond that which present job can fully utilize.
JOB ATTITUDE: Amount of interest and enthusiasm shown in work.	Attitude too poor to retain in job without improvement.	Attitude needs improvement to be satisfactory.	Favorable attitude.	High degree of enthusiasm and interest.	Extraordinary degree of enthusiasm and interest.
DEPENDABILITY: Extent to which employee can be counted on to carry out instructions, be on the job, and fulfill responsibilities.	Too unreliable to retain in job without improvement.	Dependability not fully satisfactory.	Fully satisfies dependability demands of job.	Superior to normal job demands.	Extraordinary dependability in all respects.
OVERALL EVALUATION OF EMPLOYEE PERFORMANCE:	Performance inadequate to retain in present job.	Does not fully meet requirements of the job.	Good performance. Fully competent.	Superior. Beyond satisfactory fulfillment of job requirements.	Extraordinary. Performance approaching the best possible for the job.

(OVER)

Fig 14-1.
(continued)

USE THIS ITEM ONLY IF THE EMPLOYEE IS STILL IN THE LEARNING STAGE ON THE JOB

EVALUATION OF TRAINEE PERFORMANCE:	UNSATISFACTORY	FAIR	SATISFACTORY	VERY GOOD	EXCEPTIONAL
Considering the length of time on the job, how do you evaluate the employee's performance so far?	Progress too slow to retain job.	Progressing but not as rapidly as required.	Making good progress.	Progressing very rapidly.	Doing exceptionally well. Outstanding rate of development.
	☐	☐	☐	☐	☐

1. Outstanding abilities and accomplishments.

2. Weaknesses.

Recommendations for Improvement:

3. General remarks concerning employee's performance.

4. Specific suggestions for further development.

Rated by: Date   Reviewed by: Date

TO RATER: Initial and date this space when you have discussed this rating with the employee.

_____
SUPERVISOR

*Signature of
Employee _____

*This signature merely verifies that this evaluation has been discussed with
the employee, and it does not express approval or disapproval of the above.

Fig 14–2.
A performance appraisal form constructed so that the supervisor must read each item rather than just check boxes.

CLEMENT COMMUNITY HOSPITAL

EMPLOYEE EVALUATION

EMPLOYEE _____ DATE_____

JOB TITLE _____ DEPARTMENT _____

Evaluate the employee on the job now being performed. Circle the number to the left which most nearly expresses your overall judgment on each quality. Also, in the space reserved for comments, consider the employee's performance since the last appraisal and state whether the individual has gone backwards, remained stationary, or gone ahead in each of the qualities listed. The care and accuracy with which this appraisal is made will determine its value to you, to the employee, and to the organization.

JOB KNOWLEDGE (Consider knowledge of the job gained through experience, general education, specialized training.)
5. Well informed on all phases of work.
4. Knowledge thorough enough to perform without assistance.
3. Adequate grasp of essentials, some assistance required.
2. Requires considerable assistance.
1. Inadequate knowledge.
Comments

QUALITY OF WORK (Consider neatness, accuracy and dependability of results regardless of volume.)
5. Exceptionally accurate, practically no mistakes.
4. Usually accurate, seldom necessary to check work.
3. Acceptable, usually neat, occasional errors or rejections.
2. Often unacceptable, frequent errors or rejections, needs supervision.
1. Unacceptable, too many errors.
Comments

QUANTITY OF WORK (Consider the volume of work produced under normal conditions. Disregard errors.)
5. Exceptional quantity, rapid worker, unusually big producer.
4. Turns out good volume.
3. Average volume.
2. Volume below average, often does not complete work.
1. Very slow worker cannot complete duties.
Comments

ABILITY TO LEARN (Consider the speed with which the employee masters new routine and grasps explanations. Consider also ability to retain this knowledge.)
5. Exceptionally fast to learn and adjust to changed conditions, adaptable.
4. Learns rapidly, follows instructions, retains instructions.
3. Average instruction required.
2. Requires extra instructions, necessary to repeat instructions.
1. Very slow to absorb, poor memory, cannot adapt.
Comments

INITIATIVE (Consider the tendency to contribute, develop and/or carry out new ideas or methods. Also dependability in carrying out routine assignments.)
5. Excellent initiative resulting in frequent saving in time and money, always reliable, is a leader.
4. Very resourceful, can work on own, manages time well, is reliable.
3. Shows initiative occasionally, usually reliable.
2. Lacking in initiative, has to be told to complete tasks.
1. Needs constant prodding, is unreliable.
Comments

COOPERATION AND RELATIONSHIPS (Consider manner of handling job relationships.)
5. Goes out of way to cooperate with co-workers, supervisors, and subordinates; excellent attitude; takes and gives instructions well.
4. Gets along well with associates.
3. Acceptable, usually gets along well, occasionally complains.
2. Shows reluctance to cooperate, complains.
1. Very poor cooperation, does not follow instructions, dislikes fellow employees.
Comments

Fig 14–2.
(continued)

ATTENDANCE (Consider rate of absenteeism, reasons for absenteeism, tardiness, and promptness in giving notice.)
5. Excellent, absent only for emergencies: family crisis, civic duty, illness: always on time, gives notice when absent.
4. Rarely absent or late, absent with good reason, gives notice.
3. Occasionally absent, less important reasons, usually gives notice, but not always in time.
2. Often absent, lack of adequate notice.
1. Excessive absenteeism, does not give notice, reasons are unacceptable, cannot be depended upon.
Comments

APPEARANCE (Consider neatness and appropriateness of dress.)
5. Excellent, always neat and clean.
4. Good, usually neat and clean.
3. Average appearance.
2. Poor, often dirty and careless in appearance.
1. Unacceptable, offensive.
Comments

OVERALL EVALUATION: Superior_____Good_____Satisfactory_____Unsatisfactory_____

COMMENTS (Consider need for improvement; suitability for job, contributions.   BE SPECIFIC!)

CERTIFICATION BY RATER:
I HEREBY CERTIFY THAT THIS APPRAISAL CONSTITUTES MY BEST JUDGMENT OF THE SERVICE VALUE
OF THIS EMPLOYEE AND IS BASED ON PERSONAL OBSERVATION AND KNOWLEDGE OF THE EMPLOYEE'S WORK.

Signature _____ Date _____

CERTIFICATION BY EMPLOYEE:
I HEREBY CERTIFY THAT I HAVE PERSONALLY REVIEWED THIS REPORT.

Signature _____ Date _____

Approved by : _____
              Administrator   Date

many organizations, although these forms differ somewhat in their format and approach. One of the advantages of the evaluation form shown in Figure 14–2 is that it is constructed in such a way that the supervisor must read each item rather than just check boxes in a mechanical fashion. Both forms provide space for additional comments about various aspects of an employee's performance.

Problems with Appraisal Forms. Despite the uncomplicated design of most performance appraisal forms, supervisors will encounter a number of problems when filling them out. First of all, not all raters will agree on the meaning of such terms as exceptional, very good, satisfactory, fair, and unsatisfactory. Descriptive phrases or sentences added to each of these adjectives are helpful in choosing that level which best describes the employee. Even so, the choice of an appraisal term or level depends mostly on the rater's perceptions, and this may be an inaccurate measure of actual reality.

Another problem is that one supervisor may be more severe than another in the appraisal of employees. The supervisor who gives predominantly low and harsh ratings is likely to damage the morale of those employees who feel that they have been unfairly and severely judged. At the same time, such poor ratings may also reflect negatively on the supervisor's own ability, suggesting that the supervisor has not been able to attain good performance from the employees.

On the other hand, some supervisors may be overly generous or lenient in their ratings. These supervisors do not give low ratings to their employees because they are afraid that they will antagonize the employees and thus make them less cooperative. Further, such supervisors want to be liked by their employees to the extent that they give out only high ratings, even when such ratings are undeserved.

The supervisor also should be aware of the problem of the "halo effect," namely, not allowing the rating of one factor to influence excessively the ratings of other factors.[2] If a supervisor feels that an employee is strong in one area, say productivity, he or she may tend to rate the employee high on most other factors. One way to avoid this "halo" effect is to rate all employees on a single factor before starting on the next factor. This means that the supervisor evaluates only one factor at a time for all employees, and then goes on to the next factor for all employees, and so on. By so doing, the supervisor rates each employee in relation to a standard or to each other on each factor.

Appraisal Objectivity. Every appraisal should be made within the context of each employee's particular job, and every rating should be based on the total performance of each employee. It would be unfair to appraise a sub-

---

[2]The "halo" and the "horns" problem was previously discussed in Chapter 13.

ordinate on the basis of one assignment that had been done just recently, done particularly well, or done very poorly. Random impressions should not influence a supervisor's judgment. The appraisal should be based on an employee's total record of reliability, initiative, skills, resourcefulness, capability, and any other relevant factors. Further, the supervisor must scrupulously strive to exclude personal biases for or against different individuals, which can be a serious pitfall in appraisal. Although results of performance appraisal are by no means perfect, they can be fairly objective and serve as a positive influence in influencing an employee's future performance.

The Appraisal Interview.   The second major part of an appraisal procedure is the **evaluation** or **appraisal interview.** This takes place when the supervisor who has completed the performance rating form sits down with the employee to review the ratings. Since this is a vital part of the appraisal procedure, the supervisor should develop a general plan for carrying out the appraisal interview. If poorly handled, this interview can lead to considerable resentment and misunderstanding.

Unfortunately some supervisors shy away from the appraisal interview. They simply fill out an appraisal form and turn it in to their boss or the human resources department. But the entire evaluation process loses its effectiveness if the appraisal interview does not take place. Supervisors who avoid the appraisal interview may rationalize that there is no need to discuss annual performance ratings with their employees, since they are in daily contact with employees and the "door is always open." This, however, is not enough. Employees usually know that an appraisal form about them will be (or has been) turned in, and they want to have a first-hand report on how they were evaluated. Employees also may have things on their mind that they do not want to (or cannot) discuss in everyday contacts with their supervisor. The appraisal interview gives them the opportunity to discuss such matters.

Time and Place.   Appraisal interviews (sometimes called **post-appraisal interviews**) should be held shortly after the performance rating form has been completed, preferably in an office or private setting. Privacy and confidentiality should be assured, since this discussion will include criticism, personal feelings, and expressions of opinions.

The supervisor should make an appointment several days in advance with the employee to conduct the interview. This enables the employee to be prepared for the appraisal meeting and to consider in advance what he or she would like to discuss as well.

An interesting approach to use prior to the interview is to provide the employee with a performance rating form and to ask the employee to fill out an appraisal of himself or herself. Many supervisors find that employees often are more critical of themselves than are their supervisors! This **self-rating approach** can produce positive results, since it enables employees to point out those areas where they think they have done best and those areas where they think they should improve.[3] During the appraisal interviews, supervisors can compare their employee ratings with how the employees rated themselves. Thus a basis for discussion and reconciliation of the two appraisals is established. Of course, the supervisor retains the responsibility to determine the content of the final "official" appraisal form that will be signed and become part of each person's employment record.

Conducting the Appraisal Interview. Most of the discussion on interviewing included in the previous chapter is applicable and necessary for the appraisal interview. Although appraisal interviews tend to be directive, in many situations an appraisal interview can take on characteristics of a nondirective interview, since the employee may bring up issues that the supervisor did not expect or was not aware of. On occasion, it will be difficult for the supervisor to carry through this interview successfully, particularly if the employee shows hostility when the supervisor discusses some negative evaluations. It is easy to communicate positive judgments, but it is difficult to communicate major criticisms without generating resentment and defensiveness. There is a limit to how much criticism an individual can absorb in one session without devastating results. It takes planning, practice, insight, sensitivity, and skill to conduct the appraisal interview.

After a brief informal opening, the supervisor should state that the main purpose of the interview is to assess the employee's performance in objective terms. The supervisor might point out that the performance appraisal process should help the employee to improve for his or her own benefit, as well as that of the organization. The supervisor should refer to the progress that the employee has made since the preceding evaluation interview, compliment the employee on achievements, and then proceed to the areas that need improvement. The formula of starting with praise, following it up with criticism, and ending the interview with another compliment is not necessarily the best method. As a matter of fact, "good" and "bad" may cancel each other out, and the employee may forget about the criticism. However, for most people it is better to start with praise than criticism. Most mature employees are able and willing to take deserved, fair criticism; by the same token, those who merit praise want to hear it. It is not always possible to mix good and bad in an appraisal interview without diluting the effectiveness of the interview itself.

During the interview, the supervisor should emphasize that everybody in the same job in the department is evaluated using the same standards and that no one is singled out for special scrutiny. The supervisor should be prepared

---

[3]As discussed in Chapter 7, this is usually part of any management-by-objectives (MBO) procedure that a firm may be using.

to support or document ratings by citing specific illustrations and actual instances of good or poor performance. In particular, the supervisor should indicate how the employee performed or behaved in certain situations that were especially crucial or significant to the performance of the department. This is sometimes referred to as the **critical incident method.** Of course, this means that during the year the supervisor will have written notes in a book or file whenever employees performed in an outstanding fashion or whenever their work was clearly unsatisfactory. In addition, the supervisor should relate the factors being rated to actual demands of the job, and show how the ratings were developed according to the present levels of each employee's performance. This is particularly important if an employee is doing good work; simply to tell an individual to "keep up the good work" is not sufficient.

If the supervisor has chosen to use the employee self-rating approach mentioned earlier, the interview primarily may become a matter of comparing the employee's self-rating with that made by the supervisor. This may involve considerable back-and-forth discussion, especially if there are major differences of opinion on various parts of the appraisal form. Typically, however, this is not a major difficulty, unless the employee has an exaggerated notion of his or her ability or feels that the supervisor's lower ratings were unjustified. As stated before, many employees tend to rate themselves more critically than their supervisors, and they usually are pleased to discover that their supervisor's appraisal has been more positive than expected.

Regardless of the interviewing approach used, the supervisor must include a discussion about areas for improvement and possible opportunities for the employee's future. Supervisors should mention any educational or training plans that may be in the offing or available. This means that the supervisor should be familiar with advancement opportunities open to employees, with requirements of future jobs, and with each employee's personal qualifications. Whenever discussing the future, supervisors should be careful not to make any promises or commitments for training or promotion that are not likely to materialize in the foreseeable future.

The evaluation interview also should provide each employee with an opportunity to ask questions, and the supervisor should answer them as fully as possible. In the final analysis, the value of an evaluation interview depends on an employee's ability to recognize the need for self-improvement and the supervisor's ability to stimulate in the employee a desire to improve. It takes sensitivity and skill for a supervisor to accomplish this, and it frequently is necessary for the supervisor to adapt what is to be said to each individual employee's reactions as these surface during the interview.

Closing the Appraisal.   At the time for closing the appraisal interview, the supervisor should be certain that the employee has a clear understanding of his or her performance rating. Where applicable, the supervisor and employee should agree on some mutual targets or goals in those areas where the employee needs improvement. It may be desirable for the supervisor to set a date with the employee—perhaps in a few months—to discuss whatever progress has been made toward meeting the new objectives. This reinforces the supervisor's stated interest to assist the employee to improve in the right directions.

Many organizations request employees to sign their performance appraisal forms after being interviewed by the supervisor. If a signature is requested as proof that the supervisor actually held the appraisal interview, the supervisor should so inform the employee. The supervisor should explain that, by signing the form, the employee does not necessarily agree with the ratings on the form. If this is not explained and understood, the employee may be reluctant to sign the form, especially if he or she disagrees with some of the contents of the appraisal.[4]

Some firms require the supervisor to discuss completed employee appraisals with the boss or the human resources department before the appraisal documents are placed in the individual's permanent employment record. A supervisor may be challenged at times to justify certain ratings—for example, if a supervisor has given very high evaluations for the majority of departmental employees. For the most part, if a supervisor has carefully and conscientiously appraised his or her employees, these challenges will be infrequent.

PROMOTING EMPLOYEES

Given the proper encouragement in an evaluation interview, many employees return to their jobs with renewed determination to improve their performance and eventually to be promoted. A **promotion** usually means advancement to a better job in terms of more responsibility, more privileges, higher status, greater potential, and higher pay.

Although the majority of employees want to improve and possibly advance, this is not true of everyone. Some employees have no desire to advance any further. They may feel that an increase in responsibility, pay, or status would demand too much of their time and energy, which they prefer to devote to other interests. Or such employees may be content with their seniority and security in their present positions. But the number of employees who do not want to improve or advance tend to be in the minority. Promotions are desired by most employees who have aspirations for themselves. For them, starting

---

[4]Some appraisal forms will have a line above or below the employee's signature which states that the employee's signature only confirms that the appraisal interview has taken place, and that the employee does not necessarily agree with or disagree with any statements made during the appraisal.

"at the bottom" and rising in status and income over time is part of a normal way of life.

Promotion from Within

Most organizations have policies for promoting employees into better and more desirable positions. The policy of "promotion from within" is widely practiced, and it is of considerable significance both to an organization and its employees. For an organization, it means a steady source of trained personnel for higher positions; for employees, it is a motivator and a major incentive to perform better. If employees have worked for an organization for a period of time, more is usually known about them and their attributes than even the best selection processes and interviews could reveal about outside applicants for the same job. Supervisors should know their own people well, but they do not know individuals hired from the outside until those individuals have worked for them for a certain length of time.

Occasionally a supervisor may want to bypass an employee for promotion, because the productivity of the department would suffer until a replacement has been found and trained sufficiently. This kind of thinking is short-sighted, since it would be counter to the purposes of a promotion-from-within policy.

Similarly, there would be little reason for employees to improve themselves, if they believed that the better and higher paying jobs were reserved for outsiders. Additional job satisfaction results when the employees know that stronger efforts on their part may lead to more interesting and challenging work, higher pay and status, and better working conditions. Most employees will be better motivated if they believe that they can move ahead in the organization.

In considering promotion for an employee, the supervisor should recognize that what management considers as a promotion may not always be perceived as such by the employee. For example, an engineer may believe that a promotion to administrative work is a hardship and not an advancement. The engineer may feel that administrative activities are less interesting or more difficult than technical duties and may be concerned about losing or diluting professional engineering skills. Such an attitude is understandable, and the supervisor should try to suggest promotional opportunities that do not require unacceptable compromises.

Additionally, a supervisor should be sensitive to those employees who appear to be satisfied in their present positions. They may prefer to stay with fellow employees whom they know, and retain responsibilities with which they are familiar and comfortable. These employees should not be strongly pressured nor coerced by a supervisor to accept higher-level positions. However, if a supervisor believes that such an employee has excellent qualifications for promotion, the supervisor should offer encouragement and counsel, which may make a promotional opportunity attractive to the employee for either current or future consideration.

Modifying a Promotion-from-Within Policy

Generally, a policy of promotion from within should be applied whenever possible and feasible. Although such a policy normally is preferable, situations will occur where strict adherence to this policy would not be sensible, and might even be harmful to a firm. If there are no qualified internal candidates for an available position, then someone from the outside has to be recruited. For example, if an experienced computer programmer is needed in a data processing department and if the department already is short-handed, the departmental supervisor will have to hire one from outside the organization.

At times, the injection of "new blood" into a department may be very desirable, since this discourages current employees from becoming complacent or conformists. New employees may bring with them different ideas and fresh perspectives. Still another reason for recruiting employees from the outside is that an organization may not be in a position to train employees in the necessary skills. A particular position may require long, specialized, or expensive training, and the organization may be unable either to offer or to afford such training. Thus in order to cover these types of contingencies, an absolute promotion-from-within policy must be modified as is realistic and appropriate to the situation. This is why most written policy statements concerning promotion from within include a qualifying clause such as "whenever possible" or "whenever feasible."

Criteria for Promotion from Within

Typically there are more employees who are interested in being promoted than there are openings available. Since promotions should serve as an incentive for employees to perform better, some supervisors believe that those employees who have the best records of production, quality, and cooperation are the ones who should be promoted. In some situations, however, it is difficult to measure such aspects of employee performance accurately or objectively, even when there has been a conscientious effort by supervisors in the form of merit ratings or performance appraisals.

Seniority.   One easily measured and objective criterion that has been applied extensively in an effort to reduce favoritism and discrimination is **seniority,** or **length of service.** Labor unions have placed great stress on seniority, and the use of seniority as a major consideration is widespread among organizations that are not unionized and for jobs that are not covered by union agreements. Many supervisors are quite comfortable with the concept of seniority as a basis for promotion. Some supervisors feel that an employee's loyalty as expressed by length of service deserves to be rewarded. Basing promotion on seniority also assumes that an employee's abilities tend to increase with service. Although this assumption is questionable and not always accurate, it is likely that with continued service an employee's capacities to perform should improve.

If promotion is to be based largely on seniority, then the initial selection procedure for new employees must be careful, and each new employee should receive considerable training in various positions.

Probably the most serious drawback of using seniority as the major criterion for promotion is that it discourages younger employees, that is, those with less seniority. Younger employees may believe that they cannot advance until they, too, have accumulated years of service on the job. Consequently, they may lose interest and enthusiasm and perform at only an average level, since they feel that no matter what they do, they will not be promoted for a long period of time.

Merit and Ability.   Although labor unions have stressed the seniority criterion in promotion, it is well recognized that seniority alone does not guarantee that an individual either deserves promotion or is capable of advancing to a higher level job. In fact, some employees with high seniority may lack the necessary educational or skill levels needed for advancement. Consequently, most unions understand that length of service cannot be the only criterion for advancement or promotion. They agree that promotion should be based on seniority combined with merit and ability, and this type of provision is included in many union contracts.

Merit usually refers to an employee's past job performance, whereas **ability** implies an employee's capability or potential to perform, or to be trained to perform, a higher level job. Supervisors often are in the best position to determine the degree to which merit and ability are necessary to compensate for less seniority. However, even in union contracts that mention merit and ability as "codeterminants" for promotion, the decisive criterion frequently used is seniority, particularly where merit and ability are relatively equal among several candidates seeking a promotion.

Balancing the Criteria.   Good supervisory practice attempts to attain a workable balance between the concepts of merit and ability on the one hand and seniority on the other. In selecting from among the most qualified candidates available, the supervisor may decide to choose essentially on the basis of seniority. Or the supervisor may decide that, in order to be promoted, an employee who is more capable but who has less seniority will have to be "head and shoulders" above—that is, far better than—those with more seniority; otherwise, the supervisor will promote the employee with the greatest seniority, at least on a trial basis.

Because promotion decisions can be of great significance, the preferred solution would be to combine all criteria equitably. However, promotion decisions often involve "gray" areas or subjective considerations that can lead rejected employees to be dissatisfied and file grievances. Realistically, unless there are unusual circumstances involved, it is unlikely that a supervisor will choose to promote an employee over other eligible candidates solely on the basis of merit and ability, without giving some thought to seniority.

Assessment Centers

Because of shortcomings and subjectivity associated with promotion decisions, numerous enterprises in recent years have adopted an **assessment center** approach for evaluating and possibly promoting individuals for supervisory and managerial positions. An assessment center is a place where a number of individual and group exercises are administered to candidates who are hoping to be promoted to supervision or higher management. Some large companies operate their own assessment centers; other companies send their candidates to assessment centers operated by management associations or consulting firms.

Typically, the purpose of the assessment center approach is to evaluate individuals for their potential for success in management. Exercises and activities include simulations that are designed to test and measure managerial and human relations skills. Trained assessors—sometimes including one or more psychologists—eventually come up with a composite profile of a candidate's strengths and weaknesses, which is reported back to the company or organization that sent the candidate to the assessment center. The assessment center

Fig 14–3. The assessment center approach evaluates an individual's potential for managerial success.

profile then becomes a crucial part of the firm's decision whether or not to promote this individual.

Although a detailed discussion of the pros and cons of assessment centers is beyond the scope of this text, it appears that this approach will become more widespread in future years. Many supervisors will be involved in recommending employees to be sent to an assessment center. Some supervisors themselves may be sent to an assessment center when they are being considered for promotion to a higher level management position. The advantage of the assessment center approach is that it can provide an objective, systematic evaluation of an individual's managerial potential as developed by neutral, trained observers. This, in turn, should assist a firm in making its final decisions concerning whom to promote.[5]

THE SUPERVISOR'S ROLE IN COMPENSATION

Although it is not always recognized as such, a supervisor's staffing function includes the compensation of employees. Typically, of course, wage rates and salary schedules are formulated by higher management, by the human resources department, or by union contract.[6] In this respect, the supervisor's authority is quite limited. Nevertheless, within such limitations the supervisor is responsible for determining that departmental employees are compensated appropriately.

Every supervisor has some, if only limited, responsibility in the overall problem of offering the kinds of compensation that will attract and retain competent employees. Too often wage rate schedules simply follow historical patterns, or they are haphazardly formulated. At the departmental level, wage rate inequities often develop over time due to changes in jobs, changes in personnel, and different supervisors who use varying standards for administering compensation. However, when inequitable wage situations arise, they should not be tolerated. It is part of a supervisor's role to make sure that wages paid in the department are properly aligned both externally and internally.

External Wage Alignment and Compensation Surveys

External wage alignment means that the wages offered for a job being performed compare favorably with going rates for similar jobs at other firms in

---

[5]See Leon C. Megginson, *Personnel Management: A Human Resources Approach* (5th ed.; Homewood, Illinois: Richard D. Irwin, Inc., 1985), pp. 262–265; or Sue Branscome Keel, Daniel Cochran, Kirk Arnett, and Danny Arnold, ''AC's Are Not Just for the Big Guys,'' *Personnel Administrator* (May, 1989), pp. 98–101.

[6]For government agencies, wages and salaries are usually established by legislation or government regulations.

the community. If wages within the present compensation structure are not externally aligned, the supervisor can expect eventually to lose some competent employees and to experience difficulty in attracting adequate replacements. Of course, external wage alignment implies that a firm's compensation policies are in accord with state and federal laws governing minimum wages, overtime hours, overtime premiums, and the like. These considerations usually are handled by the human resources department, although supervisors, too, should be informed about them and their meaning and application to departmental jobs.

To determine whether the compensation rates offered by a department are attractive or comparable to those of similar jobs in the area, the supervisor should request the human resources department to gather and share information from compensation surveys.[7] These surveys provide data on wages and salaries paid by other organizations for similar jobs existing within an area, as, for example, a wage and salary survey of all retail department stores in an area. Normally wage and salary information can be obtained readily from governmental, trade, industrial, or local associations. A comparison of the "going wage" paid at other establishments for similar jobs is vital to the supervisor in determining whether departmental wages are properly aligned externally. At the least, the supervisor may wish to scan the "Help Wanted" section of a local newspaper to get some general idea of the range of wages and salaries that other organizations are offering for various jobs.

Internal Wage Alignment and Job Evaluation

Internal wage alignment means that jobs within a department are paid according to what they are worth relative to each other. Unless there are extreme differences, most employees do not become as upset about questionable external wage alignment as they do with poor internal wage alignment. In part, this is because employees may not really comprehend how to compare their compensation with wages for jobs in other companies. But employees do have a good idea of the relative values of jobs within their own immediate working areas. They are more likely to become disturbed if lower skill, "easy" jobs in the department (or other nearby departments) pay more than their own jobs, which involve more difficult work. Because poor internal wage alignment can lower employee morale, it is important that supervisors monitor and strive to eliminate apparent inequities that may exist in departmental pay rates.

In order to pay jobs within a department according to what they are relatively worth, it is necessary for the human resources staff, an outside consultant, or someone in management to conduct what is called a job evaluation.

---

[7]We are not referring here to the issue of so-called comparable worth, which is discussed in Chapter 17.

Job evaluation involves rating jobs according to various factors upon which an appropriate wage rate schedule can be based. If it has not been done recently, say, within a year or so, a supervisor should request the human resources staff to undertake or assist in a job evaluation for the department.

There are several techniques of job evaluation that can be utilized. Since these can become rather specialized in nature, they will not be discussed here. The supervisor should rely upon the expertise and know-how of the human resources department to conduct an evaluation of the relative values of jobs in the department and throughout the organization. If assistance from a human resources department is not available, the supervisor should request higher management to arrange for a job evaluation, perhaps by employing outside consultants who are knowledgeable in this field.[8]

Based on the results of job evaluation, an appropriate wage and salary schedule can be implemented. Of course, problems may arise about what to do with those employees who are receiving either excessively high or low compensation in relation to others. Here, too, the human resources director or outside consultant can be helpful in solving these problems, once an equitable overall wage structure for the department has been clarified.

The Supervisor's Role in Compensation Decisions

A sound and equitable compensation structure should be of great concern to everyone in management, but, as stated earlier, it is an area where a supervisor typically has little direct authority. However, it should be the supervisor's concern to plead with higher management, if he or she becomes aware of serious compensation problems and inequities at the departmental level. Often the opportunity to make a presentation in this regard will arise as supervisors make their recommendations for wage and salary adjustments for individual employees.

Recommending Wage Adjustments. Most supervisors make recommendations to the human resources department or higher management for wage and salary adjustments for departmental employees at various time intervals. For example, many firms provide for **step intervals** at which wage increases will be made within guide rates for a job, provided that the employee has satisfactorily completed a certain period of service.

Unfortunately, too often supervisors automatically recommend full wage

---

[8]Among the most frequently used techniques are (a) Ranking—basic comparison of one job against another; (b) Classification—comparing a job against an objective scale and placing it in its proper category or classification; and (c) Point rating and factor comparison—quantitative approaches for evaluating the relative worth of jobs in an enterprise. For an expanded discussion of conducting job evaluations, see Richard Henderson, *Compensation Management* (5th ed.; Englewood Cliffs, N.J.: Prentice-Hall, Inc., 1989), pp. 168–207.

increases rather than seriously consider whether each employee deserves such a raise. Here is where employee performance evaluation becomes crucial. If an employee's work has been satisfactory, then the employee deserves the normal increase. But if the employee has performed at an unsatisfactory level, the supervisor should suspend the recommendation for an increase and discuss this decision with the employee. The supervisor might outline specific targets for job improvement that the employee must meet before the supervisor will recommend a wage increase at a future date. And if an employee has performed at an outstanding level, the supervisor should not hesitate to recommend a generous, more-than-average wage increase, if this can be done within the current wage pattern. Such a tangible reward will encourage the outstanding employee to continue striving for excellence.

Pay for Performance.   In recent years, many companies and organizations have adopted a number of types of bonus arrangements in order to better reward those who perform in a superior fashion. These approaches have collectively been referred to as **variable pay,** which is defined as any pay that is given strictly on the basis of employee or corporate performance. Among these approaches are special cash awards, bonuses for meeting performance targets, team (departmental) incentive bonuses, gain sharing for meeting production or cost saving goals, and profit sharing.

Although the specific details and formulas for variable-pay plans reflect the unique characteristics of each firm, supervisors play an important role in their implementation, especially in determining which individuals and departments are most deserving of special awards. Further, supervisors must thoroughly understand any pay-for-performance or variable-pay plan that affects the department and be able to explain to employees how the plan works in order to provide the incentives and obtain the results that are intended.[9]

Employee Benefits.   In addition to monetary compensation, most organizations provide supplementary benefits for employees, such as vacations with pay, holidays, retirement plans, insurance and health programs, tuition-aid programs, and numerous other services.[10] In general, benefits are considered as part of an employee's overall compensation, and they, too, are provided within the working environment to stimulate employee motivation and job performance. Most supplementary or additional benefits are established by higher management, by law, and by union contracts. The supervisor has little involvement in establishing benefits, but the supervisor is obligated to see to

---

[9]A survey in 1989 indicated that some three-fourths of the major firms surveyed had a variable-pay plan in effect. See, ''Pegging Payroll to Performance,'' *Management Review* (September, 1989), p. 8.

[10]On the average, the additional cost of supplementary benefits—often called ''fringe benefits''—is between 30 percent and 40 percent of wages and salaries paid to employees.

it that departmental employees understand how their benefits operate, and that each employee receives his or her fair share.

When employees have questions about benefits, the supervisor is well-advised to consult with human resources staff or higher management for advice and assistance. For example, the supervisor often will have to make decisions that involve employee benefits—such as the scheduling of departmental vacations and of work shifts during holidays. In these circumstances the supervisor must be sure that what is done at the departmental level is consistent with the organization's overall policies and rules, as well as with laws, union contract provisions, and the like.

In recent years, many companies have made numerous changes in their benefit programs. Employee stock ownership plans, changes in medical and hospitalization plans, certain forms of child-care support, and other changes and innovations are widespread. Some companies have adopted so-called **cafeteria** or **flexible benefit plans,** in which employees are permitted to choose—within cost and other limits—which benefits they will receive.[11] Again, supervisors should make every effort to stay currently informed about their firm's benefit programs and should consult the human resources or benefits office whenever necessary or as questions arise. Further, supervisors should be willing to permit and even encourage employees to visit the human resources department—or the appropriate management person—for advice and assistance about benefits. This particularly is desirable when individual employees have personal problems or questions about sensitive areas such as medical and other health benefits, and retirement and insurance programs.

SUMMARY

A formal performance appraisal system is the process of periodically rating an employee and conducting an evaluation interview thereafter. The supervisor must appraise employee performance both on a day-to-day and on an overall basis. Whatever the choice of appraisal forms, it is important that every appraisal be made within the context of each employee's particular job and be based on the employee's total performance.

Although the appraisal interview may be a trying situation, the entire employee performance appraisal system is, of no use if this aspect is ignored or not carried out properly. The appraisal interview should emphasize opportunities for further self-development of an employee interested in advancement. Some supervisors have found that the employee self-rating approach is helpful in facilitating an open discussion of an employee's own perceived strengths and weaknesses.

---

[11]See Susan J. Velleman, ''Flexible Benefits Packages That Satisfy Employees and the IRS,'' reprinted from the March, 1985, issue of *Personnel* in *Current Issues in Personnel Management*, 3d ed., edited by Kendrith M. Rowland and Gerald R. Ferris (Boston: Allyn and Bacon, Inc., 1986), pp. 195–202.

Promotion from within is a widely practiced personnel policy and is beneficial to the organization and to the morale of employees. Although it is difficult to specify exactly what should be the basis for employee promotion, there should be appropriate consideration of ability and merit on the one hand and length of service on the other.

The supervisor's staffing function includes making certain that employees of a department are properly compensated. Many of the compensation considerations are not within the direct domain of a supervisor. Nevertheless, a supervisor should attempt to ascertain whether departmental wages are in reasonable external alignment. Even more important is that a supervisor should make certain that job evaluations are conducted to ensure a proper internal wage alignment. Since supervisory responsibility and authority are limited in these areas, supervisors should work closely with the human resources staff to maintain equitable compensation offerings and to ensure that departmental employees are informed and fairly treated in regard to benefits and any bonus plans that may be available.

QUESTIONS FOR DISCUSSION

1. What is meant by a formal performance appraisal (or merit rating) system?
2. Discuss the advantages of a formal employee appraisal system to:
   a. the employee;
   b. the supervisor;
   c. the company or organization.
3. What are some of the factors that most frequently are included on employee performance rating forms? Why do most employee performance appraisal forms include space for supervisors to write comments about the employee being evaluated?
4. Outline the major aspects of conducting an appraisal interview. Include consideration of some of the major difficulties associated with this interview.
5. What is the employee self-rating approach and how can it be used as part of the appraisal interview?
6. Why do most firms try to maintain a policy of promotion from within whenever feasible? Do most firms adhere strictly to this policy? Why or why not?
7. Discuss and evaluate the issues relating to promotion based on seniority on the one hand and merit and ability on the other. Are there any clear guidelines that can be utilized by a supervisor in order to have a workable balance between these criteria?
8. What is meant by the assessment center approach? Why is this approach likely to grow in future years?
9. How is proper compensation of employees part of a supervisor's staffing function? Why do many supervisors believe that this function largely has been removed from their control?
10. Define the concepts of external alignment and internal alignment of wage rates. Which of these usually will be of most concern to the first-line supervisor? Why?
11. Define job evaluation. Discuss the supervisor's role, if any, in a firm's job evaluation program.
12. Discuss the role of a supervisor in departmental decisions involving employee wage increases, variable-pay plans, and supplementary benefits.

CASE 19

An Ethical Selection Dilemma

Charles Holmes was a supervisor in charge of pet foods production for a food processing firm located in the southeast part of the United States. In Holmes's earlier years at the company plant, he had relied on a fellow supervisor, Ellis Duvall, for assistance in learning many aspects of production and quality control and in meeting deadlines. Duvall subsequently became plant manager, and he now was Holmes's immediate boss.

Holmes was facing a difficult dilemma. Ellis Duvall had called, saying that his nephew, Rob Ling, had just graduated from college and was looking for a job. Duvall knew that Holmes's department had an opening for a quality control inspector. Holmes interviewed Rob Ling and found him to be a good-looking, reasonably intelligent young man; but Ling had absolutely no experience to do the kind of work that Holmes required in an important area. To complicate the matter further, Holmes had found out that Rob Ling's father was a buyer for a large food store chain in the region; this food store chain was a major customer of the company.

Prior to meeting with Ling, Holmes had interviewed several applicants for the position, who had been referred to him by the Human Resources Department. Three of the applicants were far more qualified than Rob Ling; the most qualified individual of all was a young woman, Susan Wilson, who had excellent credentials and who also had several years of experience as a quality control inspector. Charlie Holmes had almost hired Wilson on the spot, and now he wished he had.

Holmes decided to talk with Arleen Hunter, the human resources manager, about his dilemma. Hunter was not very helpful, stating that "I've seen jobs given as favors over and over again; you have to make up your own mind on this one. However, I would point out that your boss, Ellis Duvall, is on the management review committee, which currently is studying different ways of reducing supervisory and other managerial personnel. I think you've got a difficult choice to make."

As Charles Holmes left Arleen Hunter's office, he primarily wondered whether his job would be eliminated if he failed to hire Rob Ling.

CASE 20

The Stress Interview Approach

Bradley Products Company employed some 500 employees in its manufacturing and warehouse facility. Sterling Durbin, the director of human resources, had held this position for the past 17 years. He prided himself on his ability to conduct interviews effectively. When Patricia Sutton was hired as a new assistant human resources manager, Durbin took great pleasure in "breaking in" this recent college graduate on the practical aspects of effective interviewing.

"I can size anyone up in ten minutes or less in an interview. My record shows how good I am at this, and I'll give you a few tips," Durbin told his new assistant. "We don't use written tests anymore because of EEOC hassles with them. It's just as well, because I didn't put much faith in what those tests showed anyway. As for personal interviews, we use several interviewers for important positions to get the effect of a group interview. Everyone asks the questions that they feel are important, and they report to me anything outstanding or particularly negative that turns up. My interview with a prospective employee is the one that usually counts the most, though. I'm looking for 'hard drivers' and people who I think will succeed around here. In just a few minutes, I can tell by the way they look at me, the kind of clothes they wear, and their general confidence in themselves whether or not they're likely to be good employees. For example, you can tell a lot about a man by the kind of shoes he wears and how well they are polished. Also, I put a lot of stock in whether or not the applicants have finished the education they began, whether it's high school, junior college, or university. It shows that they can finish things and can stick to their tasks."

Durbin continued, "The best techniques I've found to separate the poor applicants from those with real promise is to ask them how they would handle the following situation. I give them two alternatives to stop employees from arguing constantly with each other. First, the employees could be told either to work it out among themselves or to get a transfer out of the department. Second, the supervisor could sit down with the employees and work the difficulties out together. Whichever approach the applicant picks, I tell them that they are wrong. If they select the first method, I tell them that their job is to develop and help employees to perform better. If they select the second, I tell them they have more important things to do than to work out personal problems between employees. By doing this, I see how applicants handle stress and find out what they're made of. A good potential employee will stick by his guns and give me some good reasons why his approach should be followed. With all this information, I can usually make a good decision in a pretty short time. I've found that I am seldom wrong."

CASE 21

From Part Time to Full Time?

Alice Tumser was supervisor of the clerical staff in the Medical Records Department of a major urban hospital. She had the authority to hire and fire for her department, and she was not affected by a union contract since the hospital had no union. She had seven employees working for her full time. Whenever a regular clerical employee did not show up, she called Helen Drew, who worked as a relief person on a part-time basis.

Recently, Drew told Tumser that she would like to work full time, since she needed the income and was now in a position to leave her two small children with a baby-sitter. This request came as something of a surprise and a problem to Tumser. She had observed that, whenever Drew came in to help out, there seemed to be friction. Apparently Drew did not get along too well with the rest of the employees, most of whom were young, unmarried people in their early twenties. Tumser did not know whose fault it was, but there seemed to be numerous complaints about Drew from the other employees. Drew's work was of high quality, however; Tumser was certain of this.

Shortly after Helen Drew had asked to be considered for a permanent position, a full-time job opened up in the department. Alice Tumser pondered whether she should offer this job to Drew. Of course, Drew would be very pleased to get this position, and she knew it was open. But Tumser was concerned about the reaction of the other employees in the department.

CASE 22

Sanders Supermarkets (#21): Orientation of a New Employee

Max Brown was one of the most promising young applicants whom Nancy Brewer had interviewed and hired in months. As the employment manager of Sanders Supermarkets, she had instructed him on company policies, pay periods, rate of pay, etc., and had given him information about the union. He then left with his referral slip to report to Store #21, a large one located in a suburban shopping center.

Before Brown went to his new job, he stopped at his favorite clothing store and bought new white shirts to conform with the company dress code described by Brewer. He then went to the barber shop for a haircut, the first he had had since graduating from high school several months ago.

Upon arriving at Store #21, Brown introduced himself to Carl Dressel, the store supervisor. Dressel then told Brown to go over to aisle #3 and tell Sean Kelly, the head stock clerk, that he was to work with him. Brown walked into aisle #3, but no one was there. Not knowing what to do next, he just waited for someone to show up. About 20 minutes later, Kelly came into the aisle with a stock truck full of cases. Brown introduced himself and said, "Mr. Dressel told me to come and work with Sean Kelly. Is that you?"

"Yeah," said Kelly, "I was just going to lunch. Here's my case cutter and price stamper. You can figure it out. I'll see you in 30 minutes or so."

Kelly then left the aisle with Max Brown standing there rather confused. "Some training program," he thought to himself. Nancy Brewer had said that there would be lockers in the store for his personal items, but he wondered where they were. Brewer had also told him about punching a time card, so he wondered where the time cards were. Since Kelly had an apron on to protect his clothes, Brown tried to figure out where he could get one, too. He thought he might look in the backroom to see if the answers to some of his questions might just be back there. Walking into the backroom, he confronted one of the stock clerks and asked where he could hang his coat, get a time card, and find an apron.

"We just throw our coats on top of the overstock, the aprons are in the office, and so are the time cards," said the stock clerk.

"At last," thought Brown. "Now I'm getting someplace." On his way to the office, he saw two other stock clerks working in aisle #1. He had seen four stock clerks so far, and only one wore a tie. Two had on plaid shirts, and the other had hair at least three inches below the collar. "I don't understand why Nancy Brewer was worried about the way I looked," he thought.

Finally, Brown found an apron and a time card. To find the time clock, he went toward the backroom again and asked one of the meat cutters where the time clock was. He was given directions to go through the meat department to the other side of the store. He went through the door he was told to go through, which had a sign on it saying, "Authorized Personnel Only." He was worried that he might not be an "authorized" person. He finally found the time clock and, with a little difficulty, he figured out how to clock in. This done, he hurried back to aisle #3 where Carl Dressel stood waiting for him. "Where the hell have you been?" asked Dressel. "And where is Kelly?"

Brown explained that Kelly had gone to lunch and that he himself had been looking for an apron, the time clock, and a place to hang his coat. "You might as well learn right away that your job is putting up the loads of stock— and fast! I don't want to hear any more excuses. Now get to work," said Dressel.

As Brown started to open the top of the first box of cases, he thought to himself, "The only thing I know for sure right now is that Nancy Brewer has never worked in the stores!"

CASE 23

The Quasi-Demotion

Frank Schneider, plant superintendent of Central Metalworks Co., had just been informed that a young man named Kirk Bell had been hired from outside the firm for the position of vice-president of manufacturing, a job that Schneider very much wanted to have. Bell was in his early thirties and had an undergraduate engineering degree, a master's degree in business administration, and some previous working experience.

Schneider was 50 years old. He had been with this firm for almost 30 years, working his way up from the bottom. Starting as a machine operator, he progressed to the positions of leadman, foreman of various departments, assistant superintendent, and his current job, which he had held for seven years. He had no formal education after finishing high school, but he had a well-recognized talent for machines, tools, and anything associated with manufacturing metal parts. He also had an excellent ability to work with people, and he was well-liked and respected by the employees.

When the president of the company, R. D. Allen, told Schneider who his new boss would be, Schneider replied, "I don't know whether I can work for a young man 20 years my junior, especially one who never dirtied his hands fixing or running a piece of machinery. What can a fellow like this possibly know about running a manufacturing plant?"

A few days later, Allen met with Bell in his office. "Kirk," said Allen, "I think you may have a serious problem with Frank Schneider. He's a good man, but his feelings are hurt, and he thinks he's been demoted. What would you propose to do to win him over?"

CASE 24

Sanders Supermarkets (#13): Who Should Be Promoted to Head Stock Clerk?

Robert Frazier was the store supervisor for Store #13 of the Sanders Supermarkets. Early one morning Jerry Stiffelman, stock clerk, approached him.

Stock Clerk: *Bob, I hear that Tim Stapleton was promoted to head stock clerk. Why didn't I get a chance at the promotion? I've been working here eight years, and he's only been here six. Doesn't seniority count as long as two people are equally qualified?*

Store Supervisor: *Jerry, you were considered for the job at one time, but now I don't feel that you are qualified to handle the job. So, you were passed over.*

Stock Clerk: *What do you mean, I'm not qualified? I've done the job several times in the past when other head stock clerks were on vacation. You've never told me before that I couldn't handle it. It was my understanding that I'd get the next promotion on the basis of my seniority. This is a hell of a time to tell me that I don't have the ability to do what I've already done before.*

Store Supervisor: *Nevertheless, that's our decision.*

Stock Clerk: *That may be your decision now, but you'll think differently when the union contacts you. (And with that, Jerry walked away.)*

Robert Frazier started to think about what Jerry Stiffelman had said and remembered certain facts that he would bring out if the union did get involved. He considered Stiffelman a satisfactory stock clerk but certainly not above average. He believed that Stiffelman lacked the ability and dependability to handle the job of head stock clerk. On several occasions that Stiffelman had relieved other head stock clerks, the store had experienced out-of-stocks as a result of his poor job of ordering. Twice Frazier had received phone calls from the police on the nights that Stiffelman had closed up the store and had accidentally set off the burglar alarm system. He further noted that Stiffelman was frequently absent from work. During the previous year, Stiffelman had been absent 20 days, offering illness as the reason for his absence.

Several days later, Frazier was confronted by his boss, Susan Kennedy. As district manager, Kennedy was responsible for seven Sanders stores. The following dialogue took place:

District Manager: *Bob, we have a grievance filed by the union on behalf of Jerry Stiffelman. The union claims that we should let him have the chance to prove he can handle the job. How well has he done as a temporary head stock clerk?*

Store Supervisor: *Terrible, Susan. The police woke me up two times because Stiffelman bungled the burglar alarm system, and we had numerous out-of-stocks from his ordering.*

District Manager: *Why didn't you tell me about this before? Did you talk to Stiffelman about these things?*

Store Supervisor: *I thought I did tell you, Susan, didn't I? But I think I did talk to him about it for sure. Customers were driving me crazy because we were out of grape jelly. He caused me a lot of headaches.*

District Manager: *Well, according to his personnel file, he has never been written up. And as far as I can see, by seniority he was in line for a promotion. In response to the union grievance, I told the human resources department that we'd consider giving the head stock clerk position to Stiffelman on the basis of his seniority over Tim Stapleton.*

Store Supervisor: *That's a big mistake, Susan, because Stiffelman cannot handle it. Besides all that, he is absent too often.*

District Manager: *What do you mean, absent too often?*

Store Supervisor: *Over the past year he has been ''sick'' 20 days.*

District Manager: *There's no mention of any sick pay granted in his file. Was he paid for sick leave?*

Store Supervisor: *Darned if I know. I don't have time to pay attention to all these paperwork details.*

District Manager: *Okay, Bob. I guess we've got a real problem on our hands. Take a look at this provision of the union contract. It says that in making promotions we must give preference to the most senior employee, provided merit and ability are equal. What do you think we should do? The union business agent told me that, if we don't promote Jerry Stiffelman, the union will take this case all the way to arbitration.*

Store Supervisor: *I think we should take a stand and stick with our original decision. Stiffelman just doesn't deserve the promotion, and I'll have nothing but trouble if he becomes a head stock clerk.*

CASE 25

What Do I Say to Him?

Jane McGraw sat at her desk preparing for an evaluation session with one of her employees. McGraw was the advertising director in the Marketing Department of a major retail department store chain; she supervised 14 employees in her unit. Several days ago, McGraw had completed a performance appraisal form for Art Gross, a copyediting employee. She was now waiting for Gross to come to her office for his evaluation interview.

McGraw was concerned about what she should say to Gross regarding his evaluation. She expected that there would be problems, because she again had rated Gross as "average" on most of the categories on the appraisal form. Only on "attendance" and "relationships with other employees" had she rated him as being "above average."

McGraw believed that Gross had not performed at anything other than a general or average level in most of his work responsibilities. In reviewing last year's appraisal form, she recognized that this was the same level that she had appraised Gross at that time. During her interview with him last year, Gross had disagreed strongly with her evaluation, because he thought he should have been rated "above average" or "excellent" on most factors. McGraw had tried to explain to him at that time why she had rated Gross as "average" on most categories, and she felt that these were proper ratings. He had responded that her evaluation was unfair, and that he felt it was discriminatory as compared to other employees. McGraw denied this, and she let the evaluation form stand as she had developed it. Gross refused to sign the form, since he was quite upset about it.

Now it was another year. McGraw recognized that she really had not given Art Gross any good specific guidance as to how to improve from a year ago. She also recognized that she had only several conversations with him during the past year; most were about certain job situations and did not relate specifically to his job performance. McGraw recognized that she should have kept much better records and developed some specific examples to discuss with Gross. But pressures of business and responsibilities of supervising a large group of employees had kept her from keeping good records.

Now she wondered what would happen this time, and what she should say to him. Jane McGraw was convinced in her own mind that Gross was at best an average employee who had not improved over the last year. As she was pondering what she should say, Art Gross entered her office.

PART 5

DIRECTING

CHAPTER 15

Supervisory Directives and the Introduction of Change

CHAPTER OBJECTIVES

1. To emphasize the importance of the managerial directing function in getting results at the supervisory level.
2. To define and discuss major characteristics of a good supervisory directive.
3. To emphasize why supervisors should explain the reasons for their directives.
4. To compare autocratic and close supervision with consultative (participative) and general supervision.
5. To suggest approaches for introducing change to employees and to higher management.

Directing is the process that managers use to achieve goal-directed behavior from subordinates; thus directing is the managerial function that initiates action. It primarily means issuing instructions, assignments, and directives (orders), but it also includes building an effective work force by encouraging employees to work willingly and enthusiastically toward the accomplishment of desired objectives. Thus directing also has been identified as *leading, motivating, activating,* or *influencing.*

Every manager—a president of a company, a regional sales manager, an administrator of a university, or a departmental supervisor—performs the directing function. However, the time and effort a manager spends in directing will vary depending upon the manager's level in the organization, the number of subordinates, and the duties the manager is expected to perform. First-line supervisors normally spend most of their time in directing, whereas top executives usually spend relatively much less time on this function.

The supervisor's directing function is closely related to each of the other managerial functions. Planning, organizing, and staffing can be viewed as preparatory or preliminary managerial functions, and controlling can be considered as a check to see whether or not goals are being achieved. The connecting and actuating link between these functions is directing.

OBSERVING UNITY OF COMMAND

Giving directives is a major part of a supervisor's daily routine. Although any supervisor can learn to issue orders in some fashion, there is general agreement that some ways of issuing directives are more effective than others. The experienced supervisor knows that poorly issued orders can upset even the best-laid plans; instead of coordination of efforts, a state of turmoil can result.

At this point it is advisable to recall the principle of unity of command, which we discussed in Chapter 9. Unity of command means that each employee has only one immediate supervisor, and that directives to an employee normally should be given only by his or her immediate supervisor—except in an emergency or in unusual circumstances. Few employees can serve two or more bosses without confusion and loss of efficiency. Following unity of command provides for a direct line of authority from a supervisor to subordinates.

Unfortunately the unity-of-command principle is frequently violated. This sometimes occurs when a supervisor is under pressure and needs to communicate with someone who reports to another supervisor. For example, a sales manager may go directly to a shipping department clerk to tell the clerk to "rush delivery" on a certain order. If the sales manager does not later "clear" this directive with the shipping department supervisor, this can lead to resentment. The shipping department supervisor will feel that he has been by-passed and his departmental authority weakened.

To repeat, therefore, it is desirable that directives observe and follow the unity-of-command principle and be issued by an employee's immediate supervisor. When this is not possible—for example, in emergencies or in matrix organizational structures (as discussed in Chapter 9)—supervisors should be careful to explain the reasons for these exceptions, both to their fellow supervisors and to the affected employees. If necessary, supervisors should seek clarification from higher level management to clear up areas of overlap in their departments, so that their direct authority and unity of command can be maintained.

CHARACTERISTICS OF GOOD SUPERVISORY DIRECTIVES

Some supervisors who "break every rule in the book" when giving directives seem to achieve excellent results. Other supervisors who use the accepted techniques and who phrase their directives in courteous language still get only grudging compliance. The question of what is the most appropriate way to give an order or directive depends on the supervisor's and subordinates' personalities and attitudes, the job situation, and other factors. More important, however, is that the directive itself must be a good one.

Since issuing directives is the primary means for a supervisor to start, modify, or stop employee activities, every supervisor should thoroughly understand the fundamental characteristics of a good, sound directive. These characteristics are: reasonable, understandable, specific and with a definite time limit, compatible with organizational objectives, and communicated with an appropriate tone and wording.

Reasonable

The first essential characteristic of a good directive is that it must be reasonable. Reasonableness obviously means that no orders should be issued requiring activities that physically cannot be accomplished or that would be personally dangerous to attempt as, for example, to lift a steel bar that weighs 500 pounds. To judge whether a directive reasonably can be accomplished, the supervisor should appraise it from his or her own point of view, as well as the employee's. The supervisor should not issue a directive if the employee receiving it does not have the capability or experience necessary to comply with what is wanted.

There are occasions when a supervisor may issue unreasonable directives. For example, in order to please higher management, a supervisor may promise the completion of a job at a particular time. The supervisor proceeds to issue orders without consulting with the employees who are to do the work and without checking to determine whether other required resources to meet the commitment are available.

Therefore, before issuing directives, supervisors first should mentally

Fig 15–1.
The effective supervisor does not issue unreasonable directives.

place themselves in the position of the employees and thoughtfully consider whether compliance can reasonably be expected. There are some borderline cases where directives actually are intended to stretch the employees' capabilities a bit beyond what previously has been requested. In such instances the question of reasonableness becomes a matter of degree. Generally speaking, however, a prime requirement of a good directive is that it can be accomplished in the desired manner by the employee to whom the directive is given.

Understandable

A directive should be intelligible and understandable to those who receive it. This essentially is a matter of communication as was discussed in Chapter 6. The supervisor should make certain that an employee understands a directive by speaking in words and terms that are familiar to the employee and by using the technique of feedback. Instructions should be clear but not necessarily lengthy. What is clear and complete to the supervisor is not always clear and complete to the employee.

Specific and with a Definite Time Limit

Specificity of a directive means that it states exactly what is expected of the employee who receives it, especially when quantity and quality of work performance are involved. If a directive contains several steps to be performed, the supervisor may find it desirable to put the directive in writing and then discuss the steps with the employee to clear up possible ambiguities.

A good directive should also specify a time limit within which it should be carried out and completed. A reasonable amount of time must be allowed, since the quality of work may depend on the time allotment. Where the time factor needs to be agreed on, the supervisor and employee should discuss how the directive can be carried out within a reasonable time. If the supervisor needs to impose a time limit, perhaps this can be done with the understanding that the time limit can be modified if circumstances dictate. Generally it is undesirable to simply tell an employee to do something "when you find time to get around to it." This invites procrastination and confusion.

Compatible with Organizational Objectives

A good directive should be compatible with the purposes and objectives of the organization. If it is not, employees may be reluctant to carry out the directive adequately or may not execute it at all. For example, assume that the employees of a utility company have been told over and over again that serving customers is the major purpose of the company. Then one day, their supervisor, under pressure to reduce costs and avoid overtime work, simply tells them to "stop work and let the customer wait for service until the following day." This directive may conflict with the employees' previous understanding that customer service always had top priority. Therefore, if a supervisor issues a directive that appears to employees to be in conflict with organizational objectives or contrary to what is done normally, he or she must explain the reasons why such a directive may be necessary.

Of course, any directive must be in compliance with policies, regulations, and stated ethical standards of the organization. Any directive that would require or permit employees to falsify documents or reports, claim undeserved expenses, and the like, is obviously unacceptable. In fact, a supervisor who issues such directives may eventually be "found out" by higher management, and this can be grounds for the supervisor's dismissal.

Appropriate Tone and Wording

The tone and wording of a directive can significantly affect the employees' acceptance and performance. A polite, considerate tone is more likely to encourage willing response and acceptance. Further, supervisors should avoid using the term "order," and instead should use terms such as assignments, requests, instructions, suggestions, or directives.[1] Phrasing an order as a request does not reduce its character as a directive, but there usually will be a difference in the reaction a request will inspire as compared to an "order" or "command."

---

[1] An exception would be a health-care facility or a military organization, where the term "order" is customarily used.

Commands.   Some individuals must be told firmly what to do. At times, a direct order or command to these individuals may be needed to get things done. For example, a supervisor might have to say, "George, we are running behind schedule. You must get five units out today." Everyone remembers commands from parents and school teachers as a part of growing up. Most employees feel that they are grown up and should be treated as adults. Therefore, a supervisor should avoid commands and orders whenever possible; in most instances there are better ways to communicate what is needed.

Requests.   A directive may be phrased as a request. For the majority of employees, a request is all that is needed or wanted. It is a mature way of stating what needs to be done, especially with those employees who have been working for the supervisor for some time and who are familiar with the supervisor and the job. A request usually works better with this kind of employee, and it will not "rub the wrong way." For example, a supervisor could say, "George, would you see if you can get five units out today? We seem to be behind schedule."

Suggestions.   In other instances a directive can be phrased as a suggestion, which is even milder than a request. The suggestive form of the preceding directive could be stated, "George, we are five units behind schedule today." Suggestions usually accomplish their purpose when they are grasped by responsible employees. Many employees take the initiative to get the job accomplished when the need is communicated to them. However, a suggestive type of directive would not be advisable if the supervisor is dealing with new employees who do not have sufficient training and familiarity with the department's routine. Further, suggestions generally are not an effective way to give assignments to employees who are incompetent or undependable.

EXPLAINING REASONS FOR DIRECTIVES

Unless just routine activities are involved, and whenever it is appropriate and time is available, supervisors should thoroughly explain the reasons behind their directives and why certain things have to be done. Admittedly it is difficult for a supervisor to issue a directive so completely as to cover all contingencies and leave no room for interpretation or adaptation. But employees who know the purpose and reasons behind a directive usually are better prepared to use good judgment and perform in a manner that will produce the desired results. Without knowing the "why" of directives, employees may experience anxiety-producing situations, particularly if they encounter unforeseen circumstances while carrying them out.

There is an old story that illustrates the importance of explaining the reasons behind directives. A supervisor instructed a crew of workers to dig holes at random in the factory yard. During the morning, each time two workers had dug a hole four feet deep, the supervisor came over to inspect the hole and then ordered the workers to fill it up again. After the lunch break, the work crew threatened to refuse continuing the job, since they thought it to be useless and stupid. At this point the supervisor told them that the blueprints for an old water main had been lost and that they were searching for this water main. Having heard the explanation, the workers were content to resume their job. Obviously, the supervisor could have avoided this conflict by explaining the reason for the job right at the beginning. Further, as each hole was dug, the workers themselves could have searched for the water main, and the supervisor would not have had to inspect each hole.

In a desire to explain reasons behind directives, a supervisor may overdo a good thing. Explanations should include enough information to give employees sufficient background without overwhelming them. If a directive involves only a minor activity and if not much time is available, the explanation should be brief. For example, a data entry clerk might ask her supervisor to explain why a completely new data record must be entered into the computerized payroll system of the company because of a minor change in state tax rates. All the supervisor needs to explain is the how and why of the task, rather than to launch into a twenty-minute discussion of computers and the theory of taxation! Further, the supervisor should avoid using extremely technical language in trying to explain the meaning of each data record entry or the clerk might become even more confused.

Supervisors must use good judgment in deciding how far to go in explaining reasons for their directives. Much will depend on factors such as the content of the directive, the supervisor's attitude, the time available, the employee's capacity to understand, and previous training.

APPROACHES TO SUPERVISORY DIRECTING

In Chapter 4 we discussed employee motivation and the concept of a hierarchy of human needs, along with Theory X, Theory Y, and other styles or approaches to management that reflect different assumptions about motivation in relation to these needs. In other chapters we introduced concepts of broad and narrow delegation of authority and participative decision making. We expand these concepts in this chapter in order to relate them to day-to-day approaches that a supervisor may utilize when issuing directives.

Generally speaking, the basic approaches, or styles, of supervisory direction range from **autocratic and close supervision** (based on Theory X assumptions) to **consultative and general supervision** (based on Theory Y assumptions). In a textbook discussion, these two approaches can be presented as extremes.[2] However, in practice the supervisor usually depends on shadings and blendings of these approaches. The proportions and applications will vary, depending on the supervisor's skill and experience, the employees involved, the situation at hand, and other factors. No one style of supervision is equally correct or incorrect in all situations. Every supervisor should be sensitive to the needs of each situation and adjust his or her style as necessary to accomplish the objectives at hand.

Autocratic and Close Supervision

Autocratic and close supervision implies direct, clear, and concise orders with detailed instructions to subordinates. Little or no room is allowed for initiative on the part of employees. Autocratic supervisors delegate as little authority as possible. They believe that they know how to do the job better than any of their employees, and that employees are ''not paid to think'' but to follow orders. These supervisors further believe that since they have been put in charge and are being paid for it, they should do the planning and decision making. Since they are quite explicit in telling employees exactly how and in what sequence things are to be done, they follow through with close supervision.

Some autocratic supervisors do not necessarily distrust their employees; they believe that without detailed instructions, employees could not carry out directives. There are some autocratic supervisors who assume that the average employee does not want to do the job; therefore, close supervision and threats of loss of job or income are required in order to get employees to work (Theory X). These supervisors feel that if they are not on the scene ''breathing down their employees' necks,'' the employees would stop working.

Probably the major advantages of autocratic and close supervision are that it is quick and easy to apply, and that it usually gets rapid results in the short run. However, the autocratic method of supervision is not conducive to developing employee talents, and tends to frustrate those employees who have ambition and potential.

Effects of Autocratic and Close Supervision.　For many employees the consequences of autocratic and close supervision are negative. They tend to lose interest and initiative; they stop thinking for themselves because there is little need or occasion for independent thought. They may be obedient, but it is difficult for them to remain loyal to the organization and the supervisor. Given an alternative, ambitious employees will not remain in positions where

---

[2]In Chapter 3 these broadly defined supervisory styles were discussed in relation to delegating authority with responsibility

the supervisor is not willing to delegate some degree of latitude and authority. Any employee who is willing to learn and who wants to progress will resent constant, detailed instructions.

In some cases individual employees or groups of employees may develop hostilities toward an autocratic supervisor and perhaps even resist carrying out the supervisor's directives. The resistance may not even be apparent to the supervisor when it takes the form of slow work, mistakes, and poor quality of work. If the supervisor makes a mistake, they secretly rejoice over it!

When Autocratic and Close Supervision Is Appropriate.   Under certain circumstances and with some employees, autocratic and close supervision is both logical and appropriate. Some employees do not want to think for themselves and prefer to receive orders. Others lack ambition and do not wish to become much involved in their daily jobs. This is often the case where jobs are very structured, highly mechanized, automated, or routinized, so that employees may prefer a supervisor who mainly issues orders to them and otherwise leaves them alone.

There are also employees who have been reared by authoritarian parents or in authoritarian environments, and who expect a supervisor to be a boss who is firm and totally in charge. However, these types of employees usually are in the minority. In the American culture, most men and women have been reared in a democratic society from their early school days, and they tend to resent order-giving by autocratic bosses, which they view as being contrary to the democratic way of life.

Consultative and General Supervision

The opposite of autocratic and close supervision is consultative and general supervision. In this text we associate **consultative supervision** with employees' participation in decision-making situations regarding their jobs and **general supervision** with situations where directives are issued for regular, repetitive, and routine assignments. Both operate from the premises of Theory Y and can be practiced simultaneously by the supervisor.

The Meaning of Consultative Supervision.   Consultative supervision also could be called **participative management** in supervision. The supervisor who uses this approach discusses with employees the feasibility, workability, extent, and content of a problem before making a decision and issuing a directive. Consultative supervision does not lessen or weaken a supervisor's authority; the right to decide remains with the supervisor, and the employees' suggestions can be rejected. Consultative supervision means that a supervisor expresses personal opinions in a manner that indicates to employees that these opinions are subject to critical appraisal. Consultation means a sharing of ideas and information between supervisor and employees and thorough discussion of alternative solutions to a problem, regardless of who originates the solutions.

More important than the exact approach is the supervisor's attitude. Some supervisors are inclined to use a pseudo-consultative approach simply to give employees the "feeling" that they have been consulted. These supervisors ask for ideas or suggestions, even though they already have decided on a definite course of action. They use this approach to manipulate employees to do what will be required with or without their consultation. However, employees can sense superficiality and will usually perceive whether a supervisor is genuinely consulting on a problem. If employees believe that their participation is fake, the results may be worse than if the supervisor had practiced autocratic supervision.

If consultative supervision is to be successful, not only must the supervisor be in favor of it, but also the employees must want it. If the employees are individuals who believe that "the boss knows best" and that making decisions and giving directives is none of their responsibility or concern, there is little likelihood that an opportunity to participate will induce higher motivation and better morale. Further, employees should be consulted only in those areas where they are capable of expressing valid opinions and where they can draw on their own fund of knowledge. The problems involved should be consistent with the employees' experiences and abilities. Asking for participation in areas that are far outside of the employees' scope of competence may have the adverse effect of making them feel inadequate and frustrated.

Advantages of Consultative Supervision.   Perhaps the greatest advantage of consultative supervision is that a supervisor's directive can be changed from that of an order to a solution that employees themselves discovered or, at least, one in which they participated. This normally leads employees to cooperate with more enthusiasm in carrying out the directive. Further, employee morale is apt to be higher when their ideas are desired and valued. Active participation provides an opportunity to make worthwhile contributions. Still another advantage is that consultative supervision permits closer communication between employees and the supervisor, so that they learn to know and respect each other better.

Organized Participative Management Programs.   In Chapter 4 we discussed a number of organized types of participative management programs that currently are being used and followed by many companies and organizations. These programs are called *quality circles,*[3] *quality-of-work-life pro-*

---

[3]See Edward E. Lawler III and Susan A. Mohrman, "Quality Circles after the Fad," *Harvard Business Review* (January–February 1985), pp. 65–71.

grams, employee participation teams, and the like. In essence, all of these efforts employ principles and premises of consultative supervision, and they have most of the same attendant advantages. When such a program is in place, the supervisor by definition is "forced" to practice consultative and participative management, which may go considerably beyond mere consultation. Some of these programs call for active employee involvement in making and implementing decisions; most of these are concerned with problems stemming from work operations at the departmental level. However, some of the issues and problems may even involve company-wide situations and interdepartmental relationships.

The Meaning of General Supervision.   As stated earlier, general supervision primarily is identified with routine or daily tasks for which employees are trained and with which they are well acquainted. General supervision means permitting employees—within prescribed or agreed-upon limits—to work out the details of such tasks and to make many or most of the decisions about how tasks will be performed. In so doing, the supervisor believes that employees want to do a good job and will find greater satisfaction in making decisions for themselves. The supervisor communicates the desired results, standards, and limits within which the employees can work and then delegates accordingly.

For example, a maintenance department supervisor might assign a group of employees to paint the interior walls of a plant. The supervisor tells the group where to get the paint and other materials, and reminds them that they should do the painting without interfering in the normal operations of the production department. Then the supervisor suggests a target date for completing the project and leaves the group to work on their own. The supervisor may say that he or she will occasionally check back with the group to see whether they are encountering any problems or need help.

General supervision is not the same as no supervision. Under general supervision, employees are expected to know the routine of their jobs and what results are expected. But the supervisor avoids giving detailed instructions that specify precisely how results are to be achieved.

General supervision also means that the supervisor, or the supervisor and employees together, should set realistic standards or performance targets. These should be high enough to represent a challenge, but not so high that they cannot be achieved. Such targets sometimes are known as **stretching standards.** Employees know that their efforts are being measured against these standards. If they are unable to accomplish the targeted objectives, they are expected to inform the supervisor so that the standards can be discussed again and perhaps modified.

Consultative and General Supervision as a Way of Life.   When practiced simultaneously, consultative and general supervision is a way of life that must be followed over a period of time. A supervisor cannot expect sudden results by introducing this type of supervision into a situation where employees have been accustomed to autocratic and close supervision. It may take considerable time and patience before positive results are evident.

Successful implementation of consultative and general supervision requires a continuous effort on a supervisor's part to develop employees beyond their present skills. Employees tend to learn more when they can work out solutions for themselves rather than when they are given solutions. Further, they learn best from their own successes and failures.

The participative type of supervisor spends considerable time encouraging employees to solve their own problems and to participate in and make decisions. As employees become more competent and self-confident, there is less need for the supervisor to instruct and direct them. A valid way to gauge the effectiveness of a supervisor is to study how employees in the department function when the supervisor is away from the job.

Although a supervisor may use consultative and general supervision whenever possible, from time to time he or she will have to demonstrate firmness and authority with those employees who require close and autocratic supervision. Consultative and general supervisors must be as performance conscious as any other type of supervisor. It is merely the style they use that differentiates them from authoritarian supervisors.

THE INTRODUCTION OF CHANGE[4]

Another challenging aspect of a supervisor's directing function occurs whenever the need exists to introduce change. Change is expected as part of everyday life, and the survival and growth of most enterprises depend on change and innovation. The introduction of change—such as a new work method, a new product, a new work schedule, or a new personnel policy—usually involves the issuance of supervisory directives at the departmental level. In the final analysis, it is the supervisor who typically has to bring about the change.

Reasons for Resistance to Change

Some supervisors are inclined to discount the existence and magnitude of human resistance to change. They fail to recognize that what may seem like a trifling change may bring strong reaction from the employees. Supervisors should remember that employees seldom resist change just to be stubborn. They resist because they believe a change threatens their positions socially,

---

[4]For a practical, extensive discussion of introducing change, see Murray M. Dalziel and Stephen C. Schoonover, *Changing Ways* (New York: AMACOM, 1988).

psychologically, or economically. Therefore, the supervisor should be familiar with the ways in which resistance to change can be minimized and handled successfully.

Most people pride themselves on being modern and up to date. As consumers, they expect and welcome changes in material things such as new automobiles, homes, clothing, appliances, or gadgets. But as employees, they may strenuously resist changes on the job or changes in personal relationships, even though such changes are vital for the operation of the organization. If an organization is to survive, it must be able to react to prevailing conditions by changing and developing directives which will incorporate and implement necessary adjustments.

Change tends to disturb the environment in which people exist. Prior to a change, employees become accustomed to a work environment where patterns of relationships and behavior have reached a degree of stability. When a change takes place, new ideas and new methods may be perceived as a threat to the security of the work group. Many employees fear change because they cannot predict what the change will mean in terms of their own positions, activities, or abilities. It makes no difference whether the change actually has a negative result. What matters is that the employees believe or fear that negative consequences will be experienced as a result of the change.

For example, the introduction of new machinery or equipment is usually accompanied by employee fears of loss of jobs or skills. Even though the supervisor and higher management announce that no employees will be laid off, rumors and fears circulate that layoffs will occur and existing jobs will be

Fig 15–2. Many people fear change because they cannot assess or predict what the change will mean in terms of their own positions.

downgraded. It may not be until months after the change has been in place that employee fears will subside.

Changes affect individuals in different ways. A change that causes great disturbance to one person may create only a small problem for another. A supervisor must learn to recognize how changes affect different employees and to observe how individuals develop patterns of behavior that serve as barriers to accepting change.

Reducing Resistance to Change

Probably the most important factor in gaining employee acceptance of new ideas and methods is the personal relationship that exists between the supervisor who is introducing the change and the employees who are affected by it. If a relationship of confidence and trust exists, the employees more likely will accept the change readily.[5]

Provide Adequate Information.   First of all, a supervisor should explain as early as possible what will happen, why, and how employees and the department will be affected by a change. If appropriate, the supervisor should emphasize how the change either will leave employees no worse off or may even improve their present situation. This information should be communicated to all employees who are directly or indirectly involved, either individually or in a meeting. Only then can employees assess and understand what a change will mean in terms of their positions and activities. This will be facilitated if the supervisor consistently has tried to give ample background information for all directives.

Employees who are well acquainted with the underlying factors that surround departmental operations will better understand the necessity for change. They probably will ask questions about a change, but they then can adjust to it and go on. When employees have been informed of the reasons for a change, they know what to expect and how their jobs will be affected. Instead of blind resistance, usually there will be intelligent adaptation. Instead of insecurity, there will be a feeling of relative confidence. In the final analysis, it is not the change itself that usually leads to resistance. Rather, it is the manner in which the supervisor introduces the change. Thus resistance to change that comes from fear of the unknown can be minimized by supplying all the information that the employees consciously and subconsciously want and need to know in order to minimize or dispel their fears.

Participation in Decision Making.   Another technique for reducing resistance to change is to permit the employees affected by the change to share in

---

[5]For an expanded discussion of this topic, see Gordon F. Shea, *Building Trust in the Workplace* (New York: AMACOM, 1984).

making decisions about it. If several employees are involved in a change, group decision making is an effective way to overcome or reduce employee fears and objections. When employees have an opportunity to work through new ideas and methods from the beginning, usually they will consider the new directives as something of their own making and then give their support. The group may even apply pressure on those who have reservations about going along with the change, and it is likely that each member of the group then will carry out the change once there is agreement on how to proceed.

Group decision making is especially effective in those changes where the supervisor is indifferent about the details, so long as the change is implemented. Here the supervisor must set the limits within which the group can decide. For example, a supervisor may not be concerned how a new departmental work schedule is divided among the group so long as the work is accomplished within a prescribed time, with a given number of employees, and without overtime.

Proposing a Change to Higher Management

In many organizations higher management complains that supervisors are too content with the status quo and are unwilling to suggest new and innovative ways of improving departmental performance. Supervisors, on the other hand, complain that higher management is not receptive to ideas that they have suggested for their departments. There is probably some truth to both complaints.

If supervisors wish to propose changes, it is important that they understand how to present ideas not only to their employees but also to higher management. "Selling" an idea to a boss involves the use of certain concepts and the art of persuasion. A good salesperson uses many of these same concepts in selling a product or service to a reluctant customer!

Obtain Needed Information. The supervisor who has a good idea or who wishes to suggest a change should first ask, "What aspects of the idea or change will be of most interest to the boss?" Higher management usually will be interested if a change might improve production, increase profits, improve morale, or reduce overhead and other costs. It is important to do considerable homework to see whether a proposed change is feasible and adaptable to the departmental operation. By carefully thinking through the idea and getting as much information as possible, the supervisor will be in a better position to argue strong and weak points of the proposal. In addition, the supervisor should find out whether any other departments or companies have used the proposed idea—either successfully or unsuccessfully. Doing this will impress the boss that the supervisor has invested time and effort in checking out the idea in other work environments.

Consult with Other Supervisors. In order to get an idea or proposal beyond the discussion stage, the supervisor should consult with other supervisors and personnel who might be affected and get their reactions to the proposed change. Checking it out with them gives them a chance to think the idea through, to offer suggestions and criticisms, and to "work out some of the bugs." Otherwise some supervisors may resist or resent the change if they feel they have been ignored.

If possible, it is helpful to get the advance approval or tentative commitment of other supervisors. It is not always necessary to obtain their total commitment or approval. Yet, higher management will be more inclined to consider the idea if it has been discussed at least in preliminary form with knowledgeable people in the organization.

Formal Written Proposal.   At times a supervisor will be asked by the boss to put the proposed idea in writing, so that copies may be forwarded to higher management, other supervisors, or other personnel. This requires hard work and effort. The supervisor may have to devote considerable study outside of normal working hours to obtain all the information that is needed. Relevant information on costs, prices, productivity data, and the like should be included in the proposal, even if some data are only educated guesses. Highly uncertain estimates should be labeled as tentative, and exaggerated claims and opinions should be avoided. Risks, as well as potential advantages, should be acknowledged in the formal proposal.

Formal Presentation.   If a supervisor is asked to make a formal presentation of the proposal to a group or at a meeting, ample planning and preparation again are required. The presentation should be made thoroughly and in an unhurried fashion, allowing sufficient time for questioning, which inevitably will occur.

The supervisor who has carefully thought through an idea should not be afraid to express it in a firm and convincing manner. The supervisor should be enthusiastic in explaining the idea, but at the same time be patient and empathic with those who may not agree with it. A helpful technique in a formal presentation is to utilize some type of chart, diagram, or visual aid that will dramatize the presentation.

Acceptance or Rejection of Change by Higher Management

A supervisor who is able to persuade higher management and other supervisors to accept a proposed change will realize a feeling of inner satisfaction. Of course, any good idea typically will require careful implementation, follow-up, and refinement, as necessary. Rarely does a change follow the exact blueprint that has been suggested. Follow-up and working out the problems with others are important aspects of making any change effective.

Despite a supervisor's best efforts, the idea presented may be rejected, altered greatly, or shelved. This can be frustrating, particularly to a supervisor who has worked diligently to develop an idea that he or she believes would lead to positive results. The important thing here is to avoid becoming discouraged and developing a negative outlook. There may be valid reasons why the idea was rejected, or perhaps the timing was not right. A supervisor should resolve to try again, perhaps to further refine and polish the idea for resubmission at a future date.

A supervisor who has developed an idea for change, even if it has not been accepted, usually will find that such efforts were appreciated by higher management. Further, the experience of having worked through a proposal for change is one that will make the supervisor a more valuable member of the organizational team, and there will be many other opportunities to work for the introduction of change.

SUMMARY

The managerial directing function forms the connecting link between planning, organizing, and staffing on the one hand and controlling on the other. Directives issued by a supervisor should normally follow the principle of unity of command.

Among the characteristics that good supervisory directives should possess are: (a) reasonable, (b) understandable, (c) specific and with a definite time limit, (d) compatible with organizational objectives, and (e) appropriate tone and wording.

A supervisor may direct using approaches ranging from autocratic and close supervision at one extreme to consultative and general supervision at the other extreme. Autocratic supervision is effective for certain occasions, employees, and conditions. However, for most situations it is better to use applications of the consultative (participative) and general supervision techniques. Consultative supervision is particularly adaptable for new job assignments, whereas general supervision is appropriate for routine assignments and daily tasks.

In order to successfully cope with employees' normal resistance to change, supervisors must understand why resistance surfaces and what can be done to help employees adjust and accept changes that must be implemented. A supervisor also should learn the principles of ''selling'' change to higher management. This typically involves persuading the boss, higher management, and other supervisors that the acceptance and adoption of a proposal will benefit them and the total organization.

QUESTIONS FOR DISCUSSION

1. Define the managerial function of directing. Why is directing the function that most involves day-to-day supervisory activities?
2. Should the unity-of-command principle always be followed in issuing directives? Discuss.
3. Review each characteristic of a good supervisory directive, and discuss how these characteristics relate to communication concepts.
4. Distinguish between autocratic and close supervision on the one hand and consultative (participative) and general supervision on the other. What theoretical

differences are implied in each of these approaches? (Relate these to concepts concerning delegation of authority and motivation.)

5. Is autocratic and close supervision always negative in its consequences? Why or why not?

6. Why are employee attitudes and expectations important if consultative supervision is to be successful?

7. Why can current participative management programs—such as quality circles and quality-of-work life—be considered as organized adaptations of consultative supervision?

8. How does general supervision differ from "no supervision" in determining targets and standards?

9. Discuss the statement: "When practiced simultaneously, consultative and general supervision is a way of life that must be followed over a period of time." What are some of the major advantages to supervisors and employees when consultative and general supervision is practiced realistically?

10. Discuss supervisory approaches for the effective introduction of change to employees. How are these approaches related to some of the common barriers that cause employees to resist change?

11. Discuss the principles of proposing change to higher management. How do these compare with those utilized when introducing change downward to employees?

CHAPTER 16

Work Groups and Maintaining Morale

CHAPTER OBJECTIVES

1. To discuss why work groups form and function and the influence they have on employee performance.
2. To suggest supervisory approaches for managing work groups, which are consistent with behavioral research findings.
3. To emphasize the importance of employee morale and its relationship to teamwork and productivity.
4. To introduce certain programs that organizations are using to assist employees with personal and work-related problems.
5. To discuss techniques to assess the level of employee morale including the use of employee attitude surveys and follow-up of survey results.

In Chapter 10 we presented a brief overview of the "informal organization," with particular reference to the supervisor's relationship with informal work groups and their leaders. We mentioned that informal work groups can exert a positive or a negative influence on employee motivation and performance. Further, throughout this book we have emphasized that a supervisor's decisions must be concerned not only with employees as individuals, but also with how they relate to groups of employees both within and outside the supervisor's own department.

An individual's motivations and clues to behavior are often found in the context of the person's associates, colleagues, and peers. On the job, an employee's attitudes and morale can be shaped to a large degree by co-workers, at times even more so than by the supervisor or other factors in the work environment. Therefore, a supervisor should be sensitive to and aware of work groups and how they function. Moreover, a supervisor needs to develop a keen understanding of how morale influences employee performance, and what can be done to maintain a high level of morale at the departmental level.

UNDERSTANDING WORK GROUPS[1]

There are many reasons why work groups form and function in work settings. Among the most commonly identified reasons are:

1. *Companionship and identification.* The work group provides a peer relationship and a sense of belonging, which help satisfy the individual employee's social needs.
2. *Behavior guidelines.* People tend to look to others, especially their peers, for motivational guides to acceptable behavior in the workplace.
3. *Problem solving.* The work group may be instrumental in providing a viable means by which an individual employee may solve a personal problem.
4. *Protection.* The old adage of "strength in numbers" is not lost on employees who often look to the group for protection from outside pressures, such as supervisors and higher management.

Much behavioral research has focused on factors and situations that tend to make work groups tightly knit, cohesive, and effective. The following are among the most prominent:

1. Where the group members perceive themselves to have a higher status as compared to other employees, as for example, in matters of job classification or pay.

---

[1]For an expanded discussion of group processes in organizations, see Richard M. Steers, *Introduction to Organizational Behavior* (3rd ed.: Glenview, Illinois: Scott, Foresman and Company, 1988), pp. 322–343.

2. Where the group is generally small in size.
3. Where the group tends to share similar personal characteristics such as age, sex, ethnic background, off-the-job interests, etc.
4. Where the group tends to be located relatively distant from other employees, such as geographically dispersed work groups or groups located away from the home office or plant.
5. Where the group has been formed due to outside pressures or for self-protection, such as a layoff or disciplinary action taken by management.
6. Where group members can communicate with one another relatively easily.
7. Where the group has been successful in some previous group effort, which encourages the group members to seek new objectives again on a group basis.

Of course, a supervisor will never be completely aware of the kinds of forces that are most prevalent in the group dynamics of the department. However, an alertness and sensitivity to the considerations just described can be helpful in approaching and dealing with work groups more effectively.

Classification of Work Groups

Quite a few years ago, Leonard Sayles defined four major clusterings of employee work groups that exist in most organizations.[2] These classifications are still valid and useful and are defined as: command groups, task groups, friendship groups, and special-interest groups. Since there is some overlap in these classifications, a supervisor should recognize that individual employees may be members of several such groups simultaneously.

Command Group.   The **command group** essentially is a grouping of employees according to the authority relationships shown on the formal organizational chart. For example, at the departmental level a command group consists of the supervisor and the employees who report to this supervisor. Throughout the organization there will be interrelated departments or divisions of command groups that reflect the formal authority structure.

Task Group.   Consisting of employees from different units or departments of an organization, a **task group** comes together to accomplish a particular job. For example, in order for a telephone to be operative in a customer's home, the telephone company's employees and supervisors from a number of departments—such as customer service, construction, plant installation, central office equipment, accounting, and test center—may come into contact with one another to accomplish the job. Another example would be a hospital,

---

[2]Leonard R. Sayles, "Work Group Behavior and the Larger Organization," as reproduced in I. L Heckmann and S. G. Huneryager, *Human Relations in Management* (Cincinnati: South-Western Publishing Co., 1960), pp. 231–243.

where numerous interdepartmental task relationships and communications take place among hospital personnel from departments such as admitting, nursing, laboratory, dietary, pharmacy, physical therapy, medical records, and others, in order to care for a patient.

Friendship Group.   The **friendship group** is an informal group of people who have similar personalities and social interests. Many friendship groups are related primarily to common factors such as age, sex, ethnic background, outside interests, and marital status. Of course, the presence of command and task groups may be instrumental in bringing clusters of friendship groups together.

Special-Interest Group.   The **special-interest group** exists to accomplish in a group something that individuals feel incapable of or unwilling to pursue on an individual basis. Such a group can be either temporary or permanent. A temporary special-interest group might be a committee of employees who wish to protest an action taken by a supervisor or management, to promote a charitable undertaking, or to organize an employee picnic. A labor union is an example of a more permanent special-interest group, since it is legally and formally organized. A labor union brings together employees from different departments and divisions to unite them in striving for economic and other objectives.

As stated earlier, an employee may be a member of a number of groups in the workplace, and the supervisor who understands the nature of these different groups more likely will be in a position to influence them. Some research studies have suggested that a supervisor has a better chance to influence an individual employee's behavior as a member of a work group than to deal with that employee on an individual basis (that is to say, without having the work group's influence in mind). Some concepts in this regard will be presented later in this chapter.

The Hawthorne Studies Are Still Relevant for the 1990s

Numerous behavioral studies have been made of work groups and how they function. The studies that probably have had the most lasting influence during this century were conducted in the late 1920s and early 1930s at the Western Electric Company's Hawthorne plant near Chicago, Illinois.[3] Known as the Hawthorne Studies, they remain even today a comprehensive and authoritative source on the subject of work-group dynamics as related to employee productivity and morale.

---

[3]For an expanded discussion of the Hawthorne studies and their impact, see David J. Cherrington, *Organizational Behavior* (Boston: Allyn and Bacon, 1989), pp. 52–56.

A brief synopsis of two of the major experiments at the Hawthorne plant is given here. These are the relay assembly room experiment and the bank wiring observation room experiment.

Relay Assembly Room Experiment.   In the relay assembly room experiment, a group of six female employees worked on jobs consisting of assembling electrical relay equipment. They were closely observed in a special room while being subjected to varying working and other conditions. For about two years, researchers experimented with a number of scheduling arrangements, such as changes in rest and lunch periods, in workday arrangements, and in the workweek. Regardless of whether the changes instituted were favorable or unfavorable to the group, the outcome was that the employees' performance generally improved. By the end of this experiment, overall productivity had risen to about 30 percent over the pre-experiment level!

The researchers found that the primary reasons for the marked improvement in work performance were the attitudes and morale that had developed the employees into a solid, cohesive group. The employees became involved in the changes that were contemplated and implemented, and they felt that they were part of a team. The employees said that they felt that their supervision was much more informal and relaxed than they had experienced previously. Equally important was the fact that they considered the experiment to be an important part of a major project in the company. Since their work took on new importance, they developed their own norms for doing their jobs better. The research results clearly showed that a work group can be a positive influence on job performance, if the group believes that it is part of a team and that what they are doing is important.

Bank Wiring Observation Room Experiment.   A second group research experiment at the Hawthorne plant occurred a little later in time and lasted for almost a year. It involved 14 male employees whose work was to attach and solder banks of wires to telephone equipment. These employees and an observer were placed in a special room. The purpose of this experiment was to determine the impact of a series of wage incentive plans on employee productivity. The result of this experiment, however, revealed that a work group can have a negative influence on job performance. It turned out that the bank wiring observation room employees, as a group, developed an entirely different approach to their jobs than did the women in the relay assembly room experiment. The men decided to restrict output and keep it at a constant standard (or norm), which they referred to as the "bogey." It was learned from observation and interviews with the men in this group that there was strong pressure on the group members not to do anything more than the standard agreed upon by them. In effect, their approach was to maintain production at a level considered sufficient to keep the company "satisfied," but not nearly as much as the employees could do. In fact, the employees believed that if they increased production significantly, it would not mean higher wages but would instead lead to a management "speedup" without additional compensation and some employees might be laid off.

In today's businesses, many supervisors complain that their employees would perform at higher levels if it weren't for work groups that place considerable pressure on individual employees "not to do too much." The on-going challenge to today's supervisor is to encourage positive attitudes among work groups to perform at superior levels, such as that exhibited many years ago by the relay assembly room group at the Hawthorne plant.

Approaches for Managing Work Groups

A number of approaches for managing work groups effectively have been suggested. Although the following are by no means certain to produce the desired results, they are consistent with behavioral research findings concerning work group dynamics and group behavior.[4]

Assigning Compatible Employees.   Generally, it is preferable for a supervisor to assign employees who are friendly with each other to work together or at adjoining work stations. Human nature is such that trying to force people who dislike each other to work together—or even in close proximity—will usually lead to trouble or disruption. A number of studies have shown that employees who like each other tend to perform better as a team than those who are antagonistic toward each other. Further, it may be possible for the supervisor to allow some employees to choose from among themselves those who will work together on certain tasks. For example, several studies in the construction industry showed that when carpenters and bricklayers were allowed to pick their co-workers on work projects, these teams outproduced comparable groups who were selected and assigned to work solely by a supervisor. A caution, however, is that the supervisor must see to it that friendship does not lead to too much socializing, which interferes with job duties.

Counseling the "Loners."   Another approach is to be on the alert for individual employees who seem to be "loners" or who have difficulty in adjusting to their co-workers. By having a private counseling session with such an individual, the supervisor may be able to uncover the reasons for this situation and be able to take actions designed to help this individual gain acceptability by his or her peers. This is especially important if the "loner" is a new employee. As was discussed in Chapter 13, it may be desirable to assign a

---

[4]For a more extensive discussion, see George Strauss and Leonard R. Sayles, *Personnel: The Human Problems of Management* (4th ed.; Englewood Cliffs, New Jersey: Prentice-Hall, Inc., 1980), pp. 117–136.

senior employee to help a new employee "get to know the ropes" and be brought into the social functioning of the department.

Rotating Assignments.   Another technique that can foster a sense of teamwork in the department is to rotate work assignments within a group.[5] Having employees fill in on different jobs or do some of the more difficult and challenging jobs often helps to provide them with a greater sense of identity with the group. For example, many restaurant managers train their waiters and waitresses to help one another in the overall job of serving customers. Even though they may have their own specific table assignments, they help each other by cleaning tables, pouring water, or performing other service duties. If better service is provided, then these waiters and waitresses should receive more generous tips from appreciative customers.

Maintaining A Managerial Perspective.   Regardless of which approach is used, supervisors must maintain their perspective and role as managers. This means that a supervisor should not become too close to employee work groups, that is, the supervisor should not become too personally or deeply involved in their individual problems and feelings. Becoming too close to any individual or work group within a department may lead a supervisor to lose objectivity in decision making. It may also open a supervisor to criticism for showing favoritism to certain employees. As the old line has described it, "You can't be a buddy and a boss!"

Generally, it is more desirable for supervisors to socialize on the job with other supervisors and members of management, although this may not be comfortable for some supervisors. Ideally, supervisors need to demonstrate a balance of loyalty to higher management and to their employee work groups. This is not an easy task. But the supervisor who is sensitive to work groups and who maintains a sound managerial perspective can usually figure out ways to manage work groups effectively and, at the same time, have a cordial relationship with them.[6]

UNDERSTANDING AND MAINTAINING EMPLOYEE MORALE

Although there are many definitions of morale, a basic one is that it is a state of mind and emotions.[7] **Employee morale** consists of attitudes and feelings of individuals and groups toward their work, their environment, their supervi-

---

[5]Refer to the discussion of job rotation, job enlargement, and job enrichment in Chapter 4.

[6]See Raymond L. Hilgert, "Divided Loyalties: The Perennial Supervisory Problem," *Supervision*, Vol. XXXIX, No. 12 (December, 1977), pp. 4–5.

[7]Webster's dictionary defines the word *morale* as: "the mental and emotional condition (as of enthusiasm, spirit, loyalty) of an individual or a group with regard to the function or tasks at hand."

sors, top management, and the organization. Morale is not a single feeling, but a composite of feelings, sentiments, and attitudes. It affects employee performance and willingness to work, which in turn affect individual and organizational objectives. When employee morale is high, employees usually do what the organization would like for them to do; when it is low, the opposite tends to occur.

Two large-scale polls in 1989 revealed that the majority of employees were unhappier with many aspects of their jobs than were employees ten to fifteen years earlier. Much of this lowered morale was attributed to a belief that employers generally were not loyal to their employees, that employees were therefore not loyal to their employers, and that employees were likely to change jobs much more frequently than otherwise would be the case.[8]

There should be little doubt that employee morale is an important supervisory consideration. Yet some supervisors simply believe that morale is something that employees either have or do not have. Actually, morale is always present in some form and can be positive (high) or negative (low). High morale obviously is a desirable objective. Employees with high morale find satisfaction in their positions, have confidence in their abilities, and usually work with enthusiasm and to the extent of their abilities. High morale cannot be ordered, but it can be fostered by certain conditions in the work situation that are favorable to its development. High morale is not the cause of good human relations; it is the result of good human relations. High morale is the result of positive motivation, respect for people, effective supervisory leadership, good communication, participation, counseling, and desirable human relations practices. The state of employee morale reflects to a large degree how effectively a supervisor is performing his or her managerial responsibilities.

Morale Should Be Everyone's Concern

Every manager, from the chief executive down to the supervisor, should be concerned with the morale of the work force. It is a managerial duty to develop and maintain employee morale at as high a level as possible without sacrificing the company's objectives. The first-line supervisor, probably more than anyone else, influences the level of morale in day-to-day contacts with employees.

Bringing morale to a high level and maintaining it there is a continuous process, which cannot be achieved simply through short-run devices such as pep talks or contests. High morale is slow to develop and difficult to maintain. The level of morale can vary considerably from day to day, and it can be as changeable as the weather. Morale is contagious in both directions, because both favorable and unfavorable attitudes spread rapidly among employees.

---

[8]See *Time Magazine* (September 11, 1989), p. 54; and *U.S. News and World Report* (September 18, 1989), p. 77.

Unfortunately it seems to be human nature that employees tend to quickly forget the good and long remember the bad when it comes to factors influencing their morale.

The supervisor is not alone in desiring high morale. Employees are just as much concerned with morale, since it is paramount to their work satisfaction. High morale helps to make the employee's day at work a pleasure and not a misery. High morale also is important to an organization's customers. They usually can sense whether employees are serving them with a positive level of morale and interest or just going through the motions with a ''care-less'' attitude.

Relationships Among Morale, Teamwork, and Productivity

Teamwork is often associated with morale, but the two terms do not mean the same thing. Morale refers to the attitudes and emotions of employees, whereas **teamwork** implies coordinated and purposeful activities achieved by a motivated group. Good morale is helpful in achieving teamwork, but it is possible that teamwork can be high when morale is low. Such a situation might exist in times when jobs are scarce and when employees tolerate authoritarian supervision for fear of losing their jobs. On the other hand, teamwork may be absent when morale is high. For example, employees working on a piece-work basis or salespeople being paid on a straight commission basis typically are rewarded for individual efforts rather than for group performance.

Most supervisors tend to believe that high morale usually is accompanied by high productivity. Much research has been done to study this assumption. Although there are many ramifications and some contradictions in research results, there is substantial evidence to suggest that in the long run high-producing employees do tend to have high morale.[9] That is to say, well-motivated, self-disciplined groups of employees tend to do a more satisfactory job than those from whom the supervisor tries to ''force'' such performance. Further, high employee morale usually is accompanied by lower employee turnover, absenteeism, and tardiness rates.

There is little question that a high level of morale tends to make work more pleasant, particularly for the supervisor!

Factors Influencing Morale

Virtually anything can influence the morale of employees either positively or negatively. Some of these are within the control of the supervisor; others are not. These factors generally can be classified as two broad types: external and internal.

---

[9]For a discussion of research studies in this regard, see Dale S. Beach, *Personnel: The Management of People at Work* (5th ed.; New York: The Macmillan Company, 1985), pp. 307–312 and 332–347.

External Factors.   Those factors that are associated with events and influences outside the organization generally are beyond the supervisor's control. Nevertheless, they may significantly affect the morale of employees at work. Examples of external factors are family relationships, associations with friends, a breakdown of the car, sickness or death in the family, outside hobbies, and the like. What happens at home changes an employee's feelings very quickly. An argument before leaving for work may set an emotional tone for the rest of the day. Even headlines in the morning newspaper may be depressing or uplifting.

Because external factors are beyond the supervisor's direct control, the supervisor should be alert to sense them and to do whatever is possible to mitigate their effects. If an external factor has lowered an employee's morale, the supervisor should try to help the employee forget or resolve the incident as soon as possible. One way to erase or reduce the negative effects of an outside occurrence is to encourage the employee to talk about it openly in a **counseling interview.**[10] By being a good listener, the supervisor can find out what happened and may help the employee develop alternatives. Take, for example, an employee who is upset because of a sudden financial crisis. The employee is depressed, and her work performance shows a marked decline from normal. She spends more time thinking about how to solve her financial problems than she does thinking about her work. The supervisor may serve as an empathic listener by helping the employee consider several avenues to obtain financial assistance. The supervisor should be cautious about offering specific advice which might bring unexpected and unwanted repercussions. Should the employee feel dissatisfied with the results obtained by following a supervisor's advice, she may blame the supervisor for her problems. This can only complicate a difficult situation. If the problem is beyond the supervisor's range of experience, perhaps the supervisor can arrange for the employee to get help from a professional. We discuss this possibility further later in this chapter.

Aside from this sort of private counseling interview, there is little a supervisor can do to cope with the outside factors that affect an employee's morale. The supervisor's main role is to help get the employee's morale back to a more positive level. At the same time, the supervisor must be careful not to pry into the employee's private affairs.

Internal Factors.   Examples of internal factors that influence employee morale are compensation, job security, the nature of work, relations with coworkers, working conditions, recognition, and so on. These factors are partially or fully within the realm of the supervisor's control. When compensation is adequate, other factors may assume a more significant role. But even when wages are good, morale can sink quickly if working conditions are neglected.

---

[10]This is essentially a nondirective interview, as defined and discussed in Chapter 13.

The critical factor here is whether or not the supervisor attempts to improve working conditions. Employees often will perform very well under undesirable conditions and still maintain high morale, if they believe that their supervisor is seriously trying to improve conditions wherever possible.

The Supervisor's Influence.   It is well-recognized that a significant influence on employee morale is the supervisor's general attitude and behavior in day-to-day relationships. If a supervisor's behavior indicates suspicion about the employees' motives and actions, a low level of morale will likely result. If the supervisor acts worried or depressed, employees tend to follow suit. If the supervisor loses his or her temper, some employees may also lose theirs. Conversely, if the supervisor shows confidence in the employees' work, they react accordingly.

This does not mean that a supervisor should overlook difficulties and troubles that arise from time to time. Rather, it means that if something goes wrong, the supervisor should act as a leader who has the situation in hand. The supervisor should demonstrate an attitude that the employees will be relied on to correct the situation and to do what is necessary to prevent occurrence of a similar situation.

Supervisors should not relax in their efforts to build and maintain high employee morale. However, they should not become discouraged if morale drops from time to time, because there are so many factors beyond their control that can cause this. Supervisors can be reasonably satisfied if employee morale is high most of the time.

Fig. 16–1.
A supervisor's general attitude, more than anything else, can result in good or poor employee morale.

Assisting Employees with Personal and Work-Related Problems

As discussed in a previous section, supervisors at times will hold a counseling interview with those employees who are exhibiting low morale or experiencing certain personal or work-related problems. By being an empathic and sincere listener, the supervisor may help such employees to "work out" their own solutions or suggest avenues of professional advice or assistance. In many organizations, the supervisor alternatively may refer the employee to the human resources department or some designated management person, who will hold the counseling interview and suggest possibilities for help.

In recent years, many organizations—especially large corporations and governmental agencies—have adopted what usually are called **Employee Assistance Programs (EAP).** These programs typically involve a special department and staff personnel to whom supervisors may refer employees with certain types of problems.[11] Additionally, employees on their own may seek help from the EAP office, or they may be referred to the EAP by other sources, such as their labor union. Among the major areas of counseling and professional services provided for in most employee assistance programs are: help for alcoholism and substance abuse; marriage, child-care, and family problems; financial questions; and other personal, emotional, or psychological problems that may be interfering with job performance. Figure 16–2 is a policy statement included in the EAP booklet provided to employees of a major corporation, which illustrates the typical elements of this type of program.

Another approach for assisting employees with special work-related problems is that of the so-called **corporate ombudsman.** This, too, for the most part is available only in large organizations; the person or persons serving in the ombudsman role may or may not be part of an EAP program or human resources staff. Frequently, the ombudsman is part of a separate department, which might be identified as the "personnel communications department" or the "liaison department." Employees who have work-related problems are encouraged to come to this department to be interviewed on a confidential basis. Often the employee has a problem or conflict with his or her supervisor, which the employee is afraid to discuss with the supervisor. Or perhaps the employee is dissatisfied about something that has happened—for example, being passed over for a promotion, being disciplined, being given unfair work assignments or schedules, and the like. The ombudsman listens to the employee's concerns, and then may choose to follow a number of alternatives in an effort to resolve the problem. The ombudsman does not have any direct authority, but acts as a type of "third party" or "neutral service" when, for example, he or she meets with the employee's supervisor to discuss the matter and to see what—

---

[11]See Donald W. Myers, *Establishing and Building Employee Assistance Programs* (Westport, Ct.: Greenwood Press–Quorum Books, 1984); or Diane Kirrane, "EAPs: Dawning of a New Age," *HR Magazine* (Vol. 35, No. 1, January 1990), pp. 30–34.

EMPLOYEE ASSISTANCE PROGRAM

Introduction

The Employee Assistance Program (EAP) was adopted to provide confidential, professional assistance to employees and their families. The program also provides managers and union representatives with a constructive way to help employees and reduce the adverse economic impact to the company that occurs when personal problems interfere with job performance.

HOW THE PROGRAM WORKS

There are essentially four ways that a person may enter the EAP — self-referral, management referral, union referral or medical referral.

SELF-REFERRAL

Any employee or family member may call the EAP office for information or to make an appointment to discuss a personal problem. The contact, as well as what is discussed, is handled in strictest confidence.

MANAGEMENT REFERRAL

Managers and supervisors may suggest to an employee that he or she seek help when there is a noticeable decline in the employee's work performance that is not correctable through usual supervisory procedures or where there are specific on-the-job incidents which indicate the presence of a personal problem.

UNION REFERRAL

Official union representatives are encouraged to ask their members to make use of the services provided by the EAP. Union officials may call the EAP office and speak with the counselor or provide the employee or family member with the EAP office telephone number.

MEDICAL REFERRAL

Medical referrals to the EAP will be based upon either the identification of a medical symptom or disorder which is normally associated with a personal problem or on a request from the employee for advice or assistance regarding a personal problem.

if anything—should or might be done. In this regard, the ombudsman is acting as a communications link, which often becomes the most important aspect of resolving or at least reducing the magnitude of the problem or conflict.[12]

Techniques for Assessing Morale

Some supervisors pride themselves on their ability to "size-up" morale intuitively, but most supervisors would be better advised to approach this effort systematically. Although employee morale cannot be measured directly, there are techniques for assessing prevailing levels and trends. The two most frequently used are study and observation, and attitude surveys.

---

[12]For an expanded discussion of the ombudsman and similar types of employee problem assistance approaches, see Mary P. Rowe and Michael Baker, "Are You Hearing Enough Employee Concerns," *Harvard Business Review* (May–June 1984), pp. 127–135.

Study and Observation.   By observing, monitoring, and studying patterns of employee behavior, a supervisor often will discover clues to employee morale. The supervisor should closely monitor such key indicators as job performance levels, tardiness and absenteeism, the amount of waste or scrap, employee complaints, and accident and safety records. Any significant changes in the levels of these indicators should be analyzed, since they often are interrelated. For example, excessive tardiness and absenteeism seriously interfere with job performance. The supervisor should find out why employees are often tardy or absent. If reasons are related to morale, are the causes within the supervisor's control, or should the employee be referred somewhere for counseling or assistance?

It is relatively easy to observe the extremes of high and low morale; however, it is quite difficult to differentiate among intermediate degrees of morale—or to assess when morale is changing. For example, an employee's facial expression or shrug of the shoulder may or may not reflect that person's level of morale. Only an alert and sensitive supervisor can judge whether this employee is becoming depressed or frustrated. Supervisors must attempt to sharpen their powers of observation and be careful not to brush indicators of change conveniently aside.

The closeness of daily working relationships offers numerous opportunities for a supervisor to observe and analyze changes in employee morale. However, many supervisors do not take time to observe, and others do not study or analyze what they observe. It is only when an extreme, obvious drop in the level of morale has taken place that some supervisors recall the first indications of change. By then, the problems that led to this lowered state of morale probably will have magnified to the point where major corrective actions will be necessary. As so often is the case in supervision, "an ounce of prevention would have been worth more than a pound of cure."

Attitude Surveys.   Another approach for assessing employee morale is to request employees to fill out **attitude surveys,** also called **opinion** or **morale surveys.**[13] Employees are asked to express their opinions about major aspects of organizational life, usually in the form of answers to questions printed on the survey form. The survey questionnaire elicits employee opinions about such factors as management and supervision, job conditions, job satisfaction, co-workers, pay and benefits, job security, advancement opportunities, and so on. Employee attitude surveys are rarely initiated by a supervisor. Usually they are undertaken by top management and prepared with the help of the

---

[13]Many companies conduct *exit interviews* with individuals when they leave employment with the firm. Exit interviews are usually conducted by a human resources staff person, who asks various questions that may be similar to questions on employee attitude survey forms. Results of exit interviews are often used to assess the state of morale that exists in the firm or in certain departments of the firm.

human resources department or an outside consulting firm. The survey questionnaire should be prepared and written in language that is relevant and appropriate for most of the employees.

Attitude surveys, or questionnaires, may be completed on the job or in the privacy of the employee's home. Some organizations prefer to have employees answer these questionnaires on the job, because a high percentage of questionnaires that are mailed out are never returned. On the other hand, a possible advantage of filling out the questionnaire at home is that employees may give more thoughtful and truthful answers. Regardless, completed questionnaires should not be signed so that they remain anonymous, although some surveys may request employees to indicate their departments.

Many attitude survey forms offer employees the choice of answering questions from a given list of answers. Other forms are not so specific and provide employees the opportunity to answer as freely as they wish. Since some employees may find it difficult to write down their opinions in sentences or to complete started sentences, better results usually are obtained with a survey form on which the employees simply check the printed responses which correspond to their answers. Figure 16–3 is an example of this type of attitude survey form.

Survey Results and Follow-up.   The tabulation and analysis of questionnaires usually are assigned to the human resources department or to an outside consulting firm. Survey results are first presented to top-level and middle-level managers and eventually to departmental supervisors. In some organizations survey results are used as discussion materials during supervisory training, especially when they provide clues or information about ways to improve employee morale.

Attitude surveys may reveal certain identifiable deficiencies that the supervisor can eliminate. For example, a complaint that there is a "lack of soap in the washroom" can be solved easily. But frequently the responses are difficult to evaluate, as for example, a complaint that "communication channels are not open to employees." Such complaints raise more questions than answers and may necessitate a careful study of existing policies and procedures to see if corrective actions are warranted.

If the attitude survey reveals a correctable problem at the departmental level—perhaps with an individual supervisor—the solution should be developed and implemented by the supervisor involved. On the other hand, a broader problem that requires the attention of higher management should be reported to the appropriate manager so that actions may be taken at the higher level. Unless supervisors and higher management make needed changes as a result of a survey, the survey was a waste of time and money. In fact, if no changes or improvements materialize, or if changes are not communicated to the employees concerned, a decline in morale may occur after the survey. Employees may feel that their problems and suggestions have been ignored. Thus,

Fig 16-3.
Attitude survey
questionnaire.

AJAX CORPORATION

EMPLOYEE OPINION SURVEY

We are all interested in maintaining sound personnel policies and practices. You can help by contributing your opinions through this questionnaire.

We would appreciate your frank, straight-from-the-shoulder answers. There are no right or wrong answers. Please read each question carefully. Then check the one answer which most nearly reflects your personal opinion.

This survey is completely anonymous. Questionnaires will be tabulated and analyzed by an outside firm. Please do not put your name anywhere on the questionnaire. When you have finished, please return the questionnaire in the enclosed envelope addressed to Ellen Rolfe, Director of Human Resources.

Thank you for taking the time to give us your opinions.

(1) How much information do you receive about what is going on in your department?

1. _____ I get more than enough information.
2. _____ I get all the information I am interested in.
3. _____ I get almost as much information as I am interested in.
4. _____ I get about half the information I am interested in.
5. _____ I get very little of the information I am interested in.

(2) How well do you know what is expected of you in your job?

1. _____ I have only a very vague idea.
2. _____ I have a somewhat vague idea.
3. _____ I have a pretty good idea.
4. _____ I have a very good idea.
5. _____ I know exactly.

(3) When your supervisor makes decisions and commitments about your work, how is it handled?

1. _____ It is almost always discussed with me first.
2. _____ It is usually discussed with me first.
3. _____ It is discussed with me about half the time.
4. _____ It is sometimes discussed with me first.
5. _____ It is rarely or never discussed with me first.

Fig 16–3.
(continued)

(4) Does your supervisor ask for your advice about changes that will affect your job?

1. _____ My opinion is always sought.
2. _____ My opinion is usually sought.
3. _____ My opinion is sought about half the time.
4. _____ My opinion is rarely or never sought.
5. _____ This does not apply to me.

(5) How sincere is your supervisor's interest in getting your opinions and suggestions?

1. _____ My supervisor has a very sincere interest in my opinion.
2. _____ My supervisor has considerable interest in my opinion.
3. _____ My supervisor has some interest in my opinion.
4. _____ My supervisor has little or no interest in my opinion.
5. _____ I don't know whether my supervisor is interested in my opinions.

(6) What attention or emphasis is given to the following by your supervisor?

	Too Much Attention	About Right	Too Little Attention	Doesn't Apply
The quality of your work	_____	_____	_____	_____
Costs involved in your work	_____	_____	_____	_____
Meeting schedules	_____	_____	_____	_____
Getting your reactions and suggestions	_____	_____	_____	_____
Giving you information	_____	_____	_____	_____
Making full use of your abilities	_____	_____	_____	_____
Safety and housekeeping	_____	_____	_____	_____
Training and development	_____	_____	_____	_____
Innovations, new ideas	_____	_____	_____	_____
Effective teamwork among employees	_____	_____	_____	_____

wherever possible, dissatisfactions that have been expressed in an attitude survey should be addressed promptly by managers and supervisors, or at least employees should be informed that management is aware of the dissatisfactions and what may be done to change things by some future date.

Attitude Surveys and Organizational Development. Some companies have found it advantageous to follow up their attitude surveys with feedback meetings and conference sessions with groups (or teams) of employees and supervisors. Typically these meetings are conducted by an outside consultant, or by a staff person from the human resources or some other department. In these meetings, results of attitude surveys are openly discussed and debated. Further, the groups are expected to develop recommendations for improvement, which are forwarded on an anonymous basis to higher management for consideration and possible implementation.[14]

This type of approach is often part of a broader concept that also has become rather widespread in many large enterprises and governmental and other establishments. Usually known as **organizational development (OD),** it involves having scheduled group meetings under the guidance of an internal or external conference leader. The groups may involve just employees, employees and supervisors, just supervisors, just higher level managers, or whatever composition is decided on as being appropriate. For the most part, the meetings focus on solving problems that may be hindering effective work performance or causing disruption, poor coordination, fouled-up communications, and strained personal relations. When there is honest and frank discussion in a relatively open and informal atmosphere, individuals tend to "open-up" about what really is on their minds and what might be done to resolve problems and reduce conflict. Organizational development efforts can take numerous forms and directions, which are beyond the scope of this text.[15] Suffice it to say, however, that many supervisors in the future will be involved in organizational development programs, since these types of programs are still another effort that can contribute to the improvement of morale and organizational effectiveness.

SUMMARY

Work groups typically are formed to provide companionship and identification, behavior guidelines, problem-solving help, and protection. Various factors can contribute to the cohesiveness and functioning of the work group, such as the group's status, size, personal characteristics, location, and previous success.

---

[14]See Hugh J. Arnold and Daniel C. Feldman, *Organizational Behavior* (New York: McGraw-Hill Book Company, 1986), pp. 99–107.

[15]See Andrew J. DuBrin, *Human Relations: A Job Oriented Approach* (4th ed.: Englewood Cliffs, N.J.: Prentice-Hall, 1988), pp. 420–428.

At any time, an employee may be a member of a command group, task group, friendship group, or special-interest group. The Hawthorne research studies demonstrated that work groups can have either a positive or negative influence on employee performance. Supervisors who are alert and sensitive to the nature of and forces behind work groups can use better approaches for managing them more effectively.

Employee morale is a composite of feelings, sentiments, and attitudes of individuals and groups toward their work environment, supervision, and the organization as a whole. Morale can vary from very high to very low and can change considerably from day to day. A concern for morale should be felt by everyone in the organization.

Morale and teamwork are not synonymous; but generally it is believed that, in the long run, high morale will be associated with high productivity. Morale can be influenced by factors from outside the organization as well as by on-the-job factors. There is relatively little a supervisor can do to change the effects of external factors. However, the supervisor's general attitude and behavior can significantly influence employee morale. Further, in efforts to assist employees who have certain types of personal and work-related problems that a supervisor would not be able or competent to handle, some organizations have employee assistance programs or ombudsmen available. These efforts, too, are designed to deal with problems and issues that affect employee morale, and to assist employees to solve problems that detract from their job performance.

Astute supervisors can sense a change in the level of morale by studying and observing employees and key indicators that are readily available.

Another means of assessing levels of employee morale is to conduct an attitude survey. Once an attitude survey has been conducted, supervisors and higher management should—if possible—correct those problems that have been brought to their attention through the survey. It is also desirable to discuss the results of an attitude survey in meetings with groups of employees and supervisors and to encourage them to recommend changes and improvements.

QUESTIONS FOR DISCUSSION

1. What are some of the most common reasons for forming work groups? What are some factors that tend to make a work group a more cohesive entity?
2. Define each of the following classifications of work groups:
   a. Command group.
   b. Task group.
   c. Friendship group.
   d. Special-interest group.
3. What were the principal aspects and results of the relay assembly room experiment and the bank wiring observation room experiment conducted as part of the Hawthorne Studies? Discuss the relevance of these findings to modern supervision.
4. Discuss various approaches that supervisors can implement in order to manage their work groups more effectively.
5. Define the concept of employee morale. Evaluate the statement: "High morale is not the cause of good human relations; it is the result of good human relations."

6. Why should employee morale be of concern to everyone in the organization?

7. Discuss the relationships between: (a) morale and teamwork and (b) morale and productivity. Is it possible for employees to have low morale and still perform at a high level of work performance? Discuss.

8. Differentiate between external factors and internal factors that influence employee morale. What should a supervisor do to minimize the influence of external factors on an employee's work?

9. Why is the supervisor a significant influence on employee morale?

10. Discuss the increasing use of employee assistance programs and corporate ombudsmen, especially in large-scale enterprises. Why would such approaches probably not be ''cost-effective'' in small companies?

11. How can study and observation be a basis for assessing employee morale at the departmental level?

12. Discuss the use of employee attitude surveys in assessing employee morale. Why is follow-up on survey results vital if an attitude survey is to be worth anything? What types of follow-up can managers and supervisors utilize? Discuss.

CHAPTER 17

Supervision of Legally Protected Employees

CHAPTER OBJECTIVES

1. To identify the major categories of legally protected employees.
2. To discuss several considerations that affect the supervision of racial/ethnic minority employees.
3. To discuss factors that are particularly important when supervising women employees.
4. To discuss considerations involved when supervising older workers, the handicapped, employees of different religious views, and Vietnam-era veterans.
5. To recognize several pressures faced by supervisors who themselves are members of legally protected groups.
6. To understand the issue of reverse discrimination and to reiterate what should be the overriding concern in supervision of all employees.

Earlier in this text, we stressed the fact that employees are individuals shaped by a variety of forces from within and without the organization. In the previous chapter, we discussed how employees tend to form groups and why supervisors should be aware of group dynamics. In this chapter we focus on the need for supervisors to develop a special awareness, sensitivity, and adaptability to protected-group employees, a term that we use primarily in a legal sense but which also has social and psychological dimensions.

IDENTIFYING "PROTECTED-GROUP" EMPLOYEES

The identification of employees who have been afforded special legal considerations comes primarily from civil rights legislation, equal employment opportunity regulations, and numerous court decisions. Various laws and regulations that govern employment policies and practices today were listed in Table 12–1. The term **protected-group employees** has evolved to describe groups of individuals primarily according to their:

1. Racial/ethnic origin.
2. Sex (i.e., women).
3. Age (i.e., over 40).
4. Physical status (i.e., handicapped).
5. Religion.
6. Military record.

The underlying philosophy of this term is that certain employees in these classifications have been unfairly or illegally discriminated against in the past or that they are entitled to special protection and consideration because of certain past or present aspects of their situations.

Regardless of personal biases or views, supervisors must be sensitive to possible illegal discriminatory actions and to adjust their supervisory practices accordingly. In this chapter we highlight some of the important considerations that supervisors of "protected-group" employees should take into account while carrying out their directing function.[1]

The OUCH Test in Supervision of "Protected" Employees

The OUCH test, which we discussed in Chapter 13 as a guideline in selecting employees, also applies to day-to-day supervision. This test should remind supervisors that their actions as supervisors should be:

---

[1] Our discussion in this chapter reflects laws, court rulings, administrative policies, and federal guidelines that were in effect at the time of writing of this text. Also, we are not considering aspects of discrimination involving protections for employees who are involved in labor union activities. These considerations are addressed in Chapters 21 and 22.

O—<u>O</u>bjective
U—<u>U</u>niform in application
C—<u>C</u>onsistently applied
H—<u>H</u>ave job relatedness

For example, assume that a work rule specifies a disciplinary penalty for being tardy three times in one month. The supervisor should give the same penalty to *every* employee who is late the third time in one month, regardless of whether the employee is in a protected-group category. By so doing, this supervisory approach would meet the OUCH test, because the tardiness is an observable behavior that is objectively measured for all employees. The penalty is the same for all employees, is consistently applied, and is clearly job-related.

A myth occasionally voiced by some supervisors is that certain categories of employees cannot be disciplined or discharged because of government regulations. That view is false. Laws and regulations do not prevent a supervisor from taking disciplinary action against protected-group employees. However, they do require that such employees be treated on the same basis as other employees whenever disciplinary actions are taken. Therefore, it is extremely important that supervisors be careful in meeting the OUCH test and in justifying their actions through adequate documentation. We discuss this in more detail in both Chapters 18 and 22.

Fig 17–1.
One myth occasionally voiced by some supevisors is that protected-group employees cannot be disciplined or discharged.

SUPERVISING MINORITY EMPLOYEES

Most major employers have developed nondiscrimination and/or affirmative-action policies or programs for employment of certain racial/ethnic minorities. A major thrust of most of these policies and programs is to ensure that minorities, as well as certain other "protected-group" individuals, receive special consideration when jobs are filled or promotion decisions are made. The philosophy underlying affirmative-action plans is to overcome the impact of past discriminatory practices and to provide greater opportunities for "underrepresented" groups to participate more fully throughout the work force.

Effects of Previous Discrimination

It is not surprising that some minority persons who have experienced unfair or prejudiced treatment are skeptical of or resentful toward supervisors of different racial/ethnic backgrounds. The most common area of tension continues to be between black employees and white supervisors and managers. Even though nondiscrimination laws have been in place for several decades, annual data compiled by the federal Equal Employment Opportunity Commission (EEOC) show that minority persons file tens of thousands of complaints about unfair treatment because of their race. Typically, alleged discriminatory discipline and discharge have been the most frequent bases for these complaints.

Since responsibility for initiating discipline and discharge actions usually rests with supervisors, such decisions play a significant role in generating charges of discrimination. Investigations of charges require extensive time, effort, and involvement of supervisors, human resources and legal specialists, and others. Thus supervisors must be sensitive to the feelings and attitudes of minority employees who may have experienced discriminatory treatment in the past or who believe that they currently have been discriminated against in some way. Supervisors should respond with empathy and understanding to minority employees who display or harbor lingering resentment and suspicion. More important, the supervisor must be fair and considerate when making decisions that affect these employees. By demonstrating that minority employees will be supervised in the same manner as other employees, the supervisor can contribute to overcoming—or at least reducing—the negative effects of past discrimination.

Cultural Differences

A continuing debate about human behavior is how much heredity as compared to environment shapes on individual. Obviously, heredity is a major factor in the physical and ethnic makeup of a person. Further, because members of various races or ethnic origins often have different environmental experiences, somewhat unique subcultures have tended to develop for each racial/ethnic minority group. For example, the ties that American Indians have to their heritage reflect their subculture. Persons of Asian/Oriental descent have distinctive values and traditions that reflect their heritage and cultures.

Unfortunately, differences in cultural backgrounds can contribute to prejudicial attitudes and treatment of minority employees by supervisors. For example, a minority employee's values about the importance of work and punctuality may be different from those held by a supervisor. If a minority employee has not grown up in an environment that stresses the importance of being punctual, especially in a work situation, the supervisor must be prepared to spend extra time explaining to that employee the reasons for good and punctual attendance and the consequences of tardiness and absenteeism. Regardless of what cultural differences exist, it is the supervisor's job to exert special efforts to overcome these differences—or at least to mitigate their effects—so that the minority person can become a fully contributing member of the department.

Language Difficulties

Another consideration in supervising minority employees relates to different languages that may be spoken in a work environment. Some Hispanic Americans and native Mexicans who legally work in the United States may speak Spanish fluently but have much difficulty with English. Or a native of Southeast Asia may speak Vietnamese but hardly any English. It has even been observed that some black Americans have unique dialect variations of American English and that they use certain words that are unfamiliar to most white people.

Some employers have held training programs to sensitize supervisors and managers to better understand minority language patterns. For example, one large firm held a series of one-day training sessions for supervisors, managers, and professional staff to make them more knowledgeable about the culture and language backgrounds of black Americans. The training program focused on language expressions and speech habits with which nonblacks are generally not familiar.

The other side of the language problem has been addressed by some employers who sponsor English improvement and business English courses for minority employees. These programs focus on development of writing and speaking skills needed for job improvement and advancement.[2]

---

[2]It is anticipated that the need for so-called workplace literacy training programs will escalate dramatically during the 1990s. See *The Bottom Line: Basic Skills in the Workplace,* a joint publication of the U.S. Department of Labor and the U.S. Department of Education (Washington, D.C.: U.S. Government Printing Office, 1988).

At one time, some employers attempted to prevent employees from using their native languages at work. However, such restrictions today are viewed by courts and enforcement agencies with skepticism, unless interpersonal communication is a critical part of the job. For example, a manufacturing company's refusal to hire a Spanish-speaking worker on an assembly line might be ruled as prejudicial, since on this job communication skills may be much less important than manual dexterity skills. However, for a salesperson in a department store, or for a nurse working in an emergency room, adequate interpersonal language skills would be essential. In some parts of the United States, such as Miami, Florida, or San Antonio, Texas, a bilingual (Spanish-English) person would be a valuable asset. The extensive number of Spanish-speaking persons in those areas represents a major pool of potential clients who could be better served by a bilingual person. In summary, supervising racial/ethnic minority employees requires a high degree of sensitivity and even "extra fairness" when the supervisor is not a member of that minority.

SUPERVISING WOMEN

Throughout the decades of the 1970s and the 1980s, both the number of women and the percentage of women in the labor force have increased dramatically. The reasons for this are many dimensioned, but some of the reasons mentioned most often are: changing values regarding personal fulfillment through work; wider career opportunities; the feminist movement; higher educational levels; growth in single-parent and single-adult households; and economic pressures. As of 1990, women comprised slightly under one half of the U.S. labor force. During the 1990s, it is expected that almost two thirds of new entrants to the labor force will be women; by 2000, three out of five of all "working age" women will hold paying jobs.[3]

Both men and women supervisors should be aware of a number of important concerns that affect the supervision of women. While not all-inclusive, the areas to be discussed here represent a range of issues that supervisors should recognize and deal with appropriately.

Entry of Women into Many Career Fields

The combined effects of antidiscrimination laws, affirmative-action programs, and the increasing number of women in the labor force have led to the movement of women into many jobs that were traditionally dominated by men. For example, in greater numbers than ever before women are financiers, scientists,

---

[3]U.S. Department of Labor, as reported in "Demographics Breeding Changes and Challenges" *St. Louis Post-Dispatch* (May 14, 1989), p. 6E.

engineers, utility repair specialists, sales and technical representatives, accountants, and managers. However, a high percentage of women still work predominantly in clerical and service jobs. Figure 17–2 illustrates these trends, which are expected to continue for the foreseeable future.

The entry of women into jobs requiring hard physical labor and craft skills has been comparatively limited, but when women do assume craft or other physically demanding jobs, changes often occur. Experiences of a number of firms indicate that some equipment may have to be modified. For example, one utility company found that it had to change the shape of some wrenches and tools to accommodate the smaller hands of women. Telephone companies have changed the mounting position for ladders on trucks used by outside repair employees to make them easier for women to reach and have bought light-weight ladders that are easier to carry. Further, special clothing and shoes were developed so that women employees could have the proper protective equipment.

If many women seek to move out of service and clerical jobs, one effect may be a shortage of these types of employees. For example, a chronic shortage of nurses is likely for the foreseeable future. Further, a number of authorities have estimated that there will be a major shortage of qualified secretaries

Fig 17–2. Women in occupational fields, 1972 to 1987.

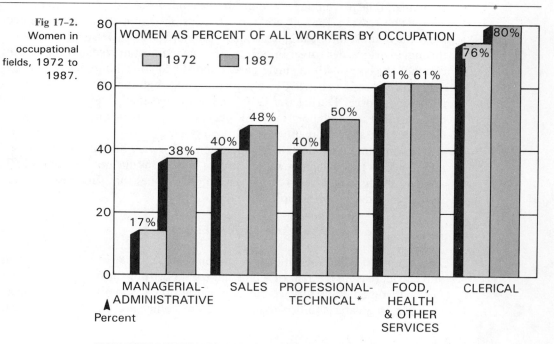

*INCLUDES ACCOUNTANTS, DOCTORS, ENGINEERS, LAWYERS, TEACHERS, AND NURSES.

SOURCE OF DATA: U.S. Department of Labor and U.S. Department of Commerce.

in the 1990s. To prepare for this shortage, supervisors may have to take advantage of technological advances in word processing equipment and modify some of the traditional secretarial duties. The secretarial position may require a different mix of skills and capabilities, and it may be upgraded to that of an administrative assistant or a skilled technical position that requires little direct supervision.

Although women have successfully broken down many of the "barriers" that previously limited their entry into male-dominated positions, there are still problems that occur, especially at the departmental level. For example, a supervisory consideration when a woman takes a job traditionally held by men is the reaction of the current male employees. Some of the men may harbor resentment and may even openly express negative reactions and criticism. The supervisor should be prepared to deal with such attitudes in order to enable the woman to perform her job satisfactorily. The supervisor should first inform the men about the starting employment date of the woman so that her presence does not come as a surprise. Then the supervisor should make it clear to the men that disciplinary action will be taken if this woman—or any women employees in the future—is ignored or subjected to abuse or harassment.

Further, the supervisor should make it clear that any woman taking a previously all-male job will be afforded a realistic opportunity to succeed or fail based on her capabilities to perform the job.

Issues of Sexual Harassment and Sexual Stereotyping

In recent years, a growing number of civil rights and court cases in the United States have dealt with problems of sexual harassment. Sexual harassment usually consists of actions in which a female employee must respond or submit to sexual language, touching, or sexual advances by a male employee or a male supervisor. If a female employee resists or protests such behavior by a male supervisor, she may fear being discriminated against when the supervisor is considering pay raises or promotions. It is important to note that a female supervisor also can be charged with sexual harassment of a male employee. However, sexual harassment of women by men has been the focus of most of the cases heard by federal agencies and the courts.

Court decisions have generally held that an employer is liable if sexual harassment of employees is condoned, overlooked, or does not lead to corrective actions by management. Reprimand and discipline of offending employees and supervisors are recommended courses of action. Consequently, supervisors should avoid and discourage sexual language, innuendos, and behavior that are inappropriate in the work situation. Supervisors who use their positions improperly in this regard are engaging in conduct that certainly is unacceptable and could lead to their own dismissals.

Sexual sterotyping consists of language or judgments that demean women. For example, a department store supervisor may find that women buyers may strongly resent being referred to as "the girls." Or a supervisor may imply that women are more emotional, less rational, and less reliable than men.

Some assertions and concepts about women employees as compared to men employees are inaccurate. For example, one large firm examined the absenteeism records of both their male and female employees. This firm found no significant difference in absentee rates between the two sexes and that their women employees with children had a lower absentee rate than single men. Thus the supervisor should not make supervisory decisions based primarily on sexual stereotypes.

It is important to note that many job titles have been changed to avoid sexist tones. For example, the job title "fireman" is now "fire fighter"; a "mailman" is now a "letter carrier"; a stewardess is now a "flight attendant"; and so forth.

Training and Development Opportunities for Women

Women employees should be offered equal access to available training and development activities, and those who have potential should be encouraged to develop their skills. This is especially important for the upgrading of women to supervisory and other managerial positions.

A number of research studies have found that women employees often benefit from special training and development opportunities that focus on enhancing their self-esteem, communication skills, and career development. For women who already are managers and supervisors, many firms provide special programs that include such topics as personal awareness, assertiveness training, managerial barriers to success, time management, delegation, and special problems encountered by women in managerial positions.

Pregnancy and Family-Care Policies

In the not-so-distant past, many public school systems and other employers prohibited a pregnant woman from working when her pregnant state became obvious. However, such policies are no longer permitted because of the passage of the Pregnancy Discrimination Act of 1978. This act, which is an amendment to the 1964 Civil Rights Act, requires that pregnancy be treated no differently than illnesses or health disabilities if an employer has medical benefits or a disability plan. In addition, about half of the states in the United States have laws that require certain considerations on pregnancy benefits for employed women. In response, many employers have adopted policies that allow a pregnant employee to work as long as she and her physician certify is appropriate. These policies also grant the pregnant employee a leave of absence until she can return to work. To prevent abuse of pregnancy leaves—

or any type of leave for that matter—many employers require a physician's statement to verify a continuing disability.

Women who take a pregnancy (or maternity) leave usually are assured a job upon their return to work. Many employers, however, do not assure a woman of her same job and rate of pay if her leave extends past 60 or 90 days. In the interest of equal treatment, some employers have granted paternity leaves in order for male employees to assist their wives after delivery and to take care of other family responsibilities.

Supervisors must see to it that pregnant employees are treated in a nondiscriminatory manner, although they are not required to give pregnant employees easier job assignments. A more difficult problem for the supervisor is a pregnant employee's uncertainty about returning to work after her pregnancy is over. This situation affects supervisors in scheduling work and anticipating future staffing needs. Supervisors may have to hire part-time or temporary help, schedule overtime work, or take other temporary actions until the woman definitely decides if and when she will return to work. This is not an unduly burdensome problem, if a supervisor plans well in advance to accommodate the temporary absence of a pregnant employee.

Family Care and the Workplace.   As we discussed in Chapter 1, a major problem in recent years that has accompanied the growth of women in the labor force has been the conflict between the job demands placed on women and their family responsibilities. Women with children often must cope with demanding responsibilities at home, which are not always shared equally by their husbands. Further, many women for a variety of reasons head so-called single-parent households in which they are the primary provider for their families.

Because of concern over this problem, many employers have adopted flexible policies concerning work schedules, leaves, and other arrangements in order to accommodate employees—especially women—in meeting their various obligations. At the time of writing of this text, a number of proposals were before the Congress of the United States that would require employers to grant certain types of parental leave and other leaves to cover situations of adoption, illness of a child, and employee disability. Another proposed law would provide grants to assist in the development of various arrangements for child care of children of employees who must work and for whom no other care would be available. Regardless of the outcome of this legislation, it appears that the tension between family and job responsibilities is one that employers and supervisors will have to address throughout the 1990s. Supervisors should become very familiar with their firm's policies regarding family- and child-care assistance and endeavor to resolve whenever possible those conflicts that interfere with the employee's capacity to carry out her or his job responsibilities.

Equity of Compensation

Statistically the pay received by women employees in the United States work force generally has been below that of men.[4] In an effort to combat this disparity, the Equal Pay Act was passed. This federal law requires that men and women performing equal work must receive equal pay. For example, a female bookkeeper and a male bookkeeper in the same firm who have approximately the same seniority and performance levels must be paid equally. Although equal pay has not always been interpreted to mean "exactly the same," a firm would probably be in violation of the Equal Pay Act if it paid the female bookkeeper $1.00 an hour less than her male counterpart.

A more complex reason for the disparity in the pay of men and women has been the issue of comparable worth. **Comparable worth** occurs when jobs that are distinctly different, but which require similar levels of skills and abilities, have different pay scales—especially if one job is predominantly held by men and another is predominantly held by women. For example, compare the job of medical technologist, which is held predominantly by women, with that of electrician, which is held mainly by men. Both jobs require licensing or certification, but medical technologists typically have more formal education. Now assume that the pay scales for medical technologists in a hospital are about one-third lower than those for electricians working in the same hospital. A comparison of these dissimilar jobs might suggest that unequal pay is being given for jobs of comparable worth.

However, a probable major cause for the difference in such pay scales is the labor market in the area. If unionized electricians in the area are paid $18 per hour by other employers, the hospital would have to set its pay scale at this level in order to compete for electricians. Similarly, if the going rate for nonunionized medical technologists is $12 per hour, the hospital is likely to pay its medical technologists this rate.

Although the concept of comparable worth has received much attention from certain women's groups, it has received little support from most employers and mixed support from government agencies, legislatures, and the courts. The difficulty of determining which jobs are comparable, as well as the role of supply and demand for different jobs, have been the major reasons why most employers question this concept. Also, differences in pay may be attributable to numerous factors, including the supply or shortages of women in certain jobs. In the example cited, the reason why the job of electrician is predominantly held by men is that, in the past, few women sought or were permitted to become electricians. Only by providing training and entry for qualified women to become electricians will the disparity in pay be eliminated.

---

[4]Although estimates vary, the statistical median for women's salaries was about 66 percent of that for men in the late 1980s.

Likewise, men with the appropriate interests and abilities could be encouraged to become medical technologists.

It is important for supervisors to understand the issue of comparable worth, which may become a major issue in the future.[5] However, it is even more important for supervisors to identify and support qualified women to train and develop for higher paying jobs that have been held predominantly by men. Supervisors should be willing to encourage, select, and assist these women as they progress into higher paying positions of greater skill and responsibility.

OTHER "PROTECTED GROUPS" AND THE SUPERVISOR

In addition to racial/ethnic minorities and women, there are a number of other "protected-group" categories with which supervisors should be familiar. Since a discussion of all the aspects of and issues for each of these categories is beyond the scope of this text, in this section we only highlight some of the additional supervisory considerations applicable to employees who are older, are handicapped, have different religious beliefs, and are Vietnam-era veterans.

Older Employees

As mentioned in Chapter 1, a significant trend in the composition of the U.S. population is the increasing number of older persons. This trend includes more employees in the "older" age categories and the need to generate replacements for them as they retire.

The Age Discrimination in Employment Act, as amended in 1986, prohibits discrimination in employment policies for most individuals beyond 40 years of age. Consequently, mandatory retirement ages (such as at age 70) no longer are permissible for most employees. Nevertheless, many workers still retire at age 65 or earlier. In part, this is because of the existence of improved retirement programs and pension plans, including plans that allow early retirement. Some early-retirement plans permit employees who have 30 years of service to retire before age 60.

Decisions Involving Age Discrimination. When making decisions to hire, promote, or discharge, supervisors may be directly affected by the Age Discrimination in Employment Act. For example, selecting a 35-year-old person for a sales position instead of a 55-year-old with more selling experience might

---

[5] See Rod Willis, "What's New With Comp Worth?" *Management Review* (March 1986), pp. 40–43.

result in an age discrimination lawsuit. Laying off a 50-year-old engineer while keeping a 30-year-old engineer on the payroll during a reduction in force might be age discrimination, unless the younger engineer is far superior in abilities to the older one.

Supervisory decisions to demote or terminate older employees should be documented with sound, objective performance appraisals. Terminating a 62-year-old clerical worker simply for "poor job performance" might be discriminatory if this employee's work performance was not objectively measured and compared with all employees in the department. Some supervisors complain that greater costs and inefficiencies are incurred if they are required to "carry" older workers who no longer can do the job. Whether or not this complaint is valid, the supervisor must appraise the performance of all employees in an impartial, objective way before making decisions that adversely affect older workers. As emphasized in Chapter 14, performance appraisal is a significant part of any supervisor's job, but it is especially important when older workers are in the department.

The Question of Declining Abilities.   Supervisors often express concern about those older workers who show a decline in physical and mental abilities. While some older persons do lose some of their former strengths on the job, they may be able to compensate by using their experience. Even with a decline in physical strength due to age, most firms report that older workers tend to have better quality, safety, and attendance records than do younger employees.

Further, it may be possible, within certain limits, for supervisors to make special accommodations for some older employees. Years of dedicated and faithful service should not be disregarded by a supervisor. Adjustments in the older employee's workload, scheduling, and the like can be reasonable allowances, which will be understood and accepted by others in the work group, particularly those who are themselves advancing in years and who recognize that someday their capabilities might also diminish somewhat.

Preparation for Retirement.   Older employees who are approaching retirement present another problem that requires sensitivity on the part of supervisors. Some employees who have worked for 30 years or more look forward to retirement as a time to enjoy a greater variety of activities and leisure. However, others view retirement with anxieties about the security of a daily routine, steady income, and established social relationships.

Supervisors should be supportive and understanding as older employees near retirement. These employees should be encouraged to take advantage of preretirement planning activities that may be available in the company or through outside agencies. Some companies allow employees nearing retirement to attend retirement-related workshops during working hours without loss of pay. In other companies, members of the human resources department or a benefits specialist will spend considerable time with each employee nearing retirement to discuss pensions, insurance, social security, and other financial matters. Supervisors should also encourage recent retirees to attend company social functions and to maintain contact with their former supervisors and co-workers wherever possible. Such contacts are valuable aids in making the transition to retirement more comfortable for these persons.

Handicapped Persons

A handicapped person has been defined as one who has a physical or mental impairment that substantially limits one or more of life's major activities, who has a record of such impairment, or who is regarded as having such an impairment.[6] Thus people who are lame, crippled, blind, deaf, and mentally retarded are classified as handicapped.

Although many companies have long made special efforts to provide employment for handicapped persons, there has been greater emphasis in this direction in recent years. The federal Rehabilitation Act of 1973 and other laws and government regulations have identified handicapped persons as another group that must receive special consideration in employment and other organizational activities. These laws require that certain employers doing business with government agencies must develop affirmative-action programs and make reasonable accommodation for the employment of handicapped persons. At the time of writing of this text, legislation was pending in the U.S. Congress that more generally would make discrimination based on disability unlawful in employment and that would further broaden and extend requirements on employers for reasonable accommodation to employ the handicapped.

Thus in addition to employing the handicapped, reasonable accommodation is another responsibility that employers must assume. By **reasonable accommodation** is meant making adjustments in the work situation to make it possible for otherwise qualified handicapped persons to perform useful work at a satisfactory level of performance. However, such accommodation does not require the employer to assume extraordinary additional costs or totally change business operations. For example, reasonable accommodation means making buildings accessible to handicapped persons by the building of ramps, the removal of barriers such as steps or curbs, and the alteration of restroom facilities. Reasonable accommodation may mean that the arrangement of desks and the width of aisles have to be altered to allow persons in wheelchairs access to job locations.

In some situations job duties have been altered to accommodate handicapped persons. For example, in one company an employee who assembled

---

[6]Gopal C. Pati, ''Countdown on Hiring the Handicapped,'' *Personnel Journal* (March 1978), p. 148.

small component units was also expected to place the completed units in a carton at the end of the assembly process. Several times a day the full carton had to be carried to the shipping area. In order for an employee in a wheelchair to perform this assembly job, the supervisor arranged for a shipping clerk to pick up completed units at designated times each day. Thus the supervisor made a reasonable accommodation so that a physically impaired employee could handle this job. Another supervisor added a flashing warning light to a piece of equipment that already contained a warning buzzer so that an employee with a hearing impairment could safely be employed.

The type of handicap that an employee has may affect the managerial style used by a supervisor. For example, employees who are mentally handicapped may require close and direct supervision. However, a physically handicapped employee who uses a wheelchair while working as a proofreader would probably be better supervised in a more general and participative style. In general, much research has shown that handicapped employees can make excellent employees, provided that they are placed in job situations where their abilities can be adapted and used appropriately.[7]

Accommodation of Different Religious Views

Since the passage of the Civil Rights Act of 1964, most employers are required to afford nondiscriminatory treatment to employees who hold different religious views. Although EEOC and court decisions have not always clearly defined religious discrimination, the principle has evolved that employers must make reasonable accommodation for employees who hold differing religious beliefs.

In this regard, work and holiday schedules have been the major focus for employers. For example, some employees who follow the orthodox Jewish faith consider Saturday as the day for their religious observance instead of Sunday. Requiring such employees to work on Saturday would be the same as requiring employees who are members of some Christian denominations to work on Sundays. A supervisor might be able to accommodate the religious views of such employees by scheduling their workweeks in such a way that their religious preferences are accommodated. Allowing Jewish employees to take holidays on Rosh Hashana and Yom Kippur instead of Christmas and Easter would be another example of accommodation.

Supervisors may find that they will be confronted with situations where it will be extremely difficult to accommodate all of their employees' religious preferences and still schedule the work to be done. If this happens, a supervisor would be well-advised to discuss the problem with his or her boss and with

---

[7]See *Ready, Willing, and Available: A Business Guide for Hiring People with Disabilities* (Washington, D.C.: U.S. Government Printing Office Publication #239–825, 1989).

the human resources staff to determine whether scheduling alternatives are available that might accommodate the employees and yet not be too costly or disruptive.

Vietnam-Era Veterans

Vietnam-era military veterans are another group that has been identified for certain employment protection. After the end of the Vietnam War, with so many men and women released from military service in the 1970s, legislators and political leaders felt that Vietnam-era veterans were entitled to assistance to facilitate their reentry into the civilian labor force. The Vietnam-Era Veteran's Readjustment Act of 1974 was passed, which applies primarily to employers who have contracts with the federal government. This law requires employers to have affirmative-action programs for the hiring and advancement of veterans. Other laws and regulations—particularly in public and government employment—provide for preferential hiring policies for veterans.

Supervision of military veterans usually involves fewer special considerations than does supervision of other legally protected employees. Except for those veterans who experienced mental or physical impairment during the war and who may continue to show some effects, most veterans cannot be distinguished from nonveterans. Consequently, once they have been employed and have adjusted to the work environment, veterans generally should be supervised just like everyone else. Further, as the 1990s progress, it seems likely that this "protected group" will need less special consideration by employers than in the earlier post–Vietnam years.

"PROTECTED-GROUP" SUPERVISORS

Thus far we have discussed how the supervision of legally protected employees requires both awareness and sensitivity to a variety of factors. Additionally, problems can arise for supervisors who themselves are members of a legally protected category, e.g., minorities and women, and who may experience resistance and resentment in their supervisory positions.

For example, it is common today to find a woman supervisor whose subordinates primarily are men, especially in office and sales departments. Skepticism about the qualifications of the woman supervisor may be voiced in men's comments such as, "She didn't deserve the job" or "She got it because she's female." A woman supervisor in such a situation may feel that she has to accomplish more than a male supervisor might be expected to achieve in a similar job situation. However, past experiences of many women supervisors indicate that, once they have proven their competence, most of this initial complaining or skepticism will fade away.

Another example might be a black production supervisor in a manufacturing plant who supervises black employees and who may be faced with a dilemma. Because the supervisor is of the same race, some black employees may attempt to take advantage of the situation, perhaps by taking more extended break periods than allowed. On the other hand, the black supervisor may put greater pressure on black employees to perform and to obey the rules so that no charge of favoritism can be justified.

Similarly, the woman supervisor who feels obliged to accomplish more than her male counterparts and who wishes to avoid charges of favoritism toward female subordinates may put greater pressure on female employees. This tendency has led some female employees to say that they would rather work for male supervisors, because female supervisors are "tougher" on them than are men.

On the other hand, research studies have suggested that, in general, supervisors tend to be able to communicate better with subordinates who are of the same race or the same sex as the supervisors. For example, a black supervisor is likely to understand better the culture, speech patterns, and attitudes of black employees.

Problems or potential problems such as those cited are not unusual, and they should even be anticipated by supervisors or potential supervisors. It is helpful if such issues are openly discussed in supervisory training and development meetings. In addition, "protected-group" supervisors—just like all other supervisors—must have performance expectations, policies, and decisions that are applied consistently and uniformly to all employees, regardless of race, sex, and other such considerations.

UNDERSTANDING "REVERSE DISCRIMINATION"

The attitudes and reactions of employees who are not members of a legally protected group represent another challenge to supervisors. These reactions are often associated with so-called reverse discrimination. **Reverse discrimination** is often charged when a more senior or qualified person is denied a job opportunity or promotion because preference was given to a "protected-group" individual who may be less qualified or junior in seniority.

For example, in a significant U.S. Supreme Court case, a white male with higher seniority was denied admission to a company–union training program because a specific number of openings were designated to be filled by black employees with less seniority. The Supreme Court decided that the white male had not been discriminated against illegally because the company and the labor union had negotiated a voluntary affirmative-action program. Although the court indicated that there were times that such reverse favoritism might be illegal, it did not identify those instances. Thus the court upheld the idea of affirmative action but did not clearly rule for or against the issue of reverse discrimination.

The impact of equal employment opportunity and affirmative-action programs most often is felt by white male employees. Some white males feel that they do not have an equal or fair opportunity to compete for promotions or higher paying jobs. Further, some of them interpret the existence of numerical goals in affirmative-action programs as "quotas" that have to be met by hiring and promoting unqualified or less qualified women or minorities.

Supervisors of integrated racial groups and male and female employees may be apprehensive about their situations. For example, supervisors may become reluctant to discipline anyone so as to avoid charges of favoritism or discrimination. Another difficulty is that conflicts and distrust among these various groups may arise, which place stress on interpersonal relationships and which may affect performance of the department. Such problems are not easily overcome. However, communication between the supervisor and all groups of employees is absolutely essential, and the supervisor should try to correct misperceptions about any employee's abilities and qualifications as they occur. Whether "reverse discrimination" exists is not really important. Rather, what is important is the supervisor's approach in responding to the feelings and attitudes of all groups and individuals in an understanding, empathic, fair, and objective manner.

Good Supervision: The Overriding Consideration

It is likely that the types of issues and considerations that we have discussed in this chapter will be of concern to supervisors for years to come. Additional legislation and court decisions will specify or clarify other considerations for legally protected groups that now exist and, perhaps, for other groups to be identified in the future.

It is apparent that supervisors must adapt their ways of managing their departments to meet the requirements and considerations afforded to legally protected employees. In this effort supervisors should always recognize that the best way to manage *all* employees in their departments—protected or not— is to constantly apply the principles of good supervision as presented throughout this text.

SUMMARY

The classifications of "protected-group employees," such as those based on racial/ethnic origin, sex, age, physical limitations, religion, and military record, heighten the importance of being aware of some additional considerations that complicate the supervisor's job.

When supervising minority employees, supervisors should endeavor to overcome the impact of past discrimination. Awareness of cultural factors and recognition of language differences are important aspects in supervising minority employees.

The growing role of women in work organizations means that supervisors must ensure that women are not adversely affected as they move into a greater variety of career fields and positions. Avoidance of sexual harassment and stereotyping is mandatory. Human resources policies should stress training and development opportunities for women, nondiscriminatory treatment during pregnancy, flexibility in resolving family-care conflicts and problems, and equitable compensation.

When making decisions to hire, promote, or discharge, supervisors should objectively appraise the qualifications and performance of older workers. Supervisors should also understand and try to adjust to reduced abilities of older workers, if at all possible. Further, supervisors should assist those employees who are nearing retirement to prepare for it.

The principle of reasonable accommodation should be followed when supervising handicapped workers and employees of different religious beliefs. Reasonable adjustments are made to allow such employees to be employed or to continue their employment. Vietnam-era veterans are to be afforded special consideration when hiring decisions are made, but they usually require only regular supervision after they have adjusted to their work environment.

The supervisor who is a member of a protected group may encounter pressures from both ''protected-group'' and ''nonprotected-group'' employees. Nevertheless, he or she should see to it that all employees are given equal treatment and have equal performance expectations. Also, this supervisor should be sensitive to the feelings and attitudes of some employees about so-called reverse discrimination.

QUESTIONS FOR DISCUSSION

1. Who are classified as ''protected-group'' employees? Does ''protected group'' mean the same as a ''special group'' of employees? Discuss.
2. Identify a particular racial/ethnic minority (other than the examples given in the text) and discuss some cultural factors and language differences that a supervisor might need to consider in supervising this minority group.
3. Why have many employers given women access to special training and development opportunities and moved them into jobs that might require the modification of existing tools or equipment?
4. Give several examples of sexual stereotyping and sexual harassment (other than those given in the text) that supervisors must cope with.
5. Discuss how women can be affected by pregnancy, family-care, and compensation policies. What legal requirements are imposed, and not imposed, for employers in these areas?
6. Assume that a supervisor has a 60-year-old secretary whose performance has slipped recently. What considerations should affect the supervisor's actions toward this employee?
7. What does reasonable accommodation mean? How does it apply to handicapped employees and members of different religious groups? Are there limits to reasonable accommodation? Discuss.
8. Discuss the statement that supervision of Vietnam-era veterans usually requires few special considerations once they are employed and have adjusted to the job.

9. ''Protected-group supervisors tend to be more demanding on employees who are of the same protected group.'' Discuss this statement.
10. What is meant by the concept of reverse discrimination? Is it a valid concept, a new stereotype, or a myth? How does it affect the practice of supervisory management?
11. Why should the application of the principles of good supervision be the overriding concern of a supervisor in charge of a department that is racially mixed and has both male and female employees?

CHAPTER 18

Building Positive Discipline

CHAPTER OBJECTIVES

1. To emphasize the importance of positive self-discipline in an organization.
2. To identify situations that call for disciplinary action.
3. To discuss disciplinary processes and approaches that will be conducive to ensuring that a disciplinary action is taken for just (proper) cause.
4. To discuss the concept and application of progressive discipline.
5. To explain the ''hot stove rule'' approach for disciplinary actions.
6. To stress the need to document disciplinary actions and to provide the right of appeal to employees.

It is well recognized that the term discipline is used and understood in several different ways. Many supervisors associate it with the use of authority, force, or punishment. In this text, however, we prefer to consider **discipline** as a condition of orderliness, that is, the degree to which members of an organization act sensibly and observe the organization's standards of acceptable behavior. Discipline is positive (or good) when employees generally follow the rules and meet the standards of the organization. It is negative (or bad) when they follow the rules reluctantly or when they actually disobey regulations and violate the prescribed standards of acceptable behavior.

Discipline is not identical with morale. As discussed in Chapter 16, morale consists of attitudes and a state of mind, whereas discipline is primarily a state of affairs. However, there is some correlation between morale and discipline. Normally there will be fewer disciplinary problems when morale is high; conversely, low morale is usually accompanied by more disciplinary problems. Yet it is conceivable that a high degree of positive discipline could be present in spite of a low level of morale; this could occur primarily as a result of insecurity, fear, or sheer force. Nevertheless, it is unlikely that a high degree of positive employee discipline will be maintained indefinitely, unless there is an acceptable level of employee morale.

THE BASIS OF POSITIVE SELF-DISCIPLINE

The best type of discipline is *positive self-discipline*. It is based on the normal human tendency to do what needs to be done, to do one's share, and to follow reasonable standards of acceptable behavior. Even before they start to work, most mature persons accept the idea that following instructions and fair rules of conduct are normal responsibilities in any job.

Positive self-discipline of employees is based on the premise that most employees want to do the right thing and can be counted on to exercise self-discipline. They believe in performing their work properly, coming to work on time, following the supervisor's instructions, and refraining from fighting, using drugs, drinking liquor, or stealing. They know that it is natural to subordinate some of their own personal interests and desires to the needs of the organization. As long as company rules are communicated to them and are reasonable, most employees usually will observe the rules.

Unfortunately, there are always some employees who, for one reason or another, fail to observe established rules and standards even after having been informed of them. In recent years, there have been numerous reports of employee theft from employers, which amounts in the aggregate to several tens of billions of dollars of loss annually. When added to other forms of employee fraud and dishonesty—including misuse or "stealing" of company time on a

Fig 18–1.
Self-discipline
must exist at
the supervisory
level before it
will exist at the
employee level.

habitual basis by unwarranted absenteeism, tardiness, and doing personal business and socializing on company time—the cost of employee theft and dishonesty to American businesses has been estimated to be over 200 billion dollars a year.[1]

Despite such unfortunate statistics, supervisors should maintain a balanced perspective that employees at the departmental level will take most of their cues for self-discipline from their supervisors and managers. Ideally, positive self-discipline will exist throughout the entire management team, beginning at the top and extending through the supervisors. Supervisors cannot expect their employees to practice positive self-discipline if they themselves do not set a good example. As we have stated several times previously, a supervisor's actions and behavior are easy targets for the employees to either emulate or reject. Further, if the supervisor is able to encourage the vast majority of the employees in the department to show a strong sense of self-discipline, usually they will exert group pressure on the dissenters. For example, if a "no smoking" rule is introduced in an office work area, usually someone in the group itself will enforce this rule by reminding any smoker to leave the work area before lighting a cigarette. Thus the need for corrective action by the supervisor is reduced when positive self-discipline is evident and practiced.

[1]Banning K. Lary, "Why Corporations Can't Lock the Rascals Out," *Management Review* (October 1989), p. 51.

THE IMPORTANCE OF WRITTEN RULES AND REGULATIONS

In Chapter 7, we discussed the need for and importance of policies, procedures, methods, and rules as standing plans that cover many aspects of ongoing operations. These are particularly vital in informing employees concerning what standards of behavior are expected and what types will not be acceptable.

Most organizations provide their employees with a written list of rules or codes of conduct. These are sometimes included in an employee handbook; otherwise they will be provided as a separate booklet or memorandum, which will be available or posted in each department. The supervisor must ensure that employees have read and understand the general and departmental rules, which may include safety and technical regulations depending upon the activities of a department.

Written rules and regulations provide a common code or standard that should assist the supervisor in encouraging and maintaining employee self-discipline. Some companies spell out very detailed lists of rules and infractions, and may include classifications of the likely penalties that will be meted out for violations. Other companies and organizations—probably the majority—prefer to list their major rules and regulations but without tying down the consequences for violations of various rules. (An example of such a list as used by a manufacturing plant is shown in Figure 18–2). Regardless of what type or how detailed a list is used, the supervisor is the person most responsible for

Fig 18–2. Partial list of plant rules and regulations of a manufacturing company.

PLANT RULES AND REGULATIONS

The efficient operation of our plants and the general welfare of our employees require the establishment of certain uniform standards of behavior. Accordingly, the following offenses are considered to be violations of these standards and employees who refuse to accept this guidance will subject themselves to appropriate disciplinary action.

1. Habitual tardiness and absenteeism.
2. Theft or attempted theft of Company or other employee's property.
3. Fighting or attempting bodily injury upon another employee.
4. Horseplay, malicious mischief, or any other conduct affecting the rights of other employees.
5. Intoxication or drinking on the job; or being in a condition which makes it impossible to perform work in a satisfactory manner.
6. Refusal, or failure to perform assigned work; or refusal, or failure to comply with supervisory instructions.
7. Inattention to duties; carelessness in performance of duties; loafing on the job, idling, sleeping, or reading papers during working hours.
8. Violation of published safety or health rules.
9. Possessing, consuming, selling, or being under the influence of illegal drugs on the premises.
10. Unauthorized possession of weapons, firearms, or explosives on the premises.
11. Requests for sexual favors, sexual advances and physical conduct of a sexual nature toward another employee on the premises.

the consistent application and enforcement of both company and departmental rules. In fact, the degree to which employees follow the rules in a positive, self-disciplined way is usually more attributable to the supervisor's role than to any other single factor.

CONFRONTING DISCIPLINARY SITUATIONS

Despite a supervisor's best efforts to prevent infractions, it is almost inevitable that a supervisor at times will be confronted with situations requiring some type of disciplinary action. Among the most common recurring situations that require supervisory disciplinary actions are: infractions of rules regarding time schedules, rest periods, procedures, safety, etc.; excessive absenteeism or tardiness; defective or inadequate work performance; and poor attitudes that influence the work of others or damage the firm's public image.

At times a supervisor might experience open insubordination, such as an employee's refusal to carry out a legitimate work assignment. It may even happen that a supervisor is confronted with disciplinary problems that stem from employee behavior off the job. For example, an employee may have an excessive drinking problem or may be taking illegal drugs. Whenever an employee's off-the-job conduct has an impact on his or her job performance, the supervisor must be prepared to respond to such a problem in an appropriate fashion. Situations that call for disciplinary action are certainly not pleasant, but the supervisor must have the courage to deal with them rather than to ignore them, hoping they will go away. If the supervisor does not take responsible action when it is required, some borderline employees might be encouraged to try to "get away" with similar violations.

The supervisor should not be afraid to draw on some of the authority inherent in the supervisory position, even though the supervisor might prefer to overlook the matter or "pass the buck" to higher management or the human resources department. Further, a supervisor who finds it expedient to ask the human resources department to take over all departmental disciplinary problems is shirking responsibility and undermining his or her own position of authority.

Normally a good supervisor will not have to take disciplinary actions frequently. But whenever it becomes necessary, the supervisor should be ready to take the proper action no matter how unpleasant the task may be.

THE DISCIPLINARY PROCESS

Any disciplinary action must be undertaken with sensitivity and sound judgment on the supervisor's part. The purpose of a disciplinary action should not be to punish or seek revenge but rather to improve the employees' future behavior. In other words, the primary purpose of a disciplinary action is to avoid similar infractions in the future.

In this chapter we do not consider directly those situations where union contractual obligations may restrict the supervisor's authority in taking disciplinary action. Nevertheless, the ideas discussed here are generally applicable in most unionized as well as nonunionized organizations.[2]

Disciplinary Action Should Be for Just Cause

Most employers accept the general premise that disciplinary action taken against an employee should be for *just cause*. The overwhelming preponderance of labor union contracts specify a "just-cause" or "proper-cause" standard for discipline and discharge. Similarly, many cases decided by government agencies and by the courts have required employers to prove that disciplinary actions taken against legally protected employees (as discussed in the previous chapter) were not discriminatory but were for just cause.

Although the ramifications of a just-cause standard for disciplinary action can be rather complicated, the guidelines presented in this chapter are consistent with the principles and requirements necessary to justify any disciplinary or discharge action. The supervisor who follows these guidelines in a conscientious way normally should be able to meet a just-cause standard, irrespective of whether it involves a unionized firm, a nonunionized organization, or a potential area of legal discrimination.[3]

Precautionary Questions and Measures

As a first consideration in any disciplinary situation, a supervisor should guard against undue haste or taking unwarranted action based on emotional response. There are a number of precautionary questions and measures that a supervisor should consider and follow before deciding on any disciplinary action in response to an alleged employee offense.

Investigate and Study the Situation. Before doing anything, a supervisor should study and investigate what happened and why. The following questions, while not comprehensive, might be used as a checklist as the supervisor investigates and considers what should be done:

[2]Special considerations involving labor unions are discussed in Chapters 21 and 22.

[3]See Arthur A. Sloane and Fred Witney, *Labor Relations* (6th ed., Englewood Cliffs, N.J.: Prentice-Hall, Inc., 1988), pp. 458–464; or Adolph M. Koven and Susan L. Smith, *Just Cause: The Seven Tests* (Dubuque, Iowa: Kendall/Hunt Publishing Company, 1985).

1. Are all or most of the facts available and are they reported accurately? That is, can the alleged offense be proved by direct or circumstantial evidence, or is the allegation based merely on suspicion?
2. How serious (minor, major, or intolerable) is the offense? Were others involved or affected by it? Were company funds or equipment involved?
3. Did the employee know the rule or standard? Does the employee have a reasonable excuse, and are there any extenuating circumstances?
4. What is the employee's past disciplinary record, length of service, and performance level? Does the offense indicate carelessness, absentmindedness, loss of temper, etc.? How does this employee react to criticism?
5. Should the employee receive the same treatment others have had for the same offense? If not, is it possible to establish a basis for differentiating the present alleged offense from past offenses of a similar nature?
6. Is all the necessary documentation available in case the matter leads to outside review?

Investigatory Interviews.   As part of the supervisor's investigation of an alleged infraction, it may be necessary for the supervisor to question the employee involved, as well as other employees who may have relevant knowledge or information to offer. In general, such interviews should be conducted in private and on an individual basis. This is usually less threatening to an employee who may be reluctant to tell what he or she knows, unless it is in private and perhaps stated on a confidential basis. This also helps to avoid having what employees say being unduly influenced by each other's versions and interpretations.

If an employee who is to be interviewed believes that he or she may be subject to disciplinary action, this employee may request that a union representative or co-worker be present during the investigatory interview.[4] Normally the supervisor should grant such a request; of course, if the employee is to have a witness present, the supervisor is well-advised to have a fellow supervisor also present to serve as a supervisory witness to the interview.

In conducting an investigatory interview, most of the principles of interviewing discussed in Chapter 12 are applicable. The supervisor should ask both directive and nondirective questions that are designed to elicit specific answers concerning what happened and why. Above all, the supervisor should avoid making any final judgments until all the interviews have been held and other relevant information has been assembled.

---

[4]In 1975, a Supreme Court ruling (commonly known as the Weingarten decision) held that a union employee has the right to have a union representative present during an investigatory interview if the employee reasonably believes that the investigation may lead to disciplinary action. In 1982, a decision of the National Labor Relations Board extended this right to nonunion employees by holding that an unrepresented employee had the right to have a co-worker present during an investigatory interview. However, in 1985 the National Labor Relations Board reversed itself and held that only employees represented by a labor union had the right to representation during an investigatory interview! Irrespective, however, a representative or co-worker witness cannot disrupt an investigatory interview or answer questions in place of the employee being interviewed.

Maintaining Self-Control.   Regardless of the severity of an employee violation, a supervisor must not lose self-control. This does not mean that a supervisor should face a disciplinary situation half-heartedly or indifferently. But if a supervisor feels that he or she is in danger of losing control of temper or emotions, the supervisor should delay the investigatory interviews and not take any action until calming down. A supervisor's loss of self-control or a display of anger could compromise fair and objective judgment.

Generally, a supervisor should never lay a hand on an employee in any way. Except for emergencies, when an employee has been injured or becomes ill or when employees who are fighting need to be separated, any physical gesture could easily be misunderstood. A supervisor who engages in physical violence, except in self-defense, normally would be subjected to disciplinary action by higher management.

Privacy in Disciplining.   When a supervisor finally decides on a course of disciplinary action, the supervisor should communicate the discipline to the offending employee in private. A public reprimand not only humiliates the employee in the eyes of co-workers but also can lead to loss of morale in the department or even a grievance.[5] If in the opinion of the other employees a public disciplinary action is too severe for the violation, the disciplined employee might emerge as a martyr in the view of every employee in the department.

Only under extreme circumstances should disciplinary action be taken in public. For example, a supervisor's authority may be challenged directly and openly by an employee who repeatedly refuses to carry out a reasonable work request. Or an employee may be drunk or fighting on the job. In these cases it is necessary for the supervisor to reach a disciplinary decision quickly—for example, by sending the offending employees home on suspension pending further investigation. The supervisor may even have to do this in the view of other employees in order to regain control of the situation and to maintain their respect.

Disciplinary Time Element.   When a supervisor decides to impose a disciplinary action, the question arises as to how long the violation should be held against an employee. Generally, it is desirable to disregard minor or intermediate offenses after a year or so has elapsed since they were committed. Thus an employee with a poor record of defective work might be given a "clean bill of health" by subsequently compiling a good record for six months or one year.

---

[5]Many union contracts require that employees who are to be disciplined for an infraction have the right to request the presence of a union representative. In unionized organizations, it is desirable to have more than one management person present—for example, the supervisor, the supervisor's boss, and perhaps the human resources director. Thus both management and the union have witnesses to the disciplinary action, even when it takes place in a private area.

In this regard, some companies have adopted "point systems" to cover certain infractions—especially absenteeism and tardiness—by which employees can have points removed from their records if they have perfect or acceptable attendance during later periods.

There are situations when the time element is of no importance. For example, if an employee is caught brandishing a knife in a heated argument at work, the supervisor need not worry about any time element or previous offenses. This act is serious enough to warrant immediate discharge.

Practicing Progressive Discipline

Unless a serious wrong, such as stealing, physical violence, or gross insubordination, has been committed, the offending employee rarely is discharged for a first offense.[6] Although the type of disciplinary action appropriate to a situation will vary, many organizations practice the concept of **progressive discipline,** which provides for an increase in the severity of the penalty with each offense. The following steps comprise a system of progressive disciplinary action: informal talk, oral warning, written warning, disciplinary layoff (suspension), transfer or demotion, and discharge. An example of such a system is illustrated by the "Corrective Action Policy" for a hospital shown in Figure 18-3.

Informal Talk.   If the offense is of a relatively minor nature and if the employee has had no previous disciplinary record, a friendly and informal talk will clear up the problem in many cases. During this talk, the supervisor should try to determine the underlying reasons for the employee's unacceptable conduct. At the same time, the supervisor should reaffirm the employee's sense of responsibility and acknowledge his or her previous good behavior.

Oral Warning.   If a friendly talk does not take care of the situation, the next step is to give the employee an oral warning (sometimes known as "counseling"). Here the supervisor emphasizes the undesirability of the employee's repeated violation in a straightforward manner. There is no need for the supervisor to lament the fact that the employee's fine reputation has been tarnished. Although the supervisor should stress the preventive purpose of dis-

---

[6]For certain gross violations, such as stealing, narcotics use, and violence, an organization may call in law enforcement authorities to conduct an investigation and to take appropriate action. Some firms will employ a consultant to administer a polygraph test in an effort to determine who committed the violations, particularly in matters involving theft. The use of the polygraph, however, has been restricted somewhat as a result of a 1988 federal law. This statute prohibits random polygraph testing, but permits an employer with "reasonable suspicion" of employee wrongdoing to use a polygraph test provided certain standards are met. Supervisors, for the most part, do not make the decision to use a polygraph; such a decision is normally made by someone in higher management, or the human resources staff, after consultation with legal counsel.

Fig 18–3.
Progressive
disciplinary
policy for a
hospital.

HOSPITAL CORRECTIVE ACTION POLICY

POLICY

Corrective action shall progress from verbal counseling to written reprimand, suspension and termination. All actions taken shall include a reference to the specific policy or procedure which has been violated, the adverse consequence resulting from the violation, the type of behavior expected in the future, and the corrective action which will be taken if further violations occur. A copy of a written corrective action form shall be given to the employee. The following are guidelines for corrective action procedure:

A. *Verbal Counseling* — A verbal counseling shall be given for all minor violations of Hospital rules and policies. More than two verbal counselings, within the last twelve month period, regarding violations of any rules or policies warrants a written reprimand.

B. *Written Reprimands* — Written reprimands shall be given for repeated minor infractions or for first-time occurrences of more serious offenses.

Written reprimands shall be documented on the Notice of Corrective Action form, which is signed by the department head or supervisor and the employee.

C. *Suspension* — An employee shall be suspended without pay for one to four scheduled working days for a critical or major offense or for repeated minor or serious offenses.

D. *Termination* — An employee may be terminated for repeated violations of Hospital rules and regulations or for first offenses of a critical nature.

cipline, the supervisor should also emphasize that unless the employee improves, more serious disciplinary action will be taken. In some organizations a record of this oral warning is made in the employee's files. Or the supervisor may simply write a brief note in a supervisory log book to document the fact that an oral warning took place on a particular date. This can be important evidence in the event that the same employee commits another infraction in the future.

Some supervisors feel that oral reprimands are not very effective. However, if oral warnings are carried out skillfully, many employees will respond and improve at this stage. The oral warning should leave the employee with the feeling that there must be improvement in the future.

Written Warning.   A written warning contains a statement of the violation and the potential consequences of future violations. It is a formal document, which becomes a permanent part of the employee's record. The supervisor should review with the employee the nature of this written warning and again stress the necessity for improvement. The employee should be placed on clear notice that future infractions or unacceptable conduct will lead to more serious discipline, such as suspension or discharge.

Written warnings are particularly necessary in unionized organizations, because they can serve as evidence in grievance procedures. Such documentation is also important if the employee is a member of a legally protected group,

Fig 18–4.
A program of
disciplinary
action will often
begin with an
informal talk.
With repeated
offenses,
penalties will
become more
severe.

such as minorities or women. The employee usually receives a duplicate copy of the written warning, and another copy is sent to the human resources department. Figure 18–5 is an example of a written warning used by a major supermarket chain. The form even provides space for the supervisor to note if the employee refuses to sign it.

Disciplinary Layoff (Suspension). If an employee has committed offenses repeatedly and previous warnings were of no avail, a disciplinary layoff would probably constitute the next disciplinary step. Disciplinary layoffs involve a loss of pay and usually extend from one day to several days or weeks. Because a disciplinary layoff involves a loss of pay, most organizations limit a supervisor's authority at this stage. Most supervisors can only initiate a disciplinary suspension, which then must be approved by higher management after consultation with the human resources department.[7]

Employees who are not impressed with oral or written warnings usually find a disciplinary layoff to be a rude awakening. The layoff may restore in them the need to comply with the organization's rules and regulations. However, managers in some organizations seldom apply suspension or layoff as a disciplinary measure. They believe that laying off a trained employee will hurt their own production, especially in times of labor shortages. Further, they rea-

---

[7]A disciplinary layoff, like all other disciplinary measures, is usually subject to an appeal procedure, as discussed later in this chapter and in Chapter 22.

Fig. 18–5. Example of a written warning used by a supermarket firm.

EMPLOYEE CORRECTIVE ACTION NOTICE

Employee's Name _____ Date of Notice _____

Store Address _____ Store # _____ Dept. _____ Job Classification

This notice is a: First Warning Second Warning Third Warning Final Warning
                        ☐   ☐   ☐   ☐

Reason for Corrective Action: (Check below)

☐ Cooperation/Interest   ☐ Cash register   ☐ Insubordination
                               discrepancy

☐ Quality/Quantity of   ☐ Dress code   ☐ Time card violation
   work

☐ Tardiness/Absenteeism   ☐ Disregard for safety   ☐ Other causes (Explain)

Explanation must accompany reason checked above:

_____

_____

_____

I HEREBY SIGNIFY THAT I HAVE RECEIVED A FULL EXPLANATION OF MY
FAILURE TO PERFORM AS EXPECTED. THE COMPANY AND I UNDERSTAND THAT
FURTHER FAILURE ON MY PART WILL BE DUE CAUSE FOR DISCIPLINARY
ACTION UP TO, AND INCLUDING, DISCHARGE.

_____ _____   _____ _____
Employee's signature   Date   Supervisor's signature   Date

                                   _____ _____
                                   Store Manager's signature Date

REFUSAL OF EMPLOYEE TO SIGN THIS NOTICE SHOULD BE SO NOTED HEREON.

Note: Prepare original and three copies. Send original and one copy to the Human
Resources Director. Send one copy to the Store Manager and one copy to the
employee.

son that the laid-off employee may return in an even more unpleasant frame of mind. Despite this possible reaction, in many employee situations disciplinary layoffs can be an effective disciplinary measure.

Transfer. Transferring an employee to a job in another department typically involves no loss of pay or skill. This disciplinary action is usually taken when an offending employee seems to be experiencing difficulty in working for a particular supervisor, in working at a current job, or in associating with certain other employees. The transfer may bring about a marked improvement if the employee adjusts to the new department and the new supervisor in a positive fashion. If a transfer is made simply to give the employee a last chance to retain a job in the company, the employee should be told that he or she must improve in the new job or else be subject to discharge. Of course, the supervisor who accepts the transferred employee should be informed about the circumstances surrounding the transfer. This will help the supervisor in assisting the transferred employee to make a successful transition.

Demotion. Another disciplinary measure, the value of which is open to serious question, is the demotion of an employee to a lower-paying job. This course of action is likely to bring about dissatisfaction and discouragement, since losing pay and status over an extended period of time is a form of constant punishment. The dissatisfaction of the demoted employee can also spread to other employees. Therefore, most organizations avoid demotion (or downgrading) as a disciplinary action.

Demotion should be used only in unusual situations where a disciplinary layoff or a discharge are not better alternatives. For example, a long-service employee may not be maintaining the standards of work performance required in a certain job. In order to retain seniority and other accrued fringe benefits, this employee may accept a demotion as an alternative to discharge.

Discharge (Termination). The most drastic form of disciplinary action is discharge (or termination). The discharged employee loses all seniority standing and may have difficulty obtaining employment elsewhere. Discharge should be reserved only for the most serious offenses and as a last resort.

A discharge involves loss and waste. It means having to train a new employee and disrupting the makeup of the work group, which may affect the morale of other employees. Further, in unionized companies management becomes concerned about possible prolonged grievance and arbitration proceedings. Management knows that labor arbitrators are unwilling to sustain discharge except for severe offenses or for a series of violations that cumulatively justify the discharge. If the discharge involves an employee who is a member of a legally protected group, such as minorities and women, management will have to be concerned about meeting appropriate standards for nondiscrimination. Therefore, because of the serious implications and consequences of discharge, many firms and organizations have taken the right to discharge away from the supervisor and have reserved it for higher management. Other organizations require that any discharge recommended or initiated by a supervisor be reviewed and approved by higher management or the human resources department.

The preceding is true even for those employers who traditionally have had the freedom to dismiss certain employees "at will," at any time, and for any reasons except for discrimination, union activity, and the like, or where there are restrictions imposed by a contract, a policy manual, or some form of employment agreement. This has been called the **employment-at-will theory,** and it still is generally considered applicable from a legal point of view.[8] However, as stated before, most employers do recognize that a discharge action should have some basis, such as economic necessity, or should be for just (proper) cause. By following the principles of progressive disciplinary action coupled with good supervisory practices, employers usually will not have to resort to employment-at-will to decide whether to terminate an employee who has not performed in an acceptable manner.

The "Hot Stove Rule"

Taking disciplinary action may place the supervisor in a strained, difficult position. Disciplinary action tends to generate employee resentment, and it is not a pleasant experience. To assist the supervisor in applying the necessary disciplinary measure so that it will be least resented and likely to withstand challenges from various sources, many authorities have advocated the use of the **hot stove rule.**[9] This rule draws a comparison between touching a hot stove and experiencing discipline, both of which contain four elements: advance warning, immediacy, consistency, and impersonality.

Everyone knows what will happen if he or she touches a red-hot stove *(advance warning)*. Someone who touches a hot stove gets burned right away, with no questions of cause and effect *(immediacy)*. Every time a person touches a hot stove, that person gets burned *(consistency)*. Whoever touches a hot stove is burned because of the act of touching the stove, regardless of who the person is *(impersonality)*. These four elements of the hot stove rule can be applied by the supervisor when maintaining employee discipline.

Advance Warning.   In order to maintain proper discipline and to have employees accept disciplinary action as fair, it is essential that all employees

---

[8] In recent years, some employers have been confronted with "wrongful discharge" or "unlawful discharge" lawsuits, which have challenged the employment-at-will theory in certain circumstances. See Lawrence E. Dube, Jr., "Planning for Defensible Discharges," *Management Review* (March 1986), pp. 44–48; or Daniel Murnane Mackey, *Employment at Will and Employer Liability* (New York: American Management Association, 1986).

[9] Douglas McGregor, who postulated the Theory X and Y styles of management discussed in Chapter 4, is generally credited with the "hot stove" analogy for disciplinary action.

know in advance what is expected of them and what are the rules and regulations. Employees must be informed clearly that certain acts will lead to disciplinary action. Many organizations use orientation sessions, employee handbooks, and bulletin board announcements to inform employees about the rules and how they are to be enforced. In addition, supervisors are responsible for clarifying any questions that arise concerning new and old rules and their enforcement.

Some companies find it effective to utilize sections of an employee handbook, which every new employee receives. As part of orientation, the supervisor should explain to each new employee the departmental rules and the rules that are part of the employee handbook. Some organizations require employees to sign a document that they have read and understood the company's rules and regulations.

Unfortunately, in some organizations there are rules on the books that have never been enforced or that have been ignored. For example, there may be a rule prohibiting smoking in a certain area, which the supervisor has not previously enforced. Of course, it would be most improper if the supervisor suddenly decides that it is time to enforce this rule strictly and tries to make "an example" by taking disciplinary action against an employee found smoking in this area.

Yet the fact that a certain rule has not been enforced in the past does not mean that it can never be enforced. To enforce such a rule, the supervisor must inform and warn the employees that this rule will be strictly enforced from here on in. It is not enough just to post a notice on the bulletin board, since not everyone looks at this board every day. In this situation, the supervisor should issue a clear, written notice and supplement it with oral communication.

Immediacy.   After noticing an offense, the supervisor should proceed to take disciplinary action as promptly as possible. At the same time, the supervisor should avoid haste, which might lead to unwarranted reactions. The sooner the discipline is imposed, the more closely it will be connected with the offensive act.

There will be instances when it is clear that an employee is guilty of a violation, but the supervisor may be doubtful as to the degree of penalty which should be imposed. For example, incidents such as fighting, intoxication, or insubordination often require an immediate response from the supervisor. In these cases the supervisor may invoke **temporary suspension,** which means that the employee is suspended pending a final decision. The temporarily suspended employee is advised that he or she will be informed about the ultimate disciplinary action as soon as possible or at a specific date.

Temporary suspension in itself is not a punishment. It protects both management and the employee. It provides the supervisor with time to make an investigation and an opportunity to cool off. If the ensuing investigation indicates that no disciplinary action is warranted, then the employee is recalled and does not suffer any loss of pay. If a disciplinary layoff eventually is applied, then the time during which the employee was temporarily suspended will constitute part of the disciplinary layoff. The obvious advantage of temporary suspension is that the supervisor can act promptly. However, it should not be used indiscriminately.

Consistency. Appropriate disciplinary action should be taken each time an infraction occurs. The supervisor who feels inclined to be lenient every now and then is, in reality, not doing the employees a favor. Inconsistency in imposing discipline will lead to employee insecurity and anxiety and create doubts as to what they can and cannot do. This type of situation could be compared to the relations between a motorist and a traffic police officer in an area where the speed limit is enforced only occasionally. Whenever the motorist exceeds the speed limit, the motorist experiences anxiety because he or she knows that the police officer can enforce the law at any time. Most motorists would agree that it is easier to operate in a location where the police force is consistent in enforcing or not enforcing speed limits. Employees, too, find it easier to work in a situation where the supervisor is consistent in applying disciplinary action.

However, being consistent in applying disciplinary action does not necessarily mean treating everyone in exactly the same manner. Special considerations surrounding an offense may need to be considered, such as the circumstances, the employee's productivity, job attitudes, length of service, and the like. The extent to which a supervisor can be consistent and yet consider the individual's situation can be illustrated with the following example. Assume that three employees become involved in some kind of horseplay. Employee A just started work a few days ago, Employee B has been warned once about this, and Employee C has been involved in numerous cases of horseplay. In taking disciplinary action, the supervisor could decide to have a friendly informal talk with Employee A, give a written warning to Employee B, and impose a two-day disciplinary layoff on Employee C. Thus each case is considered on its own merits, with the employees being judged according to their work history. Of course, if two of these employees had had the same number of previous warnings, their penalties should be identical.

Imposing discipline consistently is one way in which a supervisor demonstrates a sense of fair play. Yet this may be easier said than done. There are times when the department is particularly rushed and the supervisor may be inclined to conveniently overlook infractions. Perhaps the supervisor does not wish to upset the work force or does not wish to lose the output of a valuable employee at a critical time. This type of consideration is paramount, especially when it is difficult to obtain employees with the skill that the offending employee possesses. Most employees, however, will accept an exception as fair if they know why the exception was made and if they consider it justified. Further, the employees must feel that any other employee in exactly the same situation would receive similar treatment.

Impersonality.   All employees who commit the same or a similar offense should be penalized. Penalties should be connected with the offensive act, not with the personality of the employee involved. Of course, it is only natural for an employee who has been disciplined by a supervisor to feel some resentment. Yet the supervisor can reduce the amount of resentment by making disciplinary action as impersonal as possible. This means that once the disciplinary action has been taken, the supervisor should treat the employee the same as before the infraction, without being apologetic about the disciplinary action.

DOCUMENTATION AND THE RIGHT TO APPEAL

Whenever a disciplinary action is taken, it is essential for the supervisor to keep records of the offense committed and the decision made including the reasoning involved in the decision. Documentation is necessary because the supervisor may be asked at some future time to substantiate the action taken, and the burden of proof is usually on the supervisor. It is not prudent for the supervisor to depend on memory alone. This is particularly true in unionized firms where grievance-arbitration procedures often result in a challenge of disciplinary actions imposed on employees.

The **right to appeal** means that it should be possible for employees to appeal a supervisor's disciplinary action to higher management. If the employee belongs to a labor union, this right is open through a grievance procedure. In nonunionized companies the appeal should be directed to the supervisor's boss, thus following the chain of command. Many nonunion firms have provided for a hierarchy of several levels of management through which an appeal may be taken.[10]

The right of appeal must be recognized as being a real privilege and not be merely a formality. Some supervisors tell their employees that they can appeal to higher management but that it will be held against the employees if they do so. This attitude is indicative of a supervisor's own insecurity. Supervisors should not be afraid to encourage their employees to appeal to higher management if the employees feel that they have been treated unfairly. Nor should supervisors feel that an appeal threatens or weakens their position as departmental managers. For the most part, a supervisor's boss will be inclined to support the supervisor's original action. If the supervisors do not foster an open appeal procedure, employees may enlist aid from outside, such as a

---

[10]The human resources department may become directly involved in an appeal procedure. Complaint procedures in nonunion firms and grievance procedures in unionized organizations are discussed in Chapter 22.

union would provide. Management's failure to provide a realistic appeal procedure is one of the reasons why some employees have resorted to unionization.

In the course of an appeal, the disciplinary penalty imposed or recommended by a supervisor may be reduced or reversed by the supervisor's boss. The supervisor's decision might be reversed because the supervisor has not been consistent in imposing disciplinary action or has not considered all the necessary facts. Under these circumstances the supervisor may become discouraged and feel that the boss has not backed him or her up. Although this situation is unfortunate, it is preferable for the supervisor to be disheartened than for an employee to be penalized unjustly. This is not too high a price to pay in order to provide every employee the right to appeal. Situations such as these can be avoided if supervisors adhere closely to the principles and steps discussed in this chapter before taking disciplinary action.

"DISCIPLINE WITHOUT PUNISHMENT"

In recent years, a number of companies have experimented with or adopted disciplinary procedures called **discipline without punishment programs, positive discipline,** and the like. The major thrust of these approaches is to stress extensive coaching, counseling, and problem solving and to avoid confrontation. A significant (and controversial) feature is the so-called paid decision-making leave in which an employee is sent home for a day or more with pay to decide whether he or she is willing to make a commitment to meet the expected standards of performance that the employee heretofore has not met. If the employee makes a commitment to improve but fails to do so, the employee is then terminated.

In general, these approaches replace warnings and suspensions with coaching sessions and reminders by the supervisors of the expected standards. The "decision-making leave" with pay is posed as a decision to be made by the employee, namely, to "improve and stay, or quit."

Those organizations that have implemented these approaches successfully have reported various benefits, particularly in the area of reduced complaints and grievances and improved employee morale. We believe that it is too early to predict whether "discipline without punishment" programs will be extensively adopted, since it is not clear that these programs are really that different in concept and outcome from progressive disciplinary action as discussed in this chapter.[11]

---

[11]For a discussion of a successful "positive discipline" program, see Alan W. Bryant, "Replacing Punitive Discipline with a Positive Approach," *Personnel Administrator* (February 1984), pp. 79–87.

SUMMARY

Employee discipline can be thought of as a state of affairs. It is likely that if employee morale is high, discipline will be positive and less need will exist for the supervisor to take disciplinary action. Supervisors should recognize that most employees want to do the right thing and that most discipline is self-imposed.

When infractions occur, the supervisor is expected to take disciplinary action. Before doing this, however, a supervisor first needs to investigate thoroughly the situation at hand and think it through appropriately. Emotional and physical responses should be avoided, and disciplinary actions for the most part should be administered to the offending employee in private.

A number of progressively severe disciplinary actions, ranging from an informal talk to discharge, are open to a supervisor as alternative choices, depending on the nature of the infraction. The supervisor's purpose in taking disciplinary action should be the improvement of the employee's behavior.

Taking disciplinary action usually is an unpleasant experience for both the employee and the supervisor. In order to reduce the distasteful aspects, each disciplinary action should fulfill as much as possible the requirements of the ''hot stove rule.'' These are advance warning, immediacy, consistency, and impersonality. To further ensure that discipline is fair and just, the right of appeal should exist for all employees.

QUESTIONS FOR DISCUSSION

1. Define the concept of employee discipline as a state of affairs. In this context, differentiate between good discipline and poor discipline.
2. Discuss the relationship between discipline and morale.
3. Evaluate the following statement: ''The best type of discipline is positive self-discipline.''
4. Discuss the need for written rules and regulations.
5. What is meant by the concept that disciplinary action should be for just cause?
6. Discuss the importance of each of the following precautionary questions and measures that supervisors must bear in mind when taking disciplinary action:
    a. Careful study and investigation.
    b. Considerations in conducting investigatory interviews.
    c. Avoiding emotional or physical outbursts.
    d. Privacy in administering discipline.
    e. Observing the time element.
7. Define and evaluate each of the following steps of progressive discipline:
    a. Informal talk.
    b. Oral warning or reprimand.
    c. Written warning.
    d. Disciplinary layoff.
    e. Transfer.
    f. Demotion.
    g. Discharge.
    Why is demotion considered to be the least desirable form of disciplinary action?

8.   What should be the purpose of any disciplinary action?
9.   Define and evaluate each of the following elements of the ''hot stove rule'':
     a.   Advance warning.
     b.   Immediacy.
     c.   Consistency.
     d.   Impersonality.
10.   Discuss the following statement: ''Discipline should be directed against the act and not against the person.'' Why is this sometimes difficult for a supervisor to accomplish?
11.   Why should a supervisor document any disciplinary action that is taken?
12.   What is meant by the right to appeal? How can this right be implemented in a nonunion organization? Discuss.
13.   Are ''discipline without punishment'' approaches significantly different from regular progressive discipline? Discuss.

CASE 26

The "Theory Triple X" Manager

Otto Wood was an engineering technologist for the Waite Conveyor Company. He was busy working on the final stages of the installation of a sophisticated computerized conveyor system in the Webster Department Stores. A sales engineer, Warren Clark, was in charge of the overall project from the time it was sold until it would be turned over to the Webster Department Stores. Clark had negotiated a deadline for installation, which was ten days away. The sales contract provided for a severe price penalty in case of late delivery.

Wood's immediate boss was Will Meyers, head of the Installation and Inspection Department. Last night, Wood phoned Meyers and told him that he was quitting immediately. He had had all he could take from Warren Clark, and he had decided to leave the firm. Wood told Meyers that Clark had been ''breathing down his neck'' continuously and that he had been pressuring him needlessly to get the job completed. Wood assured Meyers that he had been doing his best but that, in a sophisticated installation of this sort, many things create problems and interfere with getting quick results. Wood said that he didn't attempt to explain the problems to Clark because, in Wood's words, ''Mr. Clark knows next to nothing about the intricate nature of the problems involved.'' The ''straw that broke his back'' was a threat from Clark to lock him in the building until the installation was operable, even if he had to bring him his food. Wood said he realized that Clark did not intend to do this; but Clark's threat, after everything else he had done, was too much to take. In Wood's view, Clark was a Theory Triple X manager all the way!

Meyers wondered what to do. He knew that people with Otto Wood's skills were hard to find. Particularly at this stage of the project, it would be next to impossible to get a replacement employee who could come in to pick up the installation where Wood had left off and complete the project on time. Meyers understood the meaning of a penalty for late delivery. The next morning Will Meyers decided to meet with Warren Clark to discuss the situation.

A Group Decision Baffles the Supervisor

Shirley Rice was the supervisor of the Packing Department of the Amcee Novelty Company. She supervised 15 employees, predominantly young workers in their twenties, whose job it was to wrap finished products in tissue paper, put them into cardboard boxes, and then glue labels to the outside of the boxes. She was known as an experienced and firm supervisor. After observing and timing the operations frequently, she had arrived at what she considered to be a fair standard of how many items each employee could box during an eight-hour day. However, this standard was seldom reached. In order to improve the situation, after additional studies she installed a different layout, rearranged the work benches, simplified the procedures, and did all she could to raise the output of the department. But output remained considerably below her expected standard.

As a last resort, Rice decided to try an idea that had greatly impressed her. During the last two months, once a week, the company had made it possible for all supervisors to attend a series of lectures given at a local university. These lectures covered the basics of good supervisory management. During the last lecture, the professor had discussed the advantages of group decision making and group discussion, including the advantages of decisions that are worked through and reached by those who will be concerned with the outcome. The professor stated that, in such cases, the subordinates do their utmost to carry their decisions through to a successful conclusion. He compared them with decisions handed down unilaterally by supervisors, which often are only grudgingly complied with by subordinates.

Rice therefore decided to apply this method and called a meeting of the workers in the department. She told them that the current standard of output was too low and that a new standard of output had to be set. Instead of establishing the new production standard by herself, however, she wanted them to decide as a group what it should be. Of course, she hoped—but she did not say this—that they would arrive at a higher standard than the level at which they had been operating.

Several days later, much to Shirley Rice's amazement, the group arrived at a standard that was significantly lower than the current one. The group claimed that even with the new work arrangements, the current standard was too high. Shirley Rice realized that she now had a more serious problem than before.

CASE 28

Preferential Treatment

George Mason was foreman of the Production Department of a small manufacturing company. Most of the time, he supervised about eight to ten people. One of his employees was Paula Whisler, a black woman who was a widow with five small children. She was a very good worker, but she almost always was late for work in the morning. Mason had spoken to her numerous times about tardiness, but to no avail. She assured him that she tried hard to be at work on time, but she "just did not seem to be able to make it" at 7:30 A.M. since she had to get her children off to school and to the babysitter. She argued that she worked twice as hard as anyone else and that she stayed over in the evening to make up for the time she lost in the mornings. There was little doubt in Mason's mind that Whisler did produce as much or more than anyone else and that she did stay later in the evening to make up the time she lost by being late in the morning.

One Thursday morning, however, Paula Whisler's tardiness was holding up a job that had to be finished by noon. Regardless of how hard she might work during the morning, it would be difficult to finish the job on time, since the production material had to dry for three hours before it could leave the department. Although some other worker could have performed the operation, George Mason felt that Whisler was most qualified to do it. But should she not come in at all or be quite late, again the entire production schedule would be thrown out of balance. All of this was going through Mason's mind when he heard one of the workers say to a co-worker, "That gal Whisler is getting preferred treatment. Why should a black be given any favors like she's better than the rest of us?"

Sure enough, Paula Whisler arrived 45 minutes late. George Mason realized that the situation required action on his part, but he didn't know what it should be.

CASE 29

The Speedy Stock Clerk

Gary Powell, age 19, had recently been hired as a stock clerk for a major discount department store in an urban center. Powell was black, and this was his first full-time job after graduation from high school. He was quite excited about being hired, since he felt that the job offered potential for future advancement if he did good work in his entry-level position.

Powell was assigned to work from 11:00 P.M. to 7:00 A.M., the so-called "graveyard" shift, as part of a group of some six other stock clerks. These stock clerks reported to a supervisor, Sylvia Prater; they were responsible primarily for replenishing and arranging merchandise stock throughout the store.

One evening about three weeks after Gary Powell had begun his job, he asked if he could talk with Sylvia Prater in her office. "Sylvia", said Gary, "I'm really upset about what has happened the last few evenings on the job. I've had several of my fellow employees tell me that I was working too fast, filling too many of the store's aisles and that I was making the rest of them look bad. One employee even told me that if I didn't slow down that 'something might happen' which I wouldn't like, especially if I kept on making the rest of the clerks look bad."

"Why that's terrible," replied Sylvia Prater. "Give me the names of the employees who talked to you in this fashion, and I'll put a stop to it immediately."

"Oh, I can't do that," replied Gary Powell, "because then I'm sure that no one would have anything to do with me. I'm the only black stock clerk, you know, and it's tough enough trying to be accepted by my fellow employees as it is without giving you names of the ones who have been pressuring me to slow down. In fact, I'm sort of worried about coming to you with this in the first place. If the word gets back to the rest of the group that I've complained to you, things may get worse rather than better."

Prater realized that she had a problem. Powell seemed to be a conscientious employee who was being pressured by his fellow clerks about his good work performance. Yet she realized that she would have to be very careful in how she approached the problem so as not to make it worse than it already was.

"Thank you, Gary, for coming to me with your concerns," said Sylvia Prater. "I'll think about it and see what I can do to straighten this problem out. In the meantime, Gary, keep working as you have been doing, the best you know how. And if someone says something to you again, just try to laugh it off and kid them about it rather than to make an issue over it." With that, Gary Powell left Sylvia Prater's office.

CASE 30

Sexual Harassment in the Accounting Office

Charlie Gillespie was office manager of a group of accountants and accounting clerks in the corporate budget office of a large utility company. He was known to be a "happy-go-lucky" supervisor, who found it very difficult and unpleasant to confront inappropriate behavior or take disciplinary action. Charlie normally tried to avoid conflict by turning his head and looking the other way, pretending that he didn't observe inappropriate conduct.

On a number of occasions, Gillespie had observed one of his accountants, Oliver Olson, making crude and suggestive comments to a group of female accounting clerks in the department. Although Gillespie did not like what he heard and observed, he thought that most of the employees understood Olson for what he was and really did not take him seriously.

However, one day an accounting clerk named Julie Lowe came to Gillespie's office. She claimed that Olson's comments were a form of sexual harassment. Lowe stated that she understood the company had a policy prohibiting sexual harassment and that, even though Olson himself had not made any direct sexual overtures to any of the female employees, his vulgar language and crude questions no longer could be tolerated by the women in the office. Gillespie responded that Olson was just a "good old boy," and that the women should ignore him and the problem would take care of itself.

Several weeks later, Lowe resigned her position with the company without giving an explanation as to why she had resigned. One week after leaving her job, the company received a notice that Julie Lowe had filed charges with the Equal Employment Opportunity Commission claiming that she had been discriminated against because of her sex. In her complaint, she had stated that there was an "atmosphere of sexual harassment in the office"; that because of this continued harassment the "hostile work environment caused her severe tension and distress," which she no longer could tolerate and which forced her to end her employment with the company.

Gillespie had received a copy of Lowe's discrimination and harassment charges from Pamela Richter, the company's director of human resources. Richter requested that Charlie Gillespie come to her office to discuss what the company's response to these charges should be.

CASE 31

Under the Influence?

Carl Kloski had been employed as a laborer for eight years in the warehouse division of a major wholesale appliance distributor. His record over the years indicated the following disciplinary actions:

1. Three written reprimands for failure to report absences.
2. One one-day suspension for reporting to work under the influence of alcohol.
3. One five-day suspension for reporting to work under the influence of alcohol.
4. One one-day suspension for failure to report to work.

One Friday morning, Kloski reported to work at abut 7:30 A.M. Sometime prior to the beginning of the shift, Kloski's lead man, George Ramsey, noticed that Kloski appeared to be under the influence of alcohol, since he was talking loudly and walking about in a confused manner. Ramsey reported this to his boss, the warehouse supervisor Steven Bell. Bell sent Ramsey and the rest of the crew out to perform their normal duties, but he ordered Kloski to stay behind to do clean-up work in the employee lunch room. About an hour or so later, Bell noticed that Kloski had done very little clean-up work in the lunch room. Bell approached Kloski and asked him why he had not followed his instructions. Kloski objected to this questioning, and he continued in a loud manner that the supervisor was always "picking on him" and "being discriminatory."

In response to these accusations, Bell took Kloski into his office to review his file for past performance appraisals and disciplinary actions. A lengthy discussion followed in which Kloski continued talking in a loud and angry manner. Both Bell and the office clerk, Marilyn O'Toole, believed that they could smell liquor on Kloski's breath.

Finally, Bell said, "Carl, I think you're under the influence of alcohol again, and with your past record, I ought to terminate you immediately!"

Kloski exploded, "What in the hell do you mean 'under the influence?' You assigned me to work over an hour ago, and you've got no proof whatsoever. You're just mad because I don't jump when you say, 'Jump!' "

Steven Bell pondered what his next response would be.

<hr>

CASE 32

Go Home, Suzy

Laura Skinnard was a supervisor in the General Accounting Department of a large insurance firm. Skinnard supervised 12 employees (all women) who worked on various aspects of processing and accounting for payments of insurance claims.

One day Skinnard received a report from several of her employees that Suzy Turner, a clerk in the department, had a severe cold and cough and was disturbing other employees in the department. The employees told Skinnard that Turner's "wheezing and coughing" were annoying and that they feared catching her cold. Subsequently, Skinnard approached Turner and suggested to her that she go home and get some rest in order to improve her condition. Turner replied, "I'm not ill; I've got a little cough, but that's all." At this point Skinnard stated, "Suzy, I think you should go home, because other employees are complaining about your condition." Turner replied, "You can't make me go home. I'm not ill. Besides, I've used up all my allowed sick leave days for this year, and you'll probably discipline me for being off again if I go home today.'' Skinnard replied, ''Are you telling me, Suzy, that you won't go home like I've told you to do?'' Turner responded, ''If you try to force me out of here, I'll go to human resources and top management with this, because it just wouldn't be right for you to send me home! You're always complaining about people being off from work, and here I'm at work and you're making a big issue over a little cough.'' Laura Skinnard pondered what she should say and do next.

CASE 33

Locker Room Theft

For a number of months, Charlie Blair, the supervisor of a large warehouse servicing a major retail food distributor, had been concerned about reports of missing valuables from the lockers of employees in the employee dressing room in the warehouse. The company provided metal lockers for employees to use, but they had no locks. Employees shared these lockers on a rotating-shift basis, and the company never considered it necessary to assign lockers to individuals. The lockers were provided mainly for the convence of employees to leave their clothing and other items while they were working in the warehouse.

Blair had reminded employees on a number of occasions about not leaving valuables in the lockers. He told the employees that the company assumed no responsibility for any loss, and he also told them that anyone who would be found guilty of stealing a valuable that belonged to another employee would be immediately terminated for theft. This was in accordance with posted company rules in the warehouse.

However, for the last several months Blair had received reports of numerous items being missing from employees' lockers. These reports included items such as a sweater, a lunch pail, food from several lunch pails, and a baseball glove.

For a number of reasons, including several rumors that had been circulated to Blair, he was suspicious of a fairly new warehouse employee named Eric Raleigh. Raleigh was a young warehouse worker who operated a tow truck. He was about 22, and he had been employed by the company about six months previously. Coincidentally, the reports of missing items from the locker room seemed to have become more frequent the last several months.

On a Tuesday morning, Blair received a report from a warehouse employee named Willie Jeffries that a small transistor radio was missing from his locker. Jeffries stated that he had placed it in his locker when he reported to work at 7:30 A.M., and he noticed it missing when he came to his locker during his morning coffee break.

Upon receiving this report, Blair decided to conduct a search of Raleigh's locker while all the employees were in the warehouse working. At about 11:00 A.M., Charlie Blair went into the locker room and searched the locker where Raleigh had his clothing and lunch pail. At the bottom of the locker underneath a number of magazines, Blair found a transistor radio. Blair returned to the office and summoned Jeffries to identify the radio. Jeffries identified the radio as his own; Blair did not disclose to Jeffries where he had found it.

Shortly thereafter, Charlie Blair asked Eric Raleigh to come to his office. Blair explained to Raleigh the nature of the report he had received, what he had done, and how he had found the missing radio in Raleigh's locker. Charlie Blair did not directly accuse Raleigh of theft; but he suggested that perhaps Raleigh might want to consider resigning from the firm because of the suspicions that had been circulating about his connection to the other missing items in the lockers.

At this point Raleigh became very angry. He stated that he would not resign because he was innocent; he felt that someone else had been stealing the items from the employee lockers and that whoever it was had planted the radio in his locker in order to place the blame on him. Raleigh insisted he was innocent, and he said that he would be willing to take a polygraph (lie detector) test to prove his innocence. He told Blair, "If the company decides to fire me for this, I'll get the union and a lawyer to sue the company for everything it has for false accusation and unjust termination." With that, Eric Raleigh left Charlie Blair's office and returned to his job.

Blair was somewhat taken aback by Raleigh's adamant denial of any involvement in locker room theft. Blair was not sure what he should do in this situation; he recognized that the union contract for employees in the warehouse required that any disciplinary action must be for "just cause." Charlie Blair decided that he would discuss the situation with Elaine Haas, the company's director of human resources.

PART 6

CONTROLLING

CHAPTER 19

Fundamentals of Controlling

CHAPTER OBJECTIVES

1. To understand the nature and importance of the managerial controlling function.
2. To identify several types of control mechanisms according to the time factor: preliminary, concurrent, and feedback.
3. To explain the essential characteristics of effective controls.
4. To describe and emphasize the essential steps in the control process.

Although the word *control* often causes negative reactions, control is a normal part of daily life. At home, at work, and in the community everyone is affected by a multiplicity of controls, such as alarm clocks, thermostats, coffee makers, fuel and electronic gauges, traffic lights, police officers directing traffic, and the like. Controls are also a necessity and play an important role in all organizations. Without controls, very little would be accomplished in comparison with what was planned and expected. Every manager—from the chief executive down to the supervisor—must develop and apply controls that regulate the organization's activities in order to achieve the desired results.

The managerial function of **controlling** consists of checking to determine whether employees are adhering to established plans, ascertaining whether proper progress is being made toward objectives, and taking appropriate actions where necessary to correct any deviations from established plans. Controlling is essential whenever a supervisor assigns duties to subordinates, because the supervisor does not escape responsibility by assigning work and delegating authority to those subordinates. The responsibility remains with the supervisor. If all plans set in motion would proceed according to design without interference or disturbance, there would be no need for the controlling function. As every supervisor knows, this is not the case in real life. Thus it is part of every supervisor's job to keep activities in line and, where necessary, to get them back "on the track." This is done by controlling.

NATURE OF THE CONTROLLING FUNCTION

Controlling is one of the five primary managerial functions. It is so closely related to the others that a line of demarcation between controlling and the other functions is not always clear. However, the controlling function is most closely related to the planning function. In planning the supervisor sets objectives, and in turn these objectives become standards against which performance is checked and appraised. If there are deviations between performance and standards, the supervisor must carry out the controlling function by taking corrective action, which may involve new plans and different standards.

Since the discussion of the controlling function comes last in this book, controlling might be perceived as something that the supervisor performs after all other managerial functions have been executed. This perception could convey the impression that controlling is concerned only with events *after* they have happened. It is true that the need for controlling is noticeable after a mistake is made. However, it is much better to view controlling as a function that goes on simultaneously with the other managerial functions. As we discuss later in this chapter, there are control mechanisms that are utilized before, during, and after an activity.

Fig 19–1.
After developing
standards of
performance,
the supervisor
must be alert
for any
deviations from
these
standards.

Employee Responses to Controls

Employees often view controls negatively, because the amount of control that exists within the department may determine how much freedom of action they have in performing their jobs. Yet most employees understand that a certain amount of control is essential to regulate behavior and performance in most situations. They know that without controls, confusion, inefficiency, and even chaos would result.

In a behavioral sense, controls and on-the-job freedom are seemingly conflicting conditions. However, when controls are well designed and properly implemented, they can be a positive influence on employee motivation and behavior. The supervisor should exert considerable effort to design and apply control systems that will be accepted and not resented by the employees but which also will be effective in monitoring performance in the department.

Controlling Should Be Forward-Looking

There is nothing the supervisor can do about the past. For example, if work assigned to an employee for the day has not been accomplished, controlling cannot correct the results of the day. Yet some supervisors believe that the main purpose of controlling is to rebuke or blame someone who is responsible for negligence or mistakes. This attitude is not sound, since the supervisor primarily should look forward rather than backward. Of course, the supervisor should study the past in order to learn what and why something has happened and then take steps so that future activities will not lead to the same mistakes or dilemmas.

Since the supervisor should be forward-looking while controlling, it is essential that he or she discovers any deviations from established standards as quickly as possible. Setting up controls within a process or within an established time frame of an activity—rather than at its end—will enable the supervisor to take prompt corrective action. For example, instead of waiting until a day is over, the supervisor could check at midday to see whether a job is progressing satisfactorily. Even though the morning is already past and nothing can change what has happened, there may be time to correct a problem before the damage becomes excessive.

Controlling and Closeness of Supervision

It is essential for a supervisor to know how closely to check and monitor the work of an employee. The closeness of supervisory follow-up is based on such factors as an employee's experience, initiative, dependability, and resourcefulness. Permitting an employee to work on an assignment without close supervision is both a challenge and a test of the supervisor's ability to delegate. This does not mean that the supervisor should leave an employee completely alone until it is time to inspect the final results. But it does mean that the supervisor should avoid watching every detail of every employee's work. By being familiar with and aware of each employee's abilities, the supervisor can develop a sensitivity as to how much leeway can be given and how closely the supervisor has to follow up and control.

TIME FACTOR CONTROL MECHANISMS

Before we discuss the steps of the controlling process, it is important to distinguish between three types of control mechanisms. These are classified according to the time factor as: preliminary (or preventive, anticipatory) controls, concurrent (or in-process) controls, and feedback (or after-the-process) controls.

Preliminary (Preventive, Anticipatory) Controls

Since controlling has forward-looking aspects, the purpose of **preliminary controls** is to anticipate and prevent potential sources of deviation from standards by considering in advance the possibility of any malfunction or undesirable outcomes. A preventive maintenance program, designed so that equipment will not break down at the height of production, is an example of preliminary control. Other examples include devices such as safety posters, fire drills, disciplinary rules, checklists to follow before starting up certain equipment, and the policies, procedures, and methods drawn up by management when planning operations.

Concurrent (In-Process) Controls

Controls that are applied while operations are going on and which spot problems as they occur are called **concurrent controls.** Examples of concurrent control mechanisms are on-line computer systems, numerical counters, automatic switches, gauges, and warning signals. Where these types of aids are not in place, a supervisor will monitor activities by observation and instruction, often with the assistance of departmental employees.

Even though preliminary controls have been set up, it is essential that concurrent controls be available in order to minimize the negative consequences in the event that preliminary controls should fail.

Feedback (After-the-Process) Controls

The purpose of a **feedback control** is to measure or assess a process or operation when it is finished and to prevent any future deviations. Examples of feedback controls are those that measure the quality and quantity of units produced, various kinds of statistical information, accounting reports, visual inspections, and the like. Since these controls are applied after a task, process, or product is finished, they are the least desirable control mechanisms if damage or mistakes have occurred. If no damage or mistakes took place, feedback controls are used as a basis for further improvement of the process or the finished product. Feedback controls are probably the most widely used category of controls at the supervisory level. Too often, however, they are used primarily to determine what went wrong and where to fix blame, rather than to prevent recurrence of the problem in the future.

CHARACTERISTICS OF EFFECTIVE CONTROLS

For control mechanisms to work effectively, they should be *understandable, timely, suitable* and *economical, indicational,* and *flexible.* These characteristics are required of the controls used in all supervisory jobs—in manufacturing, retailing, office work, health care, government service, banks, other services, etc. Because there is such a diversity of activities in different departments, these characteristics will be discussed only in a general way. Each supervisor will have to tailor control mechanisms to the particular activities, circumstances, and needs of his or her department.

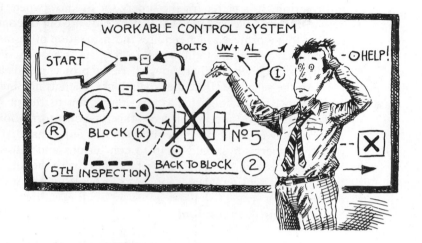

Understandable

All control mechanisms—preliminary, concurrent, and feedback—should be understood by the managers, supervisors, and employees who are to use or generate them. At higher management levels, control mechanisms may be rather sophisticated and based on management information systems, mathematical formulas, complex charts and graphs, and detailed voluminous reports. At the top levels, such controls may be needed and should be understandable to all of the managers who utilize them. However, controls should be much less complicated at the departmental level. For example, a supervisor might use a brief—perhaps one page—report as a control device. This report might show the number of units produced and the number of employee hours worked in the department on a given day. It is uncomplicated, straightforward, and understandable. If a supervisor's control mechanisms are confusing or too sophisticated for the employees, the supervisor should devise new control systems that will meet departmental needs and that will be understandable to everyone who uses them.

Timely

Control mechanisms should indicate deviations without delay, and such deviations should be reported to the supervisor promptly. Obviously, the sooner a supervisor is made aware of any deviations, the more quickly the deviations can be corrected.

It usually is desirable to have deviations reported promptly even if they are

substantiated only by approximate figures, preliminary estimates, or partial information. It is better for the supervisor to know when things are about to go wrong than to learn later that they already are out of control. For example, assume that a project which requires the installation of certain equipment must be completed within a tight schedule. The supervisor should have reports on a daily or weekly basis that show where the project stands and how this compares to the schedule. Potential roadblocks, such as missing parts or absences from work, which might delay the completion of the project should be on these reports. The supervisor needs this type of information early in order to take corrective steps before the situation gets out of hand. This does not mean that the supervisor should jump to conclusions and resort to drastic action hastily. Generally, the supervisor's familiarity with the job and experience will be helpful in sensing when a job is not progressing the way it should.

Suitable and Economical

Controls must be suitable for the activity to be watched. A complex information systems control approach that is necessary for a large corporation would not be applicable in a small department. The need for control exists just the same, but the magnitude of the control system will be different. Whatever controls the supervisor applies, it is essential that they be suitable, adequate, and economical for the job involved. There is no need to control a minor assignment or task as elaborately as a manager would control a major capital investment project.

For example, the head nurse in a hospital will usually control the supply of narcotics with greater care and frequency than the number of band-aids on hand. Or, in a small department of three employees doing clerical work, it would be inappropriate and uneconomical to have someone assigned full time to check the work of these employees for word processing and other clerical mistakes. It is better to make each employee responsible for checking his or her own work or, possibly, to make employees responsible for checking each other's work. However, in a very large department involving the work of several hundred employees who are mass-producing a small unit product, it makes considerable sense to have full-time inspectors or quality control specialists to check the results. Typically, this is done on a sampling basis, since it is impossible to check every item that goes through the production process. There are many in-between situations where supervisors must use good judgment as to the suitability of the controls that may be utilized.

Controls also must be economical; that is, they must be worth their expense, even though it may be difficult to determine how much a control system costs and how much it is worth. In such a situation, it is advisable to consider the consequences that could result if controls were not in place. For example, think of the value of an elaborate, expensive control system in a company producing pharmaceuticals as compared to an enterprise manufacturing rubber bands.

Indicational

It is not enough for controls just to expose deviations as they occur. A control mechanism should also indicate who is responsible for the deviation and where the deviation occurred. If several subassemblies or successive operations are involved in a work operation or process, it may be necessary for the supervisor to check performance after each step has been accomplished and before the work moves on to the next work station. Otherwise, if end results are not up to standards, the supervisor may not know where to take corrective action.

Flexible

Since work operations occur in a dynamic setting, unforeseen circumstances can play havoc with even the best laid plans and systems. Therefore, controls should be flexible enough to cope with unanticipated changing patterns and problems. Control mechanisms must permit changes when such changes are required; otherwise the controls will be strongly resented and are bound to fail. For example, if an employee encounters significant changes in conditions early in a work assignment—such as an equipment failure or a shortage of materials—the supervisor must recognize this and adjust the plans and standards accordingly. If these difficulties are due to conditions beyond the employee's control, the supervisor also must adjust the criteria by which the employee's performance will be appraised.

STEPS IN THE CONTROL PROCESS

The control process involves three sequential steps. The first step (which usually is part of the planning function) begins with the setting of appropriate standards for what should be accomplished. Next, actual performance must be measured against these standards. If performance does not meet the standards, the third step is to take corrective action. These three steps must be followed in the sequence presented if controlling is to be effective and achieve desired results. (See Figure 19–3.)

Setting Standards

Standards may be defined as units of measurement or specific criteria against which to judge performance or results.[1] Standards indicate the targets that should be achieved; they are criteria against which performance will be com-

---

[1] For purposes of brevity, we use the term "standards" in this chapter to generally include other terminology that we have used in previous chapters, such as objectives, goals, results, targets, and the like. Many organizations use these terms more or less interchangeably.

Fig 19–3.
Steps in the
control process.

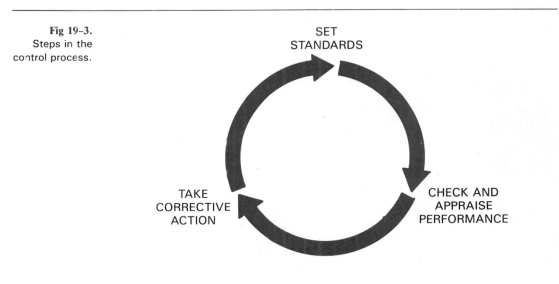

Fig 19–3. Steps in the control process.

pared for exercising control. Standards must be set before any meaningful evaluations can be made about a person's work, a finished product, or a service.

There are many types of standards that can be established, depending on the areas of performance or results that need to be measured. For example, **tangible standards** can be set to measure such things as quantity of output, quality of output, costs of direct and indirect labor, overhead expenses, time spent in producing a unit, market share, and the like. However, it is usually more difficult to establish **intangible standards** in numerical or precise terms. Intangible standards cover such areas as a company's reputation, employee morale, and the quality of humane, loving care of patients in a health-care center or nursing home.

The most frequent tangible standards that supervisors determine (or must follow) pertain to the operations of the department. For example, in a production department standards can be set for the number of units to be produced, the labor hours per unit, and the quality of the product in terms of durability, finish, and closeness of dimensions. In a sales department, standards might be set for the number of customers contacted, the sales dollars realized, and the number and types of customer complaints.

In setting departmental standards, a supervisor can be guided by experience and knowledge of jobs to be performed. Through experience and observation, most supervisors have a general idea about how much time it takes to perform certain jobs, the different resources that are required, and what constitutes good or poor workmanship. By study and analysis of previous budgets, past production, and other departmental records, supervisors should be able to develop workable standards of performance for most aspects of the department's operations.

Motion and Time Studies.   A more thorough and systematic way to establish standards for the amount of work that employees should accomplish within a given period is to have industrial engineers—assuming they are available—perform motion and time studies. A **motion study** involves an analysis of how a job currently is performed with a view to improving, eliminating, changing, or combining certain steps to make the job easier and quicker to perform. Typically, **flow process charts** are designed, which analyze each step taken in performing the job. After a thorough analysis of the work motions and layout, the industrial engineer will develop what he or she considers to be the "best" current method for doing this job.

Once the "best" current method has been designed, a **time study** is performed in order to determine a time standard for the job. This is accomplished in a systematic and largely quantitative manner by selecting certain employees for observation, by observing the times used to accomplish various parts of the job, by applying correction factors, and by making allowances for fatigue, personal needs, and unavoidable delays. When all these factors are combined properly, a time standard for performing the job is the result.

Although this approach attempts to be quite objective, considerable judgment and approximations are part of the established time standard. A time standard determined by motion and time study is neither wholly scientific nor beyond dispute, but it does provide a sound basis on which a supervisor can set realistic standards.[2] Standards developed by motion and time studies can help the supervisor distribute work more evenly and judge each employee's performance fairly. Such standards also assist the supervisor in predicting the number of employees required and the probable cost of a job to be done.

When a new job is to be performed in the department, the supervisor can set tentative standards based on similar operations in this or other departments. If the new job is not being performed elsewhere and if no industrial engineers are available to conduct motion and time studies, the supervisor should observe the operation while it is being performed and then develop a motion and time study as best he or she can in order to arrive at a tentative standard.

Participation of Employees.   Some employees resent and resist standards, especially those arrived at through motion and time studies. This resent-

---

[2]For a more detailed description of work measurement techniques, see Thomas E. Hendrick and Franklin G. Moore, *Production/Operations' Management* (9th ed.; Homewood, Illinois: Richard D. Irwin, Inc., 1985), pp. 611–627; or Donald Fogarty, Thomas Hoffmann, and Peter Stonebraker, *Production and Operations Management* (Cincinnati: South-Western Publishing Company, 1989), pp. 332–369.

ment is part of a long-standing fear that "efficiency engineers" use motion and time studies primarily to speed up the workers' ouput. However, the main purpose for setting performance standards should be to create realistic targets, that is, objectives that can be achieved and that are considered fair by both the supervisor and the employees. Workers are more apt to accept standards as reasonable and fair if they have had some active part in the formulation of those standards.

One technique for having employee participation in establishing standards is to form a committee of workers to assist the supervisor and/or industrial engineer in carrying out a work measurement program. The employees selected for this committee should be those who, in the supervisor's judgment, consistently do a fair day's work.

In addition, the supervisor and industrial engineer should make every effort to explain to all employees what is involved in motion and time studies, including those areas where judgment is involved. Employees should be given opportunities to challenge any standard that they consider to be unfair, perhaps even to have a job restudied and retimed if necessary. Most workers will accept performance standards, if they feel that the supervisor has sincerely tried to help them understand the basis for the standards and has been willing to reconsider and adjust those standards that appear to be unreasonable.

Strategic Control Points.   The number of standards needed to determine the quantity and quality of performance within a department may become larger as the department expands. As operations become more complex and as functions of a department increase, it becomes time-consuming and impractical for a supervisor constantly to check against every conceivable standard. Therefore, a supervisor usually will find it advantageous to concentrate on certain strategic control points against which overall performance may be monitored. **Strategic control points,** or **strategic standards,** consist of a limited number of key indicators that give the supervisor a good sampling of overall performance. There are no specific rules on how to select strategic control points. Because the nature of a department and the makeup of the supervisor and employees will differ in each situation, only general guidelines can be suggested.

A major consideration in choosing one standard as being more strategic than another is its timeliness. Time is essential in control; therefore, the earlier a deviation can be discovered, the better it can be corrected. A supervisor needs to recognize at what critical steps operations should be checked during a given overall process. For example, a strategic control point might be established when a subassembly operation is finished but before the product is put together with other parts and spray painted.

A supervisor should be careful that the selection of a strategic control point does not have a significant adverse effect on another important standard. For example, excessive control to increase the quantity of production may have an adverse effect on the quality of the product. Moreover, if direct labor expenses are selected as a strategic control point, both quality and quantity standards conceivably could deteriorate. To illustrate, a laundry department supervisor in a nursing home must not sacrifice the high standards set to prevent infections simply to achieve a goal of reducing expenses to a certain cost of laundering linen per pound. Thus decisions about strategic control points will depend to some extent on the nature of the work in the department. What serves well as a strategic control point in one department will not necessarily apply in another.

Another example of applying the concept of strategic control points would be the supervisor who wishes to assess the quality of his or her departmental employee relations. The supervisor might decide to use the following indicators as strategic control standards:

Number of employees' voluntary resignations and requests for transfer;
Levels of absenteeism, tardiness, and turnover;
Accident frequency and severity rates;
Number and types of grievances and complaints.

By closely watching trends and changes in these indicators, the supervisor should be able to spot problems or situations where follow-up and corrective action may be necessary. If the trend of most or all of these selected indicators is unfavorable, this would suggest the need for major supervisory attention.

As mentioned previously, there are also standards of an intangible nature that should be monitored closely, even though it is difficult to set precise standards for them. For example, the state of employee morale is typically an important element of departmental operations, which a supervisor may decide to appraise and assess as a strategic control standard.[3]

Checking Performance Against Standards

The second major step in the control process is the checking of actual performance against established standards. This is an ongoing activity for every supervisor. The primary ways for a supervisor to do this are by personal observations, by requesting and studying oral and written reports, and by making spot checks.

Personal Observation. For monitoring employee performance, there is no substitute for direct observation and personal contact by a supervisor. The opportunity for inspection and close personal observation of employee performance is an advantage the supervisor has over top management. This is

---

[3]Techniques for measurement and evaluation of employee morale were discussed extensively in Chapter 16.

because the further removed a manager is from the "firing line," the more the manager will have to depend on reports from others. The supervisor, however, has ample opportunity for direct observation all day long.

When supervisors find deviations from expected standards, they should assume a questioning attitude but not necessarily a fault-finding one. Although supervisors should not ignore mistakes, they should raise questions about mistakes in a prudent manner. For example, instead of just criticizing what happened, supervisors first should ask whether there is any way in which they can help the employees do their jobs more easily, safely, or efficiently. Supervisors also should elicit suggestions from employees concerning what should be done to correct existing problems. Where standards are stated primarily in general terms, supervisors should look for specific unsatisfactory conditions, such as inadequate output, sloppy work, or unsafe practices. It is not enough just to tell an employee that his or her work is "unacceptable" or "not satisfactory." If the supervisor can point to specific instances or cite actual recent examples, the employee more likely will recognize and acknowledge the deficiencies that exist and must be corrected.

Checking employee performance through personal observation does have limitations. It is time-consuming, and it may require spending hours away from the office and desk. Also, it may not be possible to observe some of the important activities at the critical times. There always will be those employees who perform well while being observed, but who revert to poorer, less diligent habits when the supervisor is not around. Nevertheless, personal observation still is the most widely used and probably the best method of checking employee performance at the supervisory level.

Oral and Written Reports.   If a department is large, operates in different locations, or works around the clock, oral and written reports become necessary. For example, if a department operates around the clock and its supervisor has the overall responsibility for more than one shift, the supervisor will have to depend on reports submitted by employees in order to appraise the performance of those shifts during which the supervisor is not present.[4]

Wherever reports are required, the supervisor should insist that they be clear, complete but concise, and correct. If possible, it is preferable to have written reports submitted along with an oral presentation. Reports are also more effective when they are substantiated with statistical data.

Most employees will submit reasonably accurate reports, even when they contain unfavorable outcomes. Of course, much of this depends on the supervisor's reaction to reports and the existing relations between the supervisor and employees. If the supervisor handles adverse reports in a constructive and

---

[4]Where a department operates multiple shifts and different supervisors are in charge on different shifts, it is usually desirable for each supervisor to arrive somewhat early in the department in order to get a first-hand report from the supervisor who is completing the previous shift.

helpful manner, appreciating honesty instead of just giving demerits, employees will be encouraged to submit reliable and accurate reports even if the reports show them in an unfavorable light.

In checking reports, supervisors usually will find that many activities have been performed according to standards and that these can be passed over quickly. As a result, many supervisors use the **exception principle** by concentrating on those areas in which performance is significantly above or below standard. Supervisors may even request employees to forego reporting on activities that have for the most part attained the established standards and to report only on those activities that are exceptionally below or above standards. Obviously, if performance is significantly below standard, supervisors will have to move to the third stage of the control process, namely, taking corrective action. Where performance is significantly above standard, supervisors should study why and how such exceptional performance was achieved in order to determine if what was done can be applied and repeated in the future.

Spot Checks.   If the employees' work routine does not lend itself to reports, the supervisor may have to rely on periodic spot checks. For example, a data systems supervisor who is responsible for a centralized computer department that works round the clock six days a week should, from time to time, make a spot check to see what goes on in the department during the different shifts. In those situations where the supervisor has little or no opportunity to observe or perform spot checks, usually the supervisor will have to depend on reports.

Taking Corrective Action

Where no deviations from established standards occur, the process of control is fulfilled by the first two steps—setting standards and checking actual performance against the standards. But if there are discrepancies or deviations that have been noted through personal observation, reports, or spot checks, then the supervisor will have to take the third step of taking corrective action in order to bring performance back into line.

Prior to taking specific corrective action, a supervisor should bear in mind that there are various reasons why discrepancies or deviations from standards can occur in any job. Among these are:

1. The standards could not be achieved, because they were based on faulty forecasts or assumptions; or an unforeseen problem arose that distorted the anticipated results.
2. Failure already occurred in some other job (or activity) that preceded the job in question.
3. The employee who performed the job either was unqualified or was not given adequate directions or instructions.

4. The employee who performed the job was negligent or did not follow required directions or procedures.

Therefore, before taking corrective action, the supervisor should analyze the facts of the situation to determine the specific causes for the deviation. Only after sufficient analysis of the problem should the supervisor decide what remedial actions are necessary to obtain better results in the future. For example, if the reason for the deviation lies in the standards themselves, the supervisor must revise the standards accordingly. If the employee who performed the job was not qualified, additional training and closer supervision might be the answer. Or if the employee was not given the proper instructions, then the supervisor should accept the blame and improve his or her own techniques for giving directives.

In the case of sheer negligence or insubordination on the part of the employee, corrective action may consist of a discussion with the employee or a verbal or written reprimand. At times, more serious forms of disciplinary action may have to be taken, including suspending or replacing the employee. Under such circumstances, the disciplinary procedures discussed in Chapter 18 should be followed.

SUMMARY

Controlling is the managerial function that determines whether plans are being followed and performance conforms to standards. Control should be forward-looking, since nothing can be done about the past.

Control mechanisms can be categorized according to the time factor as preliminary, concurrent, and feedback. To be effective, controls should be understandable, timely, economical, indicational, and flexible.

In performing the controlling function, a supervisor should follow three basic steps. These consist of setting standards, checking actual performance against standards, and taking corrective action if necessary. Standards may be set for both tangible and intangible areas. A supervisor's own experience and knowledge can serve to develop certain performance standards. More precise work standards can be accomplished through motion and time studies. Many supervisors focus their control efforts on selected strategic control points (or strategic standards), which provide major indicators of performance.

The supervisor should check and appraise performance against the established standards. In some instances the supervisor will have to depend on reports, but in most cases personal observation and inspection will be appropriate for checking departmental employee performance. At times, the supervisor may apply the exception principle, which means concentrating on those areas where performance is significantly below or above the expected standards. Where discrepancies from standards are revealed, the supervisor must take the necessary corrective actions to bring the performance back in line and to prevent future deviations.

QUESTIONS FOR DISCUSSION

1. Define the managerial function of controlling and discuss its relationship to the other managerial functions.
2. Why do many people view controls in a negative manner?
3. If control should be forward-looking in nature, does this mean that looking backward is improper in the controlling process? Discuss.
4. Evaluate the statement: ''Permitting an employee to work on an assignment without close supervision is both a challenge and a test of delegation.''
5. Define and give examples of each of the following:
   a. Preliminary controls.
   b. Concurrent controls.
   c. Feedback controls.
6. Define and discuss the characteristics of effective controls and how these are interrelated:
   a. Understandable.
   b. Timely.
   c. Suitable and economical.
   d. Indicational.
   e. Flexible.
7. Define and discuss each of the primary steps in the control process:
   a. Setting standards.
   b. Checking actual performance against standards.
   c. Taking corrective action.
8. Define and discuss the following terms:
   a. Tangible and intangible areas for setting standards.
   b. Motion study.
   c. Time study.
   d. Time standard.
   e. Strategic control points.
   f. The exception principle.
9. How does controlling relate to disciplinary action?

CHAPTER 20

Accounting, Budgetary, and Other Controls

CHAPTER OBJECTIVES

1. To identify several accounting controls with which supervisors should be familiar.
2. To emphasize the importance of budgets, with particular reference to supervisory participation in budget making and controlling through budgets.
3. To discuss the supervisor's role in maintaining cost consciousness and in responding to higher management's orders to reduce costs.
4. To identify additional managerial control areas and to show how the controlling function is closely related to the other management functions.

Sooner or later, and certainly in the final analysis, all of the activities that an organization undertakes will be reflected in monetary terms. Consequently, not-for-profit as well as profit-seeking organizations must establish financial controls through accounting and budgeting processes. The purpose of this chapter is not to discuss the technical and legal framework of accounting statements or budgets, since these aspects usually are not the responsibility of first-line supervisors. Rather, the focus is on the overall significance of basic accounting and financial controls and other control areas as they affect supervisors. Further, we review briefly several aspects of the controlling function that have been discussed in different contexts in other chapters of this text.

CONTROLLING THROUGH ACCOUNTING

Financial information about an organization must be expressed in accounting terms. **Accounting** is the system of recording, classifying, and summarizing business transactions and interpreting the summarized information.

In order to keep accurate and detailed cost summaries of economic transactions of the organization, the *accounting department*[1] will establish a number of accounts to which various activities are charged. Each of these accounts is given a title and a number. For example, the business transaction of purchasing office supplies might be charged to the following account: ''715—Office Supplies.'' Other transactions, such as purchases of raw materials, wages and salaries, payment for utilities, and the like will have their own account numbers and titles. Thus when keeping departmental records that may eventually be submitted to the accounting department, supervisors must know to which particular account(s) they should charge certain expenditures in their departments.

Summarized financial information prepared by the accounting department usually comes in the form of financial statements. The two most common financial statements that supervisors may come in contact with are the income statement and the balance sheet.

Income Statement

The **income statement** summarizes the incomes and the expenses of the organization for a stated period of time, such as a year, six months, a quarter, or a month. It is also known as the **operating statement,** or the **profit and loss statement.**[2] The profit or loss is the difference between income (sales revenue

---

[1]This department is often called the *controller's* office, the *comptroller's* office, or by other designations.

[2]In not-for-profit organizations, such as hospitals, educational institutions, and government agencies, the term ''operating statement'' is used. The difference between their incomes and expenses is reported as ''surplus'' or ''deficit.''

Fig 20-1.
An income
statement.

HAIHIL CORPORATION
Income Statement
For the Year Ended December 31, 1990

Sales		$600,000
Cost of goods sold		360,000
Gross profit..		$240,000
Expenses..		
Wages and salaries	$77,250	
Rent..	10,500	
Insurance..	2,250	90,000
Income before taxes..		$150,000
Local, state, and federal taxes		75,000
Net income		$ 75,000

and other sources of income, if any) and expenses (the cost of doing business). It is when the income statement shows losses or low earnings that top management will frequently press supervisors to watch or reduce costs in their departments. Figure 20-1 is an example of an income statement for a small firm.

Balance Sheet

The **balance sheet** is a statement of an organization's financial condition at a particular point in time. Although the format of this statement varies from one organization to another, it will consist of two main sections: (a) assets and (b) liabilities and stockholders' (or owners') equity. The items that the organization owns, such as cash, accounts receivable, inventory, land, buildings, and equipment, are classified as **assets. Liabilities** consist of items that the organization owes, such as notes payable, accounts payable, and other debts. **Stockholders' equity,** which frequently is designated as **shareholders equity,** typically consists of the amount of capital stock and earnings that have been retained in the business. On a balance sheet, an example of which is shown in Figure 20-2, the total assets will be equal to the total of the liabilities and stockholders' equity.

BUDGETARY CONTROL

Among the available tools for financial control, the budget usually is the one with which supervisors will have the most frequent contact. A **budget** is a

HAIHIL CORPORATION
Balance Sheet
December 31, 1990

ASSETS

Current assets:

Cash	$89,550	
Accounts receivable	85,500	
Inventory	157,500	
Total current assets		$332,550

Plant assets:

Land	$60,000	
Building	150,000	
Equipment	450,000	
Total plant assets		$660,000
Total assets		$992,550

LIABILITIES AND STOCKHOLDERS' EQUITY

Current liabilities:

Notes payable	$30,000	
Accounts payable	77,550	
Total current liabilities		$107,550

Long-term liabilities:

Mortgage note payable	$60,000	
Bonds payable	375,000	
Total long-term liabilities		$435,000

Stockholders' equity:

Capital stock, $10 par, 30,000 shares issued	$300,000	
Retained earnings	150,000	
Total stockholders' equity		$450,000
Total liabilities and stockholders' equity		$992,550

written plan expressed in numerical terms covering anticipated resources and expenditures for a period of time such as a month, a quarter, six months, or a year. Although most budget items are expressed in dollars and cents, some are expressed in units of measure such as pounds, liters, or yards. Budgets pertaining to employment requirements may be expressed in numbers of employee-hours allocated for certain activities, or numbers of workers needed for each job classification. Eventually, however, the various nonfinancial budgets are converted into monetary figures—an operating budget—which is a statement by which the organization's overall activities are summarized and through which managers can plan and control the use of financial and other resources.[3]

All managers, from the chief executive officer down to the supervisors, must learn how to plan budgets, live within their limitations, and use them for control purposes. The term **budgetary control** refers to the use of budgets by supervisors and higher level managers to control operations so that they will be in compliance with various standards that have been established by the organization in the making of the budgets.

Budget Making

The making of a budget, whether it is expressed in monetary or other terms, involves considerable effort. It means that the budget maker must quantify estimates about the future by attaching numerical values to each budgeted item. The numerical figures in the final overall budget become the desired financial standards of the organization. Similarly, the numerical figures in the final departmental budgets become the standards to be met by each department and departmental supervisors.

Most annual budgets are projections for the following year based on the previous year's budget. This approach for making a budget is known as **traditional** or **incremental budgeting.** Another approach, which has gained some acceptance in recent years, is **zero-base budgeting.** If an organization practices zero-base budgeting, all budgets must begin "from scratch," and each budget item must be justified and substantiated. In zero-base budgeting, the previous budget does not constitute a valid basis for a budget being prepared for a future period. The advantage of zero-base budgeting, sometimes also called **zero-base review,** is that all ongoing programs, activities, projects, products, and the like, are reassessed by management in terms of their benefits and costs to the organization. This avoids the tendency of simply extrapolating expenditures from a previous budget period without much consideration. The disadvantage of zero-base budgeting is that it involves a large amount of paperwork, and it is very time consuming. Further, in actual practice it is difficult to apply the concept to some departments and types of operations.[4]

---

[3]See Richard Steers, Gerardo Ungson, and Richard Mowday, *Managing Effective Organizations* (Belmont, Calif.: Kent Publishing Company—Division of Wadsworth, Inc., 1985), pp. 216–225.

[4]For additional discussion of zero-base budgeting, see Charles T. Horngren and George Foster, *Cost Accounting—A Managerial Emphasis* (6th ed.; Englewood Cliffs, N.J.: Prentice-Hall, Inc., 1987), pp. 382–383; or Robert Anthony and James Reece, *Accounting* (8th ed.; Homewood, Illinois: Richard D. Irwin, 1989), pp. 896–897.

Supervisory Participation in Budget Making

The budget that most concerns supervisors is usually the departmental **expense budget,** which covers the variety of expenditures to be incurred in the department.[5] To many supervisors, this budget has a negative connotation of arbitrariness, inflexibility, conflicts, and problems. If the budget is perceived in this manner, it will tend to breed resentment and discontent. This is why it is desirable that expense budgets be determined with the participation and cooperation of those who are responsible for executing them. Preferably supervisors should have an opportunity to submit their own departmental budgets and participate in making them. When higher management allows supervisors to do this, it becomes essential for a supervisor to be familiar with both general and detailed aspects of budget preparation. Even in those cases where a budget is just handed down to the supervisor by higher management, it is necessary for the supervisor to understand the budget and the reasoning behind each budget figure.

In order to participate successfully in budget making, supervisors should endeavor to demonstrate the actual need for each amount they request and document their requests with historical data wherever possible. Frequently the final budget will contain lower figures than those first submitted. A supervisor should not consider this as a personal rejection or defeat, because other supervisors also are making their own budget requests and having them cut. It is rarely possible for higher management to grant everyone's requests. Much will depend on how realistic supervisors have been and how well their budget needs are documented or substantiated. Each supervisor can only hope that the final budget will be close to what was requested and will give each supervisor some room to "turn around in" while operating his or her department.

Budgetary Control by Supervisors

Budget making falls under the managerial function of planning, but carrying out the budget—or living with the budget—is part of the controlling function. Supervisors must manage their departments within budget limits and utilize their budgets to monitor and control their operations.

When a budget is approved by higher management, the supervisor is allocated specific amounts of money for each item in the budget. Expenditures in the supervisor's department must be charged against various budget accounts. At regular intervals—for example, monthly—the supervisor must review the budgeted figures and compare them with the actual expenses incurred. This

---

[5]In the text discussion that follows, we presume that a firm uses traditional (or incremental) budgeting practices. We do not refer to budgeting procedures in public-sector organizations, where budgets are usually determined by governmental bodies under applicable statutes.

Fig 20–3.
A departmental monthly cost summary.

Models Assembled In Dept. 4	No. of Units	Materials		Labor		Overhead	
		Budget Standard Per Unit	Budgeted Total Materials Costs	Budget Standard Per Unit	Budgeted Total Labor Costs	Budget Standard Per Unit	Budgeted Total Overhead Costs
Model 101	10	$315	$3,150	$462	$4,620	$462	$9,240
109	8	420	3,360	368	2,944	368	5,888
113	11	641	7,051	441	4,851	441	9,702
154	20	199	3,980	407	8,140	407	$16,280
Total	49		$17,541		$20,555		$41,110
Actual costs in November			17,152		21,063		42,225
Variances from budget Standard			$ +389		$ −508		$ −1,115

comparison is usually reported to the supervisor by the accounting department. Figure 20-3 is an example of a departmental monthly cost summary prepared by the accounting department.[6]

If the supervisor notes that actual expenditures for a specific item greatly exceed the budgeted amount, he or she must immediately find out what happened. Investigation could reveal a logical explanation for the discrepancy. For example, if the amount spent on labor in a manufacturing department exceeded the budgeted amount, this could be due to an unanticipated demand for the company's product, which required working overtime in order to meet this demand. If the excessive deviation from the budgeted amount cannot be justified, the supervisor must take whatever actions are necessary to bring the "out of control" expenditures back to where they should be—at least from that point on. Excessive deviations usually have to be explained by the supervisor to higher management or the accounting department. Therefore, in order to avoid this unpleasant task, a supervisor is well-advised to make regular comparisons of actual expenditures with budgeted amounts and to keep expenses close to the budget.

Budget Flexibility

Budgets should not be so detailed that they become cumbersome. Rather, they should allow the supervisor some freedom to accomplish departmental objec-

---

[6]Many firms utilize computer-based cost and financial control systems. Income and cost projections and reports are produced in the form of computer printouts, which may be prepared and distributed by the data processing or information systems department.

Fig 20–4. Budget flexibility means that the budget figures are not "carved in stone."

tives with a reasonable degree of latitude. Flexibility does not mean that the supervisor can change budget figures unilaterally or that the supervisor can take them lightly. Rather, it means that the supervisor should not be led to believe that budget figures are carved in stone. The supervisor must understand that budgets are guides for management decisions and not substitutes for good judgment.

Sometimes certain expenses can be charged to more than one account. For example, assume that the expense of attending a seminar out of town can be charged to either the travel expense account or the educational expense account. Knowing the status of both of these accounts can provide the supervisor some leeway in determining where to charge the expense of attending the seminar. If the travel expense account is already exhausted and the educational expense account is not, the astute supervisor may take advantage of the flexibility of the budget and charge the expense to the latter account.

To prevent a budget from becoming a straitjacket, most organizations provide for regular **budget reviews** to be undertaken by supervisors together with higher levels of management. These reviews should take place about every three months—or every six months at the very least—in order to ensure a proper degree of flexibility. If operating conditions have changed appreciably since the budget was established or if there are valid indications that the budget cannot be followed in the future, a revision of the budget is in order. For example, unexpected price increases or major fluctuations in the general economic climate might be reasons for revising the budget. Usually there is enough flexibility built into a budget to permit common-sense departures in order to accomplish the objectives of the department and the total organization.

COST CONTROL AND THE SUPERVISOR

Competition from domestic companies and from abroad and the changing economic environment require most organizations to strive continuously to control and minimize their costs. Sooner or later most supervisors become involved in some way with **cost control,** because higher management constantly reminds them of their role in controlling costs. Thus **cost consciousness,** or **cost awareness** or **cost containment,** should be an ongoing concern of supervisors, just as cost control is an ongoing problem for higher management. Occasional or sporadic efforts to curtail costs, crash programs, and economy drives seldom have lasting benefits. Although many organizations employ specialists or consultants who are trained along the lines of work efficiency and cost control, in the final analysis it remains the supervisor's duty to look at cost consciousness as a permanent part of the departmental job.

Maintaining Cost Awareness

Because cost consciousness should be of ongoing concern to the supervisor, plans should be made concerning how to achieve cost awareness throughout the department. Here is where planning and controlling again become closely interrelated. By setting objectives and defining specific results to be achieved within a certain time frame, cost priorities can be set.

After having given these matters considerable thought, the supervisor should involve the employees who are in positions that will be most affected. Employees often can make valuable contributions. The supervisor should fully communicate cost-reducing objectives to employees and get as much input from them as possible. The more that employees contribute to a cost-control program, the more committed and involved they will tend to be. It may also be advisable to point out to employees that eventually everyone benefits from continuous cost awareness. They should be trained to see cost containment as being part of their jobs and in their own long-term interest. Most employees will try to do the right thing and will seek to reduce waste and costs if their supervisors approach them in a positive way.

Responding to a Cost-Cutting Order

Reducing costs is part of the nature of most businesses, and it is frequently brought on by foreign and domestic competitors. It is likely that within an enterprise, at one time or another, an order will come from top management to ''cut all costs across the board'' by a certain percentage. At first glance such a blanket order could be considered fair and just; however, this may not be so, since it could affect some supervisors much more severely or directly than others. Some supervisors are continuously aware of costs and operate their departments efficiently, while others are lax and perhaps even wasteful. How should a supervisor react to such a blanket order?

There are some supervisors who will read the order to mean that everything and anything should be done now to bring about the desired percentage of cost reduction. They might hold "pep rallies" with employees or, at the other extreme, engage in harsh criticism of employees and others. Some supervisors might stop buying supplies, leading eventually to work delays. Others might eliminate preventive maintenance work, even though this eventually could lead to breakdowns of the production line or other work flow. Although these actions may bring about some cost reductions, they may be more expensive in the long run.

Other supervisors merely will follow management's cost-cutting directive half-heartedly; they have seen economy drives like this come and go. They probably will make minimal efforts here and there to give the appearance that they are "doing something" about costs. Such efforts are not likely to impress the employees, who in turn also will make only a half-hearted effort. This type of supervisory response will not bring about an adequate contribution to a cost-control program.

An across-the-board, cost-reduction order may work a hardship on the diligent, cost-conscious supervisor whose department is working efficiently. Nevertheless, this supervisor will strive to take some action by looking again at those areas where there still is "some fat to be boiled out." This supervisor will call for suggestions and help from employees, because they are the ones who can bring about results. For example, there may be some paper work that can be postponed indefinitely. Or there may be certain operations that are not absolutely necessary, even if they are performed efficiently. The supervisor should point out to the employees which are the most expensive operations and let them know what these actually cost. It is possible that an employee may suggest a less expensive way of doing a job; if so, the supervisor should not criticize the employee for not having thought of it before, but instead welcome the suggestion. The supervisor should be committed to the cost-reduction campaign and should set a good personal example whenever possible. Although it may be difficult for such a supervisor to come up with large savings, at least he or she will have made a diligent and honest effort to support the company's cost-cutting drive.

OTHER CONTROL AREAS

In addition to accounting and budgetary controls, there are other areas of management control that exist in many organizations. Typically these control areas are supervised by specialized departments and usually are outside the realm of most supervisors' direct authority and responsibility. Nevertheless, supervisors should be aware of these control areas, and, if necessary, should familiarize themselves with the techniques and methods employed by the specialists who perform these control activities. Often such specialists are attached to the organization in staff positions.

Specialized Controls

Inventory control is concerned with keeping watch over raw materials, supplies, work in process, finished goods, etc. Maintaining sufficient but not excess inventory on hand, keeping records of the status of all inventory, ordering economic lot sizes, and many other problems connected with inventory policy are part of inventory control.

Quality control consists of maintaining the quality standards set by a firm for its products or services. These must be continually tested in order to make certain that quality is maintained. Quality control of products is often accomplished by sampling procedures in which quality control specialists closely examine randomly selected items to determine if quality standards are being met.

Production control usually consists of a number of activities to maintain overall operations on schedule. It involves routing of operations, work flow through various departments, scheduling with necessary time elements involved and, if necessary, expediting of the work flow. Elaborate charts and network analyses may be utilized. For example, the production control department may start with a **Gantt-type** chart, which is a diagram or pictorial representation of the progress and status of various jobs in production. If practical, this can lead to a network analysis making use of computers. Two of the most widely used analyses are PERT (program evaluation review technique) and CPM (critical path method). A discussion of these techniques is beyond the scope of this text; they usually are not the responsibility of departmental supervisors, although supervisors may have input or involvement in their application.[7]

Controlling and the Other Managerial Functions

Throughout this text, we have discussed numerous aspects of effective managerial controls from different perspectives. At this point we recall and review several of them as they relate to the controlling function.

In Chapters 4 and 7 we discussed the system of MBO (management by objectives) in connection with motivation and planning. The MBO process involves setting objectives and standards, evaluating results, following up, and

---

[7]For a discussion of these and other computer and network models, see Harold Koontz and Heinz Weihrich, *Management* (9th ed.; New York: McGraw-Hill Book Company, 1988), pp. 520–535.

revising previous objectives if necessary. Obviously evaluation of results, follow up, and establishment of new objectives contain the element of control.

We also discussed standing (repeat use) plans, such as policies, procedures, methods, and rules, in Chapter 7 primarily in regard to managerial planning. However, when standing plans are not working or are not followed, the supervisor must take the necessary corrective actions to bring things back in line. Thus these types of standing plans may be seen as forward-looking control devices.

Performance appraisal, which we discussed under the staffing function in Chapter 14, also has a place as a control mechanism. During a performance appraisal interview, the supervisor evaluates an employee's performance against predetermined objectives and standards. At the same time, the supervisor and the employee may agree on steps for corrective action, as well as new objectives and standards. Again, the element of supervisory control can be detected throughout a performance appraisal cycle.

In Chapter 18 we treated the subject of maintaining employee discipline as part of the directing function of management. If a supervisor takes disciplinary measures when established rules are not followed by employees, such measures serve as control techniques.

These managerial activities show how intrinsically related the controlling function is to all the other managerial functions. As stated previously, controlling is a function that typically is performed simultaneously with the other managerial functions. The better the supervisor plans, organizes, staffs, and directs, the better will be the supervisor's ability to control the activities and employees in the department. Thus controlling takes a forward-looking view, even though it has been discussed as the "final" managerial function in this text.

SUMMARY

Supervisors need to have some familiarity with the various accounting and budgetary controls their organizations have in place. At the very least, supervisors must know the accounts to which they will charge various expenses and uses of resources. Supervisors may also come in contact with financial statements prepared by the accounting department, such as the income statement and the balance sheet.

The most widely used financial control device is the budget. The preparation of a budget primarily is a planning function. However, the application, supervision, and living with the budget are part of the controlling function. Supervisors should have an opportunity to participate in preparing budgets for their departments, regardless of whether the enterprise practices traditional or zero-base budgeting. Virtually all budgets need some built-in flexibility to allow for adjustments when necessary. When significant deviations from the budget occur, a supervisor must investigate and take whatever actions are appropriate to bring expenditures back in line.

Cost control and cost consciousness should be a continuing high-priority concern of all supervisors. When top management issues cost-cutting orders, supervisors should avoid taking extreme measures that may in the long run be more costly than the savings themselves.

Many organizations have specialists who concentrate on inventory control, quality control, and production control. These types of control systems usually are not under the direct authority of most departmental supervisors but are handled by staff specialists. Other managerial concepts, techniques, and approaches used by departmental supervisors contain aspects of the controlling function. Among these are MBO, use of standing plans, maintenance of discipline, and performance appraisal of employees. Thus controlling is intimately interrelated with all the other managerial functions.

QUESTIONS FOR DISCUSSION

1. Define and discuss the importance of the following to supervisors:
   a. Account numbers and titles.
   b. Income statement.
   c. Balance sheet.
2. Why can a budget be described as a "projected financial statement"?
3. What is meant by zero-base budgeting? How realistic is this approach?
4. To what degree should supervisors be permitted to participate in the budget-making process? Discuss.
5. Discuss the supervisor's duty to take appropriate action when accounting reports indicate that actual expenditures are significantly above or below budget allocations.
6. Can there be too much flexibility in budgets in view of the fact that budgets are often criticized for being too rigid? Discuss.
7. Why should cost consciousness be of major concern to a supervisor? How should the supervisor react to top management's periodic orders to reduce costs on an across-the-board basis?
8. Define each of the following:
   a. Inventory control.
   b. Quality control.
   c. Production control.
9. Discuss how each of the following approaches are control techniques, even though they were discussed in earlier chapters under other managerial functions:
   a. Management by objectives (MBO).
   b. Standing plans (policies, procedures, methods, and rules).
   c. Employee performance appraisals.
   d. Disciplinary rules and actions.
10. Try to identify other managerial concepts and approaches that have been discussed in previous chapters and analyze how they may also contain elements of the controlling function.

CASE 34

Sanders Supermarkets (#16): What Happened to Control?

Juan Sanchez was store supervisor at Store #16 of Sanders Supermarkets. For about three months he had been talking to his district manager, Milton Greenberg, about a major renovation for the grocery section in the store. At long last Greenberg called Sanchez to tell him that a meeting at the corporate main office would be held to discuss the renovation project for Store #16.

The meeting was attended by supervisors from the sales department and construction department, several district managers, and the corporate operations manager. By the end of the meeting, it was generally agreed that Store #16 should be reorganized (called "reset" in the language of the company), including moving and relocating several main aisles. The supervisor of the reset crew and the construction supervisor were to submit final plans and a cost estimate at the next meeting of the group, which was scheduled for a week later.

During his next visit to Store #16, Greenberg told Sanchez about the meeting. Greenberg informed Sanchez about the plans for Store #16, although he added that "nothing is finalized yet." Greenberg, however, failed to mention that part of the reset would include moving some of the aisles.

The next week, completed plans and costs were submitted to and given a final approval by the corporate operations manager. Since new shelving had to be ordered and schedules made, the supervisor of the reset crew and the construction supervisor were assigned the job of putting the necessary paperwork into motion. Milton Greenberg then called Juan Sanchez and said, "The reset project for your store has been okayed. I'll let you know more as soon as I hear."

One month later, as Sanchez was driving to work, he made a mental note to call Greenberg to ask about the reset project. However, when Sanchez arrived at Store #16, he soon forgot about this plan. He walked into the store to find three major problems: the frozen food case had broken down, the floor scrubber was malfunctioning, and the grinder in the meat department had quit working. After some checking, he found that no maintenance calls had been made, because each of his two assistant supervisors, Jane Oliver and Wally Withers, had thought the other was going to do it. The floor scrubber had not worked well for three days, the frozen food case had broken down the previous afternoon, but the meat grinder had just conked out.

"It just doesn't pay to take a day off," Sanchez muttered to himself as he headed for the telephone. He called the maintenance department, explained what had happened, and requested immediate service. While waiting for the maintenance person, Sanchez called Jane Oliver and Wally Withers to talk to them about letting him and each other know about these kinds of problems and how to control them. "All it takes," he said, "is working together, communication, and follow-through to ensure that our customers get the best service available. We can't be out of merchandise, especially frozen food. And we have to make sure that when we are busy, as we will be this week, that our customers aren't stepping over workers in the aisles."

At about that time, Sanchez was called to his office. When he arrived, he was greeted by five carpenters and laborers. "We just wanted to tell you we're here, and we'll get started right away," said the carpenter in charge.

"How come it takes this many people to fix a frozen food case?" asked Sanchez.

"We're not here to fix a frozen food case," said the carpenter. "We're here to move the shelving in the aisles and to reset the store."

"Today?" replied Sanchez. "Nobody told me that you guys were doing this today. I can't have you moving aisles during the day. What are my customers going to do?"

Sanchez then called Greenberg. "Milt, did you know that they were going to start the reset project in the store today?"

"No," said Milt, "I wasn't notified either."

"Why wasn't I consulted on this?" exclaimed Sanchez. "First of all, the first week of the month is always too busy a time for laborers to be working in the aisles. Second, this type of work must be done at night. Maybe other stores can handle this in the daytime, but my customers will not tolerate that kind of inconvenience."

"OK," said Milton Greenberg, "it sounds like things are really out of control at your store right now. What are *you* going to do about it?"

"Milt, don't you mean, what are *we* going to do about it?"

CASE 35

Resistance to a Work Sampling Program

Debbie Quarter, a new staff engineer for the C. W. S. Manufacturing Company, had been assigned the responsibility of administering the plant's work sampling program. This was the first assignment of this nature in her career. Her only knowledge of the program until this time came in the form of comments from friends working as plant foremen or supervisors. She recalled that they referred to the work sampling program as "bird dogging." They seemed universally to regard the program as unfair, a waste of time, and a personal affront. She realized that only the line superintendents supported the program, and even some of them regarded it as a necessary evil.

Details of the Program

The work sampling program, or ratio-delay as it is sometimes called, involved the statistical sampling of the activities of hourly production and maintenance department employees, which included approximately two thirds of the plant's 2,000 employees. The sampling was conducted on a continuous basis by a full-time observer who walked through the plant via a series of randomly selected, predetermined routes. The observer's job was to record the activity of each worker as the worker was first observed. An activity could fall into one of seven categories, which in turn were subclasses of either "working," "traveling," or "nonworking." The data were compiled monthly, and results were charted for each group and sent to the various supervisors and superintendents.

The program had been in effect for about five years at the plant. At the time it was initiated, management stated the purpose of the program as threefold: (1) it was to be used as an indication of supervisory effectiveness; (2) it was to be of help in identifying problems interfering with work performance; and (3) it was to be a control measure of the effect of changes in work methods, equipment, facilities, or supervision.

Meetings on the Program

Realizing the widespread resistance to the program, Debbie Quarter began immediately to conduct informational meetings for all line foremen and supervisors. In these sessions she discussed the purpose of the program and the mechanics of conducting it. She also attempted to answer any questions raised. The foremen and supervisors were most vocal in expressing their negative opinions about the program, and after a few meetings she noted that certain comments were being repeated in some form by almost every group.

Most supervisory groups identified some particular aspects of the sampling program that they thought biased its results against them. The most common complaint of this type was that the sampling was too often conducted during periods when work was normally lightest, that is, during coffee breaks and early or late in the day. Since the method of scheduling visits was quite complex, efforts to explain the concept of randomness and how fairness was ensured had never been accepted. Some basic statistical training had been attempted in the past but with little success—especially among the foremen who had traditionally come up through the ranks and had little technical background.

Another frequently repeated complaint was that activities normally considered as work were not recorded as such. Examples of this were going for tools or carrying materials. The reason for this, as had been explained to the foremen, was to allow identification of those factors not directly accomplishing work, since these were the areas where improvements could be made.

Several maintenance foremen complained that results were repeatedly used to pressure them to "ride" their workers. When they would tighten down, these foremen said, the workers would resist, and less was accomplished than before. One foreman quoted his boss as saying that, "These figures (work sampling results) better be up next month, or I'm going to have three new foremen in here!" It was general knowledge that the superintendents placed quite a bit of emphasis on these results when appraising the supervisors and foremen.

Virtually no one at any level of supervision had a good understanding of how results could be affected by sample size. Small groups with few samples said they had experienced wide fluctuations in results that "just couldn't happen." This, of course, reinforced their distrust of sampling methods.

There had been few, if any, changes initiated by first-line supervisors as a result of work sampling results. Several staff projects had been generated—some of which were quite popular with the workers (for example, motorized personnel carriers)—but these were not generally associated with work sampling results.

After the first few sessions, Debbie Quarter wondered whether her meetings with the foremen and supervisors were perhaps doing more harm than good. The meetings seemed to get everyone "heated up," and anything that was learned was probably lost in the emotional discussion. She pondered what she should do next.

CASE 36

Who's Telling the Truth about Quality Control?

Bartholomew Equipment Co. was a major manufacturer of complex electronic data processing equipment. The company had very strict delivery schedules, which had to be kept in order to preserve its good image with its customers. Currently, the company was involved in manufacturing an extremely high-cost computer with specific data characteristics, which was to be submitted to one of Bartholomew's largest customers, the Kee Corporation.

Preparation of the Data Package

The project manager for the company, Ray Edwards, was responsible for gathering all the necessary data that would be incorporated into the final design "data packages" for various computers. Edwards had an engineer, Stan Neil, to whom he had assigned major responsibility for the Kee project. Neil had been with the company for only six months, but he had steadily gained knowledge of data packages and had carefully tried to understand what was required.

During the collection of various data, representatives of the Kee Corporation visited the Bartholomew plant to check on the progress of the data package. The representatives held meetings with Neil and Edwards, explaining what they wanted and various changes they required. Neil believed that these meetings had developed the full requirements for this customer's data package.

Inspection by Quality Control

Neil continued to gather the data in a timely manner. The deadline was drawing near, and some items were not complete. He felt that a major obstacle to completion on time could be the Quality Control Department, which had the reputation of having been unable to meet scheduled inspection deadlines on other projects. In order to get the quality control people to recognize the urgency for meeting deadlines on the Kee project, he thought it might be beneficial to provide them with a portion of the data package that was already complete. He went to the Quality Control Department to meet with Rick Chang, one of the inspectors. Chang accepted the drawings and data after being informed of the urgent requirements for the package. Chang said he would do all he could to expedite the matter.

Conflict Between the Departments

Neil went back to Edwards and told him that the Quality Control Department would be entirely too slow in doing its work. He stated, "Rick Chang wants us to do work that the customer has not said is necessary. We'll never meet the delivery date if he continues to delay the inspection and approval of the data package!"

Edwards, who had not had a good working relationship with the quality control people in the past, took Neil at his word. Edwards complained to the company president about quality control's position and slow work. As a result, the company president, Marcus Finley, decided to call a meeting with Edwards, Neil, and Vic Johnson, the supervisor of the Quality Control Department. The three men were notified to attend a meeting in Finley's office, although Finley did not inform them as to what the meeting would cover.

At the meeting, the trend of the conversation was directly aimed at quality control. Marcus Finley told Vic Johnson that his department was delaying the important Kee project, and this had to stop. Johnson became very defensive and told Finley, "I have no idea what is going on. I don't know who is responsible for this job or what the status of it is. You did not tell me what this meeting was going to cover. I feel very concerned about the way this meeting is being handled. I will not make any statements until I talk to my people about this job.'' At this point Johnson asked to be excused. He said he could be of more help after he had more of the facts.

Marcus Finley and Vic Johnson had a private meeting that afternoon. Finley apologized for the way the meeting was handled and asked Johnson to check into the problem.

Two days later, the Kee data package was approved by Rick Chang in quality control. However, Johnson sent a memo to Finley stating that, ''The engineering done on this data package was horrible.'' Johnson added that his department was not furnished the proper or complete drawings and data and that Edwards and Neil had been most uncooperative. He also mentioned Edwards and Neil specifically as having ''very poor customer attitudes.''

When Ray Edwards received a copy of this memo, he was beside himself. He considered whether he should write his own ''poison pen'' letter to tell his side of the story.

CASE 37

Intolerable Working Conditions

Background

At 10:00 A.M., Dan Michaels, a production supervisor at Monarch Chemical Company's Bromwich Plant, received a phone call from Russ Stern, president of the plant local union. Stern requested that a meeting be set up immediately with himself and Julie Casten, a shift operator in the Raw Material Preparation Unit of the plant.

The Bromwich Plant was divided into two major manufacturing areas, one of which was the Calcium Phosphate Chemicals Department. This area consisted of six major operating units. Management personnel included a production supervisor, a staff engineer, two departmental foremen, and four shift foremen. The hourly work force in the area consisted of 80 employees, who performed operating, packing, and manual labor jobs.

The entire plant had undergone a series of automation projects, which had reduced the number of operating employees by 33 percent in four years. The automation projects had created several air-conditioned control centers throughout the plant from which the operating employees performed many of their new job functions.

The Raw Materials Preparation Unit (one of the six departmental units) occupied a five-story building and was composed of two operating sections and two control center areas. Its function was to receive a rock-like raw material, and by a series of crushing, mixing, heating, and adjusting steps, convert it into slurry form for use by the remaining operating units in the plant. The unit had been among the first to be automated, and the resultant job combinations reduced the number of operators required from two to one per shift.

It was the operator's duty to make sure that all equipment and instruments were functioning properly, to run frequent checks on product quality, and to adjust the converted raw materials as required by these checks. In addition, the operator was required to spend at least 30 minutes per shift cleaning up the area; this was the only manual labor involved in the job. The operator was responsible for the entire five-story building and was the only person in the building. The operator had access to an elevator and could telephone a central plant shift supervisor's office whenever trouble occurred.

The job was not considered to be undesirable, except in the summer when heat and humidity often raised temperatures to 110°–115° during the day in some areas of the unit. During periods of major breakdowns in the unit (about once every two weeks), severe dusting occurred for periods of up to an hour or more. This caused anyone working in the building to wear a dust mask in order to breathe without irritation. The building's control centers had not been air-conditioned during the automation project, since it was felt that the operator would be moving continually throughout the building.

The raw material used in the department had just been changed to one that was 70 percent of the cost of the former material. It was slightly harder to handle than the original raw material and involved the use of more equipment. The plant was set up to handle this raw material on an interim basis. Plans were being formulated to install permanent handling facilities for the material.

The Issues

Russ Stern, Dan Michaels, and Julie Casten met at 10:30 A.M. the following morning on the lower floor of the unit's building. Casten opened the meeting, obviously upset, with the statement that the "dust, heat, and noise conditions of the fifth floor are intolerable," and that she felt that she and other shift operators had a right "to refuse to work under such conditions." A discussion was then conducted on each of these complaints.

With regard to dust conditions, Casten felt that there were several dust sources in the building, particularly the conveyors and the duct work. Stern pointed out another major dust area. At this point, Michaels stated that it was management's intention to install a dust-collecting device to control major dusting in this area; the installation was to be completed within the next six weeks.

The complaint next voiced by Casten was that the equipment noise level was very high, and it could be harmful. Michaels asked whether the noise was worse than in the past.

Casten responded, "Yes, it sure is worse, especially on the fifth floor! Why don't you try it out for a while yourself?"

Concerning the heat, Casten stated that all the operators felt that the heat on the fifth floor was excessive, although she acknowledged that it probably was no worse than in the past. She complained that the exhaust fans on that floor had not worked for several days, and that this had been reported to the shift supervisor, but nothing had been done to fix the fans. Even if the heat was no worse than in the past, Casten felt it was a severe problem that had been "lived with" and should be corrected now.

Casten stated, "Just because the country boys put up with the heat for years is no reason I have to. I'm a city gal! Besides, times have changed, and I don't have to work in a 'sweat shop' anymore."

The meeting continued with further questions and discussion as to why this issue of working conditions had more or less risen all of a sudden. Casten said that the operators had gotten together and discussed their problems, and they felt that it was time to take a stand.

"All the other operating personnel, with the exception of one other group, now have air-conditioned control centers in which to spend all or part of their time. Besides, Monarch is going to save a lot of money in the next few years by using a new type of raw material, so why can't the operators have an air-conditioned room built on the fifth floor in which to 'cool-off'? Besides, we have plenty of time to spend in it."

The Response

The meeting adjourned with Dan Michaels promising to present management's answer within a week. Six days later, Stern and Michaels held another meeting on the subject. Michaels stated that all the dust leaks had been fixed, except the worst one on the third floor, which was scheduled to be fixed soon. A noise survey had indicated that no excessively serious problem existed on the fifth floor. The exhaust fans had been fixed, and a heat survey would be taken during the summer months to determine whether a serious problem truly existed. Stern replied that the raw material unit's operators needed an air-conditioned room and that, if management would not give them one, the union would have to file a formal grievance. If necessary, the union would take the issue to arbitration. Stern also said, "If this doesn't do it, we're going to file a formal complaint with OSHA about all this; I'm sure that you'll get more than you bargained for with them!" The meeting adjourned on that statement. Dan Michaels tried to determine his next move.

CASE 38

Long Lunch Periods and the Senior Employee

Ries Company was a food manufacturer that sold its product lines throughout the United States. One of the company's six plants was located in a large midwestern city, and it produced four of the eight major Ries products. In addition, it served as a warehouse and distribution point for an area that included most of the central United States.

The Materials Handling and Shipping Department had the task of storing products manufactured in the plant, as well as creating temporary storage facilities for products imported from other plants. Because of somewhat limited space in the warehouse, the supervisors in this department were under constant pressure to make maximum use of available space. In order to accomplish this, the department was responsible for loading as many boxcars each day as required to meet the company's shipping and space necessities.

The Supervisor's Problem

Don Rube was hired by the Ries Company after he received a business administration degree from a midwestern university. He was working as a trainee foreman in the Materials Handling and Shipping Department in order to obtain experience at the "grass roots" of the company. He hoped to advance to a department head position either at this plant or at one of the other company plants.

Since Rube believed that his advancement would hinge on how well he performed at his present job, he was now grappling with a serious problem concerning his work group of 15 men. The workers had been leaving for their lunch periods from five to ten minutes early each day. This disturbed him because he had always been quite liberal in enforcing the time allowed for lunch. Although the union contract provided a paid 30-minute lunch period, Rube and the other shift supervisors had always allowed the workers an extra ten minutes. The supervisors figured that this extra time was needed by the workers to get to the lunch room from their work stations and back.

A quick investigation revealed that one of the older workers, Mike Lange, usually left for his lunch period 15 to 30 minutes early. Since the other employees (most of whom were younger) observed this, they thought that they could do the same.

Lange had been employed continuously by the Ries Company for 28 years. He started to work at the plant after graduating from high school. He unquestionably was the hardest working and most productive person in Rube's work group. Lange knew only one way to work—and that was to drive himself every minute he was on the job. He was very critical of most of the younger employees, often telling Rube that "the younger kids these days are lazy and would never have lasted in the old days."

Diana Royse, the director of human resources, told Rube of an incident that had taken place some years ago. In Lange's zest to complete a job in the shortest time possible, he drove his towmotor at rather reckless speeds around the warehouse. When the plant supervisor sternly reprimanded Lange about his work habits, Lange responded by organizing a work slowdown. As a result, everyone in the department worked at half speed for an entire week so that their output for that week was an all-time low in the department. The slow-down caused the warehouse to become so clogged that products from other plants could not be unloaded. This situation had brought considerable criticism from the home office.

From discussions with several older supervisors, Rube also learned that the slightest criticism could cause Mike Lange to become very upset. Lange invariably would state that "management didn't know how fortunate they were to have a person of his abilities still around."

The Supervisor's Alternatives

Rube felt that the output of the average worker in the department was already below standards. If he tried to force Mike Lange to observe the proper time to leave for lunch, he might lose Lange's extraordinary productive ability. Furthermore, Rube did not wish to contend with a possible work slowdown that Lange might instigate again.

On the other hand, Rube could allow the lunch period situation to continue in order to avoid alienating anyone. This action, however, would mean the continued loss of considerable work time.

Could Rube appeal to the union? He thought this action might be futile because Lange's seniority placed him in a "privileged class" among the union membership.

Don Rube preferred not to discuss this problem with his department head, as this might imply that he could not handle the job. He pondered what to do.

PART 7

LABOR RELATIONS

CHAPTER 21

The Labor Union and the Supervisor

CHAPTER OBJECTIVES

1. To emphasize the importance of good supervisory management practices where a labor union does not exist.
2. To outline procedures for supervisors to follow if confronted with a union-organizing effort.
3. To discuss the limited but important role of the supervisor in negotiating the labor agreement.
4. To discuss the major role of the supervisor in the interpretation and application of the labor agreement at the departmental level.
5. To emphasize the importance of a good relationship between the supervisor and the shop steward.

As of 1990, about 16 percent of the labor force in the United States was represented by labor unions and employee associations. Although there is a technical distinction between the terms "labor union" and "employee association," in this text we use the terms **labor union** or **labor organization** interchangeably to describe any legally recognized organization whose major function is to negotiate and administer a **labor agreement** with an employer that covers terms and conditions of employment for its members.[1]

Historically, labor unions most often were identified with so-called blue-collar employees. However, in recent years labor organizations have made gains in obtaining representational rights for white-collar employees, such as office workers, salespeople, nurses, teachers, and even engineers. Many government employees, who generally do not have a legal right to strike and whose bargaining rights are somewhat limited, have achieved the right to form and join labor organizations. In fact, the public sector of the work force in the United States has been one of the few growing segments of the labor movement in recent decades.

Although many unions have lost memberships since the late 1970s and the percentage of workers in labor organizations has declined significantly, labor unions remain an important element of the work force, which supervisors should know about and be prepared to deal with appropriately. This is especially true where employees are represented by a labor union, and supervisors must abide by the requirements of a labor agreement.

It is beyond the scope of this text to cover the history of labor relations in the United States or to discuss the federal and state labor laws that govern union–management relations.[2] Rather, the thrust of this and the following chapter is to discuss the general obligations and rights of supervisors who are confronted with (a) employee attempts to unionize or (b) with union activities in a company or enterprise whose employees are already represented by a union. Supervisors who are part of management do not have legal protection to join labor unions themselves.[3] However, as management's first-line representatives, supervisors play a major role in determining whether a group of employees will turn to a labor union in order to achieve certain objectives.

---

[1] The labor agreement is also called a union contract.

[2] For an overview of labor relations laws and issues in the United States, see William B. Werther, Jr., and Keith Davis, *Human Resources and Personnel Management* (3rd ed.; New York: McGraw-Hill Book Company, 1989), pp. 499–544. For a collection of articles and readings pertaining to contemporary labor relations, see Alan Glassman, Naomi Berger Davidson, and Thomas Cummings, *Labor Relations—Reports from the Firing Line* (Plano, Texas: Business Publications, Inc., 1988).

[3] Those "supervisors" who are not part of management—such as working supervisors and lead persons—may join the same labor union as their fellow employees.

UNDERSTANDING EMPLOYEE EFFORTS TO UNIONIZE

A number of years ago, a major union official made the following comment to one of the authors of this text: "Labor unions don't just happen; they're caused. And it's the management, not the unions, which causes them!" This labor official was quite candid about his opinion that labor unions were a direct response to failures of management to respond to certain needs of employees. Further, he implied that the sentiments of workers are usually determined more by the conditions existing in their work situations than by a union organizer's campaign. Many studies of employee and labor relations have generally verified the opinion of this union official. These studies recognize that good management and supervision, particularly as exemplified by positive human relations approaches, are usually the most important determinants in preventing the unionization of a work group.

Numerous aspects of good supervision and management that contribute to a climate that deters unionizing efforts have been discussed previously throughout this text. Among the factors that are rooted in good employee relations and which make it more difficult for a union organizer's appeal to succeed are:

1. When wages and benefits are good and reasonably comparable to those offered by other companies.
2. When personal facilities for employees are generally satisfactory or improving.
3. When a stable employment pattern has been followed (that is, no severe ups and downs in hiring and layoffs of large numbers of employees have taken place).
4. When supervisors communicate well with their employees and treat them with dignity and respect.
5. When employees have been well trained and see opportunities for advancement to higher paying or upgraded positions. This is especially important for employees in low-level jobs who do not like to feel that they will be in "dead-end" positions forever.
6. When supervisors demonstrate a participative approach to management, which allows their employees to share in making certain decisions about their jobs.
7. When employees feel that they are treated fairly by being given an opportunity to air any complaints they may have through a complaint or grievance procedure.

For the most part, the economic conditions surrounding wages, benefits, and employment patterns are not within a supervisor's direct control. However, it should be apparent from the preceding list that the supervisor has a significant role in most of the other factors that may cause employees either to join or not to join a labor union.

It does happen that some employees turn to a labor union even though their employer has worked diligently in developing and implementing policies and procedures consistent with those listed. Employees may join a labor union primarily to achieve economic objectives such as higher wages and greater benefits. Or they may join a labor union to satisfy objectives of a psychological or sociological nature. For example, some employees feel that membership in a labor union provides them with greater security and better control over their jobs through a seniority system. Other employees feel that it is important for a union to be present in processing grievances and complaints in order to get a fairer settlement of their problems or disputes. Still others find a greater sense of identity when they are part of a labor union. If a union already is in place, employees may have to join it as a requirement under a **union shop** provision of the labor agreement.[4] Even though such employees initially are required to join the union through the union shop provision, eventually most of them become loyal to the union because they believe that they can achieve more collectively than they would on an individual basis. Further, in many companies and organizations that do not have a union shop requirement, all or most of the employees may belong to the union, because they want to be part of the overall, combined group effort of fostering and protecting employees' rights and interests.

UNION-ORGANIZING EFFORTS AND THE SUPERVISOR

Union-organizing efforts can take place both outside and within a firm. If a supervisor notices that union-organizing activities are taking place among employees in the department or elsewhere in the company, the supervisor should report what he or she observes to higher management or to the human resources department. This must be done so that the company's response to the union-organizing efforts can be planned. In the meantime, the supervisor should be very careful not to violate—either by actions or statements—the labor laws governing union-organizing activities. Since these labor laws are quite complicated, many companies will hire a consultant or attorney who will advise higher management and supervisory personnel about what they should and should not do under these circumstances.

The following guidelines, although not comprehensive, are recommended for supervisors during a union-organizing period:

1. Supervisors should not question employees either publicly or privately about union-organizing activities in the department or elsewhere in the company.

---

[4]A union shop provision in a labor agreement requires an employee to join the union as a condition of employment after a certain period of time, usually 30 days. However, as of 1990, 21 states have passed "right to work" laws which prohibit the union shop. Further, labor organizations representing employees within the federal government are not permitted to have a union shop.

Doing this—even merely out of curiosity—can be a violation of labor laws, which provide employees the right to choose a union to represent them without interference or discrimination by the employer.

2. Supervisors should not make any threats or promises that are related to the possibility of unionization. Any statement that can be construed as a threat (for example, loss of job or loss of privileges if the union succeeds) or a promise (for example, some favor or benefit will be forthcoming to the employee if the union fails) is a violation of federal labor law.

3. Supervisors can and should respond in a neutral manner when employees ask for their opinions on the subject of unionization.

4. Supervisors have the right to prohibit union-organizing activities in work areas if these take place during work hours and interfere with normal work operations. Supervisors may also prohibit outside union organizers from coming into the department to distribute union bulletins and information. However, employees who are supporting the union have the right to distribute these materials to other employees during lunch periods and break periods, so long as this does not interfere with work operations. If in doubt about what can be done to control union-organizing activities within the department, supervisors should first consult higher management or the human resources department.

5. Supervisors should not look at any union authorization cards that employees may have signed. This, too, is considered illegal interference with the employees' rights to organize.

6. Supervisors should continue to do the best supervisory management job possible.

A union-organizing campaign often results in a representational election conducted by the National Labor Relations Board or some other government agency. If the majority of the employees vote for the union, the union becomes the exclusive bargaining representative for these employees. If the union loses the representational election, this means only that the employees will not have a union for the immediate future—perhaps for a minimum of one year. Many companies have found that employees, after having rejected a union in previous elections, later will vote it in.

THE SUPERVISOR'S INVOLVEMENT IN UNION–MANAGEMENT RELATIONSHIPS

Labor unions long have been recognized as being a permanent part of our free-enterprise economy. A union, just like any other institution, has the potential for either advancing or interfering with the common efforts of an organization. Thus, with rare exceptions, it is in the self-interest of management to establish and develop a union–management climate that directs these potentialities toward constructive ends. However, there are no simple or easy formulas for fostering such a climate overnight. It takes patience, sensitivity, and hard work for all managers in an organization to show in their day-to-day relationships that the union is accepted as the official and responsible bargaining representative for the employees.

In any mutual efforts to create and maintain a constructive pattern of relationships between management and the union, often the most important link is the supervisor. It is the supervisor's daily relationships with employees and union representatives that make the labor agreement a living document for better or for worse. This is why it is essential that supervisors should be trained in the fundamentals of collective bargaining and be knowledgeable about the labor agreement. For the most part, the supervisor's involvement in union–management relations consists of two phases: (a) a limited role in negotiating the labor agreement; and (b) a major role in applying the terms of the agreement on a day-to-day basis.

The Supervisor's Limited Role in Labor Agreement Negotiations

Negotiations for a labor agreement in a previously nonunionized company may be a trying experience for employees, supervisors, and higher management. Usually emotions run high, and the grapevine is active with rumors and speculation. Because of this climate, negotiations between management and union representatives are usually held away from the company premises, such as at a lawyer's office or a conference room in a hotel. If a committee of employees is participating in the negotiations, a line of communication with the other employees will be established. Supervisors usually will be excluded from this line of communication, although higher management may keep them informed through communiques.

Most labor agreements cover a period of one, two, or three years. As time goes on and new agreements are negotiated, the supervisor's role becomes an increasingly important one. Most supervisors do not sit at the negotiating table, but it is desirable for higher management to consult with them about (a) how provisions of the existing agreement have worked out and (b) what changes they would like to see in the next agreement. This exchange of information between higher management and supervisors is essential prior to negotiations, and at times it even may be needed during the negotiation proceedings.

Supervisors should have some influence on negotiations, because they bear a major responsibility for carrying out provisions of the agreement in day-to-day operations of their departments. Many issues discussed during contract negotiations stem from relationships that the supervisors have experienced with their employees. For example, problems concerning work assignments between job classifications, work-shift schedules, seniority rights, working conditions, and transfer and promotion of employees can become important issues for negotiation. Therefore, it is to the supervisors' as well as the company's advantage that provisions in the agreement be written in such a way that supervisors have as much flexibility as possible in running their departments.

In order to supply relevant information, supervisors should be keenly aware of what has been going on in their departments. Their views will be considered more credible, if they have facts available to substantiate their observations. This again highlights the importance of keeping ample records of grievances, productivity, and disciplinary problems. Supervisors should report and discuss with higher management and the human resources department problematic situations with the union that management should consider in developing an overall bargaining strategy. Thus, even though the primary responsibility of negotiating a labor agreement rests with higher management, supervisors should be prepared to provide some input to the negotiations. Unless supervisors are willing to express their opinions and substantiate them with documents and examples, it will be difficult for management's representatives to negotiate desirable changes in the agreement at the bargaining table.

The Supervisor's Major Role in Applying the Labor Agreement

The labor agreement that has been agreed upon by representatives of management and the union becomes the document under which both parties will operate during the life of the agreement. Although no two labor agreements will be exactly alike, most agreements cover wages, benefits, working conditions, hours of work, overtime, holidays, vacations, leaves of absence, seniority, grievance procedures, and numerous other matters that have been agreed upon by management and union representatives.

A labor agreement sets forth an outline for union–management relationships. In essence, it is a policy manual that provides rules, procedures, and guidelines—as well as limitations—for both management and the union. To make it a positive instrument for fostering constructive relationships, the agreement must ''become alive'' with appropriate and intelligent supervisory decisions. The best written labor agreement will be of little value if it is poorly applied by the supervisor. The supervisor—by decisions, actions, and attitudes—gives the agreement meaning and life.

Compliance with the Labor Agreement.   All supervisors are obliged to manage their departments within the framework of the labor agreement. This means that supervisors should know the provisions of the agreement and also how to interpret them. One way to accomplish this is for higher management or the human resources department to hold meetings with supervisors to brief them on contents of the agreement and to answer questions about any provisions that they do not understand. Copies of the contract and clarifications of various provisions should be furnished to the supervisors so that they know what they can and cannot do while managing their departments.

Supervisors should recognize that a labor agreement has been negotiated,

Fig 21-1.
The supervisor must know what the provisions of the labor agreement are and how to interpret them.

agreed upon, and signed by both management and union representatives. Even if a provision or provisions in the agreement may cause a supervisor problems, the supervisor should not try to "beat the contract" in the hope of doing the company a favor. For example, assume that a provision specifies that work assignments must be made primarily on the basis of seniority. Although this provision may limit the supervisor in assigning the most qualified workers to certain jobs, the supervisor should comply with it or be prepared to confront probable conflict with the union. If a labor agreement provision is clear and specific, the supervisor should not attempt to ignore or circumvent what it requires. If supervisors are not clear about certain provisions, they should ask someone in higher management or the human resources department to provide necessary explanations before they attempt to apply the provisions that they do not understand.

Adjustments for the Union.   A labor agreement does not fundamentally change a supervisor's position as a manager. Supervisors still must accomplish their goals and objectives by planning, organizing, staffing, directing, and controlling. Supervisors retain the right to require subordinates to comply with directives and to get the jobs done in their departments. The major adjustment required when a union is present is that supervisors must perform their managerial duties within the framework of the labor agreement. For example, a labor agreement may spell out some limitations to the supervisor's authority, especially in areas of disciplinary action, job transfers, and assignments. Or the labor agreement may specify procedures concerning the seniority rights of employees with regard to shift assignments, holidays, and vacations. Supervisors may find these provisions in a labor agreement not to their liking. However, they must manage within such provisions and learn to minimize the effects of contractually imposed requirements or restrictions by making sound decisions and by relying on their own managerial abilities.

As members of management, supervisors have the right and duty to make decisions. A labor agreement does not abrogate management's right to make decisions. However, it does give a union the right to protest or challenge a supervisor's decision that the union believes to be a violation of the labor agreement. For example, virtually all labor agreements specify that management has the right to discipline and discharge for "just" (or "proper") cause. Thus to take disciplinary action remains a managerial responsibility and right, but it must meet the just-cause standard. Since a challenge from the union may occur, the supervisor should have a sound case before taking disciplinary action.[5] If a supervisor believes that disciplinary action is called for when an employee breaks a certain rule, the supervisor should examine thoroughly all aspects of the problem, take the required preliminary steps, and think through the appropriateness of any action. All of the principles discussed in Chapter 18 are essential whenever a supervisor is confronted with a disciplinary problem in a unionized situation.

Supervisory Decision Making and the Labor Agreement.   In practice, the supervisor frequently expands on and clarifies provisions of the labor agreement by decisions that interpret and apply them to specific situations. By so doing, the supervisor may establish precedents that arbitrators usually consider when deciding grievances which come before them.[6] It would be impossible for management and the union to negotiate an agreement that anticipated every possible situation that could occur in union–management relations and to specify directives to solve each situation. Therefore, the supervisor's judgment becomes paramount in applying the agreement to certain situations. Since the supervisor is part of management, an error in the supervisor's decisions becomes management's error. By interpretation and application, a super-

---

[5]Unless there is a contractual requirement to the contrary, the supervisor or manager normally will carry out the disciplinary action independently of union involvement. However, some labor agreements require that a supervisor notify a union representative prior to imposing discipline or that a union representative be present when the disciplinary action is administered.

[6]An **arbitrator** is someone who is called in by the union and management to render a final and binding decision in a grievance when the union and management are unable to settle the grievance themselves. Procedures for arbitration of grievances are included in most labor agreements. A **grievance** is a complaint that has been formally presented by the union to management. Most labor agreements have several steps as part of a grievance procedure before a grievance goes to arbitration. See Figure 22–1 for an example of a typical grievance–arbitration provision in a labor agreement.

visor's decisions may take on dimensions that could go well beyond the department itself.

A labor agreement usually contains contractual provisions that are concerned with handling designated areas or specific issues. Examples are those associated with work schedules, distribution of overtime, transfers, promotions or demotions, and other recurring matters. Usually the labor agreement specifies certain limits or procedures for handling these types of issues. For example, many agreements have provisions that require the supervisor to consider both seniority and ability in decisions that involve promotion, transfer, and layoff. In these situations the supervisor's personal judgment of the abilities of the employees involved becomes vitally important. Often the opinion of the union will be at odds with the opinion of a supervisor concerning certain contractual meanings. A supervisor should not be afraid to risk the possibility that the union will file a grievance, so long as the supervisor believes that he or she understands the provisions and is complying with them.

Labor agreements also contain clauses that are even more broadly stated, such as those associated with the assignment of work between various job classifications, nondiscrimination, management rights, and disciplinary or discharge actions for "just cause." In these areas supervisors often encounter difficulty in carrying out a generalized statement in the agreement that requires narrower interpretation. If the supervisor has some doubts about the meaning or application of a broadly stated provision, he or she should first consult higher management or the human resources department. Even though the supervisor may be well indoctrinated in the content of the labor agreement, problems can develop that necessitate an interpretation beyond the supervisory level. A decision involving interpretation of the labor agreement may be long lasting in its impact. The decision may set a precedent that could become binding on both management and the union in the future. Supervisors should bear in mind that unions often base their claims on precedents, and arbitrators often base their decisions on previous decisions made by both sides.

Maintaining Employees' Compliance with the Labor Agreement.   It is also the supervisor's duty to take action whenever employees do not comply with provisions of the labor agreement. Neglect by supervisors to take action may be interpreted by employees to mean that the provisions involved are unimportant or not to be enforced. For example, if a provision specifies that employees are entitled to a 15-minute rest period at designated times during a work shift, the supervisor should see to it that the employees take a 15-minute rest period—no more and no less—during the designated times. Supervisors should make certain that employees observe the provisions of the labor agreement just as supervisors themselves must operate within the agreement. Inaction on the supervisor's part could set a precedent or be interpreted to mean that the provision involved has been set aside.

THE SHOP STEWARD AND THE SUPERVISOR

Supervisors probably will have most of their union contacts with the union shop steward.[7] A **shop steward,** also called a **shop committeeman** or **shop committeewoman,** usually is a full-time employee who is an elected or appointed representative of the union. As such, the shop steward is recognized by fellow employees to be their official spokesperson to management and for the union. This can be a difficult position since the shop steward must serve two masters. As an employee, the shop steward is expected to perform satisfactory work for the employer by following rules and directives. As a union representative, the shop steward has responsibilities to other employees and to the union. The supervisor must understand this dual role of the shop steward, because a good relationship with the shop steward can create an effective link between the supervisor and the employees.

The Shop Steward's Rights and Duties

Unless the labor agreement contains special provisions pertaining to the shop steward's position, the shop steward is subject to the same standards and regulations for work performance and conduct as every other employee of the department. The labor agreement may specify how much company time the shop steward can devote to union matters, such as meetings or discussions with members, collection of dues, and grievance handling. The labor agreement may also grant the shop steward a right to take time off to attend union conventions and handle other union matters.

A major responsibility of the shop steward is to process complaints and grievances on behalf of employees.[8] The shop steward will communicate these to the supervisor, who then must work with the shop steward to settle the complaints and to deny or adjust grievances. Labor agreements describe in great detail the procedures for handling complaints and grievances, and the shop steward and the supervisor are obligated to follow those prescribed steps.

Supervisory Relations with the Shop Steward

Some shop stewards are unassuming; others are overbearing. Some are helpful and courteous; others are aggressive and militant; some take advantage of their position to do as little work as possible; others will perform an excellent day's work in addition to their union duties. In other words, the day-to-day

---

[7]Supervisors may also have to discuss certain issues and grievances with a union **business agent,** or **business representative.** These typically are paid, full-time union officials who hold their offices with the local or national union. Some shop stewards prefer to have the business agent present when discussing union-related problems with the supervisor.

[8]The handling of complaints and grievances will be discussed in detail in the next chapter.

role and behavior of the shop steward will depend considerably on his or her individual personality and approach.

At times the supervisor may feel that the shop steward processes petty grievances in order to harass management. This may happen because the shop steward has a political assignment and may feel it necessary to assure workers that the union is working on their behalf. However, an experienced shop steward knows that normally there are enough valid grievances to be settled that it is not necessary to submit shallow complaints that rightfully will be turned down by the supervisor.

Supervisors should bear in mind that the shop steward, as the official union representative, learns quickly what the employees are thinking and what is being communicated through the grapevine. Further, the national or the local union will train the shop steward to be informed about the content of the labor agreement, management's prerogatives, and employee rights. The local union will expect the shop steward to submit complaints and grievances in such a way that they can be carried to a successful conclusion. Before submitting a grievance, the shop steward will ascertain which provisions of the labor agreement allegedly have been violated, whether the company acted unfairly, or whether the employee's health or safety was placed in jeopardy. Once a grievance has been formally submitted, the shop steward will try to win it. In most grievance matters the union is "on the offensive" and the supervisor must be prepared to respond. If the shop steward challenges a supervisor's decision or action, the supervisor must be ready to justify what he or she did or otherwise develop a remedy and resolve the grievance.

Since shop stewards are necessarily interested in satisfying the union members, their behavior may at times antagonize supervisors. It may even become difficult for supervisors to keep a sense of humor or to hold their tempers. A supervisor may not care to discuss issues with the shop steward on an ongoing basis since, in the normal working situation, the shop steward is a subordinate in the department. But shop stewards are the designated representatives of union members and should be treated as "equals" by supervisors in matters pertaining to the union. If a sound relationship is developed, the shop steward will keep the supervisor alert and literally force the supervisor to be a better manager!

SUMMARY

Good supervisory and management practices can help prevent a labor union from gaining employee representational rights. Employees turn to a labor union for representation because they see the union as a vehicle for satisfying certain needs.

When a supervisor in a nonunion organization is confronted with a union-organizing campaign, the supervisor should report the union-organizing campaign to higher management or the human resources department. The supervisor must not interfere with or threaten employees or promise any benefits in an effort to influence their choice of whether to join the union. The supervisor, however, does have the right to prohibit activities that directly interfere with job performance.

Most supervisors do not participate in labor agreement negotiations. Yet many demands that a union presents during negotiations stem from experiences that supervisors have encountered with departmental employees. Therefore, supervisors should make known their opinions and suggestions to higher management so that management can attempt to negotiate needed changes in the labor agreement.

The supervisor's major role in union–management relations lies in the day-to-day interpretation and application of the labor agreement. Although a labor agreement does not in itself change a supervisor's job as a manager, it does give a union the right to protest or challenge a supervisor's decision. The supervisor still must carry out managerial duties within the terms of the labor agreement. It is to the supervisor's advantage to seek advice from higher management or the human resources department in interpreting certain clauses of the agreement.

The shop steward should be treated as an ''equal'' by the supervisor in matters relating to the labor agreement. If a proper relationship is developed, a shop steward primarily will challenge only those actions of the supervisor that seem to be unfair or in violation of the agreement. In effect, this will force the supervisor to do a better job of managing the department.

QUESTIONS FOR DISCUSSION

1. What is the magnitude of labor union and employee representation in the United States? Why have labor unions declined in membership in recent years?
2. What are some of the major factors that typically are most crucial in preventing the formation of a labor union? Over which of these does a supervisor have the most direct control?
3. What are some of the principal reasons why employees join labor unions?
4. Discuss the proper role of the supervisor regarding union-organizing activities. Why should a supervisor generally be neutral in responding to employees' questions about the union-organizing effort?
5. Evaluate the following statement: ''The best guideline a supervisor can follow during a union-organizing campaign is to continue to do the best supervisory management job possible.''
6. What is the supervisor's role in labor agreement negotiations? What input should a supervisor have in the negotiating process?
7. Discuss why the supervisor should not attempt to ignore the labor agreement or circumvent it even if it seems like the smart thing to do.
8. Why should supervisors consult higher management or the human resources department when interpretation of a clause in the labor agreement is necessary?
9. Evaluate the following statement: ''A labor agreement does not fundamentally change a supervisor's position as a manager.''
10. How does a labor agreement complicate a supervisor's job?

11. Why does a supervisor retain the right to take action whenever employees do not comply with provisions of the labor agreement?

12. Discuss the role of the shop steward within a department. Why is this person in a key position of influence?

13. Why should the shop steward be treated as an ''equal'' by the supervisor in matters relating to the union?

CHAPTER 22

Handling Employee Complaints and Grievances

CHAPTER OBJECTIVES

1. To explain the similarities and differences between grievance procedures in unionized companies and complaint or problem-solving procedures in nonunionized organizations.
2. To emphasize the importance of open and frank communication during the initial step in the grievance or complaint procedure.
3. To present guidelines for supervisors for effective handling of complaints or grievances.

Some supervisors become irritated and confused when they experience a challenge to their authority in the form of an employee complaint or grievance. Others find it difficult to function because they feel that employee complaints and grievances reflect on their performance or perhaps that there is something wrong with them as supervisors or persons. However, employee complaints and grievances should be viewed as being an expected part of the relationship between any manager and employee group. Obviously it is not desirable for supervisors to have a constant flood of employee complaints and grievances, since this would indicate severe problems in the department. Yet, supervisors should understand that as they carry out their managerial job, it is normal to expect that on some occasions their perspectives and decisions will come into conflict with those of employees or the labor union. Therefore, a supervisor should recognize that when employee complaints and grievances occur, this is a natural component of being in the position of a supervisor.

The number and types of grievances that arise within a department can reflect the state of union–management relations. Of course, grievances can also be related to internal union politics, which usually are beyond a supervisor's control. Whether or not employees are unionized, every supervisor should be well qualified in handling employee complaints and grievances in a systematic and professional manner.[1] Skill in handling grievances, particularly in a unionized setting, is another indicator of a person's ability as a supervisor.

PROCEDURES FOR GRIEVANCES AND COMPLAINTS

A distinction can be made between the terms *grievance* and *complaint*. As commonly defined, a **grievance** is a formal complaint involving the interpretation or application of the labor agreement, which has been presented to the supervisor or another management representative by a shop steward or some other union official. A **complaint** usually consists of any individual or group problem or dissatisfaction that employees can channel upward to management. In this chapter, we use the terms complaint and grievance somewhat interchangeably. The underlying principles for handling complaints and grievances are basically the same, even though the procedures for processing them may be different. The approach suggested here should generally be followed regardless of the issue involved or whether the work environment is unionized. This includes legal issues, such as a complaint of racial or sexual discrimination.

---

[1] Parts of this chapter are adapted from Raymond L. Hilgert, ''Handling Employee Complaints and Grievances: A Supervisory Checklist,'' *Louisiana Business Survey*, Vol. XI, No. 1 (January, 1980), pp. 10–11.

Grievance Procedures

Grievances usually result from a misunderstanding, a different interpretation of the labor agreement, or an alleged violation of a provision of the labor agreement. Most labor agreements provide for several steps in a grievance procedure, beginning at the departmental level. If a grievance is not settled at the first step, it may be appealed to higher levels of management or the human resources department. The last step typically involves having an arbitrator render a final and binding decision in the matter. Figure 22–1 is an example of a grievance and arbitration procedure included in a labor agreement.

Complaint Procedures

Many nonunion companies and other organizations have adopted formal problem-solving or complaint procedures to resolve legitimate complaints that employees may bring to the attention of their supervisors. This is usually explained in an employee handbook or a policies-and-procedures manual. Even when no formal system is spelled out, it usually is understood that employees have the right to register a complaint with the possibility of an appeal to higher management. A procedure for handling complaints differs from a union grievance procedure primarily in two respects:

1. The employee normally must make the complaint without assistance in presenting or arguing the case.
2. The final decision is usually made by the chief executive or the human resources director rather than by an outside arbitrator.[2]

Figure 22–2 is an edited excerpt of a ''problem-solving procedure,'' which was established by a large firm for its nonunion employees. Note that it involves a series of steps that begins at the supervisory level.

THE FIRST STEP IN A GRIEVANCE PROCEDURE

At the first step, the shop steward usually will present a grievance to the supervisor, and the aggrieved employee (or employees) may also be present. It is essential that the supervisor listen to them very carefully. There is nothing to

---

[2]However, a number of nonunion companies are offering some assistance in processing employee complaints by providing an ombudsman or counselor to assist a complaining employee. Some companies have a ''jury'' or ''panel'' of employees or managers who serve as a form of arbitration board in their complaint procedures. These types of approaches are not widespread, but they appear to be growing in number. See Mary P. Rowe and Michael Baker, ''Are You Hearing Enough Employee Concerns?'' *Harvard Business Review* (May–June 1984), pp. 127–135.

Fig 22-1.
A grievance and
arbitration
procedure in a
negotiated
labor agreement
between a
supermarket
chain and a
retail employees
union.

ARTICLE 4—GRIEVANCES AND ARBITRATION:

4.1 Should any differences, disputes or complaints arise over the interpretation or application of the contents of this Agreement, there shall be an earnest effort made on the part of both parties to settle same promptly through the following steps:

Step 1. By conference between the aggrieved employee, the union steward and/or business agent, or both, and the store manager or owner. Store Management shall make its decision known within two (2) working days thereafter. If the matter is not resolved in Step 1, it shall be referred to Step 2 within two (2) working days.

Step 2. By conference between the business agent and the owner or a supervisor of the Employer. The Employer shall make its decision known within three (3) working days thereafter. If the matter is not resolved in Step 2, it shall be reduced to writing and referred within three (3) working days to Step 3.

Step 3. By conference between an official or officials of the Union and a designated representative of the Employer.

Step 4. In the event the last step fails to settle the complaint, it shall be referred within seven (7) working days to arbitration.

4.2 In any case in which an employee is aggrieved and the Union promptly notifies the employee that it does not intend to request arbitration after the Step 3 meeting, the time for requesting arbitration shall be stayed pending the employee's exhaustion of internal union appeals to the Union's Executive Board.

4.3 The Employer and the Union shall mutually agree to an impartial arbitrator to hear said arbitration case; however, if said arbitrator cannot be chosen within three (3) days then the Federal Mediation and Conciliation Service will be requested to furnish a panel of seven (7) names from which the arbitrator may be chosen. The arbitrator will be selected within seven (7) days after the receipt of the panel by alternately striking names. The party striking first will be determined by the flip of a coin. The decision of the arbitrator shall be binding on both parties. The expenses of the arbitrator shall be paid for jointly.

Such arbitrator shall not be empowered to add to, detract from, or alter the terms of this Agreement.

4.4 The Employer may, at any time, discharge any worker for proper cause. The Union or the employee may file a written complaint with the Employer within seven (7) days after the date of discharge asserting that the discharge was improper. Such complaint must be taken up promptly. If the Employer and the Union fail to agree within five (5) days, it shall be referred to arbitration. Should the arbitrator determine that it was an unfair discharge, the Employer shall abide by the decision of the arbitrator.

4.5 Grievances must be taken up promptly. No grievances will be considered, discussed, or become arbitrable which is presented later than seven (7) days after such has happened.

4.6 The Employer shall have the right to call a conference with a Union steward or officials of the Union for the purpose of discussing his grievance, criticisms, or other problems.

4.7 Grievances will be discussed only through the outlined procedures; except that by mutual agreement between the Union and the Employer, the time limits may be waived.

4.8 There shall be no lockout or cessation of work pending the decision of the arbitrator.

Fig 22–2.
A problem-
solving
procedure for
complaints.

— AJAX CORPORATION —
Problem Solving Procedure

OBJECTIVE — It is our purpose to provide employees with an effective means to bring problems to the attention of management and get them resolved. A problem may be any condition of employment an employee feels is unjust or inequitable. Employees are encouraged to air any concern about their treatment or conditions of work over which the Company might be expected to exercise some control.

NORMAL PROCEDURE
Step #1 — The First-Line Supervisor — Problems are best resolved by the people closest to the situation. Employees are thus asked to first discuss their concerns with their immediate supervisor. Supervisors should, of course, seek a satisfactory resolution. If the employee feels that the supervisor is not the right person to solve the problem, he or she can ignore this step.
Step #2 — The District Manager — If the problem is not resolved after discussion with the First-Line Supervisor, the employee should be referred to the District Manager (or Assistant).
Step #3 — Higher Divisional Management — If the problem has not been settled by either the First-Line Supervisor or District Manager, the employee should be referred to Higher Divisional Management.
Step #3 — Alternate — The Personnel Staff — As an alternative, the employee can discuss his or her problem with a member of the Personnel staff rather than Higher Divisional Management.
Step #4 — The President — If the matter is not adjusted satisfactorily by any of the foregoing, the employee may request an appointment with the President (or Executive Vice President) who will see that a decision is finalized.

POLICIES
1. *Freedom from Retaliation* — Employees should not be discriminated against for exercising their rights to discuss problems. Obviously any retaliation would seriously distort the climate in which our problem-solving procedure is intended to operate.
2. *Prompt Handling* — A problem can become magnified if it isn't dealt with promptly. Supervisors are expected to set aside time to discuss an employee's concerns within one working day from an employee's request. Supervisors should seek to resolve a problem within three working days of a discussion.
3. *Fair Hearing* — Supervisors should concentrate on listening. Often, hearing an employee out can resolve the problem. Supervisors should objectively determine if the employee has been wronged and, if so, seek a satisfactory remedy.

PRESIDENT'S GRIPE BOX — The President's "Gripe Box" is located on each floor or module in our Home Office buildings. Employees should feel free to use the "Gripe Box" to get problems to the President's attention expeditiously. Employees may or may not sign gripes. Written responses will be sent in response to signed gripes.

prohibit the supervisor from speaking directly with the employee in front of the shop steward. In other words, there should be frank and open communication among the parties. In the event that the shop steward does not bring the employee along, the supervisor nonetheless is obligated to listen to the shop steward.

It is unusual for an aggrieved employee to present a grievance to a supervisor in the absence of the shop steward. However, if this should happen, it is

Fig 22–3.
There should be frank and open communication among the supervisor, the shop steward, and the aggrieved employee.

appropriate for the supervisor to listen to the employee's problem and to determine whether it involves the labor agreement or the shop steward, or whether the union should be involved at all. Under no circumstances should the supervisor give the impression that he or she is trying to undermine the shop steward's authority or relationship with the employee. If the indications are that the labor agreement or union interests are involved, then the supervisor should notify the shop steward concerning the employee's presentation of the problem.

If a grievance is not settled at the first step and if the shop steward believes that the grievance is justified, the grievance will be processed to the next step. It is possible that the shop steward will carry the grievance further with some other objective in mind. In Chapter 21 we mentioned that the shop steward usually is an elected representative of the employees, is familiar with the labor agreement, and is knowledgeable in submitting a grievance. The shop steward may be eager to receive credit for filing a grievance. By making a "good showing" or by "winning" as much as possible for the employees, his or her chances of being reelected as shop steward at the next union election are enhanced.

SUPERVISORY GUIDELINES FOR SETTLING COMPLAINTS AND GRIEVANCES

Regardless of the nature of an employee complaint or grievance, a supervisor should fully investigate details of the problem and determine whether it can be resolved quickly. It is always better to settle minor issues before they grow into major ones. Although there will be cases that have to be referred to higher management, the supervisor for the most part should endeavor to settle a grievance or complaint at the first step. If many go beyond the first step, the supervisor probably is not carrying out his or her duties appropriately. Unless circumstances are beyond the supervisor's control, complaints and grievances should be handled within reasonable time limits and brought to a fair conclusion within the pattern of supervisory considerations discussed in the sections that follow.

Make Time Available

Making time available requires finding time to hear a complaint or grievance as soon as possible. This does not mean that the supervisor must drop everything in order to meet immediately with the aggrieved employee and shop steward. Rather, it means making every effort to set a time for this initial hearing. If the supervisor makes it difficult for a complaining employee to have a hearing as expeditiously as possible under the circumstances, the employee could become frustrated and feel resentful. A long delay could be interpreted by the employee or union to mean that the supervisor does not consider the problem to be important. Or it could even be interpreted as stalling and indifference on the part of management.

Listen Patiently and with an Open Mind

Too often supervisors become preoccupied with defending themselves and trying to justify their own positions without giving the shop steward and the aggrieved employee ample time to present their cases. Supervisors should bear in mind that all the principles discussed in the chapters on communication and interviewing are applicable to complaints and grievances. Both the shop steward and the employee should be encouraged to say whatever they have on their minds. If they gain the impression that the supervisor is willing to listen to them and wants to provide fair treatment, the problem may not loom as large to them as it did before. It is also possible that the more a person talks, the more likely that person is to make contradictory and inconsistent remarks that weaken the argument. Thus empathic listening by the supervisor is likely to minimize hostilities and tensions during the initial hearing.

Distinguish Facts from Opinions

Attempting to distinguish facts from opinions means being cautious in placing reliance on hearsay and opinionated statements. However, the supervisor should not try to confuse the shop steward and the employee. The supervisor should ask factual, pointed questions regarding who or what is involved; when, where, and why did the alleged problem take place; was there any connection between this grievance and another grievance? Frequently it is impossible to gather all the relevant information at once, making it inappropriate to settle the grievance immediately. Under such conditions the supervisor should tell the complaining employee and the shop steward that he or she will gather the necessary information within a reasonable time and by a definite date. The supervisor should not postpone a decision with the excuse of a "need for more facts" when the relevant information can be obtained without delay.

Determine the Real Issue

Both in union and nonunion work settings, there will be times when on the surface an employee complaint may represent a symptom of a deeper problem. For example, a complaint about unfair work assignments may really reflect personality clashes among several employees in the department. Or a complaint that newly installed machinery will not allow employees to maintain their previous incentive rates may indicate that the employees are actually having a difficult time adjusting to the operation of the new equipment after years of operating old machines. Unless the real issue is clearly defined and settled, complaints of a similar nature are likely to be raised again in the future.

Check and Consult

Checking and consulting perhaps are the most important aspects of a supervisor's role in handling employee complaints and grievances. We cannot emphasize too strongly that the labor agreement, as well as company policies and procedures, must be administered fairly and uniformly. In a unionized setting, the supervisor may not be sure whether the grievance is valid under the existing labor agreement; or provisions of the labor agreement might be unclear in reference to the alleged violation. In no case should the supervisor make a decision or commitment until after he or she has carefully reviewed the company's manual on policies and procedures and the labor agreement.

As stated previously, grievances revolve around interpretation of the labor agreement, and complaints in nonunion settings may include questions of personnel policies. Further, complaints that involve allegations of discrimination and other aspects of equal employment opportunity have legal implications. Therefore, whenever a grievance or complaint requires contractual, policy, or legal interpretation, the supervisor should tell the complaining individuals that it will be necessary to "check some things out" and that an answer will be given by a definite date. Subsequently, the supervisor should consult with the human resources department and higher management for advice and guidance on these matters.

Seeking assistance from human resources staff or higher management is neither buck-passing or revealing ignorance. Nor should it be thought of by the supervisor as weakness, because the supervisor usually is not authorized or qualified to make the policy or legal interpretations necessary to respond to certain employee complaints and grievances.

Avoid Setting Precedents

The supervisor should consult records of previous settlements and make sure that any proposed decision is consistent with established practices. If a particular issue has never been encountered in the past, the supervisor should seek guidance from other supervisors or staff personnel who may have experienced similar but not necessarily identical problems. If circumstances require a change or departure from previous decisions, the supervisor should explain the reasons why to both the aggrieved employee and the shop steward. They also should be informed about whether any exception will constitute a new precedent.

Unless there is a valid, unique reason or unless the supervisor has received approval from higher management or the human resources department, the supervisor should avoid making individual exceptions to a policy or practice. Making an exception is setting a precedent, and precedents often come back to haunt the supervisor and the company. In labor arbitration issues, most arbitrators believe that precedents can become almost as binding on a company as if they were negotiated in the labor agreement itself. Thus a supervisor should be very careful about making an individual exception, because a grievance settlement may become part of a future labor agreement.

Exercise Self-Control

Sometimes emotions, arguments, and personality clashes distort the communication between the supervisor and complaining individuals. The worst thing that the supervisor can do in these situations is to engage in a shouting match or to "talk down" to the complaining persons. Emotional outbursts usually lead to little constructive thinking; arguing and shouting may escalate a problem to far more serious proportions. Of course, there are limits to a supervisor's patience. If the employee or the shop steward persists in loud arguments, profanity, or the like, the supervisor should terminate the meeting at that point and schedule another, hoping that the problem can be discussed later in a calm and less emotional manner.

When the grievance is trivial or not even valid, the supervisor must exercise caution in not showing any personal animosity toward the shop steward or the complaining employee. The supervisor should explain why the grievance has no merit. The supervisor cannot expect the shop steward to do the explaining, since the steward is the employee's official representative.

Sometimes an employee or the shop steward may provoke an argument as a way of deliberately putting the supervisor on the defensive. Even this type of situation should not arouse open hostilities on the supervisor's part. If the supervisor does not know how to handle situations of this sort, he or she should consult with higher management or the human resources department for assistance.

Minimize Delay in Reaching a Decision

Many labor agreements require a definite time period within which a grievance must be answered. The same principle should hold true in nonunion work situations. If an employee has raised a complaint, that employee should be entitled to know—within a reasonable time—exactly when management will make a decision concerning that complaint. If the complaint can be handled immediately and if it is within the supervisor's authority to do so, of course this should be done practically on the spot. But if the complaint involves an issue that requires consultation with higher management or human resources staff, the supervisor should close the hearing with a definite commitment as to when an answer or decision will be given.

Postponing a decision in the hope that the grievance will disappear can invite trouble and more grievances. However, speed in the settlement of a grievance should not outweigh the importance of a sound decision. If delay is necessary, the supervisor should inform the parties and explain why and not leave them under the impression that they are being ignored. Since waiting for a decision is bothersome to everyone, prompt grievance handling is of utmost importance.

Explain the Decision Clearly and with Sensitivity

The supervisor should make every effort to give a straightforward, clear answer to the complaint or grievance as decided by management. In addition, the supervisor should communicate as specifically as possible the reasons for the decision, especially if it goes against the employee's case. It is quite frustrating for an employee just to get a "no" for an answer without any explanation other than that management "feels" that it does not have to do what the employee requests.

Even when the complaint was not really justified, the supervisor should not in any way convey to the employee that the problem or issue was trivial or unnecessary. There were probably good reasons in the employee's mind for raising the complaint. Therefore, the supervisor's response should be sensitive to the employee's perspective.

If a written reply to a grievance is required under the labor agreement, the supervisor should restrict it to the specific grievance and make certain that the

Fig 22–4.
The supervisor
should answer
a grievance in a
straightforward,
reasonable
manner.

Fig 22–4. The supervisor should answer a grievance in a straightforward, reasonable manner.

response is relevant to the case. References to provisions of the labor agreement or plant rules should be confined to those in question. The supervisor is well advised to first discuss the implications of a written reply with higher management or the human resources department so that it will be worded appropriately.

Keep Records and Documents

Despite good-faith efforts of supervisors or higher management to settle complaints or grievances, an employee may choose to appeal an adverse decision. If the complaint involves discrimination, the employee may file a formal complaint with a government agency for legal processing. If there is a union grievance, it may eventually go all the way to arbitration. In a nonunionized company, the company's complaint procedures may provide several steps for appeal. This is why records and documentation of all available evidence, discussions, and meetings are very important for a supervisor to file and maintain. In any appeal process, written evidence is generally superior to oral testimony and hearsay.

Keeping good records and documents is especially important when a complaint or grievance is not settled at the supervisory level. The burden of proof is usually on management to justify its position; therefore, a supervisor should be ready to explain and justify previous decisions and actions without having to depend solely on memory. Records and documentation can be very supportive in this regard.

Don't Fear a Challenge

A supervisor should make every effort to adjust a complaint or grievance at the first step without sacrificing a fair and proper decision. Unfortunately, supervisors at times are tempted to grant a questionable complaint or grievance because they fear a challenge or because they want to avoid a hassle. By giving in to an employee or the union just to avoid an argument, the supervisor may invite others to adopt the "squeaky wheel gets the grease" theory. That is, other employees or shop stewards will be encouraged to submit minor complaints because they feel that by complaining often and loudly, they have a better chance of gaining a concession. Thus a stance of "weakness" by a supervisor can establish a perception that may lead to even greater problems.

In making efforts to settle a complaint or grievance, there will always be gray areas where a supervisor must use prudent judgment. The supervisor should be willing to admit and rectify a mistake if a mistake has occurred. However, if the supervisor believes that a fair and objective decision was made, he or she should have the courage to hold to a firm decision, even if the employee threatens to appeal. The fact that the employee appeals an adverse decision does not mean that the supervisor is wrong. Even if higher management or an arbitrator should later reverse a supervisor's decision, this in itself does not imply poor handling by the supervisor. There will always be some decisions that will be modified or reversed during the appeal process, and the reasons for altering a decision may go beyond the supervisor's responsibility.

Supervisors who generally follow the guidelines discussed in this chapter and who have done their best to reach a proper and fair solution, will be backed up by higher management in most cases. At the very least, the supervisor normally should be able to handle a complaint or grievance in a professional manner and avoid having minor issues escalate into major ones. In summary, handling employee complaints and grievances is another of the many skills of effective supervision. It requires sensitivity, objectivity, and sound analytical judgment—which are the same qualities that are required in most areas of supervisory management.

SUMMARY

Two major differences usually exist between a grievance procedure in a unionized setting and a complaint procedure in a nonunionized setting. In the nonunionized setting the employee normally must make the complaint without assistance, and the final decision is usually made by the chief executive or the human resources director rather than by an arbitrator.

During the initial step in handling grievances, there should be open, frank communication between the supervisor and the complaining individuals (the employee and the shop steward). If the grievance is not settled at this step, the shop steward probably will carry the grievance further, and it may eventually be submitted to an outside arbitrator.

Whether or not employees are represented by a labor union, the supervisor should follow the same general guidelines in adjusting complaints or grievances. Among the most important supervisory considerations are: (a) make time available; (b) listen patiently and with an open mind; (c) distinguish facts from opinions; (d) determine the real issue; (e) check and consult; (f) avoid setting precedents; (g) exercise self-control; (h) minimize delay in reaching a decision; (i) explain the decision clearly and with sensitivity; (j) keep records and documents; and (k) don't fear a challenge.

QUESTIONS FOR DISCUSSION

1. How is a grievance defined in unionized companies? What are the major distinctions between a union grievance and an employee complaint in a nonunionized company?
2. Distinguish between a union grievance procedure and a problem-solving or complaint procedure.
3. Discuss the shop steward's role in the grievance procedure. Why is it generally preferable that the supervisor listen to the shop steward and the complaining employee together?
4. Review and discuss each of the eleven guidelines for satisfactory adjustment of complaints and grievances. Analyze the interrelationships among them.
5. Why should most complaints and grievances be settled by the supervisor at the departmental level? Which should be referred to higher management or human resources staff for decisions? Discuss.
6. Why is the handling of complaints or grievances a major component of effective supervisory management?

CASE 39

Can the Company Avoid Unionization?

The family-owned Royal Furniture Company manufactured and assembled office furniture in a small community in a southern state. It employed about 100 people and was operated by the principal owner, Oliver Thomas. The relationship between management and the workers had been very good in a rather paternalistic way. Wages were competitive, and the employees had numerous extra benefits, which management provided whenever the need arose. For example, wages were advanced if an employee needed money for an emergency; court fines were paid by the company if the employee did not have the funds to do so; and when a worker could not meet a monthly installment obligation, the company usually would advance the amount needed. Several times, union organizers had tried to approach the factory employees in order to organize the workers, but each time the union was unsuccessful in getting enough support.

However, in recent years the company had been experiencing more difficult economic times. Wages had not kept pace with inflation, and the company was becoming less generous in giving employees various benefits. Employees were becoming more and more dissatisfied, and a union organizer was again observed passing out union literature outside the plant.

Thomas had stated publicly on several occasions to his supervisors and some employees that, if a union would win an election, he would either sell the company or close the plant. He did not want to go through union negotiations, and he did not want his managerial prerogatives diminished.

One of the company's office supervisors, Harriet Toole, recently took a human resources management course at a local community college, where she had studied labor unions and union-organizing campaigns. She became concerned that Thomas's approach to the situation at the Royal Company could lead to unionization of the plant and that he might even be violating the law. Toole wondered what she should do.

CASE 40

What Is "Reasonable Time" for the Shop Steward?

Sandra Whitworth supervised a group of approximately 15 billing employees in the Accounting Department of Howell Stores, a major metropolitan department store chain. All office employees in the company were represented by a local union of the Office and Professional Employees Union.

One day Whitworth called Eleanor Kane into her office. Kane was a billing clerk who served as union shop steward. "Elly," said Whitworth, "it's time that we had a showdown about the amount of time you've been spending on union matters in this office. For the last two weeks you've averaged about three hours each day away from your job, allegedly to handle union grievances. This is entirely too much. I won't tolerate this anymore!"

"What do you mean, too much?" responded Kane. "The union contract says I'm allowed a reasonable time to handle union grievances, and it does not specify an upper time limit. I take only the time necessary to do my job as union steward. And lately there's been a flock of complaints and grievances which have come to my attention."

"I don't care about your union affairs," replied Whitworth. "You've got a job to do, and being away from your job more than a third of the time is unreasonable by any standards. From now on, if you're gone more than one hour each day on union matters, I'm going to dock your pay accordingly.''

"Sandra," snapped Elly Kane, "if you do that, I'll file a grievance right away and will fight you all the way to arbitration if necessary. You haven't got a leg to stand on, and you know it. Go see Larry Niland, your director of labor relations. He'll tell you the same thing. In the meantime, I'm going to report this harassment to our union business agent at our local union office!'' With that, she left Whitworth's office.

Whitworth pondered what her next move, if any, should be. She also reviewed Article 3, Section 1, of the current labor agreement, which in part stated as follows:

> A Union shop steward shall be permitted reasonable time to investigate, present, and process grievances on the Employer's property without loss of time or pay during regular working hours, provided that the steward obtains permission from his or her supervisor prior to such absence from assigned duties. Such time spent in handling grievances during the steward's regular working hours shall be considered working hours in computing daily or weekly overtime if within the regular schedule of the steward.

CASE 41

Different Hours and Rules for Union and Nonunion Employees

Oscar Pratt, superintendent of the unionized Warehouse Department of the Ashley Department Stores, was discussing a serious problem with Harmon Ashley, president of the company. According to Pratt, his foremen and the union were complaining about the different treatment of union employees from nonunion employees. For example, only union warehouse workers were docked 15 minutes' pay for 5 minutes of tardiness, while nonunion employees were seen walking in and out of the company buildings at all times. Pratt said, "Apparently the nonunion employees can arrive at any time they care to, and they don't have to comply with regular hours like the unionized warehouse workers do!''

The unionized warehouse workers also told Pratt that nonunion employees could be found in the company cafeteria at all hours of the day and were apparently not restricted to certain regular times or to 15-minute coffee breaks as were the warehouse workers. Pratt pointed out to Ashley that he had handled several formal grievances over this issue and expected even more complaints after the labor agreement expired in about a year.

Pratt urged Ashley to take steps to correct the situation so that working hours and regulations would be more uniform for both union and nonunion employees. Pratt believed that Ashley should have a serious discussion with Gail Massen, the sales manager, and Eric Engel, the assistant store manager, to bring about the desired results.

Ashley was sympathetic to Pratt's concerns. Ashley was known to believe in running a "tight" operation. As president, he reported to his desk before eight o'clock in the morning and remained until after the official quitting hour. He rarely took a coffee break himself. As he pondered what steps to take, his first reaction was to call Massen and Engel into his office and simply tell them that he wanted the nonunion employees also to put in a regular eight-hour day, to report to work on time, and to limit their break periods. But, on second thought, he realized that this would not always be possible. He was aware of the special problems of salespeople, who often had to work irregular hours to handle peak customer periods in the stores. Some sales representatives might return home late the night before from a business meeting or from entertaining a customer. Similarly, other nonunion personnel such as those in the office, advertising, and purchasing departments, including supervisors, were known to prefer some flexibility in their work schedules. They claimed that this flexibility was necessary in relation to their duties and that it contributed to good work performance and morale.

Harmon Ashley left a telephone message with Marcia Bush, the director of human resources, to come and discuss the situation with him.

CASE 42

The Unsafe Pole

Henry Floyd was the foreman of a construction crew for Municipal Power and Light Company. The crew consisted of Roy McMillan, Howard Bierman, and Mel Shostak.

One morning, while out on the job, Floyd directed Bierman and Shostak to climb a pole and remove a number of tree limbs that had fallen on a main power line carrying some 7,000 to 8,000 volts. Senior lineman Roy McMillan said, "Henry, I don't believe it's safe to climb that pole with the wind blowing the way it is. You never can tell what will happen when you have broken limbs on a power line."

Floyd responded, "Oh, come on, Roy, we've done jobs like this on many occasions and we've never had any problems." Floyd proceeded to outline how McMillan should do the job to avoid an accident. McMillan then went back to the truck, where Bierman and Shostak were gathering their tools. Shortly afterward the three of them approached Floyd.

McMillan said, "Henry, we're not going to climb that pole. We think it's unsafe. We either do it another day or we've got to have more men on the job in order to do it safely."

Floyd replied, "Now listen, fellows, we've been through this many times before. It's the supervisor who ultimately makes the decision whether or not a job is safe. We've done many jobs far more dangerous than this one without any problems."

McMillan went on, "We checked our union agreement, and the safety clause in it gives us the right to determine whether or not a job is safe." Floyd looked at the contract clause, which McMillan showed him. It read:

> All employees have the responsibility for the safety of their fellow employees and others who are affected by their work. Safety engineering and other support personnel are responsible for assisting supervisors with their safety responsibilities.
>
> All employees have the final responsibility for their own safety. They have the final control over their actions and the last possible chance of being aware of what can injure them and of doing their best to see that it does not. This is one of the job requirements for every employee of Municipal Power and Light Company.

Floyd said, "Yeah, but you're overlooking the fact that there's a clause that precedes it saying that supervisors have the direct responsibility!" With that he read the following clause:

> Supervisors have the direct responsibility for safety. Foremen, managers, superintendents, engineers, section heads, division managers, department heads, officers, and all supervisors are responsible for safety in their areas. This includes carrying out safety activities appropriate for their operations.

They continued to discuss the issue. Finally, Roy McMillan said, "Henry, we're simply not going to climb that pole. You can't make us. You can send us home if you want, but if you do we're going to file a grievance and we're also going to file an OSHA complaint for the company's failure to maintain safety standards!"

With that Henry Floyd pondered what he should do.

CASE 43

Discharge for Striking a Student

Gino Barsanti was employed as a maintenance worker at Midwest University, located in a small town in a midwestern state. Barsanti was considered to be a "handyman" who did every type of assignment ranging from manual labor to skilled carpentry and electrical work. He had been employed by the university for six years, and his work record was excellent. He had never received a reprimand, suspension, or any other type of disciplinary action during his six years of service at the university.

One day, Barsanti and two other employees were working on a broken fence adjacent to the baseball field. They were engaged in a heated discussion about religion and politics; Barsanti particularly was arguing that abortion was a mortal sin. Several students happened to be passing by and heard some of the comments being made by the employees. One of the students, Sidney Rose, decided that he would join in the conversation. Eventually Rose made several derogatory remarks about religion in general and the abortion issue in particular. Barsanti became angry that a student had entered into the conversation. Barsanti stated to him, "Who asked you to join in this discussion? Get the hell out of here." At this point Rose responded, "There's no use trying to reason with a rigid religious nut!" Barsanti became enraged. He took two steps toward the student and hit him squarely on the jaw. Rose was bleeding from the mouth when he and his fellow students left the area.

Shortly thereafter, Barsanti was summoned to the office of the maintenance superintendent, Alex Higgins. Rose had reported what had happened, and Barsanti did not deny that he had struck the student. Barsanti was sent home for the rest of the day. The next morning Barsanti was notified by Higgins that the university had decided to terminate him for striking a student, which Higgins felt was in violation of the university's strict "no fighting" policy for employees while on campus and during work hours.

On the day following Barsanti's termination, the union business representative, William Kelford, filed a grievance on behalf of Barsanti claiming that Barsanti's termination did not meet the requirement of "just cause" in the labor agreement for a discharge action to be taken against an employee. Kelford spoke with Higgins about the grievance and told him that no employee should be required to take the kind of abuse and insults from a student to which Barsanti had been subjected. Further, in view of the fact that Barsanti had never had a previous disciplinary action against him and that no specific rule covered this type of event, Kelford argued that Barsanti should be reinstated immediately. Kelford also contended that the university's so-called no fighting policy for employees was never intended to be applied to circumstances like the situation that confronted Barsanti, and therefore discharge was extreme and not justified.

Alex Higgins told William Kelford that he would study the union grievance and make a decision within the next two days.

CASE 44

Mistaken Overtime Work

Central Container Company manufactured various types of metal container products on a three-shift basis. One of the maintenance employees, Art Glenn, reported for work at 11 P.M. on a Friday night shift through an error on his part. He had not been scheduled to work and he had not been called in, although a small crew was scheduled to work this shift.

At about midnight, Glenn's regular supervisor, Gerry Fresno, entered the plant on a trouble call and questioned Glenn regarding his presence in the plant. After some discussion, both realized that Glenn had reported in error.

However, Fresno told Glenn that he could finish the shift. Glenn worked eight hours. This was Glenn's sixth consecutive day of work, and by union contract as well as by law, Glenn was to be paid at a rate of time and one half for this shift.

The next day, however, another maintenance employee, Willie Flanders, filed a grievance because Glenn had worked on a sixth day, although Glenn was junior to Flanders in seniority. Flanders claimed equal pay for the time Glenn worked (eight hours at time and one half, i.e., 12 hours of pay). Flanders and his union steward claimed that in accordance with a well-established practice at the company, overtime had to be offered first to employees in accordance with their seniority and their ability to perform the work.

At a grievance meeting held in Fresno's office, Carl Marshall, the union steward, argued that if Fresno had sent Glenn home after he found him working, no grievance would have been filed. However, since the past practice had been and still was to let the most senior employees work overtime, the union should be upheld in this case and Flanders should be paid for all time at the appropriate rate that the junior employee (Glenn) was paid.

Fresno responded that the company should not be required to pay 12 hours of pay to another employee. Out of consideration for the employee who reported by mistake, Fresno had allowed Glenn to work the full shift instead of sending him home with one hour's pay. The claim of the union was unjust and inequitable. No union employee, neither Flanders nor anyone else, suffered any loss of work or income because Fresno had acted in a considerate manner. If Glenn had not erroneously reported for work, no one would have worked in that job. Fresno claimed that his decision to allow Glenn to continue to work after he was discovered in the plant should be commended and not criticized.

Carl Marshall ended the meeting with this comment, "If that's your decision, we'll have to pursue this case further, even to arbitration if necessary. You goofed on this one, and you ought to recognize it right now!"

After Marshall left his office, Gerry Fresno decided that he had better take up the grievance with his boss and the director of human resources.

Index

Note: *n* following a page number refers to a footnote or illustration note.

Chapter Opener Photo Credits